www.wadsworth.com

wadsworth.com is the World Wide Web site for Wadsworth Publishing Company and is your direct source to dozens of online resources.

At *wadsworth.com* you can find out about supplements, demonstration software, and student resources. You can also send e-mail to many of our authors and preview new publications and exciting new technologies.

wadsworth.com
Changing the way the world learns®

The Religious Life in History Series
Charles Hallisey, *Series Editor*

Understanding Religious Life, Third Edition
Frederick J. Streng

African Cosmos: An Introduction to Religion in Africa
Noel Q. King

The Buddhist Religion: A Historical Introduction, Fourth Edition
Richard H. Robinson, Willard L. Johnson, and Sandra A. Wawrytko

The Experience of Buddhism: Sources and Interpretations
John S. Strong

Chinese Religion: An Introduction, Fifth Edition
Laurence G. Thompson

The Chinese Way in Religion
Laurence G. Thompson

The Hindu Religious Tradition
Thomas J. Hopkins

The House of Islam, Third Edition
Kenneth Cragg and R. Marston Speight

Islam from Within: Anthology of a Religion
Kenneth Cragg and R. Marston Speight

Japanese Religion: Unity and Diversity, Third Edition
H. Byron Earhart

Religion in the Japanese Experience: Sources and Interpretations, Second Edition
H. Byron Earhart

The Way of Torah: An Introduction to Judaism, Sixth Edition
Jacob Neusner

The Life of Torah: Readings in the Jewish Religious Experience
Jacob Neusner

Native American Religions: An Introduction
Sam Gill

Native American Traditions: Sources and Interpretations
Sam Gill

The Buddhist Religion

A Historical Introduction

Fourth Edition

RICHARD H. ROBINSON
formerly of the
University of Wisconsin

WILLARD L. JOHNSON
San Diego State University

Assisted by
Sandra A. Wawrytko
San Diego State University

Thanissaro Bhikkhu (Geoffrey DeGraff)
Metta Forest Monastery

Wadsworth Publishing Company
I(T)P® An International Thomson Publishing Company

Belmont, CA • Albany, NY • Bonn • Boston • Cincinnati • Detroit • Johannesburg • London • Madrid
Melbourne • Mexico City • New York • Paris • San Francisco • Singapore • Tokyo • Toronto • Washington

Religion Editor: Peter Adams
Assistant Editor: Clay Glad
Editorial Assistant: Greg Brueck
Marketing Manager: Dave Garrison
Project Editor: Jennie Redwitz
Print Buyer: Barbara Britton
Permissions Editor: Bob Kauser
Copy Editor: Michelle Filippini
Cover: Craig Hanson
Compositor: Thompson Type
Printer: Malloy Lithographing, Inc.
Cover Image: Courtesy of the Trustees of the Victoria & Albert Museum, London.

This book is printed on recycled paper.

Printed in the United States of America
4 5 6 7 8 9 10

For more information, contact Wadsworth Publishing Company, 10 Davis Drive, Belmont, CA 94002, or electronically at http://www.thomson.com/wadsworth.html

International Thomson Publishing Europe
Berkshire House 168-173
High Holborn
London, WC1V 7AA, England

Thomas Nelson Australia
102 Dodds Street
South Melbourne 3205
Victoria, Australia

Nelson Canada
1120 Birchmount Road
Scarborough, Ontario
Canada M1K 5G4

International Thomson Publishing GmbH
Königswinterer Strasse 418
53227 Bonn, Germany

International Thomson Editores
Campos Eliseos 385, Piso 7
Col. Polanco
11560 México D.F. México

International Thomson Publishing Asia
221 Henderson Road
#05-10 Henderson Building
Singapore 0315

International Thomson Publishing Japan
Hirakawacho Kyowa Building, 3F
2-2-1 Hirakawacho
Chiyoda-ku, Tokyo 102, Japan

International Thomson Publishing
Southern Africa
Building 18, Constantia Park
240 Old Pretoria Road
Halfway House, 1685 South Africa

Library of Congress Cataloging-in-Publication Data
Robinson, Richard, H.
The Buddhist Religion: a historical introduction /
Richard H. Robinson, Willard L. Johnson; assisted by Sandra A. Wawrytko,
Thanissaro Bhikkhu (Geoffrey DeGraff).—4th ed.
p. cm.—(Religious life in history series)
Includes bibliographical references and index.
ISBN 0-534-20718-9 (pbk.)
1. Buddhism. I. Johnson, Willard L. II. Wawrytko, Sandra A. (Sandra Ann)
III. DeGraff, Geoffrey. IV. Title. V. Series.
BQ4012.R6 1996 96-9605
294.3—dc20

To Sītā and Neil,
my daughter and my son,
kuladuhitre ca kulaputrāya
(R.H.R.)

In this life, hate is never
calmed by hatred,
but by love.
This is the primordial dhamma.
Dhammapada, 5
(W.L.J.)

Better than a thousand useless words
is one single word that gives peace.
Dhammapada, 100
(S.A.W.)

To Donald K. Swearer,
my first ācārya in things Buddhist
(T.B./G.F.D.)

Contents

Foreword

The Religious Life in History series introduces the richness and diversity of religious thought, practice, experience, and institutions as they are found in living traditions throughout the world.

Some of the religious traditions included in the Religious Life in History series are defined by geography and cultural arenas, while others are defined by their development across cultural and geographic boundaries. In all cases, however, the introductions seek to take full account of the variety within each tradition while keeping in sight the traits and patterns that encourage both scholars and members of various religious communities to distinguish a particular religious tradition from others around it. Moreover, as a set of introductions to quite different religious traditions, the series naturally invites comparison between different ways of being religious and encourages critical reflection on religion as a human phenomenon more generally. Thus, in addition to containing volumes on different religious traditions, the series also includes a core text on the study of religion, which is intended to aid the kinds of comparative inquiry and critical reflection that the series fosters through its introductions to religion in particular cultural and historical contexts.

The basic texts in the Religious Life in History series all provide narrative descriptions of a religious tradition, but each also approaches its subject with an interpretive orientation appropriate to its focus. Some traditions lend themselves more to developmental, others to more topical, studies. This lack of a single interpretive stance in the series is itself instructive. It reflects the interpretive choices made by the different authors, choices informed by a deep knowledge of the languages and cultures associated with the religious tradition in question. It also displays the methodological pluralism that characterizes the contemporary study of religion. But perhaps most importantly, it can serve as a useful reminder that what is considered religiously important in one context may not be so in another; indeed, what is viewed as religious in one culture may not be so regarded elsewhere.

Many of the basic texts in the series have a complementary anthology of reading selections. These include translations of texts used by the participants of a tradition, descriptions of practices and practitioners' experiences, and brief interpretive studies of phenomena important in a given tradition. In addition, all of the basic texts present a list of materials for further readings, including translations and more in-depth examinations of specific topics.

The Religious Life in History series was founded more than two decades ago by Frederick J. Streng. While Streng was editor of the series, continuous efforts were made to update the scholarship and to make the presentation of material more effective in each volume. These efforts will continue in the future through the publication of revised editions as well as with the addition of new volumes to the series. But the aim of the series has remained the same since its beginning: As Frederick Streng said, we hope that readers will find these volumes "introductory" in the most significant sense—as introductions to new perspectives for understanding themselves and others.

Charles Hallisey
Series Editor

Preface

It is always a joy to publish a book, but the joy is greatly increased when the book can be revised and reissued to incorporate the results of new research and the growing maturity of one's understanding. Rarely if ever is a scholarly work allowed to reappear in successive revised editions, but textbooks—as long as they contribute to the education of students—can appear and reappear by revising and incorporating new material to make significant improvements. Fourteen years have elapsed since the publication of the Third Edition of this text. This lapse of time is to be regretted but has allowed us to benefit from the increase of fine research on Buddhism that has appeared during this long interval.

This Fourth Edition was set in motion by a long and detailed review of the Third Edition by John Strong of Bates College, to whom we owe a profound debt of gratitude; his extensive review led to a thorough and complete rethinking of the text. Many chapters are altogether new, all the others have been substantially rewritten, and the order of chapters and subjects has been made more coherent. In addition, we have extensively cross-referenced this book to John Strong's companion Wadsworth volume, *The Experience of Buddhism.* In 1993 I asked Sandra Wawrytko to assist me on the subject of east Asian Buddhism, and in 1994–95 when I fell severely ill, Thanissaro Bhikkhu (Geoffrey DeGraff) took over the revision process and has contributed mightily to the work as a whole.

We are also very happy to have Charles Hallisey of Harvard University as the new editor of the entire Wadsworth Religious Life in History series; he guided us in the final stages of revision and production, as did Kathy Hartlove, former Religious Studies Editor for Wadsworth. We are grateful for their direction. We also wish to thank Michelle Filippini for her copyediting of the manuscript, and we thank the many reviewers of previous versions of this fourth revision, including Douglas R. Brooks, University of Rochester; Helen Hardacre, Princeton University; Karen Lang, University of Virginia; Todd T. Lewis, Holy Cross College; Dan Lusthaus, Macalester College; John Strong, Bates College; Donald Swearer, Swarthmore College; and Paul B. Watt, DePauw University. We also thank Charles Prebish; Geoff Martin; Kathryn Tsai; Dan Lusthaus; Sarah Dubin-Vaughn; the nuns and monks of Fo Kuang Shan English Buddhist College, Taiwan, especially Venerable Man Jen; Mu Soeng of the Barre Center for Buddhist Studies; Donald Swearer; and William Harman for their help.

In some ways this new edition is unlike its predecessors. We have dropped the former edition's illustrations and reduced the bibliography to allow us to develop the text more extensively. We hope that students and professors alike will appreciate this new edition, that it will assist them in their endeavors, and that it will please them as it has pleased us to revise it. We expect to produce new editions of this textbook with more regularity in the future and request that any suggestions for improvement be sent to us via the publisher.

Willard L. Johnson
San Diego State University

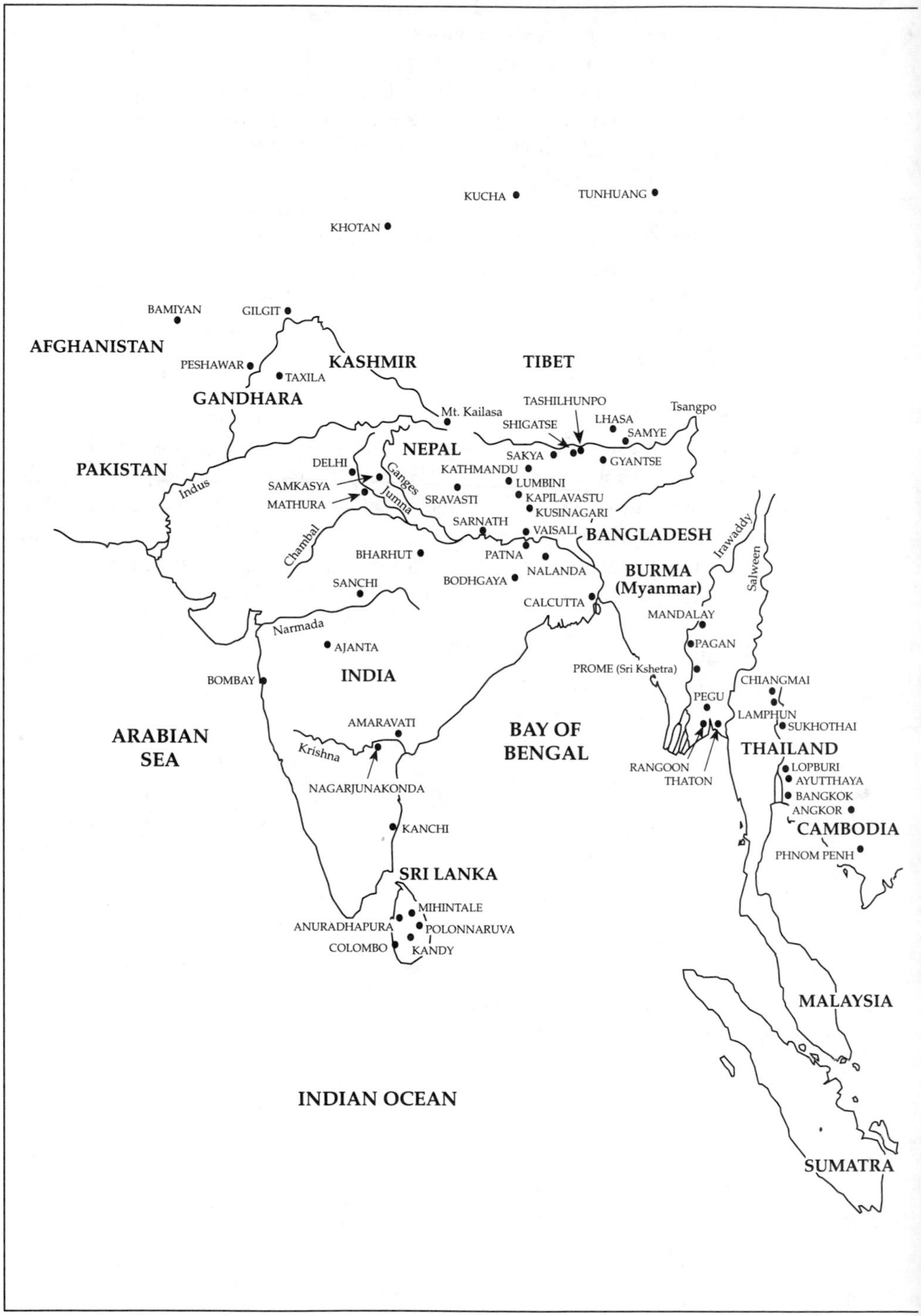

KUCHA
TUNHUANG
KHOTAN
BAMIYAN
GILGIT
AFGHANISTAN
PESHAWAR
TAXILA
KASHMIR
TIBET
GANDHARA
Mt. Kailasa
TASHILHUNPO
Tsangpo
LHASA
SHIGATSE
SAMYE
NEPAL
SAKYA
GYANTSE
PAKISTAN
DELHI
KATHMANDU
LUMBINI
SAMKASYA
SRAVASTI
KAPILAVASTU
MATHURA
KUSINAGARI
Indus
Ganges
Jumna
SARNATH
VAISALI
BANGLADESH
Chambal
BHARHUT
PATNA
NALANDA
Irawaddy
BURMA
(Myanmar)
Salween
SANCHI
BODHGAYA
CALCUTTA
MANDALAY
Narmada
AJANTA
PAGAN
BOMBAY
INDIA
PROME (Sri Kshetra)
CHIANGMAI
PEGU
LAMPHUN
SUKHOTHAI
ARABIAN
SEA
AMARAVATI
BAY OF
BENGAL
THAILAND
Krishna
RANGOON
THATON
LOPBURI
AYUTTHAYA
NAGARJUNAKONDA
BANGKOK
ANGKOR
KANCHI
CAMBODIA
PHNOM PENH
SRI LANKA
MIHINTALE
ANURADHAPURA
POLONNARUVA
COLOMBO
KANDY
MALAYSIA
INDIAN OCEAN
SUMATRA

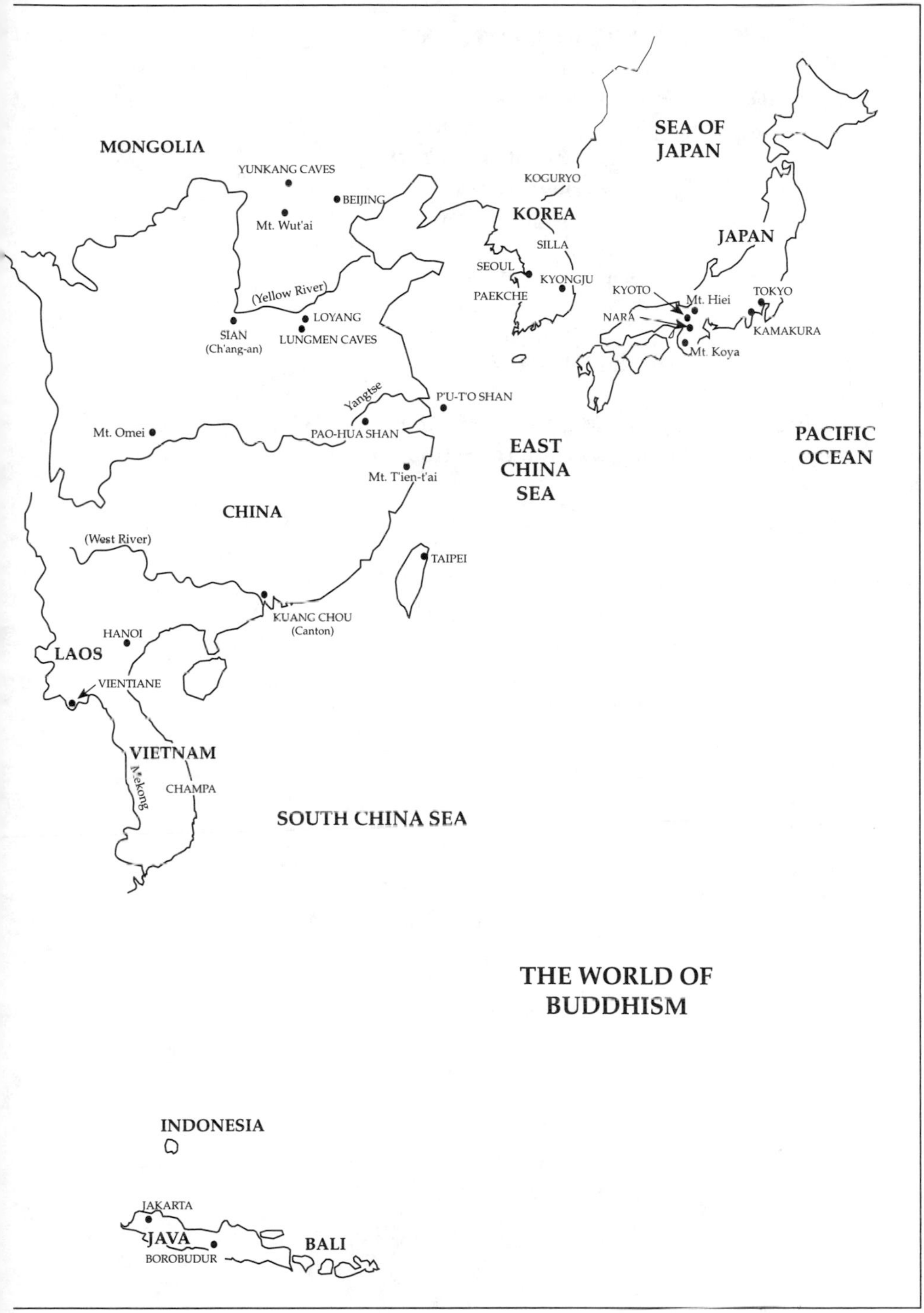
MONGOLIA
YUNKANG CAVES
BEIJING
Mt. Wut'ai
(Yellow River)
SIAN
(Ch'ang-an)
LOYANG
LUNGMEN CAVES
KOGURYO
KOREA
SILLA
SEOUL
KYONGJU
PAEKCHE
SEA OF
JAPAN
JAPAN
KYOTO
Mt. Hiei
NARA
Mt. Koya
TOKYO
KAMAKURA
Yangtse
P'U-T'O SHAN
Mt. Omei
PAO-HUA SHAN
Mt. T'ien-t'ai
EAST
CHINA
SEA
PACIFIC
OCEAN
CHINA
(West River)
TAIPEI
KUANG CHOU
(Canton)
HANOI
LAOS
VIENTIANE
VIETNAM
Mekong
CHAMPA
SOUTH CHINA SEA
INDONESIA
JAKARTA
JAVA
BOROBUDUR
BALI

THE WORLD OF
BUDDHISM

ABBREVIATIONS

Texts from the Pali Canon:

A	Anguttara Nikāya
Cv	Cullavagga
D	Dīgha Nikāya
Dhp	Dhammapada
Khp	Khuddakapāṭha
M	Majjhima Nikāya
S	Samyutta Nikāya
Sn	Sutta Nipāta

References to D, Khp, and M are to sutta. References to Dhp are to verse. References to the remaining texts are to section (*samyutta, nipāta,* or *vagga*) and *sutta.*

Introduction

Buddhism—as a term to denote the vast array of social and cultural phenomena that have clustered in the course of time around the teachings of a figure called the Buddha, the Awakened One—is a recent invention. It comes from the thinkers of the eighteenth-century European Enlightenment and their quest to subsume religion under comparative sociology and secular history. Only recently have Asian Buddhists come to adopt the term and the concept behind it. Previously, the terms they used to refer to their religion were much more limited in scope: *the Dharma, the Buddha's message,* or *the Buddha's way.* In other words, they conceived of their religion simply as the teaching of the Buddha, what the Buddha himself called *Dharma-Vinaya* (Doctrine and Discipline). Whereas Dharma-Vinaya is meant to be prescriptive, advocating a way of life and practice, *Buddhism* is descriptive in that it simply denotes the actions of people who follow a vision of Dharma-Vinaya without suggesting that the reader accept that vision or follow it, too.

This is a text about Buddhism. Although it will describe the various ways that Buddhists over the centuries have defined Dharma-Vinaya in their words and actions, it will not attempt a definition of its own. Its purpose is to portray the thoughts and actions of the large segment of the human race who have called themselves followers of the Buddha. The authors felt that this would be a worthwhile enterprise in exploring part of the range of the human condition. As Socrates once said, "An unexamined life is not worth living." One of the best ways to begin the examination of one's own life is to examine the lives and beliefs of others, so that one's unconscious assumptions can be thrown into sharp relief by the perspective offered by the assumptions, unconscious and conscious, of the rest of humanity. This text is meant to help provide a part of that perspective.

When Richard Robinson wrote the first edition of this text in 1970, he entitled it *The Buddhist Religion* in answer to a question that was very much alive at the time: Is Buddhism a religion or a philosophy? The question grew from a tendency in academic circles to identify Buddhism with a body of doctrine. Because that doctrine—unlike those of Western religions—insisted that the concept of gods or a God was irrelevant to advanced spiritual life, it bore little resemblance to what was recognized as a religion in the West. Robinson's aim was to show that when Buddhism is viewed in its entirety—in terms of devotional practices, institutional history, ritual, and meditative experience, as well as doctrine—it most certainly is a religion. The measure of his success is that the original question no longer commands the interest it once did.

Now, however, controversies in the field of Buddhist studies center on issues related to the text's subtitle: *A Historical Introduction*. Some scholars, on ideological or pedagogical grounds, have questioned whether the critical/historical method of analysis is a valid approach to understanding Buddhism at all. From the ideological standpoint, the question is whether this method makes assumptions that would be rejected by Buddhists themselves. From the pedagogical standpoint, the question is whether the historical method is equal to the task of making the bewildering variety within the Buddhist tradition intelligible. On both counts, however, a valid case can be made that the critical/historical method, even though it may not offer the final word on Buddhism, is still a useful introit to the tradition.

To deal first with the ideological issues: All Buddhists, whatever their affiliation, agree that Dharma ultimately lies beyond the temporal and social conditions of the world. As such, it does not lend itself to historical or any other kind of analysis. Nevertheless, Buddhists themselves have used words to indicate that there is an unconditioned level and to show the way to gain an experience of it, and these words surely lend themselves to historical treatment. In fact, Buddhists themselves find it necessary to explain how, for instance, Mādhyamika was a reaction to Abhidharma, and Yogācāra a reaction to Mādhyamika.

As for the conditioned level, Buddhist teachings on dependent co-arising (see Section 1.4.3) recognize two forms of causality operating on any given situation: influences from the past, and influences from the present. Thus an attempt to trace what can be learned about the past influences acting on present Buddhist practices should not pose any theoretical problems for a practicing Buddhist, although we must remember that Buddhists themselves would include among those past factors the workings of karma, which lie beyond a scholar's ability to confirm or deny.

In actual practice, Buddhists of all schools have shown a wide variety of attitudes toward historical studies and their value in the practice of their own religion. Some, such as Hsüan-tsang (see Section 8.5), have actually put their lives on the line in the quest to find reliable records of the Buddha's true teachings. Others have regarded any questioning of the tradition's current state as an act of irreverence. Although one might simply take note that these differences exist in the tradition, only a historical analysis can help provide an indication of how these differences came about; otherwise, they appear to be random, arbitrary blips on our radar screen.

This brings us directly to the pedagogical issues: As a social/cultural phenomenon, Buddhism can be subjected to two types of analysis: diachronic, dealing with events over time, and synchronic, dealing with factors abstracted from time. We have chosen primarily the diachronic approach simply because the fragmented nature of the tradition does not lend itself to synchronic analysis. Synchronic presentations help make events intelligible only when they are applied to systems whose component factors are working in interaction. Because Buddhism has developed in separate cultural spheres that are almost entirely isolated from one another, many different factors have not been interacting for several centuries. Thus a thematic analysis can simply offer up an idea of the spectrum of phenomena in the tradition, but cannot help make it intelligible. Thematic analysis can, for example, tell us the differences between Tibetan and Theravādin meditation, or between Korean and Japanese monastic life, but unlike the historical approach it cannot tell us how or why those differences came about.

Some scholars have attempted to get around this difficulty by dividing Buddhism into *Buddhisms,* teaching each as part of its cultural environment: Chinese Buddhism as a part of Chinese religion, and so forth. Although this approach has its uses, it misses the transcultural impact that the Buddha's teachings have had within Asia and beyond. Although Chinese Buddhism has been influenced by its many centuries of interaction with Taoism and Confucianism, it has also had a transformative impact on the entire nature of Chinese religious life. A full understanding of that impact can come only from a knowledge of what Buddhism was prior to its entrance into China. To use another example, we can view a thinker such as Dōgen as an example of Japanese religious thought, when in reality he saw himself primarily as a participant in the Buddhist tradition, and in this instance it is instructive to take him at his word in order to learn how he absorbed from and contributed to that tradition.

Thus this text takes a historical approach to its subject, although we have tried to be sensitive to the limits of historical method and the narrative form of presentation. Paralleling the teachings of dependent co-arising, we have augmented our diachronic narrative with synchronic depictions of cross sections in time—portraits of lay and monastic life in early Indian Buddhism; of "domesticated" Buddhism in a modern Thai farming village; of the dynamics of Tibetan ritual; and of life in a modern Korean Son monastery are but a few examples of this approach. To help draw out thematic cross sections in the Buddhist tradition, we have cross-referenced the narrative on such topics as lay practice, Buddhist linguistic theory, and the various permutations of Buddhist monastic life. We have also extensively cross-referenced the text to John Strong's anthology *The Experience of Buddhism* (henceforth referred to as Strong *EB*), in order to illuminate our account with primary sources.

Buddhism—viewed as a whole through the more than 2,500 years of its history—has been remarkably diverse. Although some writers have tried to maintain that the similarities among the various expressions of Buddhism are more important than the differences, a close look at those differences will show that they touch on issues that are most basic to the religion. Nonetheless, a continued close look at the development of the tradition shows that there have been men and women in every Buddhist country who have tried to bring their country's Buddhism into line with what they understand as the Dharma-Vinaya. Thus the attempt to reform the tradition to conform to its original sources—what modern critics of such attempts have branded "Protestant Buddhism"—is actually an integral part of the tradition itself and not simply the result of Western prejudices. As we will see in the following chapters, the history of Buddhism is in many ways the story of how the tension between these two tendencies—the need to adapt to a culture and the desire to remain true to the essence of the original teaching—has kept the religion alive. From the historian's point of view, both the tendency to adapt and the tendency to hold to an original standard qualify as valid components of Buddhism. In pointing out how a particular culture's presuppositions have shaped its perception and practice of Buddhism, or in comparing particular expressions of Buddhism with what is known of the original teachings, we are not attempting to pass judgment on the inherent worth of those expressions. Instead, we are simply attempting to provide an intellectually honest and intelligible portrait of changes and continuities in the Buddhist tradition.

In the course of writing this text, the historical method has occasionally forced us to take sides on issues that have divided Buddhists themselves. One of these issues concerns the relative ages of the various sources. Two of the "vehicles" of the Buddhist tradition—Hīnayāna and Mahāyāna—claim that their earliest texts go back to the time of the Buddha himself, whereas the third vehicle, Vajrayāna, claims that its texts go back even further in time. Comparative reading of the texts, however, reveals that the Mahāyāna texts themselves assume the preexistence of the Hīnayāna texts, and the Vajrayāna texts assume that of the Mahāyāna. At the same time, the major rules of the Prātimokṣa codes, generally recognized as being early by all schools of thought, outline a religious life that harmonizes better with the Hīnayāna discourses than with their Mahāyāna or Vajrayāna counterparts. Thus, in discussing the early history of the religion, we have given preference to the Hīnayāna accounts; Mahāyāna and Vajrayāna accounts appear at later points in the narrative. Among the Hīnayāna texts, the Pali Canon long had the field to itself as the only available source, but this situation has changed in recent years, as fragments of other Hīnayāna Canons have come to light. These fragments differ from the Pali in some details, but these differences do not touch on the major doctrines. Thus, in discussing the story of the Buddha's life, we have compared two different Hīnayāna versions—the Pali discourses, preserved by the "southern" branch of Buddhism, and Aśvaghoṣa's *Buddhacarita,* preserved by the "northern" branch—to give a sense of the variations among the Hīnayāna schools. In detailing the early doctrine, however, we have followed the Pali accounts throughout, as these come from the only complete Hīnayāna Canon extant and are thus the only sources that can provide us with a holistic picture of the relationships among the various teachings in the early centuries of the tradition. To use an archaeological analogy, the fragments of other canons resemble broken pieces of ancient statuary, whereas the Pali is an entire statue. Although the fragments can give us a sense of the range of motifs in ancient sculpture, only the complete statue can offer us a full picture of the aesthetic sense of its sculptors.

In following the Pali in this manner, we run the risk of blindly accepting the biases of the Theravāda school, which preserved the Pali; the Pali discourses, however, contradict a number of the important doctrines that became orthodox within the Abhidhamma and later texts of the school. This contradiction suggests that the school preserved the discourses relatively untouched. Discrepancies between the discourses and Pali Abhidhamma, however, have forced us to agree with some of the early Mahāyāna critiques of the Abhidhamma enterprise. As a result, there is no one school of Buddhism that we have followed throughout our narrative. And, again, we must make the point that the scholar's judgment as regards the historical reliability of a particular text is not the final word on the inherent worth of the teachings that the text may contain.

Our presentation attempts to cover five main aspects of Buddhism in as balanced a way as possible: ritual, devotionalism, doctrine, meditation practice, and institutional history. The five aspects fit rather neatly with the Triple Gem—the Buddha, Dharma, and Sangha—that serves as the basis of the religion in all its forms. Ritual and devotionalism relate to the place that the Buddha and bodhisattvas—Buddhas-to-be—assumed in the tradition; doctrine and meditation practice correspond to the Dharma; and institutional history corresponds to the Sangha. The balance among these elements varies from chapter to chapter, largely because the material available concerning the particular period or country may tend to be weighted in one direction more than others. In many cases we have given more emphasis to the Dharma, both because of its intrinsic interest and because of its pervasive influence on all other aspects of Buddhism. Rituals and institutions have meaning only when interpreted in light of the doctrine through which that meaning is articulated. In choosing this emphasis, we are honoring an assumption common to all Buddhist traditions: that the mind is the primary shaper of the world, rather than vice versa. Readers who prefer to approach the tradition from its more material aspects, such as its economic history, are directed to the bibliography.

In approaching the Buddhist tradition from the standpoint of its articulated Dharma, we find that the inherent tension between doctrine and practice goes a long way toward explaining much of the development of the tradition over the ages. This tension is present in all religions, but in Buddhism it is particularly acute. Right view, which expresses the essence of the doctrine, is meant to be used as a guide that leads ultimately to the abandonment of attachment to all views. In this sense it is therapeutic, aimed at achieving the "health" of freedom from suffering. To borrow an image from the texts, it is a raft across the ocean of suffering that is then abandoned when the ocean is crossed. On occasion there have been individual Buddhists of different eras who have regarded right view as an end in itself. Others have interpreted the result of the Path as the abandonment of views, and so regard right view as unnecessary in that one can abandon views simply by stilling the mind. This split in perspective has led to institutional splits between scholarly and meditating monastics. Much of the institutional history of Buddhism is concerned with the question of whether these two sides are working together or at cross purposes at any particular point in time.

The text falls into two parts. The first six chapters cover the history of Buddhism in India; the latter six explore Buddhism outside of India. The emphasis on India is due to the fact that Indian Buddhism forms the common stock from which all other Buddhist traditions stem. To understand the relationship between, say, Japanese and Burmese Buddhism, it is necessary to trace back through events in India. In both parts we have tried to cover what the most recent historical scholarship has been able to unearth in terms of what actually happened in the past, as well as how Buddhists in those times and places viewed their own history. In a few instances, such as the history of early Ch'an in China, we have focused more on modern than on traditional accounts simply because the traditions are already so well known in the West. In other cases, such as the thought of the Pudgalavādins, we have discussed in detail areas in which the recent discovery of sources has overthrown ideas long entrenched in the scholarly field, in order to alert students who may encounter those ideas in their reading. At the same time, however, there are areas in which we have found the latest scholarship to be less than convincing and so have inserted our reasons for adhering to more traditional accounts. We have also touched on some of the grand doctrinal syntheses—the work of Asanga, Buddhaghosa, Chih-i, Fa-tsang, Kūkai, and Tsongkhapa, among others—to show how Asian Buddhists themselves tried to deal with the bewildering wealth of their tradition. In addition, we have covered in detail the history of the meditation and devotional traditions that are now coming to the West, so that this text will be useful to students not only of Buddhism past, but also of Buddhism present and yet to come.

1

The Buddha's Awakening

1.1 THE SOCIAL AND RELIGIOUS CONTEXT OF EARLY BUDDHISM

Buddhism began with the Awakening of the Buddha (whose title means "Awakened One"), an event that took place in the fifth or sixth century B.C.E. at Bodhgaya, in the Ganges River plain of northeastern India. For Buddhists, the truths to which the Buddha awakened transcend the conditions of space and time; however, there is no denying that the social and cultural context in which he lived influenced the way he expressed his teachings and the way his contemporaries understood them. Thus the history of Buddhism must begin with an account of the events prior to the Buddha's Awakening that helped shape that context.

The sixth century B.C.E. was a period of great social and intellectual ferment in the Ganges plain. Absolute monarchs were developing new urban centers of political and economic power, based on a monetary economy supported by a rising class of merchants and property owners. In this manner, they were supplanting the traditional aristocratic and religious elites who had thrived in the earlier clan-based agrarian republics. As usually happens when elites are being disenfranchised, many sensitive members of society began questioning traditional values and opened their minds to radically new ideas regarding the ultimate meaning and goal of life.

The traditional religious beliefs and practices questioned by these members of society were those stemming from Vedic tradition. The *Vedas* were religious hymns of the Indo-Aryans, who had entered northwest India over the Khyber Pass (beginning sometime after 1600 B.C.E.), and who came to dominate the local population. These hymns had been memorized by a hereditary Aryan priestly caste called *brahmins,* who engaged in philosophical speculation and conducted empowerment rituals—often involving animal sacrifice—to bend the will of the gods in their pantheon to the wishes of their clientele. As their tradition developed on Indian soil, the patterns of the ritual came to eclipse the gods in importance, as the belief developed that the gods had no choice but to obey a ritual that was properly performed. This belief is reflected in the *Brāhmaṇas,* ritual and speculative texts that were composed in the first millennium B.C.E. and that best reflect the state of the Vedic tradition at the time of the Buddha. In contrast to the strict *orthopraxy* (rules of ritually proper behavior) advocated in the *Brāhmaṇas,* these texts contain a wide range of speculative thought concerning the origin and nature of the cosmos. Several strands of thought, however, predominate. One is that the cosmos is derived from Brahmā—conceived either as an anthropomorphic god or as a living principle—who gave birth to the cosmos through a process analogous to that of the Vedic ritual. Thus the ritual represents an order of being prior to that of the cosmos itself. Another strand is that the brahmins as a caste are descended from the mouth of Brahmā, whereas other castes are descended from more lowly parts of his body. Thus the brahmins are a higher order of being than the rest of humanity and hold a monopoly not only on ritual knowledge but also on knowledge of all ultimate truths. These strands of thought, which defined the stage of Vedism termed *Brahmanism,* became the focal point for the anti-Vedic reaction in the sixth century B.C.E.

As the social dislocations caused by the new political order became more and more acute, some members of society began to question the efficacy of the Vedic tradition, as new elites were coming into power with no access to Vedic means. New religious and philosophical groups surfaced, rejecting the basic claims of Brahmanism and asserting what they saw as truths of nature that human beings of any caste could discover through reason or meditation. These groups were called *śramaṇa* (literally, strivers). Although their original leaders were non-brahmins, they managed over time to attract some brahmins to their cause. Whether they were the result of a resurfacing of a pre-Aryan religious movement, an upsurge of dissidence from within the Aryan tradition, or a combination of both, no one knows for sure. They abandoned the family and its orthoprax ritual life, generally giving up normal work and social status to live as mendicants. These strivers, whom Siddhārtha joined at the age of 29, lived as wanderers, dwelling outside the villages and towns in forest *āśramas* (places of spiritual striving). There they formed fluid communities around masters who propounded a wide diversity of teachings, including extreme asceticism, skepticism, fatalism, and hedonism. In time, Siddhārtha became one such master, founded early Buddhism, and changed the face of Indian spiritual culture.

1.2 THE WORLDVIEW OF EARLY NORTH INDIAN THOUGHT

By the first millennium B.C.E., north Indian thought had accepted the notion—based on astronomers' calculations of planetary cycles—that time is measured in aeons, incomprehensibly long cycles that repeat themselves endlessly. The thinkers of the time presented their views of the drama of human life and the search for ultimate happiness against this vast temporal frame, but they differed widely in their interpretations of the main issues around which that drama revolved. The primary differences centered on two issues:

1. *Survival beyond death.* Most Vedic and śramaṇa schools assumed that personal identity extends through countless lifetimes in a vast cycle of repeated birth, death, and rebirth. Although early Vedic thought had expressed a positive attitude toward the idea of rebirth, by the time of Siddhārtha Gautama most of those who believed in rebirth felt that true happiness could be found only through release from the otherwise endless cycle. However, a śramaṇa band of hedonist materialists called *Lokāyata* denied the existence of any identity beyond death and insisted that happiness was to be found by indulging in the pleasures of the senses here and now.
2. *Causality.* Vedic thinkers and some of the śramaṇa schools accepted the idea that human action played a causative role in providing for one's happiness both in this lifetime and on into future lives. Views about how this causal principle worked, however, differed from school to school. For some Vedists, the only effective action was ritualistic. The Jains, one of the śramaṇa schools, taught that all action fell under linear, deterministic causal laws and acted as a bond to the recurring cycle. According to them, the only escape from the cycle lay in a life of nonviolence and inaction, culminating in a slow suicide by starvation. Some *Upaniṣads*—Brahmanical speculative texts—expressed causality as a morally neutral, purely physical process of evolution. Others stated that moral laws are intrinsic to the nature of causality, rather than being mere social conventions, and that the morality of an action determines how it affects one's future course in the round of rebirth. There is no way of knowing, though, whether these last texts were composed before or after Buddhist texts expressing this view. At any rate, all pre-Buddhist thinkers who accepted the principle of causality—however they expressed it—viewed it as a purely linear process.

On the other side of the question, the Lokāyatas insisted that no causal principle acts between events and that all events are self-caused. Thus actions have no consequences, and one may safely ignore morality and ritual orthopraxy in one's pursuit of sensual pleasure. Another śramaṇa school, the Ājīvakas, who specialized in astrology and divination, insisted that human life was entirely determined by impersonal, amoral fate; that human action played no role in providing for one's happiness or misery; that morality was purely a social convention; and that escape from the round of rebirth came only when the round worked itself out. Peace of mind could be found by accepting one's fate and by patiently waiting for the cycle, like a ball of string unwinding, to come to its end.

The divergent viewpoints on these two issues formed the intellectual backdrop for Siddhārtha Gautama's quest for ultimate happiness. In fact, his Awakening may be viewed as his own resolution of these issues, which provided a view of personal survival and the role of causality in the cosmos that proved influential for many centuries afterward, both in northern India and beyond.

1.3 THE BIOGRAPHY OF THE BUDDHA

The extant versions of the complete life of the Buddha were composed four hundred or more years after his death. Drawing on much earlier material from the canonical *Sūtras* (Discourses) and Vinaya (Discipline), they fill in the gaps in the canonical accounts with a fabric of myth (which many Buddhists believe to be true) and literary invention. The authors viewed the Buddha as an epic hero, and their purpose was to celebrate his deeds. They were not historians but poets and propagandists. For instance, Aśvaghoṣa (first century C.E.), in his epic Buddhacarita (Acts of the Buddha), depicted Gautama as a genuine human being; his narrative, even where it may not be historical, is dramatically authentic. The hero is a mortal experiencing conflicts; undergoing genuine temptations; trying, and ultimately rejecting, false courses; exercising choice at every point; and prevailing, not through fate or divine intervention, but through his own action. He is motivated by compassion for suffering humanity and exhibits the martial virtues of courage, steadfastness, initiative, and self-discipline. Throughout his ordeals he sustains a delicate sensitivity and an unshakable dignity.

How similar is this attractive character to the historical person? Probably as close as Aśvaghoṣa could manage with the data and concepts at his disposal. The quest for the historical Gautama, as that for the historical Jesus, is predestined to a measure of failure. We cannot get behind the portraits that the early communities synthesized for their founders; their reports are all we have. But although the *Saṅgha* (Community) created the image of the Buddha, the Buddha created the Sangha and in so doing impressed upon it his personality. The master exhorted his disciples to imitate him, and they formulated and transmitted an image of him, along with his teachings, as a model for later generations to emulate. Although the process of formulation entailed some distortion, the purpose of transmission ensured a measure of fidelity.

It should be noted that there is no single version of the Buddha's biography in Buddhist literature, nor can any one version be considered historical. There is no one use of the different aspects of the Buddha legend. Some accounts, in order to inspire faith in the reader, stress the miraculous acts of the

Buddha; others focus more on his personal qualities as models for Buddhists to emulate. The following account is based largely on one of the earliest extant sources—the Pali Canon as preserved by the Theravāda school (see Section 3.1)—and on Aśvaghoṣa's epic retelling of the legend.

1.3.1 Birth and Youth of the Bodhisattva

The Śākyas, the Buddha's ancestors, were members of a noble *kṣatriya* (warrior) class inhabiting a border district on the northeastern Ganges River plain just below the Himalayan foothills. For some unknown reason, they used a clan name from the brahmin class—*Gautama* (descendent of the sage Gotama). The Bodhisattva's father, Śuddhodana, was the chief aristocrat of the town of Kapilavastu, the remains of which have been tentatively identified by archaeologists on the present-day border between India and Nepal. During the later period when monarchies had become the norm in India, Buddhist chroniclers—including Aśvaghoṣa—portrayed Śuddhodana as a king, but the earlier texts reveal that he was simply one of a council of rulers of the Śākyan agrarian republic. His republic, like many republics at that time, was eventually annexed by the nearby kingdom of Kosala toward the end of the Buddha's life.

The Buddhist tradition dates the birth of Śākyamuni (Sage of the Śākyas) at around 624 B.C.E. Recent scholarship, however, places his birth at either 566 or 448 B.C.E. Buddhists celebrate his nativity on the full moon of Vaiśākha (April-May), the fourth month in the Indian calendar. According to the legend, he was conceived when his mother, Māyā, dreamed that a white elephant entered her body through the side. When her delivery time was approaching, she retired to the wooded garden of Lumbini, near Kapilavastu. There—standing with her upstretched right hand on the branch of a tree, a familiar fertility pose in Indian art—she gave birth to the Bodhisattva. The newborn child stood up, strode seven paces, and declared that this was his last birth: He was destined for Awakening. Shortly thereafter, Asita, an aged sage, examined the infant and prophesied that he would become a Buddha. Other accounts specified that he would become such only if he chose to leave the palace to become a wandering ascetic; otherwise, he would become a universal monarch, ruling over the entire Indian subcontinent. The parents named the boy Siddhārtha, "he who has achieved his ultimate goal."

The mythic elements in the nativity cycle present the Bodhisattva as innately different from ordinary people. The view holding that normal procreation and birth are impure betrays a body image that contrasts sharply with that of the *Upaniṣads,* which celebrate copulation as analogous to religious sacrifice.

Seven days after giving birth, Māyā died. Śuddhodana married her sister, Mahāprajāpatī, who brought up the young Bodhisattva. When he came of age, he was married to a bride (named Yaśodharā in most of the accounts) whom his father had selected. In due course Yaśodharā bore Siddhārtha a son, whom they named *Rāhula* (Fetter), an indication that the young father's heart was already turning away from the household life.

1.3.2 The Great Renunciation (Strong *EB*, sec. 1.3)

The Pali Suttas (=Sūtras) describe Prince Siddhārtha's youth and renunciation in simple terms. He lived a life of extreme luxury, with a separate palace for each of the three Indian seasons. On gaining maturity, however—and realizing that he, as other beings, was subject to aging, illness, and death—he lost all intoxication with youth, health, and life. Shaving off his hair and beard while his parents watched on with tearful faces, he left home for the life of an ascetic wanderer in order to seek the "unaging, unailing, deathless, sorrowless, undefiled, unexcelled security from bondage, *nirvāṇa*" (A.III.38; M.26—see Abbreviations, p. xviii).

Later accounts provide a more dramatic rendition of the events. Aśvaghoṣa relates how King Śuddhodana, from the very beginning, had tried to prevent his son from leaving the palace by tying him down with sensual pleasures, not only by arranging his marriage but also by surrounding him with young song-and-dance women and every other delight a man might desire. One day the young prince, longing to see the outside world, went out for a chariot ride through the capital city. There, for the first time, he saw a decrepit old man. Shocked, he asked his charioteer about the man's condition; the charioteer replied that such is the destiny of all human beings. The prince turned back to the palace and brooded in melancholy, taking no relish in the gaiety around him. On a second ride, he saw his first diseased man and reflected that people are foolish to revel under the constant shadow of illness. On the third trip, he saw his first corpse. Dismayed, he marveled that people could live heedlessly, forgetting the certainty of death.

Employing the conventions of Sanskrit drama, Aśvaghoṣa's poem exploits Siddhārtha's life of princely pleasure to provide an effective counterpoint to the traumatic encounters with impermanence and suffering. In an artfully composed dialogue, the king's counselor advises the young prince to disregard his disturbing encounters and to follow the example of bygone heroes and sages in pursuing the pleasures of erotic love. The Bodhisattva's reply is an eloquent statement of the ascetic case against the sensual life. Sensual joys are fleeting; death always casts its long shadow over life and blights all such transient happiness. The only true happiness would be one not subject to change. The pursuit of any lesser pleasure cannot be held up as a fulfilling or noble ideal.

The brooding prince rode out again, observed the peasants plowing, and—unlike the ordinary patrician—was moved to grief at the suffering of the toilers and oxen, and even at the slaughter of worms and insects by the plow. While meditating on the truth of suffering, he saw a religious mendicant and made up his mind to leave the household life, for only as a renunciate would he have the chance to follow rigorously the Path of mental training to see if it led to the impeccable happiness—beyond the reach of aging, illness, and death—that he sought .

The legend poignantly describes how, in the depth of night, the prince took a last look at his sleeping wife and infant son, mounted his horse, and rode out of the city, accompanied by his charioteer. After traveling a fair distance, Siddhārtha dismounted, sent his charioteer back to Śuddhodana with his ornaments and a message, then cut off his hair and exchanged clothes with a passing hunter.

The core of this episode, the Great Renunciation, is the conflict between the household and the renunciate ways of life. Far from encouraging his son, Śuddhodana had done everything in his power to prevent him from becoming a renunciate. At each crucial juncture, Siddhārtha recognized his familial duty and expressed strong affection toward his father. Aśvaghoṣa puts into the Bodhisattva's mouth a speech justifying departure for the homeless life as fidelity to an even higher *dharma* (duty or norm). Yet even in the society that spawned it, the renunciate life was a controversial ideal.

1.3.3 The Bodhisattva's Studies and Austerities (Strong *EB,* sec. 1.3)

The new mendicant, then 29 years old, went first to an ascetic teacher named Ārāḍa Kālāma, who taught a form of meditation leading to the "attainment of the state of nothingness." Gautama practiced the method and quickly attained the goal. Kālāma then set him up as his equal and co-teacher, but Gautama—concluding that this teaching did not lead to ultimate Awakening and nirvāṇa—left in search of a better teaching. He then studied under another ascetic leader, Udraka Rāmaputra, who taught the way to a higher state, the "attainment of neither perception nor non-perception." Gautama mastered this state and was proclaimed a teacher, but abandoned the method because it was inadequate for attaining his goal of "disenchantment, dispassion, cessation, tranquillity, superknowledge, Awakening, and nirvāṇa" (M.39). These seven quasi synonyms taken together reveal the main features of the goal that Gautama was seeking, and that his teachers thought they had found: pacification of mental turbulence, perfect direct knowledge, and attainment of the unconditioned state (see Section 1.4.3). Unlike the Upaniṣadic seers, they were not looking for contemplative identification of the soul and the world spirit, nor were they trying to starve out impurities through abstinence, as were the Jains. Instead, they were hoping to use meditative absorption in formless states to awaken to *nirvāṇa,* a term that literally means the extinguishing of a fire (see Section 2.3.2), but that in India was used figuratively at the time by a number of sects to denote the highest happiness, freedom, and peace.

Leaving Udraka Rāmaputra and the path of formless absorptions, the Bodhisattva then went eastward to Uruvela near Bodhgaya, where he found a pleasant spot and settled down to try the path of austerities. He practiced holding his breath in order to induce trances and was not deterred by the resulting violent headaches. Fasting, he came as close as he could to eating nothing at all, becoming utterly emaciated. He was joined in his strivings by five ascetics and continued in this painful course until the sixth year after the Great Renunciation. Then, seeing that this severe mortification had not led him to liberating knowledge, and having exhausted the various forms of ascetic practice current in his day, he tried to think of another way. He remembered an incident in his childhood: While sitting under a shady tree as his father was performing a royal plowing ritual, he had entered the first *dhyāna* (a pleasant and rapturous absorption in the inner sense of the physical body). Perhaps this might be a fruitful method, he surmised, but he realized that his body was too weak to regain that blissful concentration or to use it to gain liberating insight.

The legend goes on to say that Gautama then sat under a sacred tree. A woman named Sujātā had vowed a yearly offering to this tree if she bore a son. The wish having been fulfilled, she was preparing to offer a fine bowl of rice and milk. Her maid came upon the Bodhisattva sitting there, mistook him for the spirit of the tree, and reported the apparition to her mistress, who came and presented the food to Gautama herself. A Pali Sutta (M.36) states simply that Gautama took rice and barley gruel. The five mendicants then left him in disgust, saying that he had given up striving and was living in abundance.

Gautama's rejection of extreme austerities hinged on a critical moment when he realized that trying to gain liberation by escaping from the body through mortification was as ineffectual as attempting to escape through abstract absorptions. Caught at a dead end, he was able to open his mind to the possibility that physical pleasure of a nonsensual variety was not to be feared, and that it might form the basis for the liberating insight he sought. He went on to recognize that a healthy body is necessary for the development of discernment in order to understand the relationship of body to mind. In so doing, he took the first step on the Middle Way toward Awakening, a way that became a central feature of the Dharma (or doctrine) he later taught.

1.3.4 Temptation by Māra

After accepting the meal from Sujātā, Gautama went and sat under another tree, the *Bodhi Tree* (Tree of Awakening), facing east and resolving not to arise until he had attained his goal. Māra (the personification of death, delusion, and temptation) grew alarmed at the prospect of the Bodhisattva's attaining victory and escaping from his realm, and so tried to deflect him from his striving—an episode that later tradition lavishly embellished over the centuries. The Pali Canon (Sn.III.2) simply says that Māra tempted the Bodhisattva in two stages, first trying to plant doubts in the Bodhisattva's mind and then calling up his armies to assault him. The Bodhisattva, however, recognized Māra's 10 armies for what they were—sensuality, discontent, hunger and thirst, craving, sloth and torpor, fear, doubt, hypocrisy, self-exaltation, and the desire for fame—and this was enough to send them away in defeat. Aśvaghoṣa adds little to the legend, aside from depicting Māra's armies in grisly detail and attributing the Bodhisattva's victory over them to his persistent resolve. Legends postdating Aśvaghoṣa, however, add that Māra finally challenged the Bodhisattva's right to Awakening, in response to which the Bodhisattva touched Mother Earth to bear witness to his merit, causing her to rise up and squeeze an ocean of water out of her hair (symbolic of the cooling waters of his benevolence), washing the armies away. These legends also add a third stage to the temptation, in which Māra's daughters—Discontent, Delight, and Craving—volunteer to seduce the Bodhisattva, but they too eventually fail. As the sun sets, Māra and his retinue withdraw in defeat.

This last version of the story prevailed over the earlier versions as a favorite in Buddhist art and as a vivid allegory for the Buddhist teaching on the four determinations (or mental factors) needed in any spiritual striving: discernment, truth, renunciation, and calm (M.140). First, one must use discernment to overcome doubts that the goal is unattainable and not worth the effort involved. Then, in order to overcome fear (as tendencies that are deep-seated in one's character protest their coming destruction), one must remain true to one's resolve for the genuine good. Next, as one gains a sense of one's powers, one must practice firm renunciation to overcome the most insidious temptation of all: to divert those powers to one's own personal pleasure. Only then can the mind attain the calm needed for true understanding.

1.3.5 The Awakening
(Strong *EB,* sec. 1.3)

As the full moon rose over the river before him, the Bodhisattva focused on his in-and-out breathing and ascended the four stages of dhyāna. The first stage is a meditative absorption produced by detaching from sensual thoughts and unskillful attitudes. The mind attains a state of unity while evaluating the object to which it consciously directs its thoughts, giving rise to a sense of rapture and ease born of seclusion. The second stage is an absorption free from the activity of evaluation and directed thought. There is singleness of mind and internal assurance, in addition to rapture and ease born of composure. The third stage—dispassionate rather than rapturous—is mindful and fully aware, with a feeling of bodily ease. The fourth stage is a state of pure equanimity and mindfulness, free of elation and sorrow, pleasure and pain.

All the levels of meditative absorption are characterized by concentration and facilitate discernment—not theoretical knowledge, but direct perception. The fourth level serves as the foundation for *abhijñā* (the six superknowledges): (1) psychic powers (such as levitation and walking on water; see Strong *EB*, sec. 3.5.6); (2) the divine ear or psychic hearing; (3) knowledge of others' minds; (4) memory of one's former lives; (5) the divine eye or psychic vision; and (6) the ending of the *āsrava* (binding effluents or pollutants of the mind); namely, sensual desire, becoming (states of being), views, and ignorance. The first five superknowledges are mundane, attainable even by those who simply suppress, rather than eradicate, their mental defilements. The sixth superknowledge, however, is supramundane, realized only at the completion of the Noble Eightfold Path (see Section 2.3.1). The attainment of the sixth superknowledge distinguishes the *arhant,* or perfected saint, from the mere adept who has psychic powers within the realm of the conditioned but who lacks the ability to transcend them and attain the unconditioned.

Gautama's progress toward release from the conditions of bondage is described in terms of three forms of cognition that are identical with three of the superknowledges. During the first watch of the night (dusk to 10 P.M.), he acquired the first cognition, which is identical with the fourth superknowledge: that of knowing his many thousands of previous lifetimes, seeing them one by one. A Pali Sutta (M.4) depicts the Buddha as later describing the experience as follows: "When the mind was thus concentrated, purified, bright, unblemished, rid of defilement, pliant, malleable, steady, and attained to imperturbability, I directed it to the knowledge of recollecting my past lives. I recollected my manifold past lives, i.e., one birth, two, . . . five, ten, . . . fifty, a hundred, a thousand, a hundred thousand, many eons of cosmic contraction, many eons of cosmic expansion, many eons of cosmic contraction and expansion: 'There I had such a name, belonged to such a clan, had such an appearance. Such was my food, such my experience of pleasure and pain, such the end of my life. Passing away from that state, I re-arose there. There, too, I had such a name, belonged to such a clan, had such an appearance. Such was my food, such my experience of pleasure and pain, such the end of my life. Passing away from that state, I re-arose here [into my current life].' Thus I remembered my manifold past lives in their modes and details. This was the first knowledge I attained in the first watch of the night. Ignorance was destroyed; knowledge arose; darkness was destroyed; light arose—as happens in one who is uncomplacent, ardent, and resolute."

During the second watch (10 P.M. to 2 A.M.), the Bodhisattva acquired the second cognition: psychic vision—the fifth superknowledge—with which he surveyed the decease and rebirth of living beings everywhere. The entire cosmos, it is said, appeared to him as in a mirror. He saw that good karma leads to a happy rebirth, and evil karma to a miserable one. According to the same Sutta, the Buddha later described the experience in these words: "When the mind was thus concentrated . . . and attained to imperturbability, I directed it to the knowledge of the passing away and reappearance of beings. I saw—by means of my psychic vision, purified and surpassing the ordinary human—beings passing away and reappearing, and I discerned how they are inferior and superior, beautiful and ugly, fortunate and unfortunate, in accordance with their karma: 'These beings—who were endowed with bad conduct of body, speech, and mind, who reviled the noble ones, held wrong views and undertook actions under the influence of wrong views—with the break-up of the body, after death, have reappeared in the plane of deprivation, the bad destiny, in the lower realms. But these beings—who were endowed with good conduct of body, speech, and mind, who did not revile the noble ones, who held right views and undertook actions under the influence of right views—with the break-up of the body, after death, have reappeared in the good destinies, in the upper realms.' Thus, by means of psychic vision, purified and surpassing the human, I saw beings passing away and reappearing, and I discerned how they are inferior and superior, beautiful and ugly, fortunate and unfortunate, in accordance with their karma. This was the second knowledge I attained in the second watch of the night. Ignorance was destroyed; knowledge arose; darkness was destroyed; light arose—as happens in one who is uncomplacent, ardent, and resolute."

During the third watch (2 A.M. to dawn), the Bodhisattva acquired the third cognition (and sixth superknowledge): that of the ending of the āsravas. This involved realizing the principle of *pratītya-samutpāda* (dependent co-arising; see Section 1.4.3), the interdependent pattern of 12 preconditions whereby the asrava of ignorance gives rise not only to *duḥkha* (personal suffering) but also to the experience of the world of rebirth as a whole. By meditating on this pattern as it displayed itself directly to his awareness, Gautama was able to unravel it and gain release. In the Pali Sutta he reports: "When the mind was thus concentrated . . . and attained to imperturbability, I directed it to the knowledge of the ending of the āsravas. I discerned, as it actually was, that 'This is duḥkha. . . . This is the origination of duḥkha. . . . This is the cessation of duḥkha. . . . This is the way leading to the cessation of duḥkha. . . . These are the āsravas. . . . This is the origination of the āsravas. . . . This is the cessation of the āsravas. . . . This is the way leading to the cessation of the āsravas.' My heart, thus knowing, thus seeing, was released from the āsrava of sensual desire, released from the āsrava of becoming, released from the āsrava of views, and released from the āsrava of ignorance. With release, there was the knowledge, 'Released.' I discerned that, 'Birth is ended, the holy life fulfilled, the task done. There is nothing further for this world.' This was the third knowledge I attained in the third watch of the night. Ignorance was destroyed; knowledge arose; darkness was destroyed; light arose—as happens in one who is uncomplacent, ardent, and resolute."

In short, the Bodhisattva's remembering of his past lives during the first watch of the night allowed him in the second watch to see the mechanism of karma that determined the fates of all beings. By focusing on the source of karma in his own mind during the third night watch, he came to see the laws underlying all karma and conditioned experience and, through his insight, attained unconditioned release.

The new day dawned on Gautama, now the Buddha. According to legend, the natural world celebrated the event with miracles. The earth swayed, thunder rolled, rain fell from a cloudless sky, and blossoms fell from the heavens. Gautama's ancestors, then sages in paradise, observed his victory and offered him reverence. The Buddha thus fulfilled, at the spiritual level, the family obligation that, as a Bodhisattva, he seemed to have forsaken in the worldly sense.

1.4 AN INTERPRETATION OF THE AWAKENING

What actually happened on the night of the Awakening? The oldest account is stylized and exhibits typical mythic features. It purports, though, to be autobiographical, and there is reason to believe that at least parts of it originated with Gautama himself. First-person reporting of "peak experiences" was not a common genre in pre-Buddhist Indian literature and flourished only sporadically in later centuries. Implicit in such reports is the affirmation that the particular experiences of a historical person are of outstanding value. The dignity, economy, and sobriety of the account not only highlight the magnitude of Gautama's claims but also strongly suggest a remarkable man behind the style: composed and aware, assertive but not bombastic. If disciples put such words into the mouth of their master, then who put into their minds such an image of him?

The sequence of nocturnal watches matched with the three cognitions and the coincidence of daybreak and Awakening are mythic in style, but not necessarily fictitious. The movement from darkness to light, common to many religious traditions, is more than metaphorical. Darkness is an objective aid to sensory withdrawal without which the inner light cannot burst into radiance. The initiate into the Eleusinian and Orphic mystery cults sat in darkness until engulfed by a great light. The Eskimo aspirant to shamanhood passes long hours in solitary meditation and, in a climactic moment, feels aglow with a brain-centered light that facilitates psychic vision. The light in question—with shamans as with Buddhist monks and nuns—is a physical experience of overwhelming radiance, often described in meditation manuals in connection with states of greatly heightened sensitivity.

The full moon may be a ritualistic and symbolic element in the story. The nights of the new, full, and half moons were considered ominous in ancient India and were marked with fasts and rites. The ritual high point of the month, the night of the full moon would have seemed most appropriate for the Awakening, and the event may in fact have taken place then. One can imagine the effect of the cool, moonlit, tropical night after a hot summer day on Gautama's psyche. Symbolically, too, the night of the full moon has meaning extending back into ancient Sanskrit literature. On this one night, the ever-being-reborn moon imitates the fullness of the sun, mirroring the changelessness to be found in the midst of change.

The early texts frequently quote the Buddha to the effect that nirvāṇa is indescribable, beyond all measure or words, beyond all phenomenal flux or rest, a unique experience expressible only in metaphor. But nowhere does the Pali Canon say that the knowledge precipitating the realization of nirvāṇa is inexpressible. However splendid the insights and however exalted the state of freedom they engendered in the mind, the Awakening began with the discovery of communicable ideas: the realization through meditative absorption of the specific destinies of all living beings and of the general principles governing these destinies. The first cognition, memory of one's own former lives, is a shamanic power, documented among archaic cultures throughout the world. The second cognition, perception of living beings dying and being reborn everywhere, is also a type of shamanic power—unobstructed cosmic vision that sometimes reveals a cycle of rebirths—widely attributed to prophets and other adepts in archaic cultures. The specifically Buddhist feature is the ethical correlation of good karma—intentional deeds—with happy births and bad karma with miserable ones, together with the realization that the processes of the world as a whole stem from the factors at play in the mind's direct processing of experience. The third cognition, like the first two, is presented as a direct perception, but it goes beyond the realm of shamanic powers into a direct understanding of the causal nature of the processes of experience in and of themselves. Modern philosophy calls this approach *phenomenology* (a type of analysis in which experience is a given, and one tries to understand it from within). The description of this insight appears rather abstract, but it was clearly intended to be experiential and concrete. The universals that Gautama saw were simply the patterns of events discernible by anyone who develops the mind to the same pitch of uncomplacency, ardency, and resolution. The content of Awakening is thus two-thirds shamanism, ethically transformed, and one-third phenomenology, a feature found in civilizations but not in archaic or primal cultures.

The archaic elements here are in service to the higher ones. The first and second cognitions constitute an empirical verification of the doctrines of repeated rebirth and the consequences of intentional actions. In Gautama's view, the materialists—who say that there is no afterlife and no fruition of past deeds—were clearly wrong. What determines one's rebirth, however, is not sacrifice, as the *Brāhmaṇas* maintained, nor mere knowledge, as is claimed in the *Upaniṣads,* but rather the quality of one's entire life. Those who intentionally do good in thought, word, and deed, who speak well of the saints and hold right views, are reborn in a happy state, in heaven or on Earth. Those who intentionally do harm are reborn in a wretched state, in the lower destinies.

The idea of moral causality seems only in the sixth century B.C.E. to have become dissociated from notions of the efficacy of ritual and ascetic acts. There is no assurance that Upaniṣadic passages expressing the idea are pre-Buddhist. If, as is probable, Gautama discovered this comprehensive moral worldview, it is no wonder that the vision burst upon him with revelatory force as he saw the principle enacted in a cosmic panorama of doing, dying, and being reborn again and again.

One novel feature of early Buddhist ethics is the primacy they give to the mind, and to intention in particular. Gautama's achievement in freeing ethics from ritual and orthoprax rule was a momentous event in the history of world religion. Good and bad are not qualities of an action, as they are in Vedic ritual and Jainism, but of the intention motivating the act. Unintentional deeds have merely commonsense consequences, not karmic ones. In contrast to later Hinduism, the physical act in itself is neither pure nor impure, although certain acts—such as killing, stealing, and illicit sex—are inherently unskillful because they invariably involve at least subtle levels of wrong motivation in the mind.

Realizing that the mind is the prime mover of the cycle of death and rebirth, Gautama applied his newly found understanding of the principle of karma to the intentional processes of cognition taking place at that moment in his mind. This enabled him to see how the preconditions for suffering interacted and how they could be brought to cessation. This was the knowledge that brought about his release; while the totality of his experience of release, transcending all limitations of cosmos and self, was what guaranteed the validity of what he had come to know.

1.4.1 The Bodhisattva's Remembrance of His Past Lives and the Jātakas

The three knowledges that constituted the Awakening—remembrance of past lives, knowledge of the death and rebirth of beings, and knowledge of the ending of the āsravas—had a long-term effect on Buddhist doctrine. The Bodhisattva's remembrance of his previous lives during the first watch of the night gave rise to a large body of story literature, in many recensions, called the *Jātakas* or *Tales of the [Buddha's] Past Lives.* From the tale of Sumati, when the Bodhisattva vowed in the presence of the previous Buddha Dīpankara to achieve Buddhahood (Strong *EB*, sec. 1.4.1), to the account of his penultimate human life as the Prince Vessantara (Strong *EB*, sec. 1.4.2), the Pali Jātakas record 357 past lives as a human being, 66 as a god, and 123 as an animal. Few of the tales portray the Bodhisattva as a woman, but there is no telling whether this was the result of a bias on the part of the Buddhist compilers or a limitation in the pre-Buddhist narrative tradition from which they drew. The Jātakas have been enormously popular throughout the Buddhist world, serving as themes for painting and sculpture, from the early Buddhist *stūpas* (memorial shrines or reliquaries) onward. Some of the tales instruct Buddhists in proper ethical action, whereas others emphasize the supreme effort the Bodhisattva needed to make in perfecting the virtues required for Awakening over the course of many lifetimes. As the Jātakas portray his diverse incarnations—from ascetic, king, wonder worker, gambler, smith, and robber, to tree spirit, mountain deity, and all manner of animals, including lizard, frog, dog, pig, and rat, but never as a denizen of the lower destinies—they give a sense of the vast drama of life in which the Bodhisattva participated before his last life as Gautama. For Buddhists, the "biography" of the present Buddha consists not of one but of many lives.

1.4.2 The Wheel of Life and the Hierarchy of Beings (Strong *EB*, secs. 1.5.1, 1.5.2)

Gautama's vision of the details of *saṃsāra* (the round of existence) and karma during the second night watch—combined with the 12 preconditions for suffering (see Section 1.4.3)—was systematized in later Buddhist art in the image of the Wheel of Life. This image (see figure on p. 27) is a map Buddhists use to make the cosmos intelligible and to show the way to salvation. The earliest extant pictorial representation of the wheel is at Ajanta; it was developed especially in Tibetan Buddhist art, where the wheel was often conspicuously painted in monastery vestibules or on hanging scrolls used for meditation.

Buddhist texts present no account of creation, as saṃsāra is said to have no discernible point of origin in time. Rather, the Sūtras stress that it is more important to understand the constant re-creation of the round through one's acts of intention, for then one can find one's way out of the round. The Wheel of Life, the Buddhist cosmology, is thus the psychological equivalent of a creation myth, an attempt to account for a person's world experience in terms of the drama of personal choice and consequence. The entire wheel is held in the mouth and claws of the monster Time or Impermanence. Its perimeter is ringed with the 12 preconditions. In its nave are three animals: the cock, symbolizing passion; the snake, aversion; and the pig, ignorance. They are the propelling forces of the cycle of existence, in which karmic retribution determines where on the wheel each individual will be reborn.

The cosmos as a whole consists of three realms: in ascending order, they are the sensual realm, the realm of form, and the realm of formlessness. Within these realms are located the six major destinies: hell and the levels of hungry ghosts, common animals, human beings, and *devas* (spirits, deities) in the sensual realm; and *Brahmās* (gods) in the realms of form and formlessness. Rebirth in the three lower destinies results from evil acts; the three upper destinies reward good.

The most degraded beings are the inhabitants of the hells, which are hot and cold subterranean places of suffering that lasts for many aeons. However, Buddhist hells are purgatorial, and not places of everlasting retribution. Once the ripening of the karma is complete—a process accomplished only through the passage of time—the individuals thus punished can ascend and reach the human realm, where they again must face moral responsibility for their future. Next lowest is the realm of hungry ghosts. These beings haunt the earth's surface, continually tormented by insatiable hunger. They stand outside walls and gates, invisible to all but a few human beings, mutely pleading to be fed. The realm of animals ranks just above the hungry ghosts. Individuals reborn as animals must suffer the cruelties to which dumb creatures are subjected. This realm is somewhat confused by the inclusion of the *nāgas* (water spirits, inhabiting rivers, lakes, and oceans) and other mythical beasts and birds. The nāgas are either dragons or cobras, which may indicate that their cult is hybrid. Like human beings, they can either be protective or destructive. The enemies of the nāgas are *garuḍas* (half human and half bird of prey).

The three upper fortunate destinies reward good karma. Of these, the human destiny is considered to be the lowest but also the most important, for only here can virtue and wisdom be increased. All other realms are retributions or rewards for choices and actions taken in the human realm. Even when someone attains nirvāṇa while sojourning in a heaven, it is due to the ripening of merit won as a human being.

The highest sensual destiny is that of the devas, augmented in later versions of the wheel by the *asuras,* beings of a slightly lower order than devas who—similar to the Titans in Greek mythology—perpetually oppose them. Both of these destinies are inhabited by a diversity of beings, but all are there by virtue of their karma and, when fruits of their merit run out, are subject to rebirth. The early Buddhists inherited a diverse tradition of spirits and celestial beings from their Aryan and non-Aryan predecessors, and the early texts offer no one standard list of who's who in the lower deva realms. The lowest level contains the spirits inhabiting the earth's surface and the lower atmosphere. Prominent among these are the *yakṣas* and *gandharvas.* The yaksas were primarily tree spirits, the chief divinities of a popular non-Vedic cult. The gandharvas in the *Ṛg Veda* were spirits of the clouds and waters, and so were associated with fertility. In their aerial aspect as cloud spirits, they came to be musicians attendant upon the higher devas. Gandharvas mate with *apsaras* (celestial nymphs); such couples are frequently shown in early Buddhist art. Although many female spirits are portrayed in early Buddhist texts, only Śrī (or Lakṣmī), the goddess of fortune, is mentioned by name. She appears in Buddhist art of the second century B.C.E., standing or sitting on her lotus pediment and being bathed by two elephants.

The celestial levels of the devas are considerably more orderly than the earthly levels. The first level among the celestial devas is that of the Four Great Kings, also called World-Protectors, each of whom rules one of the cardinal points and a race of earthly devas. The most prominent of these kings is Kubera, also called Vaiśravaṇa, ruler of the North and of yakṣas. He was widely worshiped as the god of wealth, and the Buddhists portrayed him as vowing to protect all those who practice their religion. The second rank of celestial devas are the Gods of the Thirty-Three, the old pantheon of the *Ṛg Veda,* headed by Indra, more generally called Śakra in Buddhist texts. He reveres the Buddha and protects the Dharma. Buddhist propagandists presented the reformed character of the fierce warrior god of the *Ṛg Veda* as a model for their kṣatriya converts. Above the old Vedic Thirty-Three, the Buddhists imposed four more tiers of devas, of which only the second, *Tuṣita* (Satisfied), is important. The Bodhisattva spends his next-to-last life in this realm before returning to the human world to become a Buddha. His mother is reborn there after giving birth to him.

At the upper limit of the cosmos lies the Brahmā world. This world consists of 20 heavens: the first four in the realm of form—corresponding to the first four dhyānas—and the remaining ones in the realm of formlessness, corresponding to the formless levels of dhyāna. Rebirth in the Brahmā world results from great virtue, meditation, and the development of the four Brahmā Attitudes: unlimited goodwill, compassion, appreciation, and equanimity. This is the only heavenly world in which there is no gender. On occasion the Great Brahmās visit the earth to interact with human beings. One, Sahāmpati, visited the Buddha to encourage him to preach the Dharma (see Section 2.1).

The early Buddhist texts are remarkable for the sense of easy familiarity they display between the human and spirit worlds. Theirs is an attitude of polite respect for spirits, but not worship. They take the existence of spirits for granted but do not consider them especially sacred. Spirits, after all, are subject to passion, aversion, and delusion, and thus to the law of karma. In this, they are inferior to the Buddha and arhants who have overcome all mental defilements and thus create no further karma. Even the great gods of the popular religion of the time, Indra and Brahmā, were not regarded by the Buddhists as eternal persons but merely as individuals born into those positions and destined to fall from office when their karma ran out.

This gives the spirit world an ethical basis, rendering it rational and more benign. Malicious spirits were not to be appeased with sacrifice but rather tamed through the power and goodwill of a holy individual. The theme of the human sage using superior mental powers to convert ogres came to typify in later centuries the way in which Buddhism interacted with the spirit cults it encountered in every land to which it spread. As for the benign spirits, the early texts treat their foibles with a gentle humor entirely devoid of awe. For example, one of the more entertaining exchanges in the Pali Canon (D.21) is between the Buddha and a gandharva who relates how on the night of the Buddha's Awakening, when all the other deities were breathlessly awaiting the outcome, he was able to sneak off and seduce the nymph of his dreams. In another story (S.I.25), a female tree deva propositions a handsome young monk whom she spies half-naked after he emerges from bathing in a river. Yet another passage (D.11) depicts the Great Brahmā as a pompous hypocrite intent on hiding his ignorance from his adoring retinue. Thus the spirit world is viewed as not being radically different from the human world, and even its refined pleasures, like all other pleasures in the Wheel of Life, are doomed to pass away when the power of the individual's karma is depleted.

The Wheel of Life is thus not simply a map of the cosmos, but also an analysis of karma and an evaluation of its results. Human volition lies at the center of the wheel and powers its every turn. One's individual mind is the only author of rebirth in a lower or higher realm; no one else can bring about the individual's ultimate salvation. The human person stands at the center of creation with the assurance that whatever destiny is suffered or enjoyed is fully merited. Even the highest rewards the wheel has to offer, though, are doomed to pass away as the wheel turns, for all the realms of saṃsāra are impermanent and subject to recurrent death. Ultimate happiness can be found only by transcending karma and gaining release. Nirvāṇa, the goal, is nowhere on the wheel but instead utterly transcends it.

1.4.3 Dependent Co-Arising and the Cessation of Suffering (Strong *EB*, sec. 3.3.1)

As we have noted, in the third watch of the night Gautama discovered the causes and cure for bondage to saṃsāra. The variant accounts agree that the basis of this discovery was the realization of *pratītya-samutpāda* (dependent co-arising), which came to be regarded as the heart of the Buddha's Awakening. A Pali Sutta (M.28) says, "Whoever sees dependent co-arising sees the Dharma." "Dharma" here has three levels of meaning: doctrine, practice, and nirvāṇa (attainment). On the first two levels, dependent co-arising and Dharma came to be viewed as equivalent. On the level of doctrine, dependent co-arising became the basis for the standard Buddhist view of conditioned experience. Its categories formed the basic terms for analyzing experience into its ultimate components; its pattern of causality acted as the framework for understanding how the categories interacted to fuel the round of rebirth. On the level of practice, dependent co-arising functioned as the map for unraveling the causal process; through its complexity it also became the riddle that the practitioner tried to comprehend through meditation. Hence it became the primary guide for and topic of Buddhist contemplation.

On the level of attainment, the act of understanding dependent co-arising was the prerequisite for realizing the Dharma. As a Pali Sutta (S.XII.70) states, first there is the knowledge of dependent co-arising, after which there is the knowledge of nirvāṇa. For this reason, insight into dependent co-arising served as the hallmark for distinguishing the Buddhist Awakening experience from other states of altered or expanded consciousness.

The unusual pattern in which dependent co-arising is expressed can be explained by Gautama's approach to the problem of suffering, which was similar to that of phenomenology. After seeing that the processes of saṃsāra are driven by the mind, he focused his attention on the patterns of cause and effect immediately apparent to his present awareness. One of the traditional names of the knowledge he attained as a result—knowledge and vision of things as they are (*yathābhūtañāṇa-dassana*)—reflects this fact. It denotes the act of understanding the processes of experience on their own terms, as they are directly experienced, rather than trying to establish whether they correspond to anything that might be assumed to lie outside of direct experience. For the purpose of understanding the cause of suffering, the Buddha formulated several modes of analyzing direct experience, based on the insights he gained in the course of the third watch of the night.

According to the most basic mode, experience could be divided into two spheres: conditioned and unconditioned. Conditioned experience was further divided into two classes: *nāma-rūpa* (name and form), that is, mental and physical phenomena. These classes were in turn divided into two basic patterns. The first pattern was that of the six sense fields: the senses of sight, hearing, smell, taste, touch, and ideation, together with their respective objects. The first five sense fields belong to the category of form, and ideation to the category of name. In the second pattern, the five *skandha* (aggregates), form was one category, whereas name was divided into four: feelings—pleasure, pain, and neither-pleasure-nor-pain; perception (the mental act of labeling things); mental formations (thoughts, intentions, and so forth); and consciousness of the six sense fields.

The unconditioned sphere, because it was essentially simple and uncompounded, was not divided into any categories. The Buddha gave it several names—including the uncompounded, consciousness without feature or without surface, the sphere where the six sense fields cease, and the Deathless—but for the most part he did not describe it, for description would count as a perception to which one could easily become attached, thus blocking the possibility of experiencing the unconditioned. Language, being a conditioned phenomenon itself, was adequate for describing the conditioned, but totally inadequate and inappropriate for describing the unconditioned. Even terms such as *all, exists, doesn't exist, both exists and doesn't exist,* and *neither exists nor doesn't exist,* the Buddha said, could apply only to the conditioned. The unconditioned lay beyond their range. What could be usefully said about the unconditioned was that it transcended suffering and stress, that it was worth experiencing, and that there was a method for experiencing it.

Thus the early texts are quite clear on the point that the conditioned and unconditioned are radically separate. One early passage depicts the Buddha as strongly criticizing a group of monks who tried to develop a theory whereby the conditioned was derived out of the unconditioned or somehow lay within it (M.1). Duḥkha (suffering), he said, is inherent in the stressful nature of conditioned phenomena, whereas the unconditioned is totally free from suffering. Suffering could not possibly be produced by absolute freedom from suffering; because the nature of conditioning is such that causes are in turn influenced by their effects, the unconditioned could not itself function as a condition. The only way the unconditioned could be experienced would be by unraveling the conditioned from within and bringing it to cessation. To do so, one would need to know the pattern in which the various categories of conditioned experience depended on one another. This pattern the Buddha called "dependent co-arising," which is best understood as an analysis of how the various sense fields and aggregates in the sphere of the conditioned go about grouping, disbanding, and regrouping in various configurations as they influence one another in giving rise to suffering and to the conditioned world as a whole. This last point is one of the most distinctive insights of the Buddha's Awakening: the realization that personal experience and the entire conditioned universe all boil down to this single pattern, whose factors work over time but can also be directly experienced at the mind in the present.

Dependent co-arising is most commonly expressed as *nidāna* (12 preconditions). These are (1) ignorance, (2) formations, (3) consciousness, (4) name-and-form, (5) the six sense fields, (6) contact, (7) feeling, (8) craving, (9) sustenance, (10) becoming, (11) birth (that is, rebirth), and (12) aging and dying, with their attendant suffering. The pictures ringing the Wheel of Life (see figure on p. 27) represent each of these preconditions with a scene (starting from bottom left and continuing counterclockwise): (1) a blind old woman, (2) a potter making pots, (3) a monkey picking fruit, (4) a man on a journey, (5) a many-windowed house, (6) lovers touching, (7) arrows piercing the eyes, (8) eating and drinking, (9) a person picking fruit, (10) a pregnant woman, (11) a woman delivering a child, and (12) a corpse being carried away.

The interlocking chain of conditions can be analyzed in two directions: from precondition to condition, or from condition back to precondition. On the last watch of the night of his Awakening, Gautama began with the most blatant conditions and worked backward to their underlying preconditions, as follows:

12. *Aging and dying depend on birth (that is, rebirth).* If there were no birth, there would be no process exhibiting aging and death. It is important to note here, and in the following causal links, that "birth," "aging," and "dying" refer not only to the arising, decay, and passing away of the body, but also to the repeated arising, decay, and passing away of mental states, moment by moment. In fact, during the third watch on the night of his Awakening, Gautama was probably most concerned with analyzing mental states

as his primary examples of birth, aging, and death, and with gaining insight through them into how these processes functioned in the cosmos as a whole.

11. *Birth depends on becoming.* If there were no coming-to-be (through karma) of the conditions of the sensual realm, the realm of form, or the formless realm, there would be no locus for rebirth. Again, these realms refer not only to levels of being, but also to levels of mental states. Some mental states are concerned with sensual images, others with forms (such as the form of the body experienced in dhyāna), and still others with formless abstractions, such as space or nothingness.

10. *Becoming depends on sustenance.* The image here is of a fire remaining in existence by appropriating sustenance from its fuel. The process of becoming takes its sustenance from the five skandhas, whereas the act of taking sustenance is to cling to these skandhas in any of four ways: through sensual intentions, through views, through precepts and practices, or through doctrines of the self. Without these forms of clinging, the sensual, form, and formless realms would not come into being.

9. *Sustenance depends on craving.* If one did not thirst for sensuality, for coming-to-be, or for no change in what has come to be, then the process would not appropriate fuel.

8. *Craving depends on feeling.* If pleasant and painful feelings were not experienced, one would not thirst for continuing experience of the pleasant or for cessation of the unpleasant.

7. *Feeling depends on contact.* Without contact there is no pleasure or pain to be felt.

6. *Contact depends on the six sense fields.* If either the senses or their objects were absent, there would be nothing to make contact.

5. *The six sense fields depend on name-and-form.* "Name" here is defined as feeling, perception, attention, contact, and intention. Because the sense fields are equivalent to name-and-form, some lists of the preconditions omit the sense fields and interpret contact as occurring primarily between name and form.

4. *Name-and-form depends on consciousness of the six sense fields.* Without this kind of consciousness, the physical birth of the individual, which is composed of the skandhas, would abort, whereas on the level of momentary mental birth there would be nothing to activate an experience of the skandhas.

3. *Consciousness of the six sense fields depends on the forces that bring about the formation of the body, speech, and mind.* Here, on the level of physical birth, the phrase "formation of the body, speech, and mind" refers to volitional forces from the previous birth that give rise to the conditions taken on by sensory consciousness in the new life. On the level of momentary mental birth, the breath is the force that forms the body; directed thought and evaluation are the forces that form speech; and feeling and perception are

The Wheel of Life

the forces that form the mind. Without these forces, sensory consciousness would have no basis for growth.

2. *Formations come into play only because there is ignorance of the Four Noble Truths.* The Four Noble Truths are suffering, its origination (craving), its cessation, and the path of practice leading to its cessation. The knowledge that does away with this ignorance not only knows what the four truths are, but also knows the duty appropriate to each, along with the fact that one has completed that duty (see Section 2.3.1). Without this knowledge, it would be impossible to disband any force or formation that would lead to suffering.

1. *Ignorance.*

The prescription is as follows: When ignorance ceases, formations cease, and so on, until aging and dying cease. Thus is the cessation of the entire mass of suffering. This is also called knowledge of the ending of the āsravas, because the four āsravas are sensual intentions and views, both of which would fall under the category of sustenance, along with becoming and ignorance. These āsravas all cease with the unraveling of the causal process, leaving simply the experience of the unconditioned.

If ignorance is not overcome, however, the process of dependent co-arising gives rise to repeated suffering indefinitely because of its many feedback loops. For instance, the suffering of birth, aging, and death would count as feeling; as long as ignorance remains operative, this feeling could reenter the series as a mental formation (precondition 2), a factor of name-and-form (precondition 4), or as feeling itself (precondition 7). This adds a complex cyclic dimension to the series and explains how it came to be represented in Buddhist art as the Wheel of Life. Later commentaries attempted to make the causal pattern into a simple circle by asserting that the sorrow of aging and dying gives rise to ignorance. Although an early discourse does note that there are times when suffering can lead to bewilderment (A.VI.63), the series has so many points of feedback that the image of a circle does little justice to its complexity. The Pali Canon never characterizes the series as a wheel, but instead compares it to streams flowing down the mountains to fill lakes, which in turn fill rivers, which lead to the ocean (S.XII.21). This description provides a more fluid image of the interplay of interdependent forces.

The formal complexity of the series is shown by its synopsis as given in the Pali Suttas (S.XII.23): "[1] When this is, that is; [2] from the arising of this comes the arising of that; [3] when this isn't, that isn't; [4] from the cessation of this comes the cessation of that." As a theory of causation, this formula resembles modern chaos theory in that it is both linear and synchronistic. The linear pattern (taking [2] and [4] as a pair) connects events, rather than objects, over time; the synchronistic pattern ([1] and [3]) connects objects and events in the present moment. This combination of two causal patterns—influences from the past interacting with those occurring in the immediate present—reflects the relation between Gautama's second and third cognitions on the night of his Awakening. It also accounts for the complexity and diversity of causal explanations given in the Pali Canon. At the same time, these two causal patterns distinguish the Buddhist interpretation of causality from the deterministic teachings of some of its rivals. Even though the past may exert influence over the present, the possibility of modifying those influences through one's present actions means that there is an opening for free will.

Furthermore, the combination of two patterns explains a number of facts connected with the process of Gautama's third cognition itself. On the one hand, the synchronous pattern of causality explains why he experienced the Deathless at the very moment he was able to overcome ignorance of the Four Noble Truths and thus did not have to wait for some far distant time for his previous karma to run out. On the other hand, the linear pattern over time explains why he did not die at the moment of Awakening. Although he no longer created any karma, he lived out the remainder of this life on the strength of the karma he had created earlier. Old karma entered the process of dependent co-arising at the conditions of name-and-form or the six sense fields, but with no ignorance or craving to reiterate the process, it could go no further than feeling.

Furthermore, the teaching of dependent co-arising resembles a medical diagnosis in several ways. By showing that the ailment depends on a series of conditions, dependent co-arising indicates the points at which the series can be broken and a cure achieved. Craving and ignorance are the two most important links in this regard, and in the next chapter we will analyze the duties appropriate to each of the Four Noble Truths in order to show how the overcoming of ignorance and the abandoning of craving must occur simultaneously. In pointing out these causal links, the pattern of dependent co-arising counteracts the theory that suffering is a fortuitous happening, against which no remedy would be effective. It also opposes the view that the ultimate cause of suffering is some entity outside the process, such as a god or an immutable soul. Salvation or release from causally produced suffering is to be found in the process of causality itself as initiated within the mind.

For the early Buddhists, dependent co-arising inextricably entailed suffering and stress. Happiness based on causal conditions was inherently unstable and unreliable. However, although there is no refuge to be found within the interdependent dance of causally produced things, one can use the dynamics of dependent co-arising to follow a path to gain release from causality to the unconditioned sphere, and thus beyond suffering altogether. The experience of following the path to release was what convinced Gautama—now the Buddha—that he had succeeded in his quest for a happiness beyond the sway of aging, illness, and death. What remained to be seen was whether others could be brought to experience the same direct realization for themselves.

2

The Buddha as Teacher

2.1 THE DECISION TO PROPAGATE THE DHARMA

All accounts state that the Buddha spent the first seven weeks after his Awakening in the vicinity of the Bodhi Tree near Bodhgaya. During that time, two merchants en route from Orissa passed close by and were advised by the spirit of a dead relative to make offerings to the new Buddha, who was sitting at the foot of a certain tree. They offered honey cakes and sugar cane and took refuge in (formally committed themselves to the preeminence of) the Buddha and his Dharma, thus becoming the Buddha's first lay devotees in the world. In this case the Buddha did not preach Dharma to the two men but merely received their reverence and offerings. Veneration of holy persons was in many instances nonsectarian and did not necessarily involve subscribing to their ideas. Buddhist lay ritual is shown here developing naturally out of pre-Buddhist practices (Strong *EB*, sec. 2.1.1).

At first the Buddha thought that humanity, addicted to its attachments, would not understand the Dharma he had discovered. If he tried to propound his doctrines but had no effect, he would be wasting his time. Sahāmpati Brahmā, one of the highest gods in the popular religion of the time, read the Buddha's mind, left the Brahmā-world, and appeared before the Buddha, pleading, "May the Blessed One teach the Dharma. May the Well-gone One teach the Dharma. There are living beings with little dust in their eyes who fall away through not hearing the Dharma. Some of them will gain full knowledge of the Dharma" (M.26). Then, out of compassion for living beings, Śākyamuni surveyed the world with his Buddha-eye and saw that although some beings had many defilements, others had few; some had dull faculties, whereas others had keen faculties. Realizing that there was a suitable audience, he decided to teach.

Whether or not this conversation actually took place, it expresses a critical choice that the Buddha must have made. If he had not acted on his compassion and returned to teach the world, his renunciation would have been insignificant for human history. There would seem to be no need for a spirit to inform an Awakened One of something that he could have known himself through his superknowledge, but then there are many cases where perceptive people have to be told things they could have seen themselves if they had only looked. Perhaps the point of the story, though, is that the Buddha observes the etiquette of the noble gentleman in not thrusting his doctrine on those who are unready to accept it; he waits for an invitation. As he was to be the teacher of gods and men, who else but a great God was worthy to invite him?

2.2 THE FIRST SERMON
(Strong *EB*, sec. 1.6)

Having decided to proclaim his doctrine, Gautama thought first of telling his two former teachers, but a deity informed him that Ārāḍa Kālāma had died a week before, and Udraka Rāmaputra the previous night. The Buddha confirmed this with his superknowledge, then thought of the five mendicants who had been his attendants during the period of his austerities. With his divine eye he saw that they were staying near Benares, so he set out to teach them the way to Awakening.

On the road Gautama met an ascetic who, remarking on his clear eyes and radiant complexion, asked about the spiritual path he followed. The Buddha declared that he was a *jina* (victor) with no equal in the world of gods and men; that he had become Awakened and had reached nirvāṇa. The ascetic answered in one word, *hupeyya*, which means either "it may be so" or "let it be so," shook his head, and walked away. This curious encounter resembles historical fact rather than pious invention: Gautama's first proclamation of his Buddhahood was disregarded.

The Blessed One walked by stages to Benares, about 130 miles from Bodhgaya. Four miles north of the city, in the Deer Park at Sarnath, the five mendicants saw him coming and resolved not to show more than minimal courtesy to the backslider who had taken to the easy life. But his charisma was too strong for them. Against their own resolve they saluted him, took his bowl and robe, prepared his seat, and gave him implements with which to wash his feet. The effect of his spiritual presence preceded any word.

Still, they called him "Friend Gautama," but he told them not to do so, as he was now a *Tathāgata* (one who has become thus, meaning, as those Buddhas of the past); an *arhant* (one worthy of reverence); a perfectly Awakened

One. He declared that he had attained the Deathless; that he was going to teach the Dharma; and that if they practiced as he taught, they would quickly realize it for themselves. The five were dubious, protesting that one who had quit striving could not have attained the transcendent. The Buddha denied that he had given up striving, reasserted his claim, and asked them if he had ever made such a claim before. Eventually they admitted that he hadn't, and so agreed to listen receptively.

Whether the Buddha on this occasion actually preached the discourse attributed to him by canonical texts is as moot as whether Jesus pronounced the Sermon on the Mount as a single discourse. The doctrine of the Middle Way with which it begins, though, is entirely appropriate to the task of persuading the five mendicants that one who had abandoned extreme austerities had not necessarily forsaken the ascetic quest. (Here we will follow the Pali version of the text [S.LVI.11], which provides an interesting comparison with the Lokuttaravādin version translated in Strong *EB*.)

The Blessed One began by condemning each of two extremes, saying that sensual indulgence is low, vulgar, worldly, ignoble, and useless, whereas self-torture is painful as well as ignoble and useless. The Tathāgata, by avoiding these extremes, had discovered the Middle Way that produces vision and knowledge and leads to peace, higher knowledge, Awakening, and nirvāṇa. This Middle Way is the Noble Eightfold Path: (1) right view, (2) right resolve, (3) right speech, (4) right action, (5) right livelihood, (6) right effort, (7) right mindfulness, and (8) right concentration.

The Buddha then declared the Four Noble Truths. The first is the truth of duḥkha (suffering), found in every aspect of conditioned existence: birth, aging, death, grief, lamentation, pain, distress and despair; conjunction with the hated, separation from the dear; and not getting what one wants. In short, the five skandhas (aggregates) of sustenance for becoming—form, feeling, perception, mental formations, and consciousness—entail suffering. The second is the truth of the origination of suffering: the thirst or craving that leads to renewed becoming, endowed with passion and delight for this thing and that; in other words, craving for sensuality, for coming to be, and for no change in what has come to be. The third is the truth of the cessation of suffering: When craving ceases entirely through dispassion, renunciation, and nondependence, then suffering ceases. The fourth is the truth of the path of practice leading to cessation of suffering, the Noble Eightfold Path.

Each of these truths entails a task. Suffering must be thoroughly understood, the origination of suffering abandoned, cessation realized, and the Noble Eightfold Path developed. The Buddha testified that he attained supreme, perfect Awakening when—and only when—he had acquired purified true knowledge and vision of these Four Noble Truths as they actually are, and he had known and completed the task appropriate to each. As a result, he knew that his release was unassailable; that this was to be his last birth; and that there was no further becoming in store for him.

The five mendicants welcomed the discourse, and as it was occurring, one of them, Kauṇḍinya, acquired the pure Dharma-eye, seeing that whatever is subject to origination is subject to cessation. This was a momentous incident in the history of Buddhism. It indicated that the Buddha could indeed teach the Dharma to others in such a way that they would receive it and taste the results for themselves. As a result, the Buddha declared, "Kauṇḍinya knows! Kauṇḍinya knows!" Having already experienced such an Awakening himself, he could recognize it in another and so publicly indicated Kauṇḍinya's new state of mind. Kauṇḍinya asked the Buddha for full ordination, which he received with the simple formula, "Come, bhikṣu, the Dharma is well proclaimed. Follow the chaste course to the complete termination of suffering." Thus he became the first member of the *Bhikṣu Sangha*—the Order of Monks.

The texts assert that at the conclusion of the discourse, the earth deities announced to the higher heavens that the Buddha had set rolling the unsurpassed wheel of Dharma that could not be stopped by anyone in the cosmos. On hearing this, the higher levels of deities took up the proclamation until it reached the Brahmā worlds. The earth quaked, and a dazzling light illuminated the cosmos momentarily. Whether or not these events actually occurred, they are standard narrative devices conveying the point that the major events in the Buddha's life were cosmic in their importance. The reference to the wheel of Dharma, however, was used by early Buddhists with regard to this event and to no other. It is actually a play on words. On the one hand, it refers to a passage in the sermon in which the Buddha sets out a table of two sets of variables—the Four Noble Truths, and the three levels of knowledge appropriate to each: knowing the truth, knowing the duty it entails, and knowing that one has completed the duty. He then lists all 12 permutations of the two sets (not to be confused with the 12 conditions of dependent co-arising). This sort of table, in Indian legal and philosophical traditions, is called a wheel. For this reason, the wheel used as a symbol of the Dharma has 12 spokes, uniting at the hub, symbolizing the 12 permutations that unite in knowledge and vision of things as they actually are.

The wheel, however, also has political connotations. The wheel-turning monarch is one whose power is so universally acknowledged in the Indian subcontinent that the wheel of his chariot can drive from one ocean to the other unimpeded. The implication here is that the Buddha's authority as a religious leader is equivalent to the power of such a monarch; his first sermon is the establishment of that authority (Strong *EB*, sec. 2.6.1). Later movements in Buddhism adopted the turning-of-the-wheel image to indicate what they regarded as momentous developments in the Buddhist tradition—the rise of the Mādhyamika school, the Yogācāra school, and Vajrayāna—but more conservative traditions recognize only one turning of the Dharma wheel, the sermon we have just reviewed.

On the days immediately following the first sermon, the other four mendicants took turns begging alms for the group and listening to the Buddha's instruction. Very soon all four attained the Dharma-eye and received admission to the order.

The Buddha then preached a discourse on the five skandhas, briefly mentioned earlier under the First Noble Truth. Physical form, feeling, perception, mental formations, and consciousness are each *anātman* (not-self). Because they are impermanent, they entail suffering; because they entail suffering, they do not merit being regarded as "me," "my self," or "what I am." Hearing this exposition, the five monks overcame their infatuation for the five skandhas and were freed from the āsravas. Thus they too became arhants (perfected saints worthy of reverence).

2.3 COMMENTARY ON THE FIRST SERMON

All Buddhist traditions refer to the Buddha as a doctor, one who treats the spiritual ills of the world (see M.75), and this reference provides a convenient metaphor for understanding the form and content of his teaching. As noted previously (see Section 1.4.3), the Buddha's analysis of dependent co-arising resembles a medical diagnosis, pointing out both the causes of the disease of suffering and the cure to be followed to attain what counts—according to the Buddha's experience of Awakening—as the only true health: nirvāṇa. The crucial element in effecting this cure is the discernment that does away with ignorance and craving. As one of the Pali Suttas states (D.33), discernment can come from any of three sources—listening, thinking, and meditating—but only the last is sufficient for effecting the cure. These considerations placed a number of constraints on the Buddha as he undertook the task of teaching others the Path he had found. He had to convince them of the truth of his diagnosis and at the same time inspire them to administer the cure to themselves. Therefore, he prefaced his teachings by insisting on his status (as *jina*, *arhant*, *Buddha*, and *Tathāgata*, four terms current among the śramaṇa sects), for only if his listeners were receptive to his words would they benefit from them.

The claim of a mere Homo sapiens in bare feet and saffron rags to be totally Awakened is rather incredible to the post-Darwinian world and was scarcely less so to professional ascetics in the fifth century B.C.E. Unable to convince the stranger he met on the road, Gautama eventually prevailed with his old companions only by appealing to their knowledge of his responsible character. His apparent motive in self-proclamation was not vanity but a desire to prepare his listeners to receive the doctrine. He did not teach the five mendicants until they acknowledged his authority and were disposed to assent. His style in the first sermon, as in many later discourses, was didactic rather than demonstrative, elaborating the points but not attempting to prove them. The chief guarantee of their truth is the character of the teacher, the assumption being that people with keen faculties will find the points self-evident. The tone is earnest and exalted, free from sentimentality and hyperbole. Gautama's manifest desire to convince his hearers never shakes his gravity. This does not mean, however, that he was a simple ideologue. In many of his discourses his method was demonstrative—he was willing to reason and enter into dialogue—and he insisted that his listeners test his teachings for themselves, rather than accepting them solely because they are his.

Faith in the Buddha as revealer of the Dharma is a first step on the Path. The preliminary level of right view entails the belief that there are human beings who have seen the true nature of reality and can reveal it to others. Without this belief, one would lack the faith and conviction necessary to undertake the Path's remaining factors. Nevertheless, faith is not a substitute for knowledge. It is the seed that grows into confirmatory realization, formed of a willingness to take statements provisionally based on trust, confidence in the integrity of a witness, and determination to practice in accordance with instructions. As a mental state, it is accompanied not by boiling zeal but rather by the serenity and lucidity conducive to liberating insight.

2.3.1 The Four Noble Truths

The Four Noble Truths lie at the essence of that liberating insight. These truths are best understood not as the content of a belief, but as phenomenological categories, a framework for viewing and classifying the processes of experience as they are directly present to the awareness. In one of the early discourses, the Buddha refers to them as an alternative to the self/other dichotomy that most people use to categorize reality. To view experience in terms of the four truths is to regard it without the metaphysical superstructure that comes as part and parcel of the notions of "me" and "mine." Such a view also avoids many of the complicated issues that come with the notion of self: for example, the need to identify what it is, to confirm or deny its existence, and the imperative to maximize its well-being either by exploiting the "other" or by swallowing the "other" into the self by equating the latter with the cosmos as a whole. Before people can abandon these issues, however, they have to be properly prepared. The Buddha would not teach the four truths to those who were not ready for them. In some cases, this required a graduated discourse (as with Yasa; see Section 2.4), during which the Buddha would try to loosen the listener's attachment to his/her ordinary way of viewing things, first by describing the sensual rewards of generosity and virtue to be enjoyed in heaven, then the drawbacks of those ephemeral rewards, and finally the more lasting rewards of renunciation. Only then would the listener be ready for the four truths. In the case of the five mendicants, though, they first had to be weaned from their attachment to austerities. Thus the first sermon begins with a statement asserting that austerities are not different in kind from sensual indulgence, but are simply one of two ignoble and useless extremes that a śramaṇa should avoid in order to arrive at the Middle Way to true peace and Awakening.

What is the Middle Way? On one level it is, like the Greek and Chinese Golden Mean, a course of moderation in which the bodily appetites are sufficiently fed for health rather than being indulged or starved. But it comprises much more than that. The Noble Eightfold Path, the best-known expression of the way, can be subsumed under a shorter formula, called the Three Trainings: discernment (right view and resolve), virtue (right speech, action, and livelihood), and concentration (right effort, mindfulness, and concentration—see Strong *EB*, secs. 3.5.4, 3.5.5). We have already seen all three as strands in the Awakening. Discernment here means clear understanding of the Four Noble Truths and the consequent intention to act skillfully in light of the law of karma. Virtue goes beyond mere self-denial because it involves understanding and disciplining one's intentions. Concentration is achieved through specific techniques apparently known to Gautama's two teachers but not favored by the five mendicants. It requires not the mortification of the body but the cultivation of right effort and right mindfulness, leading to right concentration, which consists of the dhyānas. The Three Trainings are dependent on one another. A Pali text (D.16) states: "Concentration matured by virtue bears great fruits and benefits; discernment matured by concentration bears great fruits and benefits; the mind matured by discernment is quite freed from the āsravas."

Although this passage suggests a linear development of the factors of the Path, there are other passages in the early canon that indicate a spiraling or mutually dependent pattern. Right view on the preliminary level, as mentioned previously, begins with the belief that there are those who know the true nature of the world and who proclaim that good and evil are intrinsic to that nature, rather than being mere social conventions. Good actions are skillful in that they inherently lead to good results; bad actions are unskillful in that they inherently lead to bad. Right resolve follows naturally on this belief because the quality of an act is determined by the intention motivating it. Anyone who intends to act skillfully must begin by resolving to abstain from sensual desire, from ill will, and from harming others or oneself; these three resolves form the definition of this factor of the Path.

Right speech, right action, and right livelihood follow from these three resolves. Right speech means abstaining from the four unskillful verbal deeds: lying, divisive tale-bearing, harsh or abusive language, and idle talk. Right action means abstaining from the three unskillful bodily deeds: taking life, taking what is not given (stealing), and sexual intercourse. Right livelihood is abstention from occupations that harm living beings—for example, selling weapons, liquor, poison, slaves, or livestock; butchering, hunting, fishing; soldiering; fraud; soothsaying; and usury.

When one's speech, actions, and livelihood are free from harm, the mind is free from remorse, and this opens the way for the smooth practice of concentration. This practice begins with right effort, which means persistence in avoiding and eliminating evil and unskillful mental qualities, and nurturing skillful mental qualities in their place. To do this involves right mindfulness, inasmuch as mindfulness is the primary skillful mental quality, necessary for the development of all other important skillful qualities, such as discernment, vigor, serenity, concentration, and equanimity. If mindfulness is lacking, one cannot know clearly which other skillful or unskillful qualities are present in the mind. Right mindfulness consists of focusing on any one of four foundations or frames of reference: the body in and of itself, feelings in and of themselves, mind-states in and of themselves, and mental qualities in and of themselves (Strong *EB*, sec. 3.5.4). In the beginning stages of the practice, this means simply observing events as they occur in the course of one's attempts to master concentration. As one's mastery grows, one gains a clearer perception of causal patterns underlying these events. This gives an understanding of how unskillful mental qualities may be undercut, and how skillful ones may be fostered. Acting on this understanding leads the mind to fuller mastery of the four dhyānas, which constitute right concentration. Right concentration in turn leads to a higher level of right view—insight in terms of the Four Noble Truths—and thus the Path spirals to a higher level, leading ultimately to Awakening and release from saṃsāra. This is why the Buddha termed the four truths and the eightfold path *noble*, for he saw that they lead to a truly worthy goal (see M.26), which is not subject to change and involves no oppression of others, and that the goal transforms the mind of the person attaining it to a noble level as well.

But why did the Buddha consider knowledge in terms of the four truths to be so effective in freeing the mind from its cravings and attachments? To answer this question, it is necessary to look at the truths one by one.

The formula for dependent co-arising states that craving leads to attachment and from there to suffering. If, however, the mind can be liberated from its ignorance that the objects of its craving are unworthy of attachment, the cycle can be broken. These objects are precisely where the First Noble Truth is aimed: the five skandhas (aggregates), which cover the whole of describable and attachable reality. As the brief formula for the first truth states, attachment to any of these five aggregates constitutes the essence of duḥkha. Duḥkha is a term with no one equivalent in the English language. Suffering, stress, pain, dis-ease, distress, and unsatisfactoriness come close, but whatever the equivalent chosen, the important point is that the skandhas are unworthy of attachment because they provide no unalloyed happiness.

Buddhism has frequently been charged with being pessimistic because of its emphasis on suffering, but this charge misses the fact that the first truth is part of a strategy of diagnosis and therapy that focuses on the unsatisfactory side of life so as to provide freedom from that suffering. In this sense, the Buddha was similar to a doctor, focusing on the disease he wanted to cure. He did not deny that life has a certain measure of happiness. A Pali text (Khp.5) glowingly praises the blessings of the good householder's life—the company of the wise, honoring the honorable, living in a congenial country, erudition and skill, good manners and speech, providing for one's family, having a peaceful profession, giving alms, doing good deeds, practicing the religion, and becoming immune to worldly sorrow and defilement. The delights of life among the gods are also praised. However, the happiness of the human and heavenly worlds is yoked to suffering in that it is inconstant and impermanent. Because it is yoked to suffering, it does not lie completely under one's control, and thus does not deserve to be regarded as one's identity—one's self—or as one's possession (Strong *EB,* secs. 3.2.1–3, 3.2.6).

These three characteristics—impermanence, suffering, and "not-selfness"—are common to all conditioned things and lie at the heart of the diagnosis provided by the First Noble Truth. Like the teaching on suffering, the teaching on not-self has been controversial from early on. Opponents of Buddhism have regarded it as a metaphysical doctrine denying the existence of a self or a soul, and even many Buddhists have come to view it in that light. In the early texts, however, the Buddha pointedly refuses to answer the metaphysical question as to whether or not there is a self. (For another interpretation of one of the passages in question, see Strong *EB*, sec. 3.2.4.) He simply points out the inconsistencies of various self or soul theories and states the rewards of focusing on the not-selfness of the five skandhas. In fact, he asserts that the belief "I have no self" is as much an obstacle to Awakening as the belief "I have a self" (M.2). To believe in a permanent self, he says, is to deny the possibility of spiritual self-change. To deny the existence of a self is to deny the worth of a moral or religious life. To cling to the perception even of an impermanent self is to cling to one of the five skandhas, which would prevent a realization of the unconditioned that can be experienced only when the skandhas are relinquished.

Thus the early texts suggest that a person seeking Awakening should entirely drop the self/other mode of classifying reality in favor of the Four Noble Truths so as to avoid the pitfalls that any view dealing in terms of self would entail. For a person well advanced on the Path, the Buddha says, the question of whether or not there is a self simply would not occur. Such a person would be more involved in observing phenomena as they arise and pass away than in engaging in such speculations. All of this indicates that the not-self doctrine, like the teaching on suffering, is to be regarded as a strategy of diagnosis and therapy for undercutting craving, attachment, and the factor of sustenance in the formula of dependent co-arising. The meditator is taught simply to observe the five skandhas as they occur and to let go of them by noting that they are not his/her self. In doing so, he/she would open the way for the experience of the unconditioned, to which labels or perceptions of "self" or "not-self"—which, as perceptions, would count as a skandha—would not apply.

As stated in the first sermon, the First Noble Truth—suffering—is to be comprehended. Once it is comprehended, the Second Noble Truth—craving—has no object to latch onto and so can be abandoned. Here we must note that, contrary to some interpretations, the word *craving* covers not all desire, but only the desire leading to further becoming. The desire to escape from that becoming is said in the early texts to be part of the Path; without such a desire, no one would have the motivation to follow the Path or reach nirvāṇa. When nirvāṇa is reached, though, even this desire is abandoned, just as a desire to walk to a park is abandoned upon reaching the park.

When the Second Noble Truth is abandoned, the third—cessation of suffering—is realized. "Cessation of suffering" is a description of the goal of the practice, but its negative form should not be construed as meaning that the goal is experienced in negative terms. The standard metaphor is one of cooling. Just because cold is technically nothing more than the absence of heat, that does not mean that it cannot be intensely felt. This point is supported by the many passages in the canon in which the noble disciples express in intensely joyous terms the freedom they experience on having reached the goal (Strong *EB*, sec. 3.4).

This goal is realized by developing the Path, which we have already discussed in detail. Thus the tasks proper to each of the Four Noble Truths—comprehending suffering, abandoning its cause, realizing its cessation, and developing the Path to its cessation—are actually four aspects of a single process that, as it reaches completion, destroys any trace of ignorance concerning the Four Noble Truths at the same time that it abandons craving, the second truth. In this way, the process cuts the chain of dependent co-arising simultaneously at its two most crucial factors.

2.3.2 Practice and Attainment

How the tasks appropriate to the Four Noble Truths were to be mastered in practice can be shown by an analysis of the meditation practice most frequently recommended in the canon: mindfulness of in-and-out breathing (M.118). The meditator was to find a solitary spot, sit cross-legged, and begin focusing on the breath by noticing whether it was long or short. He/she was then to develop a whole-body awareness while focusing on the breath, and then to let the breath grow calm. At this point, if the focus was steadily maintained, feelings of rapture and ease would begin to arise. These the meditator would allow to permeate and suffuse the entire body, leading to the states of dhyāna that constitute right concentration. When the rapture and ease subsided with the attainment of the fourth stage of dhyāna, the meditator would be left with a bright awareness filling the body in a state of pure mindfulness and equanimity.

At this point, the attention would tend to focus on the sense of bright awareness together with the breath, rather than just on the breath itself. The meditator would begin to notice the ways in which the mind was steadied, uplifted, and released as it went through the various stages of absorption. This would lead to a mastery of the processes of concentration, which in turn would provide a solid basis of internally based pleasure and equanimity that the meditator could use to pry away any attachment to sensual pleasures. This process of detachment would culminate in the attainment of the stage of Awakening called nonreturning, in which sensual passion is utterly abandoned and concentration completely mastered.

The meditator would then turn inward to reflect on the processes of dhyāna itself. One text (A.V.28) describes an intermediate reflective stage of absorption, in which a meditator could analyze the various mental states in each stage of dhyāna without destroying the integrity of the stage, and some of the texts (M.111; A.IX.36) indicate that talented meditators could do this in great detail. Further contemplation would bring about a realization of the impermanence, stress, and lack of self not only in the subtle pleasures of mental absorption but also in the insights arising from reflection, all of which count as subtle forms of the five skandhas. This realization would lead the mind to perceive these phenomena in light of the categories of the Four Noble Truths, inducing a sense of dispassion, cessation, and letting go, all of which were to be observed simply as passing events. Ultimately, even right view and the other factors of the Path were to be abandoned as the last step in gaining total release. A Pali Sutta (A.X.93) makes the point that right view is unique in that it is the only form of view whose development leads to the abandoning of attachment to all views, itself included, and thus to the transcendence of all āsravas. Once these subtlest of attachments are abandoned, nothing would remain to bind one to the realm of saṃsāra, and thus the mind would attain nirvāṇa.

The word *nirvāṇa* (in Pali, *nibbāna*) literally means the extinguishing of a fire. Why the Buddha would use such a term to describe the goal of his teachings has puzzled Western scholars ever since their first encounter with the concept, largely because they have viewed it in light of their own notions of what happens to fire when it goes out. Viewed in light of the physics of the Buddha's time, however, the term is much less puzzling.

Modern etymology derives the word *nirvāṇa* from verbal roots meaning "blowing out." Traditional Buddhist etymology, however, derives it from roots meaning "unbinding." This relates to the fact that fire, in the time of the Buddha, was regarded as being in a state of agitation, dependency, and entrapment as it burned, then growing calm, independent, and released as it went out. A number of idioms reflect these notions: to start a fire, one had to "grasp" the fire-potential latent in the fuel; when a fire went out, it was "freed." Thus the term *nirvāṇa* carried no connotations of "going out of existence." In fact, there were occasions when the Buddha used ancient Vedic notions of fire—which held that fire did not go out of existence when it was extinguished, but rather went into a diffuse, indeterminate, latent state—to illustrate the notion that a person who has attained the goal is beyond all description. Just as a fire that has gone out cannot be described as having gone in any particular direction, so the person who has attained the goal cannot be predicated as existent, nonexistent, both, or neither. As for the experience of nirvāṇa, it is so totally free from any sort of limitation that the person experiencing it has no means by which he or she could say that there is a person having the experience. There is simply the experience, in and of itself.

Thus the word *nirvāṇa*, in the time of the Buddha, conveyed primarily the notion of freedom. As experienced in this life, it meant freedom from any attachment or agitation in terms of passion, aversion, or delusion; after death—when the results of all karma created prior to one's Awakening had finally worked themselves out, and input from the senses cooled away—it meant freedom from even the most basic notions or limitations that make up the experience of the describable universe. Other names the Buddha used metaphorically to indicate the goal (there are more than thirty in all) carry similar connotations, implying a subtle experience of utter transcendence and freedom from change, disturbance, danger, insecurity, or unhappiness of any sort.

The early texts describe some of the Buddha's disciples as becoming arhants (attaining total release from saṃsāra) immediately in a single experience of Awakening, whereas others attain total release in as many as four stages. In ascending order, they may become *srotāpanna* ("streamwinners"—those who have reached the "stream" to nirvāṇa), destined to reach total Awakening in no more than seven more lifetimes without ever falling to any of the lower levels of existence in the interim; once-returners, destined to be reborn once in heaven and then returning to this world once more before attaining total nirvāṇa; nonreturners, destined to be reborn in the highest Brahmā worlds, there to attain total nirvāṇa without ever returning to this world; and arhants, totally awakened, totally freed from the processes of renewed becoming and birth. Kauṇḍinya, on hearing the Buddha's first sermon, became a streamwinner through the arising of the *Dharma-eye* (the realization that all things subject to origination are subject to cessation). Other texts (Mv.I.23.5) make clear that this vision involves a glimpse of the Deathless or Unconditioned. Only in contradistinction to what is not subject to origination would the concept of "all things subject to origination" occur to the mind. In Kauṇḍinya's case, as with the rest of the five mendicants, he did not have to wait the full seven lifetimes to become an arhant, for he gained total Awakening only a few days later upon listening to the Buddha's discourse on the not-self characteristic.

The apparent ease with which many of the Buddha's early disciples attained Awakening while listening to the Dharma would seem to belie the factors of the Path as explained in the Fourth Noble Truth, but it should be remembered that the spiritual Path is not a one-lifetime affair. From the Buddhist point of view, a person may devote many lifetimes to developing *indrīya* (the mental faculties needed for Awakening)—conviction, vigor, mindfulness, concentration, and discernment—and may have them so fully matured that he/she may require only a slight impetus to focus discernment on the point that will lead to Awakening. This impetus might come from a number of external factors, such as the Buddha's charisma and his ability to know his listeners' minds so as to determine what Dharma is appropriate for them, but unless the faculties are mature, those external factors would not be enough to effect a radical change. Many of the Buddha's listeners, like the first ascetic he encountered on his way to Benares, are recorded as not having gained Awakening as a result of his teachings, although the tradition insists that they all benefited in ways that might not be immediately apparent. A Pali Sutta (A.IV.133) divides the Buddha's listeners into four types: those who will gain Awakening on hearing a brief explanation of the Dharma; those who will gain Awakening only after a detailed explanation; those who will have to take the Dharma and work at putting it into practice before achieving Awakening; and those whose understanding of the Dharma will go no further than the words, and as a result will not gain Awakening in this lifetime. This last point makes it clear that those who do gain Awakening while listening to the Dharma are not simply listening to the words, but are also reflecting on the phenomena in their own experience to which the words point.

The Buddha's confirmation that "Kauṇḍinya knows" was the first instance of a formal act that was to happen repeatedly during the Buddha's career. Having the saints identified has always been important for the Buddhist devotee, whose chief religious authority is the word of an Awakened One. Awakening is recognized by a teacher—who has achieved it—in another who has been striving for it. Those who have not gained Awakening have no criteria of their own by which they may recognize an Awakened One, aside from the negative criterion that even a streamwinner would not intentionally transgress the principles of right speech, right action, or right livelihood. Once the Buddha's Awakening is granted, as it is when one professes faith in him, it is helpful to have his or another arhant's certification that so-and-so is an Awakened One of such-and-such a degree. This is a teacher's common method of letting his students know which among them is a person whose discernment can be trusted and who is competent to carry the teachings to others. This point became increasingly important as the Buddha gained more disciples and could send them to proclaim the teaching in his place. As noted previously, the nature of his message required that the listener hold the teacher in esteem in order to benefit from hearing it. By giving his disciples what amounted to a certificate of health, the Buddha aided them in their work of conveying to others in an effective way the message that his diagnosis for their suffering was correct, the cure efficacious, and the resulting state of health well worth the effort.

2.4 FOUNDING THE BUDDHIST COMMUNITY

After the second sermon, on the not-self characteristic, there were six arhants in the world, counting the Buddha himself. Soon Yasa, son of a rich merchant of Benares, waking up during the night in a state of anxiety, went out to Sarnath, where the Buddha comforted him and taught him a graduated Dharma suitable for lay people, namely, the merits of generosity and virtue, the rewards of generosity and virtue to be enjoyed in heaven, the drawbacks of even heavenly sensual pleasures, and the blessings of renunciation. Then he preached the higher Dharma, the Four Noble Truths, to the young man, who soon afterward attained arhantship and took full ordination as a monk. Meanwhile, Yasa's father came looking for his son, happened to find the Buddha, listened to his teaching, attained the Dharma-eye, and took the Three Refuges, committing himself to the preeminence of the Buddha, Dharma, and Sangha. Thus he became the first *upāsaka* (lay devotee) in the strict sense, inasmuch as the two merchants who had brought offerings to the Buddha at Bodhgaya had not been able to take refuge in the Sangha prior to its existence. Eventually, Yasa's mother and sisters took the Three Refuges and became the first *upasikā* (female lay devotees) (Strong *EB*, sec. 3.5.1).

The Buddhist Sangha, in its *ārya* (ideal) sense, consists of all people, lay or ordained, who have acquired the pure Dharma-eye, gaining at least a glimpse of the Deathless. In a *saṃvṛti* (conventional) sense, Sangha denotes the communities of ordained monks and nuns. The two meanings overlap but are not necessarily identical. Some members of the ideal Sangha are not ordained; some monks and nuns have yet to acquire the Dharma-eye. When Yasa's family took refuge in the Sangha, all of the bhikṣus in the conventional Sangha were also members of the Sangha in the ideal sense. Thus they took refuge in the Bhikṣu Sangha, intending the word *Sangha* in both senses of the term.

This became the standard formula for taking refuge, even after the two meanings of the term *Sangha* began to diverge in the course of the Buddha's career. When the divergence became noticeable, the standard formula for expressing faith and conviction in the Three Refuges was worded to refer specifically to Sangha in the ideal sense.

The act of taking refuge, in traditional Indian culture, was a formal act of allegiance, submitting to the preeminence and claiming the protection of a powerful patron, whether human or divine. The formula of taking refuge was uttered three times to make it a solemn and formal commitment. For Buddhists, the act of taking refuge constitutes a profession of faith in the Buddha's Awakening, in the truth of his teaching, and in the worthiness of the Sangha. It is an act of submission in that one is committed to conducting one's life in line with the Dharma, principally with the doctrine of karma; it is an act of claiming protection in that one trusts that by following the teaching one will not fall into the misfortunes that bad karma engenders.

All those who take refuge in the Buddha, Dharma, and Sangha become members of the Buddha's fourfold *pariṣad* (assembly) of followers: monks, nuns, male lay devotees, and female lay devotees. Although it has been said that all Buddhist followers are members of the Sangha, this is not the case. Only the ordained are members of the conventional Sangha; only those who have acquired the Dharma-eye are members of the ideal Sangha. Nevertheless, those followers who do not belong to the Sangha in either sense of the word still count as genuine Buddhists in that they are members of the Buddha's pariṣad.

When Yasa's family became Buddhists, word spread to Yasa's friends. Many of them came, listened to the Buddha, took ordination, and gained full Awakening. There were then 61 arhants in the world. Once the Buddha had consolidated a cadre of 60 Awakened monks, he sent them out as missionaries, charging them to travel and proclaim the Dharma for the benefit of the many, out of compassion for the world and for the welfare of divine and human beings. Those with keen faculties would attain liberation if, and only if, they heard the doctrine.

The historic success of Buddhism stems from its concern for the many, regardless of race, caste, class, or gender. Compassion includes not only a sense of sympathy for the suffering of others, but also an effort to alleviate it. The foremost act of compassion is *Dharma-donation*—teaching the way to freedom from suffering. In contrast to the Brahmānical schools, who kept their teachings as secret as possible, the Buddhists broadcast their message to the multitudes, aiming it specifically at those most ready to receive it. Good Dharma-preachers, to borrow a Quaker phrase, "speak to the condition" of their audience. They aim not only to proclaim their doctrine but also to communicate it. To continue the medical analogy, their concern is less with teaching medical theory than with facilitating cures.

Only Buddhas attain Awakening without receiving the gift of Dharma from another, and even they, according to later theory, heard it many lives ago from a former Buddha. (There have been many Buddhas in the past and others are expected in the future.) Thus, no one works out personal salvation unaided. The *Dhammapada* (v.276) states: "You yourself must make an effort. Tathāgatas, for their part, are simply revealers."

The sixty missionaries were soon so successful that many converts traveled long distances to receive ordination. The Buddha noted the hardship this entailed and so granted his monks permission to confer ordination themselves wherever they went. This made the Sangha self-propagating and enabled it to spread far beyond the area within which the Buddha or any other single leader could have exercised personal control. Even during his lifetime, the Buddha entrusted his Sangha with management of its own affairs, serving as lawmaker when his disciples consulted him on problems but otherwise not imposing his authority. By the time of his decease, the Sangha was consolidated as a republican society, a loose federation bound together by a common code, a common oral tradition, and the constant coming and going of itinerant monks.

The Buddha spent the first three-month rainy season after his Awakening at Sarnath, near Benares, as the heavy rains made travel impractical. This monsoon retreat, generally observed by śramaṇas at the time, became a Buddhist institution that has been observed to the present day, particularly in Theravāda countries. After the rains, the Buddha returned to Uruvela, where he had earlier practiced austerities. The Vinaya relates that there he encountered and converted three brothers of the Kāśyapa clan, leaders of a sect of fire-worshipping ascetics, together with their one thousand disciples.

This tale demonstrates how Buddhism grew not only through individual conversions but also by incorporating whole sects. It also illustrates the role that the six superknowledges (see Section 1.3.5) played not only in the discovery of the Dharma but also in its propagation. Although the Buddha forbade his disciples from demonstrating their powers before the laity, there were occasions when he himself found it necessary to exhibit his powers in order to put his audience in the proper frame of mind to listen to and benefit from his teachings. The ascetics and yogis of pre-Buddhist India had an extensive lore concerning miraculous (or psychic) powers (in Sanskrit, *ṛddhi,* Pali, *iddhi),* and many regarded these powers as the sine qua non of a spiritually advanced teacher. The eldest Kāśyapa apparently held to this opinion, so the Buddha used a display of powers to subdue his pride: He tamed the poisonous *nāga* (serpent) living in Kāśyapa's ritual implements house; he vanished from one spot and appeared instantly in another; he prevented Kāśyapa and his disciples from chopping wood for their fires, but then caused the wood to be instantaneously chopped when they called him on the issue.

Finally, Kāśyapa saw the Buddha part the waters of a flooding river to walk in the dust of the riverbed; when he asked the Buddha to enter his boat, the latter did so by first levitating into the air. Even then Kāśyapa remained convinced of his own spiritual superiority, so the Buddha, reading his mind, confronted him, saying that he was not even on the Path to the state he believed himself to have achieved. This shocked Kāśyapa so profoundly that he asked for ordination into the Buddhist Sangha. His followers quickly followed suit.

In addition to the Kāśyapa story, the texts record many other miraculous events that occurred during the Buddha's teaching career. Once, at Sravasti, he triumphed in public debate before Prasenajit, the king of Kosala, over the leaders of six opposing śramaṇa sects. To emphasize his victory, he performed the Twin Miracle (or the Miracle of the Pairs, which he also performed on two other occasions). He levitated into the air, producing alternating streams of water and fire (or light) from different parts of his body. He created multiple images of his body and had them preach the Dharma, and performed lesser miracles as well, including causing a mango tree to spring instantaneously full-grown from a seed and creating a jeweled staircase in the sky. He then ascended to the heaven of the 33 devas to preach there for three months for his mother's benefit, converting all the inhabitants of the heaven. These episodes were portrayed on the earliest stūpas, which gives an indication of their popularity. However we may interpret these events, they are part of the wonder-worker character common to the founders of all the world's major religious traditions (Strong *EB*, sec. 2.1.6).

After converting Kāśyapa, the Buddha then went on to Rajagrha, capital of Magadha, where he was greeted by King Bimbisāra and a large crowd. Kāśyapa made a public announcement of his conversion to the Buddha's teachings, after which the Buddha gave a graduated discourse similar to the one he had given Yasa. This enabled the king, together with the majority of the crowd, to attain the Dharma-eye. On the following day, the king provided a meal for the Buddha and his followers, after which he donated the Bamboo Grove Park just outside the northern gates of the city for the Sangha's use. Soon Śāriputra of Nalanda, a town 10 miles north of Rajagrha, and his friend Maudgalyāyana were converted (Strong *EB*, sec. 2.1.3). They became the Buddha's two chief disciples, Śāriputra being foremost in discernment, Maudgalyāyana foremost in psychic powers. Both died before the Buddha did, and relics said to be theirs are now enshrined in a new temple on the ancient site at Sanchi.

Another famous disciple was Kātyāyana, a brahmin and court priest from Avanti in western India. Sent by his king on a mission to the Buddha, he returned as a bhikṣu and arhant to spread the Dharma. As the father of Buddhist exegesis, he was known as "foremost of those who analyze at length what the Buddha has stated in brief." Subhūti, foremost in dwelling free from contention and being worthy of offerings, attained arhantship by meditating on *maitrī* (goodwill). Upāli, the barber of Kapilavastu, became "foremost among those who remember the Vinaya," which he recited at the First Council (see Section 3.1). Tradition asserts that Gautama's own son, Rāhula, received ordination and became an arhant, unrivaled in his desire for training. Mahākāśyapa, foremost of those who keep the ascetic rules (Strong *EB*, sec. 2.3.3) and known for his mastery of dhyāna, convened the Council of Rajagrha shortly after the Buddha's decease and superintended the standardization of the Sūtras and Vinaya. (For a comparable list of illustrious nuns, see Section 3.4.3.)

Gautama's cousin Ānanda became a monk, attained the Dharma-eye, and served as the Buddha's constant attendant for the last 20 years of the latter's life. Ānanda figures prominently in the account of the Buddha's last weeks and was present at his death. He alone among the great disciples had not become an arhant, so there were plans to exclude him from the First Council, but finally he was admitted after gaining Awakening the night before the council was to convene. His exceptional memory reportedly enabled him to recite accurately the dialogues of the Buddha that then composed the collection of Sūtras. Earlier, Ānanda had interceded with the Buddha, on the behalf of the latter's aunt and foster mother, Mahāprajāpatī, to institute an Order of Nuns (see Section 3.4.3). Mahāprajāpatī and her attendants became its first members (Strong *EB*, sec. 2.1.4).

The early lay converts included, in addition to members of the common classes, a good array of kings, queens, princes, and wealthy merchants. Of the latter, Anāthapiṇḍika donated the land for the famous Jetavana Monastery at Sravasti. Two wealthy lay women also donated land to the Sangha, the courtesan Āmrapālī giving her orchard at Vaisali, and the matron Viśākhā giving land for a monastery near Sravasti. Thus, even during the Buddha's lifetime, his Sangha became a wealthy landowner. Arrangements were made, however, for the original donors of the land to watch over it. This left the monks free to come and go, enjoying the advantages of having established places to stay, yet unburdened with administrative responsibilities aside from helping to keep their simple dwellings in repair. With the passing centuries, though, as more and more elaborate buildings were constructed on Sangha land, converting them from parks to monasteries, the custodial and administrative responsibilities associated with the monasteries fell increasingly to the monks, making them in effect some of the most extensive landowners in a society where land was the primary measure of political power.

Even while the Buddha was still alive, the growth of the Sangha as an institution had its social and political repercussions. The Ganges Valley at the time was divided into small city-states. For the rulers of these states, the growth of a religious institution transcending caste and political barriers in their midst was obviously a matter of concern. This concern was especially marked among the states in which absolute monarchies were beginning to replace the traditional aristocratic republics, and whose new kings jealously guarded their power. Thus one of the Buddha's tasks as a religious founder was to work out a modus vivendi whereby the Sangha would not be perceived as a political threat and yet would not have to sacrifice its independence to the powers that be. To defuse the possible sense of threat, he managed to win as disciples the kings of two of the most powerful states in the Ganges Valley: Bimbisāra of Magadha and Prasenajit of Kosala. (For the story of a king not fully converted, see Strong *EB*, sec. 2.6.2.) The Buddha also advocated that his lay and monastic disciples lead their lives in line with strict moral principles, a teaching that appealed to kings not only in his time, but also for many centuries after, in that it lightened their job of maintaining law and order. At the same time, the Buddha empowered the Sangha to banish any of its monks or nuns who delivered messages or ran other errands for lay people, thus ensuring that the Sangha would not get involved in political activity.

Nevertheless, the Buddha's policy was not one of simple capitulation to the status quo. He refuted the predominant caste system, opening membership in the Sangha to all regardless of caste and refusing to allow the Sangha to use or even to mention caste rank in the course of its internal dealings. As for the Sangha's external relations with the rest of society, the Buddha realized that the smooth practice of the religion required a stable and peaceful society, which in turn depended on the wide distribution of material wealth among the people. Thus absolute monarchies, in which kings were free to confiscate and hoard wealth as they pleased, did not provide an environment conducive for the religion to prosper. Therefore, the Buddha praised the ideal society as one in which the king obeyed the law and freely dispensed seed grants of money for his subjects to use to set themselves up in business. Interestingly enough, he never mentioned this ideal to the kings who were his followers. Instead, he taught the ideal to people at large, perhaps secure in the knowledge that as it gained wider acceptance, it would ultimately affect those who actually wielded power. This in fact did occur approximately two hundred years after his death, when King Aśoka—who had ascended to the throne of an empire covering almost all of India—began putting the Buddha's social and political agenda into practice, at the same time fostering the spread of the Sangha beyond the Indian cultural sphere (see Section 3.3).

2.5 THE *PARINIRVĀṆA* (THE BUDDHA'S PASSING AWAY)

(Strong *EB*, sec. 1.7)

For 45 years the Buddha journeyed around the central Ganges River plain, receiving all callers—ascetics, brahmins, royalty, and commoners—answering their questions, displaying miraculous powers, spreading the Dharma, and aiding followers in spiritual growth.

In his seventy-ninth year, he set out on his last journey, leaving Rajagrha and walking by stages north and west until he reached Vaisali. The *Sutta of the Great Total Nibbāna* (D.16) relates how he told Ānanda that through the development of the four bases of attainment (discussed later in this section), he could stay alive for a *kalpa* (aeon), but Ānanda failed to request him to do so. Then Māra approached the Buddha and told him that the time had come for him to attain final nirvāṇa. The latter agreed, saying, "Trouble not, Evil One. Very soon the Tathāgata's *Parinirvāṇa* [total nirvāṇa, final release from saṃsāra] will take place. Three months from now he will be totally unbound."

These episodes may betray the notions of a later age puzzled by the seeming failure of the great master to avert his own death. Control of one's life span is a yogic power, and even today India and the Buddhist world are full of reports about holy persons who have lived well beyond a hundred years or who have predicted or determined the date of their death. As the Blessed One had explained to Māra, he had fully completed the task he had set for himself after his Awakening—establishing the religion on a firm foothold—so there was no reason for him to further prolong his life. Nevertheless, the monks who convened at the First Council (see Section 3.1) decided that it was Ānanda's fault for not taking the hint and asking the Buddha to live on.

The night after he relinquished his will to live, the Buddha is reported to have called a meeting of the monks, at which he listed the essential teachings in the message he had been promulgating for the previous 45 years. This list has come to be named the *bodhipakṣya-dharma* (Wings to Awakening) and is common to all schools of Buddhism. It consists of seven sets of dharmas: (1) the four foundations of mindfulness, (2) the four right exertions, (3) the four bases of attainment, (4) the five strengths, (5) the five faculties, (6) the seven factors of Awakening, and (7) the Noble Eightfold Path. Set 1 is identical with right mindfulness, set 2 with right effort, and we have already discussed set 7 in detail. Set 3 concerns types of concentration: based on desire, based on vigor, based on attention, and based on discrimination. Sets 4 and 5 are identical: conviction, vigor, mindfulness, concentration, and discernment. Set 6 is mindfulness, analysis of mental qualities (which the texts equate with discernment), vigor, rapture, serenity, concentration, and equanimity. There is an obvious overlap among the sets, and as the early texts explain, the full practice of any one set involves the practice of the others as well. What is striking about the sets is that they contain no tenets about the nature of reality or the cosmos. Rather, they deal entirely with the development of mental qualities. The Buddha seemed confident that whoever develops these qualities, focuses them on the present with reference to the foundations of mindfulness, and categorizes what is experienced in terms of the Four Noble Truths is sure to come to the same realizations that he did. Thus he felt no need to go into any great detail in his final summary as to what those realizations are. The teaching will survive, he concluded, as long as his followers agree about these qualities and put them into practice. With this statement he in effect declared to his followers that the preservation of the teachings was now up to them.

The Tathāgata's last meal was at the home of Cunda the smith. After eating a quantity of tainted pork (or perhaps mushrooms), he became very sick and suffered sharp dysentery pains. Bearing them calmly, he arose and walked a considerable distance to Kusinagari, where he lay down between two sāla trees. After night fell he received the wanderer Subhadra, to whom he recommended the Noble Eightfold Path. Only in a religion that taught the Noble Eightfold Path, he said, could members of the ideal Sangha be found. Ānanda then received this last of the Buddha's converts into the Bhikṣu Sangha.

The dying Buddha then asked the assembled monks three times whether they had any last doubts or questions regarding the teaching, but all remained silent. Then, as dawn approached, he delivered his final exhortation: "Conditioned things are perishable by nature. Be heedful in seeking realization." He then died a Buddha's death, composed and alert in meditation. Entering the first dhyāna, he ascended the dhyāna stages up to the fourth and then on through the formless dhyāna states—focused on the infinitude of space, the infinitude of consciousness, nothingness, and neither perception nor nonperception—up to the ninth, the cessation of perception and feeling (Strong *EB*, sec. 3.5.7). Then he returned, step-by-step, to the first dhyāna, and then up again to the fourth, passing into parinirvāṇa from an intermediate reflective stage just outside of the fourth dhyāna, the same level at which he had gained Awakening. The Buddha thus died in meditative calm, as he had learned to live.

The texts state that earthquakes and thunder marked the moment of death. Brahmā and Śakra recited stanzas, and the monks (except for the arhants, who understood the Deathless) burst into lamentation until the Buddha's cousin Anuruddha reminded them that doing so was not in keeping with the teaching of the impermanence of all conditioned things.

The people of Kusinagari came the next day and held a six-day wake for the Blessed One. They danced, sang, made music, and offered garlands and scents. The body was wrapped in alternate layers of cloth and raw cotton batting and placed in an iron bier filled with oil. On the seventh day, eight chiefs of the Malla clan carried the bier in through the north gate and out the east gate of the town to a tribal shrine. There they cremated the body.

When the Mallans had asked Ānanda how they should treat the remains of the Tathāgata, he replied, "Like those of a king of kings. Cremate the body and build a stūpa at the crossroads to enshrine the relics." The stūpa is a form of the round barrow, the tomb of Bronze Age chiefs and kings from Ireland to Japan. India at that time was dotted with *caitya* (shrines) and stūpas of deceased holies, at which people offered worship and veneration in hope of gaining access to the paranormal powers they felt the relics possessed.

The Buddha is reported to have said, "What is there in seeing this wretched body? Whoever sees Dharma, sees me; whoever sees me, sees Dharma." Nevertheless, the division of his cremated physical remains developed into an enduring and widespread cult centered on his relics. In fact, the single stūpa Ānanda advocated was disrupted by a dispute over who should get the relics. After almost coming to blows, the eight claimants agreed to each have a share. Gandharan artists portrayed the cremation of the Buddha, the division of his relics, and the return home of the separate relic bearers. The deposit of relics in reliquaries (special containers) is evidenced by the earliest Buddhist archaeological remains, extending back at least to the third century B.C.E. at Sanchi. Such relics were believed to empower or activate the stūpa in which they were placed. One Mahāyāna text states that, after the perfection of wisdom, relics of the Buddha are the most valuable thing in the cosmos.

Archaeologists have discovered reliquaries near Sanchi dating from the second century B.C.E.; one made of mottled steatite is in the form of an abstract stūpa. In Gandhara, reliquaries from the first century C.E. have been found, one in the form of a crystal goose, perhaps a reference to transcendence, another in a pear shape. Crystal reliquaries in Sri Lanka date from the early centuries C.E. Other reliquaries were made of copper; one made of gold set with garnets has been found. These various forms contained pieces of bone or a variety of other objects, both precious and not.

The cult of relics began early and continues today. Aśoka is said to have opened the earlier stūpas and distributed the Buddha's relics among 84,000 stūpas throughout his empire. Early chronicles record the arrival of a collarbone and a bowl relic to Sri Lanka. A medieval Sri Lankan text catalogs the characteristics of the relics of the Buddha and those of his principal disciples. The Chinese pilgrims who came as spiritual seekers to India showed great interest in famous relics of the Buddha and well-known arhants. Hsüan-tsang saw a tooth relic of the Buddha, his skull bone, hair, and nail parings, and visited the place where the Master's begging-bowl had once been enshrined. A tooth relic enshrined in Kandy, Sri Lanka, is the subject of a yearly summer festival (Strong *EB*, sec. 6.5.2); a finger bone relic exists in the Famen Temple, near Ch'ang-an, China. A Royal Air Force bombing in Southeast Asia during the Second World War resulted in the discovery of a hair relic of the Buddha. In 1956, on the 2,500th anniversary of Buddhism, the relics of Śāriputra and Maudgalyāyana, which had been removed to the British Museum during the long restoration of Sanchi, were returned and reenshrined. In the 1960s, a New Tooth Relic Pagoda was built near Peking. The great veneration with which Buddhists treat these relics is one of the clearest expressions of the religious, as opposed to the philosophical, dimension of the Buddhist tradition.

Another expression of this dimension, with similar roots in the *Sutta of the Great Total Nibbāna,* is the practice of making pilgrimages to the locations associated with four major events in the Buddha's life: his birth, his Awakening, the delivery of his first sermon, and his Parinirvāṇa (Strong *EB*, sec. 1.1). The Buddha is reported to have recommended to Ānanda that monks, nuns, and lay followers should visit these places to develop a sense of chastened dispassion. Anyone who happened to die with an attitude of true faith while taking such a pilgrimage, he said, would be assured a heavenly rebirth. This promise seems to have encouraged Buddhist pilgrims to make the journey from far distant places ever since the early days of the religion. Some of the earliest extant Buddhist artifacts are votive tablets stamped with the symbols of the four locations—a lotus for Lumbini, a Bodhi Tree for Bodhgaya, a Dharma wheel for Sarnath, and a stūpa for Kusinagari—as mementos of the trip. These have been found not only in India, but as far away as the Malay Archipelago. The volume of pilgrimage has varied over the centuries, reaching a nadir during the Muslim rule of India, during which all of the buildings erected at the holy sites, except for the great temple at Bodhgaya, were destroyed. Even though there is now little left to see at the various sites, there has been a recent upswing in the number of pilgrims, due largely to the availability of modern transportation, the relative stability of Indian politics, and the health of the Asian economy. Buddhist teachers may downplay the importance of making a pilgrimage, saying that the true Buddhist holy spot is in the present awareness of the mind, but this has not discouraged large numbers of Buddhists from taking the journey and finding inspiration in the sense of immediacy that these sites give them to the events of the Buddha's life.

3

The Development of Early Indian Buddhism

3.1 THE FORMATION OF THE CANON

The Buddha's own name for the religion he founded was Dharma-Vinaya, the Doctrine and Discipline. Shortly before his Parinirvāṇa, he reportedly told his followers that the Dharma he had taught and the Vinaya he had promulgated would serve as their teacher after he was gone. Thus the early arhants took great pains to organize, memorize, and transmit the words that were to serve as teacher for their own generation and for those to come. Nevertheless, no ungarnished collection of the Buddha's sayings has survived. The later versions of the early canon (accepted scripture) preserved in Pali, Sanskrit, Chinese, and Tibetan are sectarian variants of a still-earlier corpus that grew and crystallized during three centuries of oral transmission after the Parinirvāṇa.

Buddhist chronicles present an idealized story of the First Council *(saṅgīti,* recitation), held at Rajagrha during the first three-month monsoon retreat after the Parinirvāṇa for the purpose of standardizing the Buddha's words into tradition. Whether or not the First Council ever occurred as described, it signaled the transition from a Sangha led by a living charismatic founder to one led by his teachings. Five hundred arhants reportedly gathered, led by Mahākāśyapa, who first questioned Upāli on the Vinaya and then Ānanda on the Dharma. Their responses were accepted as the standard for the first two of the three collections, or *Piṭakas* (baskets, collections of oral traditions), that came to comprise the canon. This canon was then memorized—a prodigious feat—and passed down orally for several centuries, as writing was generally reserved for secular matters. Sects or schools sprung up, some having two divisions (Vinaya Piṭaka and Sūtra Piṭaka) in their canon, while others added a third, called the Abhidharma Piṭaka, composed of texts that interpreted and systematized *mātṛka* (lists) of essential teachings drawn from the Sūtras.

Undoubtedly, none of the extant canons date from the time of the First Council. To begin with, there is the question of language. Individuals were allowed to recite the scriptures in their own dialect, and although we do not know precisely what language the Buddha spoke, it was probably the precursor of the Magadhi dialect in which most of Aśoka's inscriptions are couched. The complete canon existing in a language closest to Magadhi is that of the Theravāda sect, which has been preserved in Pali, a literary vernacular similar to Sanskrit and perhaps spoken at the time in west India. Fragments of canons in other languages similar to Magadhi, offering slightly variant readings, also survive.

As for content, comparative textual analysis reveals that although all early Buddhist schools used essentially the same Sūtras, their Vinayas contained a fair number of variations. This may have reflected the Buddha's comment, made toward the end of his life (D.29), that differences over the Vinaya after his death should not be feared as much as differences over the Dharma. However, even though the literary form and much of the explanatory content in the Vinayas of the various schools may have originated in later centuries, most of the basic codes seem to date back to the first generation of disciples. The greatest differences among the extant canons lie in their Abhidharma texts. Although commentaries claim that early in his teaching career the Buddha delivered the Abhidharma to devas, including his former mother, in the heaven of the Thirty-Three, textual analysis reveals that the Abhidharmas we possess are, without a doubt, the final product of a centuries-long process whereby the Buddha's followers, after his Parinirvāṇa, tried to develop a systematic philosophy from his teachings.

3.1.1 The Sūtras

At the First Council, Ānanda is said to have recited in order each of the *Nikāyas* (collection of Sūtras, also called *Āgamas)* in the second collection, the *Sūtra Piṭaka* (Basket of Discourses). Four Nikāyas were recognized by all the early sects: the Long (in Sanskrit, *Dīrgha*; in Pali, *Dīgha),* the Medium *(Madhyama/Majjhima),* the Connected *(Samyukta/Samyutta),* and the Numerical *(Ekottara/Anguttara).* The Little *(Kṣudraka/Khuddaka)* Nikāya as a collection is found only in Pali and not in the Chinese translations, although many of its texts (such as the *Dhammapada*—see Strong *EB*, sec. 3.5.3) exist in Chinese as separate works or parts of other Āgamas.

The Sūtras are chiefly prose discourses, except for stanzas interspersed through the first four Nikāyas and the anthologies of verse *(Dhammapada, Sutta-nipāta,* and so on) in the fifth Nikāya. In the prose texts, the early disciples seem to have been concerned with the substantive content rather than with the precise phrasing of different discourses. Standard passages describing the basic teachings recur verbatim throughout the collections. As for the verse texts, attempts have been made to date them on the basis of meter, but because there are no known dates for when a particular meter went in or out of style—and no law against later writers deliberately using an archaic meter for stylistic purposes—the analysis can only tell us which of the verses are more or less modern in form.

Sectarian bias and misunderstandings undoubtedly led to distortions in, additions to, and omissions from the Sūtras (Strong *EB*, sec. 3.1), but a large core—including all the major Buddhist doctrines—is common to all extant versions.

3.1.2 Vinaya

The Buddha is said to have told Ānanda that, if the Sangha wished, it might revoke the minor disciplinary rules, but Ānanda neglected to ask which rules were minor, so in order to avoid controversy, the First Council decided to retain all the rules the Buddha had formulated. Upāli recited the Vinaya for the Council, and from this beginning grew the diverse versions of the Vinaya. We have six differing versions of the rules and regulations governing the monastic orders of monks and nuns. Although parts of them exist in Sanskrit, the Pali Canon contains the only complete Vinaya Piṭaka extant in an Indic language.

As with the Sūtra, modern scholars have proposed various criteria for dating the extant Vinaya texts. Archaeological evidence is the most objective criterion so far proposed, but it offers inconclusive results. All of the extant Vinayas presuppose large, settled monastic communities, but the earliest known archaeological remains from such communities—stone inscriptions and brick foundations—date back no earlier than the beginning of the common era. Based on this fact, it has been suggested that the Vinaya texts were composed in the first to fourth centuries C.E., and that they cannot provide us with a record of the earlier life of the community. This suggestion, however, ignores the fact that the typical "permanent" buildings described in the Vinayas are wattle and daub with plain dirt floors, a type of construction that would leave no archaeological traces. Thus, although brick and stone remains can tell us when brick and stone monasteries first became fashionable, they cannot tell us when the first wattle and daub monasteries were built, or when the Vinaya texts were composed.

Of the various recensions, the Theravādin Pali Vinaya is unique in that many issues included in the Vinayas of later schools were assigned by the Theravādins to their commentaries. This suggests that the Theravādins were somewhat more scrupulous than others in leaving their canonical Vinaya untouched. Sri Lankan chronicles date the closing of the canon to the second century B.C.E., and as there is no firm evidence to suggest otherwise, that is the dating we will accept for this text.

The Vinayas of all the schools are divided into two sections: the *Sūtra Vibhanga* (Analysis of the Text) and the *Skandhaka* (in Pali, *Khandhaka*—Groupings). The Skandhakas contain miscellaneous material on personal and institutional matters, including instructions on how the Sangha is to be governed. The Sūtra Vibhanga contains the rules of the *Prātimokṣa* (in Pali, *Pāṭimokkha*—Codes of Discipline), which were to be recited in assemblies of monks and nuns on the *Poṣadha* (in Pali, *Uposatha*—Observance Day), the last day of each lunar half-month. The Sūtra Vibhanga also provides background material on each rule, together with a detailed analysis of the factors determining whether an action that might come under the purview of the rule would in fact count as an offense. In the Pali recension, the five factors used in the analysis are perception, object, intention, effort, and result. The text thus encourages the individual monastics to take a persistently mindful and analytical attitude toward all of their actions, which indicates that the observance of the disciplinary code was meant not only as an external exercise for harmony within the community, but also as an integral part of training the mind in the skills needed for meditation.

3.1.3 Abhidharma

The term *Abhidharma* means "higher Dharma," the essence of the teachings in the Sūtras. Most traditional sources claim that Ānanda recited Abhidharma texts together with the Sūtras at the First Council, but as we have already noted, modern analysis shows that although the lists upon which these texts were based may have dated from the Buddha's time, the actual texts we now have were undoubtedly composed much later. By the time of the first split in the community, one hundred years after the Buddha's Parinirvāṇa, substantial Abhidharma traditions already existed. Again, only the Pali Canon contains a complete Abhidharma (in Pali, *Abhidhamma)* Piṭaka in an Indic language. Its current form can be dated no earlier than the Third Council (approximately 250 B.C.E.). It consists of seven scholastic works, among them the *Dhammasangiṇi* (Enumeration of Dharmas), which analyzes mental and physical *dharmas* (types of events), including the Wings to Awakening; the *Vibhanga* (Analysis), which discusses the skandhas, dependent co-arising, the fetters, and meditation; the *Kathāvatthu* (Subjects of Discussion), a polemical treatise discussing theses in dispute among the early schools; and the most massive of all, the *Paṭṭhāna* (Conditional Relations), which explores the almost infinite permutations of the 24 basic types of causal relationships operating among dharmas on the ultimate level of experience. Other segments of the Abhidhamma Piṭaka list the elements of experience, classify personality types in terms of passion, aversion, and delusion, and provide precise definitions of terms that would tend to crop up in sectarian debates.

In addition to the Theravādins, many other Buddhist sects also developed Abhidharma literatures, although only two others survive in their entirety in Chinese translations: the Dharmaguptaka and Sarvāstivāda Abhidharmas, which originally existed in Sanskrit. The Sarvāstivāda Abhidharma has seven texts that quite often differ from those of the Theravāda. These cover analyses of psychological events—karma in particular; polemics on time; lists of practices leading to Buddhahood; and cosmology.

Although the product of later centuries (beginning circa 300 B.C.E.), Abhidharma is an important part of the Buddhist canon and played a central role in the development of Buddhist thought and sectarianism, which we will explore further in Sections 3.2 and 4.2.

3.2 THE DEVELOPMENT OF THE EARLY SYSTEMS AND SCHOOLS

As we noted in Chapters 1 and 2, the Buddha's approach to teaching was primarily therapeutic, whereby he used a variety of strategies to induce his listeners to a realization of nirvāṇa. He mentioned at one point in his career (S.LVI.31) that the knowledge he gained in his Awakening could be compared to the leaves of a forest; the teachings he had imparted were as a mere handful of leaves. He had chosen to teach only those points that would help lead to the end of suffering. The rest of his knowledge would not have been useful for that purpose, which was why he had held it back. Thus it should come as no surprise that he did not leave behind a philosophical system. Using another image, he told his listeners that, in effect, they were in a burning house. Rather than drawing up full plans for the house, he simply marked out the escape routes. In one of his more prominent discourses (M.1), he roundly criticized monks who tried to form a philosophical system from the categories of his teaching. What he did leave behind, in addition to the memory of his discourses, was a series of matṛka (lists) of the major topics of his teachings, such as the Wings to Awakening, but these lists were not organized in any systematic way.

In the first few centuries after his Parinirvāṇa, many of the Buddha's followers came to view this lack of system as a serious defect. This feeling may have been due to outside pressures—the need to defend Buddhism from attacks of being inconsistent or inadequate—or to pressures from within the Sangha itself. Shortly before his Parinirvāṇa (D.16), the Buddha had told his followers that if anyone reported having heard that a particular teaching was his, it should be judged not by the authority cited but by its consistency with what they already knew of his teachings. After the First Council, Buddhists who had not participated in the council most likely proposed teachings that they claimed to have heard directly or indirectly from the Buddha, and thus there was a need for clear guidelines as to what the essential points of the teaching were.

The first efforts to establish these guidelines were in the form of simple lists of major topics, attributed to Śāriputra and placed in the Long Collections of the Sūtras. These were followed by early Abhidharma texts that organized the material more systematically, sorting out synonyms and redundancies in order to present the teachings as a more coherent whole. In the course of this process, apparent inconsistencies in the Sūtras came to light. The question of how to deal with these inconsistencies led the Bhikṣu Sangha to embark on original inquiries into philosophical method and formal logic. The differing answers that were devised became one of the major factors that led the Sangha to split into various schools.

If one assumes that the Buddha's teachings were primarily therapeutic, the inconsistencies are no great issue. Differing approaches were found to work for different types of problems. But if one is looking for a logically consistent system, one has to explain the inconsistencies away. The elder monks soon proposed that the Buddha's terminology had two levels: conventional, in which the Buddha used everyday language in a figurative way to discuss issues with people who would not have benefited from higher philosophical discourse; and ultimate, in which he referred directly to absolute realities in a literal sense. Ultimate terms were eventually reduced to set lists and (except for nirvāṇa) categorized under the five skandhas, together with a list of the types of relationships that operated among them. Treatises dealing with these lists and categories formed the primary Abhidharma texts. To them were added methodological handbooks and later commentaries to show how every statement in the Sūtras could be reduced to ultimate terms and relationships.

However, the explanatory power of the lists did not stop with the Sūtras. A systematic philosophy was worked out whereby the lists could be used to explain all perceivable phenomena in the cosmos. The basic terms were claimed to correspond to phenomena—both physical and mental—on the ultimate level of reality. Each term thus became a dharma, an impersonal event-type possessing its own *svabhāva* (beingness), which meant that it could exist and function without need for a personal agent. Apart from nirvāṇa, all dharmas were force-configurations that existed only temporarily, conditioning and being conditioned by one another. The hallmark of this system was the conversion of the not-self doctrine into a metaphysical principle. All events in the body, mind, and cosmos could be explained by a plurality of momentary dharmas without reference to any personal agents or abiding selves. This shift in the status of the not-self doctrine was reflected in anti-Buddhist polemics during this period. Jain Sūtras composed in the first centuries after the Parinirvāṇa complained that the Buddhists would not commit themselves to any clear position on what the self was or whether it existed; later Brahmanical treatises depict the Buddhists as stoutly defending the position that there is no self.

These developments provided the Buddhists with a systematic body of doctrine that met their needs in defending their position against outsiders and that streamlined the teaching of insiders. However, they also led to the formation of different schools of thought, as monks began to argue about what the Buddha's ultimate teachings were and how they were to be ferreted out of the massive collections of Sūtras. Before we discuss some of the more important splits, though, it is important to note that despite the divisions among various schools, there were no schisms in the early Buddhist movement. Monks belonging to different schools often lived together in harmony in the same monasteries. The Buddha's warnings against schism—two or more groups of monks living in the same monastic boundary refusing to conduct communal business together—were so strongly worded that the monks never contemplated such a drastic break. If any one group felt that its differences from its fellows were so strong that they could not live together, it would retire to another area of the subcontinent and establish itself there.

3.2.1 The Second Council and the Mahāsanghikas (Strong *EB*, sec. 3.6.1)

Although many of the differences between the various schools seem minor, they show that the early Buddhist monks were grappling with a major issue common to all religions after the death of the founder: how to extract the spirit of the founder's message from his recorded teachings in such a way as to convey it meaningfully to new generations. The first controversy is traditionally dated to one hundred years after the Parinirvāṇa, when *Sthaviras* (elders) in the western part of India learned that monks in the eastern city of Vaisali had begun making changes in the monastic code—some relatively minor (for example, making it permissible to store salt to add flavor to bland alms meals) and others more significant (allowing the use of gold and silver). A council was convened in Vaisali to address nine points of discipline and the one point of principle that underlay all of the Vaisalian practices: that it was permissible to take one's personal teacher's practices as a guide. Denouncing all the changes that had been made in the rules, the council decided that the practice of following one's teacher was sometimes permissible and sometimes not. The formal pronouncement on this last point, however, did not go into detail on how to determine when it was and was not right to follow one's teacher. The manner in which the western elders conducted the council indicated that the texts should be taken as one's final guide, but apparently the majority of eastern monks did not concur. Shortly thereafter, they held a separate council of their own at which they formed a separate school, the *Mahāsanghika* (Great Assembly).

Historical records differ as to exactly what issues precipitated this move, but a survey of the later doctrines of the Mahāsanghikas and their offshoots indicates that the general thrust was against accepting the Sūtras and Vinaya as the final authority regarding the Buddha's teachings. Some Mahāsanghika offshoots argued that arhants were fallible and thus could not be fully trusted to have remembered the Buddha's teachings correctly. One subgroup, the Katukkuṭikas, argued that the Buddha's ultimate teachings could be arrived at only through logic; that study and meditation were thus unnecessary activities; and that the only trustworthy source was their own Abhidharma. Others, especially the Lokuttaravādins, began an elaborate Buddhology, or theory of Buddhahood, arguing that even if the texts were accurate records, they were all expressed in the conventional language of the world. The Buddha's ultimate message, they said, was transcendent and thus not of this world. This line of reasoning developed further into the belief that the Buddha, in an ultimate sense, continues to exist as long as there are sentient beings and that he has the power to inspire insights in the minds of others (Strong *EB*, sec. 3.6.3). This belief provided a mechanism for justifying insights about the Buddha's message that could not be supported by the texts: The transcendent Buddha had placed such insights in the mind of the person who proposed them.

Despite the wide differences, the common denominator running through the Mahāsanghikas' positions was that the texts were not the sole authority in determining the Buddha's true teachings. However they interpreted the means of transmission, they agreed that there was the possibility of transmission outside of the texts. This point of view has continued to resurface throughout the Buddhist tradition, and is found today not only in Zen and Tibetan schools, which articulate it most clearly, but also in some Theravādin lineages. The Mahāsanghikas reportedly allowed monks who were not fully Awakened to participate in their deliberations on the proper way to interpret the Dharma. This shows that they were more inclined than the Sthaviravādins, the elders from whom they split, to give credence to the role of individual inspiration and reasoning, regardless of whether it was backed up by an experience of Awakening and could be tested against a full reading of the texts. The positive side to this approach was that it opened the door to a personal transmission of the Dharma, free from the tyranny of scholastics, patterned on the personal approach the Buddha himself used. The negative side was that it provided an opening for what has been termed "designer Buddhism," in which parts of the tradition are suppressed or denigrated because they do not fit with principles derived either from outside the tradition or from personal preferences and a mere partial reading of the texts. Although we do not have complete versions of the Mahāsanghika Abhidharmas, outside reports indicate that they denied aspects of the teaching that seem to have been central to it. For instance, they accepted only linear causal patterns and denied that the Buddha was subject to the laws of karma. All accounts indicate that the Mahāsanghikans' liberal attitude toward the tradition eventually engendered the Mahāyāna movement, which asserted that the early arhants may have not only misunderstood certain details in the Buddha's original teachings, but actually missed the entire point.

The Mahāsanghikans maintained a center in the capital at Pataliputra, but their primary strength developed in the South, especially around the great religious centers at Amaravati and Nagarjunakonda. They maintained their separate identity until the fall of Buddhism in northern India. Chinese travelers in the seventh and eighth centuries C.E. list them as one of the four major schools of Buddhism still extant in India at that time. Only a few of their texts survive.

3.2.2 The Personalist School

Because the Mahāsanghikans were united primarily around a negative position—their questioning of the authority of the canon—the wide number of subschools they developed in a fairly short time is easily explained. However, the Sthaviravādins, who remained united in their acceptance of the full canon, similarly began undergoing splits in the course of trying to develop a consistent philosophical system that could fully account for everything in the texts.

The first split was over whether, aside from nirvāṇa, all the concepts in the Sūtra Piṭaka, and in particular the concept of *pudgala* (person or individual), could be reduced to the five skandhas. The orthodox Sthaviras—with whom the Mahāsanghikas concurred on this point—said yes. The dissenting group, called the Vātsīputrīyas or, in terms of their main doctrine, the Pudgalavādins (or Personalists), said no; that the Buddha used the term *person* in three contexts in such a way that it could not be understood as merely a conventional expression for the five skandhas. However, it was also not entirely separate from them, and so was not a separate dharma.

The three contexts the Pudgalavādins cited referred to (1) the five skandhas in the present life, (2) transmigration, and (3) the attainment of Parinirvāṇa. In the first context, the Pudgalavādins cited a verse from the Sūtra stating that the person is the carrier of the burden of the five skandhas. If one did not assume such a person, they said, there was no explaining the cohesion and integrity of an individual's experiences—that things such as memory can take place and that one person's perceptions, feelings, and so forth cannot become the perceptions and feelings of someone else. With regards to the second context, if the person is not assumed to be a transmigrating principle, there is no making sense of the Buddha's teachings that a person, at death, is reborn in only one place at a time, or that the state of streamwinner, once gained, is transferred to one's following lives. And, in the third context, if the person is not assumed, there is no making sense of the statements maintaining that, when the skandhas end with the Parinirvāṇa, one will attain the Further Shore and the bliss of liberation. However, once the point of Parinirvāṇa is passed, the Pudgalavādins asserted, nothing further could be said about the pudgala, for as a concept it has descriptive power only in relation to the skandhas.

In formulating this explanation of the Sūtra, the Pudgalavādins thus introduced a third category of being—relative existence—in between the standard Abhidharma categories of ultimate reality and conventional designation. The concept of person had a relative existence to the skandhas, just as fire exists only relative to its fuel, and as such it could not be described apart from them. Thus it had to be classified as ineffable, for the terms *conditioned* and *unconditioned*, which, strictly speaking, could apply only to dharmas, could not apply to it. This introduction of a new category sparked vehement attacks from all other Abhidharmists, who refused to entertain the possibility that reality could be explained outside of the binary categories of ultimate truths and conventional expressions. Texts survive in which the Sthaviras and one of their offshoots, the Sarvāstivādins (see Section 3.2.3), attempt to force the Pudgalavādins to fit their concept into one of the two categories; the Pudgalavādins refuse to do so. This, for the Sthaviras, was proof enough that the Pudgalavādin thesis was incoherent and incomprehensible. Furthermore, they charged that the Pudgalavādin concept of person flew in the face of the not-self doctrine; that it constituted a self-identity view, and as such closed off the Path to nirvāṇa. The Pudgalavadins, for their part, were able to quote Sūtra passages to such an effect that the view "I have no self" is an annihilationist wrong view, and that the standard Abhidharma analysis thus closed off the Path to nirvāṇa as well. Their concept of a relatively existing person, they said, was not a self, as it could not be known in a way that it would function as an object of clinging. As such, it constituted a Middle Way between the Brahmanical view of an eternal self and the annihilationist view that there is no self—both of which the Buddha had attacked—and thus best preserved the sense of the Sūtras.

As might be expected, the debates reached an impasse, with neither side submitting to the logical presuppositions of the other. This impasse lasted for centuries. The Pudgalavādins survived as a school until Buddhism was wiped out of northern India in the beginning of the thirteenth century C.E. Their major offshoot, the Sāṃmitīyas, flowered in the seventh and eighth centuries C.E., largely through the patronage of the great Gupta Buddhist king, Harṣavadhana (606–647 C.E.), whose sister, Rājyaśrī, joined the school as a bhikṣuṇī. According to Chinese pilgrims at the time, it was the dominant sect in the Ganges Valley. As with the Mahāsanghikans, however, only a small number of its texts survive, mostly in Chinese translations.

3.2.3 The Third Council and the Sarvāstivādins

Theravādin sources record that another split further rent the Sthaviravādins at the Council of Pataliputra, sponsored by King Aśoka in approximately 250 B.C.E. This Third Council (the Sthaviras did not count the council that formed the Mahāsanghikas) resulted in two factions, called *Vibhajyavādins* (Distinctionists) and *Sarvāstivādins* (All-is-ists). The latter's chief thesis was that past and future things really exist, as do present things. This view was advanced to solve one of the issues that had begun to plague Abhidharma analysis after the acceptance of the belief that dharmas have only momentary existence: If such is the case, how can karma have long-term effects? The Sarvāstivādin solution was to say that dharmas have a permanent existence whose mode changes from future to present to past. Thus, even when in the past mode, a dharma is still able to exert an influence on other dharmas as they approach the momentary present mode (Strong *EB*, sec. 3.6.2). The Vibhajyavādins, whose views were seconded by the Mahāsanghikans, objected to this solution on the grounds that it constituted a denial of the Buddha's teachings on impermanence and dependent co-arising.

The Council of Pataliputra decided against the Sarvāstivādins, some of whom migrated west and north, where they established a strong center in Kashmir that flourished for a thousand years, as well as centers in Mathura and Gandhara. Buddhism flourished in this region under the Indo-Greek kings during the second century B.C.E. The greatest of these kings, Menander (in Pali, Milinda; Strong *EB*, sec. 3.4.2), is said to have become a Buddhist. The Indo-Greeks and their successors in this region—the Śakas (first century B.C.E. through first century C.E.) and the Kuṣāṇas (first century C.E. through mid-third century)—were all invaders from Bactria and Parthia. They retained their connections with central Asia and so enabled Buddhism to spread to the developing city-states along the silk route between China and the West. This put the Sarvāstivādins in a favorable position to dominate the cities on the northern branch of the trade route: Kashgar, Aksu, Kucha, and Karashahr. From there, they influenced the early spread of Buddhism into China.

Although the Sarvāstivādins took their name from their philosophic views on time and being, their primary role in Buddhist history was to nourish the doctrine of the *pāramitā* (perfections), which became a cornerstone of the Mahāyāna. The Bodhisattva, they said, fulfills six perfections: generosity, virtue, patience, vigor, dhyaana, and discernment. These qualities are frequently commended in the Sūtras, but they become perfections only when fully developed. The Jātakas, illustrated in the art of the second century B.C.E., relate how Gautama in his former lives fulfilled each perfection. For example, in one life he was an ascetic staying in the pleasure grove of a dissolute king of Benares. One day the king entered with a flock of female dancers, and when he fell into a drunken sleep the women wandered off and discovered the ascetic. On awakening, the ruler was enraged to find his women gathered round the mendicant and listening to his sermon. Asking the Bodhisattva what doctrine he professed, he was told *kṣānti* (patience). So the king summoned his executioner, had the Bodhisattva severely flogged, then asked, "What do you profess?" The answer was still "patience." So the king had his victim's hands and feet cut off, then his nose and ears. To the end, the Bodhisattva professed patience and felt no anger whatsoever. Earth, however, ran out of patience. As the tyrant was leaving his pleasure grove, the ground opened beneath his feet and threw him to the lowest hell.

Other tales exemplified the other perfections. These popular tales urged the listeners to imitate the Bodhisattva, but painted his virtues in such extreme terms that they make the bodhisattva course seem more a superhuman marvel than a practical guide to life. Only with the Mahāyāna Sūtras were people urged to become bodhisattvas themselves.

3.2.4 The Sautrāntikas and Later Schools

At an uncertain date—perhaps three centuries after the Parinirvāṇa, perhaps during the second century C.E. (see Section 4.4)—the Sautrāntikas split off from the Sarvāstivādins. This group was so called because they denied the scriptural authority of the Abhidharma and acknowledged only the *Sutrantas* (= Sūtras) as their guides. Nonetheless, in the process of defending their views against those of the Abhidharma schools, they contributed much to the development of Abhidharma thought, furnishing the Mahayana both with critiques of Sarvāstivādin doctrine and with key concepts. On the one hand, they provided telling arguments against the Sarvāstivādin teaching that past and future dharmas really exist, holding that, if this were true, conditioned things would last forever, which is an impossibility. On the other hand, they proposed several positive doctrines to supplant the Sarvāstivādin thesis, chief among them being their explanation of karma, whereby every intentional deed leaves seeds that carry effects latent in the personality stream until their time comes for fruition. This doctrine later played a major role in Yogācāra thought (see Section 4.3).

As for the Vibhajyavādins, who retained the name of the Sthaviravāda, they were united chiefly during the Council of Pataliputra by their opposition to the Sarvāstivādins, but soon they too broke into subschools. One of these, the Mahīśāsakas, was situated in the Narbada Valley (between Sanchi and Ajanta), from where it spread south to the Deccan and coastal Andhra. By the fifth century C.E. its monks, having gradually taken to the Mahāyāna, had lost their original sectarian identity.

The Dharmaguptakas separated from the Mahīśāsakas quite early and apparently were centered chiefly in northwest India and Serindia (central Asia), whence they became influential in China, where large portions of their canon are extant. They specialized in the art of *dhāraṇī,* or *mantra* (protective incantation), which must have proven popular among those traveling along dangerous trade routes. In this respect they developed a practice that plays a very minor part in the early Sūtras but that burgeoned with the rise of Tantrism (see Chapter 6).

What was left of the original Sthaviravādin group remained powerful in the Ganges Valley until the thirteenth century C.E. The only surviving group of its lineage, or of any Hīnayāna lineage for that matter, is an archaic group of Vibhajyavādins (retaining the Pali version of the original name, Theravādins) that became established in Sri Lanka, at the Great Monastery of Anuradhapura, about 240 B.C.E. For most of the second century B.C.E., Sri Lanka was ruled by the non-Buddhist Tamils who had invaded from south India, cutting the island off from developments in India. By the time Sri Lanka became independent again, Theravādin Buddhism was confirmed in the archaistic cast it has since retained.

The tables of school names, deceptively similar to grammatical paradigms, convey an impression of orderliness and exclusiveness that is contrary to fact. In the early years, when canons had to be memorized, a monk belonged exclusively to the school whose texts he had memorized. Beginning with the first and second centuries C.E., however, as written culture supplanted oral culture and the texts were written down, monks and monasteries were freed to study and even to adopt specific tenets of rival schools without risking expulsion from their own. Inscriptions reveal that monasteries "belonged" to specific schools, but any one monastery would frequently house members of different schools living side by side and would give temporary shelter to traveling monastics of all persuasions. Although scholastic affiliations may have been important to scholarly monks, they probably made little difference to monks and nuns who devoted themselves to a quiet life of meditation.

3.3 AŚOKA

In 321 B.C.E., roughly when the Mahāsanghikas and the Sthaviras were dividing, Candragupta Maurya succeeded to the throne of Magadha. His primary adviser, Kauṭalya, was the author of a treatise on political power that, because of its amoral approach to the acquisition and maintenance of power, has earned him the name of the "Machiavelli of India." Kauṭalya's advice was apparently very astute, for by 303 Candragupta had gained control of territory from Bengal to eastern Afghanistan and as far south as the Narmada River. His son, Bindusāra, acceded to the throne in 297 B.C.E. and conquered the Deccan and Mysore in central India, and the Tamil country in the far south. Bindusāra died in 272 B.C.E., succeeded by his son Aśoka, who was crowned four years later after eliminating other claimants to the throne.

Although Bindusāra was a supporter of the Ājīvika sect, whose denial of morality fit well with his approach to power, Aśoka converted to Buddhism—perhaps for political reasons, perhaps at the behest of his first wife—nine years into his reign. By his own admission, the religion did not mean much to him personally until two and a half years later, after his conquest of Kalinga in northeast India, the only major area of the subcontinent still refusing to submit to his rule. The extensive bloodshed and destruction caused by the conquest filled him with remorse. He began to study the teachings of various sects, visited monks frequently, learned from them, and formally dedicated himself as an adherent to the Sangha. As a result, he began making drastic changes both in his personal life and in his administrative policies, abandoning the amoral maxims taught by Kauṭalya and undertaking a great experiment in bringing the Dharma to bear on the running of his empire, thus earning for himself a lasting reputation in world, as well as Indian, history.

For centuries the only records of Aśoka's reign were the Buddhist chronicles, which claimed him as an exemplary supporter of the Sangha. Then in the nineteenth century, Aśokan edicts were discovered and deciphered, providing in his own words a history of his reign. In these edicts, Aśoka expresses his support for all the major religions of his time: Buddhism, Brahmanism, Jainism, and the Ājīvika sect. On the basis of this fact—together with the fact that Aśoka's expressed conception of Dharma makes no mention of particularly Buddhist doctrines such as the Four Noble Truths—some scholars have questioned whether Aśoka was in fact a Buddhist. The case for regarding him as a Buddhist, however, rests on much stronger evidence in the edicts. To begin with, there are the many edicts addressed intramurally to Buddhists; in one, Aśoka shows a close familiarity with Buddhist texts. No edicts addressed intramurally to members of other religions have been found. Second, there are the Aśokan rock pillars erected at Buddhist holy sites, an honor he did not extend to the holy sites of other religions. Although caves donated by Aśoka to the Ājīvikas have been discovered, his continued support of the Ājīvikas fits into the Buddha's instructions to major lay converts from other sects that they continue giving alms to their previous sect as before.

As for the edicts addressed to the populace at large, they are aimed at lay people, and it should be remembered that the Buddha himself often did not propound abstract doctrine to the laity. Aśoka's purpose was to give expression to an ideology that would bring his empire together. If he had tried to force his beliefs on members of other religions, it would have proven politically divisive. Thus, in these edicts he generally focuses on themes that members of all religions would accept, such as truthfulness, nonviolence, and respect for teachers and elders. Still, his language, modes of expression, and injunctions betray a Buddhist orientation. He uses the intramural word *Sangha*, rather than the extramural *Buddhists*, to refer to the Buddhist monks and nuns even in the extramural edicts. *Dharma*, for him, refers to moral values as well as the qualities of heart that underlie moral action. This too is a specifically Buddhist use of the term. The only other religion of the time that used *Dharma* in anywhere near this sense was Brahmanism, which defined it as the moral rules and ritual behavior enjoined by the Vedas. The Vedic rules, however, make no reference to qualities of the heart, and Aśoka's belittling of rituals in one of his edicts, together with his outlawing of animal sacrifices, indicates that he was not looking to the Vedas for guidance. In fact, the ideals he espouses correspond to the first four of the perfections—generosity, morality, patience (tolerance), and vigor—and the first three steps of the Buddha's graduated discourse (see Section 2.4). The attitudes he expresses fall under the four Brahmā Attitudes (see Section 1.4.2). On the whole, it seems safe to assume that Buddhists have been correct in claiming Aśoka as one of their own.

By Aśoka's own analysis, his domestic Dharma policy had three prongs: personal Dharma practice on his own part, administration in line with the Dharma, and Dharma instruction for the populace. In terms of his own practice, Aśoka ended the slaughter of animals in the royal kitchens and abandoned the sport of royal hunting excursions, replacing them with Dharma excursions on which he would take pilgrimages to holy spots, visit śramaṇas and brahmin priests, give donations to religious mendicants and to the aged, and discuss Dharma with the general populace. Appropriately, his first Dharma pilgrimage was to Bodhgaya, the site of the Buddha's Awakening (Strong *EB*, sec. 1.2). Later in his reign he visited Lumbini, the site of the Buddha's birth, where he erected a commemorative pillar that still stands today. In the same region in 253 B.C.E., he ordered the enlargement of the stūpa dedicated to the former Buddha Konamakamuni. The inscription recording this act is the earliest datable evidence for the doctrine and cult of Buddhas who had lived prior to Gautama. Aśoka's first wife came from Vidisa, which is apparently why he sponsored the first stage of construction of the still-famous stūpa on the nearby hill of Sanchi, the most extensive and perhaps loveliest of all early Buddhist holy places still standing in India. Tradition maintains that Aśoka built 84,000 stūpas altogether, but even the more modest tally of history and archaeology abundantly testifies that honoring the Buddha ranked as highly as ethical conduct in Aśoka's personal religious beliefs. As stated previously, Aśoka made donations to all sects, but his support for the Buddhist Sangha was prodigious, reportedly causing recruits to flock to the order and demonstrating the oft-repeated rule that the survival and prosperity of Buddhism have usually depended on the support of rulers.

Aśoka's administrative reforms were aimed at facilitating redress of grievances against petty officials. Inspectors were sent out to check on the fair administration of justice, especially in the newly conquered area of Kalinga. Special officials were appointed with the power to convey petitions from the populace to the king at any time, even when he was in his women's quarters.

Dispensaries and medicinal herb gardens were set up for the treatment of human and animal diseases, wells were dug, and highways improved. Aśoka noted that previous kings had also provided public works of this last sort for their subjects, but that his provisions differed inasmuch as his motivation was directed at the Dharma. This difference in motivation suggests that he was inspired by the Buddhist maxim that the practice of the Dharma fares best in a stable society, and that societies are most stable when prosperity is widely shared (see Section 2.4).

Aśoka's policy of Dharma instruction for the general populace was the most original part of his policy. According to him, it took two forms: Dharma injunctions and Dharma persuasion. The injunctions included laws forbidding animal sacrifice; prohibiting the killing of many kinds of animals, in particular those not used for food; and outlawing wasteful festivals. The persuasion consisted of the presentation of edifying performances containing moral themes for the populace, portraying the heavenly rewards of virtue, and an extensive set of royal messages aimed at persuading his subjects to live more moral lives. In 254 B.C.E. Aśoka had a series of 14 edicts on topics related to the Dharma engraved on rocks throughout his empire, and he instructed his officials to read them to the public on festival days. Thirteen years later he began issuing a similar series of seven edicts, which were inscribed on polished stone pillars. These inscriptions are the earliest surviving compositions of a Buddhist lay follower (Strong *EB*, sec. 2.6.3), and their perspective on the Dharma affords an interesting contrast to the monastic perspective recorded in the canons.

Dharma for Aśoka meant both moral action and skillful mental qualities. The actions he recommended to his subjects included obedience to and honoring of one's parents, teachers, and other elders; generosity to relatives, acquaintances, and religious persons; abstention from killing animals; moderation in spending wealth; kindness to serfs and servants; and above all, the gift of Dharma, that is, mutual admonition among friends and family members as to what is right and wrong. Mental qualities he recommended included self-control, gratitude, devotion, compassion, forgiveness, impartiality, and truthfulness. He warned against irascibility, cruelty, anger, spitefulness, and pride. The Dharma of his edicts, however, is not just humanistic morality. Aśoka asserted that he had caused deities to mingle with human beings as they had never done before. This may mean that by fostering offerings to holy individuals and deities and by promoting Dharma, he had propitiated the spirits and drawn them down to the altars and homes of his people. In addition, he extolled all the virtues he recommended as producing the merit leading to rebirth in the heavenly worlds.

In addition to promulgating edicts, Aśoka formed a new branch of the government devoted to Dharma instruction, sending Dharma officials throughout the empire to carry his message to the populace and to supervise religious activities. His interference in the life of the religious sects, Aśoka said, was motivated by a desire that each sect develop fine traditions and its religious "essence," which to him meant tolerance: not praising one's own sect to the disparagement of others. He recommended that the different schools listen to and learn from one another. To honor other sects, he said, was to honor one's own. Paradoxically, in spite of his support for tolerance, there is epigraphical evidence that Aśoka became involved in a split that was dividing the Buddhist community at this time, probably between the Sthaviravādins and their offshoot, the Sarvāstivādins, ordering that the latter group leave the community or be forcibly disrobed.

Five years after attacking Kalinga, Aśoka proclaimed a new foreign policy, one of peaceful Dharma-conquest rather than military conquest. Dharma officials were sent to proclaim Aśoka's domestic policy of Dharma practice, administration, and instruction to the people of kingdoms bordering his own—especially the Greek kingdoms on his western frontier, and the Coḷas and Sinhalese kingdoms to his south. A bilingual Greek-Aramaic Aśokan inscription at Kandahar in Afghanistan records, for the benefit of the people living in his neighboring kingdoms, the measures he had taken to "make people more pious" and concludes, "Acting in this way, during their present life and in their future existence they will live better and more happily together in all things." Aśoka's aim in his policy of Dharma-conquest was that other kingdoms would follow his example. This, he said, would be a source of greater joy than military conquest could ever provide. One of his edicts states that in 256 and 255 B.C.E. he sent Dharma-envoys to the Greek rulers of Syria, Egypt, Macedonia, Cyrene, and Epyrus, as well as to the Tamils in south India. Buddhist tradition records that he also sent missions to Sri Lanka and Southeast Asia. His missionaries left no documentable impression on the Mediterranean world, but they had more impact closer to home. In particular, his mission to Sri Lanka was an outstanding success. Legend reports that he sent not only Dharma-officials but also his own son and daughter—Mahinda and Saṅghamittā—who went as monk and nun, rather than as prince and princess, and who succeeded in converting the entire island to Buddhism.

Scholars have debated over the possible ulterior motives for Aśoka's Dharma policies. Although his edicts convey sincere concern for the welfare of his own and his neighbors' subjects more clearly than any other royal pronouncements of the ancient world, it would be a mistake to regard Aśoka as a starry-eyed idealist with his feet planted firmly in the clouds. He had inherited a large, multicultural empire, and thus needed a transcultural policy, inculcating moral behavior in his subjects, that would tie it together more firmly than the cynical maxims of amoral statecraft could possibly do. In addition, his strong bureaucratic state not only regulated commerce, industry, and agriculture, but also acted as an entrepreneur itself. Craftsmen and merchants, whose interests were tied to the Maurya enterprises, especially supported Buddhism. Thus Aśoka, in supporting that religion, was strengthening a bond with an already loyal class; in pursuing a policy of Dharma-conquest, he ensured the peace and stability needed for the profitable functioning of the government enterprises; in formulating and propagating a Dharma policy that transcended any particular religion, he created an ideological common denominator that could tie his far-flung empire together.

According to tradition, Aśoka's successors showed no interest in continuing his policies, and the fall of the Mauryas half a century after his death may have been due, in part, to their shortsightedness. Aśoka's main success was in his contribution to the Buddhist tradition. His example established an extremely influential model of the ideal but practicable Buddhist state and the dedicated lay person—a model that later Buddhists never forgot. Thus, alongside the Sangha and its monastic ideals, there developed a parallel tradition whose goals involved achieving the Dharma's ends in social and political contexts.

3.4 RELIGIOUS LIFE IN THE EARLY CENTURIES

The early canons provide an account of the practices of the community, lay as well as monastic, during the second century B.C.E. The Vinaya Piṭaka prescribes the correct life for the monks and nuns, and describes, in telling the origin of each rule, the colorful abuses against which the order had to protect itself. In doing so, it paints a detailed and quite realistic picture of the monastic community, along with its relations with the laity. At the same time, passages from the Vinaya and Sūtra also disclose the norms for lay Buddhist practice. Archaeological evidence, in the form of art and architectural remains, completes this picture by indicating cultic aspects of religious life in the early years of the tradition.

3.4.1 The Code of Discipline for Monks

The *Bhikṣu Prātimokṣa* (in Pali, *Bhikkhu Pāṭimokkha*), the central code of discipline and the heart of the Vinaya Piṭaka, defines five classes of offense, prescribes rules of deportment, and establishes procedural guidelines for the peaceful running of the community in a way that is at the same time conducive to the individual training of the mind. A similar code governed the lives of nuns. The following account draws from the Pali and Mahāsanghika versions, which differ only in minor details.

Four offenses warrant immediate and permanent expulsion: fornication, grand larceny, killing a human being (this includes recommending abortion), and falsely claiming spiritual attainments (Strong *EB*, sec. 2.3.1). Thirteen offenses require a formal meeting of the Sangha chapter and are punished with probation. The first five of these concern sex: intentional ejaculation, touching a woman with lustful intent, speaking suggestively to her, telling her that she would benefit spiritually by yielding sexually to a man of religion, and serving as a matchmaker. Two rules deal with the prescribed size and the approved site of monks' dwellings. Six pertain to concord in the order. For example, it is an offense to falsely accuse a fellow monk of an offense that merits expulsion or to support such an accusation with misleading testimony. It is an offense for a monk to persist in fomenting schism within the Sangha after the assembly has formally warned him three times to desist. It is also an offense for other monks to persist in supporting a schismatic and for a monk to persist in being obtuse and refusing to accept admonition after the third warning. The thirteenth offense of this class is for a monk who, having been banished from a community for having an evil influence on the laity, criticizes the monks who imposed the banishment on him. In each case, a formal meeting of the Sangha is called and the offending monk is placed under probation for at least six days.

The probationer forfeits many privileges. He must not allow monks in good standing to offer salutation, provide seats for him, carry his robe or bowl, or massage him. Every day he must announce to the monks in the monastery the reason for his probation, repeating this announcement whenever newcomers arrive. He is required always to take the lowest seat, the worst bed, the worst room, and to sit at the end of the line when food is being distributed. He may not leave the monastery unless accompanied by four monks of good standing. When the probation period is over, he may be reinstated only by a Sangha of 20 monks or more. This class of rules is followed by two dealing with how to handle a case when a monk has been sitting in private with a woman and is accused of an offense; the assembly must meet to review the case, deciding what penalty, if any, is called for.

Thirty rules deal with improper use or acquisition of an article, requiring confession and forfeiture of the article involved. For the most part the rules concern robes, alms bowls, and seat-rugs. The monk must not have more than one of each of these at a time. However, when his begging-bowl develops five cracks, he may exchange it for a new one. He must not get a nun to do his laundry, give him a robe (except in exchange), or prepare wool for a rug. He may store medicinal foods for only seven days. He may not receive gold or silver, buy, sell, or barter.

Ninety-two of the rules require simple confession. The list is quite miscellaneous: lying, verbal abuse, divisive tale-bearing, stealing another monk's sleeping space, sporting in the water, or eavesdropping while other monks quarrel. It is prohibited to dig the ground, destroy plant life, or sprinkle water with living creatures in it. These rules, ostensibly to protect worms and bugs, also safeguarded the religious against lapsing into peasanthood or becoming solitary hermits, growing their own food. Another group of rules prohibits the monk (except for good cause) from going near an army drawn up for battle, staying with an army for more than two or three nights, and watching other military activities. The idea seems to be that the monk should not be an accessory to bloodshed, although the prohibitions were probably also intended to protect him from accusations of engaging in espionage or diplomatic intrigue. As opposed to killing a human being, deliberately taking animal life does not warrant expulsion but does require confession. The monk must not even drink or otherwise use water that contains living things that would die from his using it. He must not eat food after noon or before dawn, nor is he to store food overnight. However, eating meat is not forbidden, as long as the monk does not know or suspect that the animal was killed specifically to feed him. Drinking liquor—even as much as the tip of a blade of grass—is an offense to be confessed.

A monk who tells a lay person of his actual spiritual attainments commits an offense requiring confession, as does one who informs an unordained person of a fellow monk's grave offense. Nevertheless, every monk is duty-bound to inform the assembly of any serious transgression committed by a fellow monk because an unconfessed sin is considered an affliction that grows aggravated the longer it goes unabsolved; therefore, the informer is doing the accused a kindness. However, the code treats false accusation as a serious offense and forbids harrying another with insinuations that he is transgressing. These rules taken together demand that the Sangha keep its own counsel, shun both the adulation and reproach of outsiders, and compel honesty, conformity, and goodwill from its members.

Rules of deportment—75 in the Pali, 67 in the Mahāsanghika recension—regulate the conduct of the monk while going on his begging rounds among the homes of the laity, receiving alms, eating, and excreting. He must at all times be properly clothed, keep his eyes downcast, not sway his limbs or body, refrain from loud laughter and noise, and observe good table manners: neither stuffing his mouth, smacking his lips, nor talking with his mouth full. He must not excrete while standing up, onto cultivated plants, or into potable water. This set also includes rules forbidding the monk to preach Dharma to a listener whose deportment is disrespectful, for example, carrying a parasol, staff, sword, or weapon in the hand; wearing slippers or sandals; wearing a turban or other head-covering; occupying a higher seat than the monk; sitting while the monk is standing; or walking on a path in front of him.

The overall purpose of the rules of deportment is to render the monk worthy of reverence and offerings. The monk must himself maintain impeccable conduct and allow the laity to choose their response. If they revile him, he suffers it with gentle dignity (Strong *EB*, sec. 2.4.2). If they behave as swine, he withholds the pearls of the Dharma. The good monk is indifferent to worldly success and failure, gain and loss. He sticks to his principles even when so doing places his life in danger. Monks and nuns have starved; died of disease; been killed by robbers, tyrants, and ferocious beasts; been sexually assaulted; and been mocked and humiliated by hostile unbelievers. But wherever the Vinaya has been observed in spirit and in letter, the Sangha as a whole has earned respect and prevailed.

In themselves, some of the rules of deportment seem trivial and quaint. The Sangha, it must be remembered, accepts recruits from all backgrounds. It has to refine vulgar ordinands and civilize uncouth barbarians. Etiquette alone does not suffice, of course, but it is a necessary part of the complete discipline that shapes character and attracts outsiders to the Dharma. A noteworthy feature of the Vinaya rules is that they are utterly free from taboos of the sort so common in the Brahmanical and Near Eastern law books. There is no idea that certain foods are impure, that bodily wastes pollute spiritually, that certain acts or objects are lucky or unlucky, or that certain plants and animals are taboo because of their association with particular divinities.

Another noteworthy feature is the prominent role the Vinaya gives to intention, in line with the general Buddhist teachings on the importance of intention in shaping one's experience of the cosmos. In most cases, an unintentional infraction of a rule does not count as an offense. Two dominant ethical concerns of the code are nonviolence and celibacy, which derive from the principles of right resolve in the Noble Eightfold Path (see Section 2.3.1). *Ahimsa* (nonviolence) develops the virtue of compassion, whereas ascetic continence avoids desire and lust, directing the force of Eros to spiritual goals.

The Vinaya does not view the monk as working out his own salvation unaided (see Section 2.4). Rather, each monk is his brother's keeper. When the ordinand joins the Sangha, he surrenders some liberties and submits to the collective authority of the community (Strong *EB*, sec. 2.3.2). The Khandhakas (see Section 3.1.2) lay down disciplinary procedures for bringing the obstinate and the wayward to conformity, with punishments ranging from censure to suspension from the Sangha. All these acts lapse when their object has mended his ways.

The Vinaya insists throughout on due process of law. The offender is warned, reminded of the rules, and, if his unacceptable behavior persists, is formally charged and duly tried by a jury consisting of the whole chapter. A transgressor may not be penalized for an act he does not admit doing, cannot be tried while absent, and may speak in his own defense. Once sentence has been passed in line with the proper procedure, however, he must accept it and try to mend his ways. The code, like the Talmud and the New Testament exhortations, is designed to compel confession of mistakes and reconciliation of conflicts. Although stringent, the punishments prescribed in the Vinaya constitute a middle ground between laxity and harshness.

The discipline presupposes a high degree of earnestness and integrity. It will work only if most candidates enter voluntarily and in good faith. For this reason, full *upasampadā* (ordination) is granted only to those who are at least 20 years of age and who have formally requested admission to the Sangha. Eight years, however, is the minimum age for the *pabbajā* (novitiate ordination), which even adult candidates must undergo—albeit briefly—before proceeding to full ordination. In the "going forth" ceremony, the ordinand has his head shaven, is invested with the ochre robes, and takes the Three Refuges and Ten Precepts to abstain from (1) taking life; (2) stealing; (3) sexual intercourse; (4) lying; (5) drinking liquor; (6) eating after noon; (7) watching dancing, singing, and shows; (8) adorning himself with garlands, perfumes, and ointments; (9) using a high bed or seat; and (10) receiving gold and silver (Strong *EB*, secs. 3.5.1, 3.5.2). The ordinand is thereafter a novice and has left the household life. If under the age of 20, he must live with a preceptor until he disrobes or gains full ordination upon coming of age. The preceptor must have passed 10 years since full ordination and must be of good character, knowledgeable, and competent. The novice may also, at his preceptor's discretion, receive instruction from a tutor, who must meet the same qualifications as the preceptor himself.

Full ordination is conferred by an assembly consisting of a quorum of at least 10 monks if it is held in the middle Ganges Valley, and 5 if held anywhere else. The candidate, accompanied by one of his tutors, comes before the senior member of the assembly, whom he asks to be his preceptor. His two tutors then examine him to ascertain that he has his bowl, under robe, upper robe, and outer cloak, after which they send him to stand a short distance outside the assembly, his alms bowl strapped onto his back. Approaching him there, they ask him whether he is free from certain diseases and whether he is a free human male (Strong *EB,* sec. 2.2.1), debtless, exempt from military service, furnished with his parents' permission, and at least 20 years of age. The candidate is then made to go forward, kneel, and ask the assembly for ordination. The tutors put him through the interrogation again. They then announce formally that the candidate desires ordination, is free from disqualifications, has a bowl and a set of robes, asks for ordination, and that the assembly grants ordination. The public proclamation is made: "Whoever approves should remain silent. Whoever objects should speak." When the assembly remains silent through the third repetition of this proclamation, the two tutors announce that the candidate has received ordination. The date and the hour are then noted, as seniority in the order commences from the time of ordination.

The preceptor then gives the new monk an exhortation, telling him that henceforth his four basic reliances are to be on alms for food, on old rags for clothing, on the shade of a tree for shelter, and on cow's urine for medicine. He mentions, however, that more luxurious requisites are also allowed, and normal monastic life usually entails the allowances; the laity prepare good food for the monks and donate new robes and other needs as necessary. The new monk is then informed of the four offenses requiring expulsion and told that he should avoid them for the rest of his life. Finally, he is directed to train himself in heightened virtue, heightened concentration, and heightened discernment so as to realize the end of craving, dispassion, cessation, and nirvāṇa. This concludes the ceremony. (For another version of the ceremony, see Strong *EB*, sec. 2.2.2.)

Once ordained, the new monk is to live in apprenticeship to a mentor—his preceptor or another teacher—for a period of at least five years. He is to regard his mentor as his father and treat him accordingly, acting as his personal attendant and applying himself diligently to a life of study and meditation. In return, the mentor is to regard the new monk as his son and to provide for his needs and training. The new monk, however, does not take a vow of obedience to his mentor. If he feels that his mentor does not have his best interests at heart, he is free to search for another senior monk to act as his mentor. Only when his knowledge of the Dharma and Vinaya are sufficiently extensive, and his behavior sufficiently reliable, is he freed from apprenticeship and allowed to set out on his own.

A Buddhist nun's ordination was similar in most respects to a monk's except that she had to be accepted twice: once by the assembly of nuns with whom she planned to live, and again by the local assembly of monks. She, too, had to undergo a period of apprenticeship to a senior nun, although hers was for four years: two as a postulant before her ordination, and an additional two afterward.

3.4.2 The Life of the Monks

From the very beginning of the tradition, the life of the monks combined two modes: *eremitic* (solitary wandering) and *cenobitic* (settled communities). The Vinaya presents a picture in which the ideal monk followed both modes by wandering during the dry season of each year and then settling down with fellow monks during the rains. During the dry season he might live—alone or with small groups of his fellows—under a tree, in a cave, on a hillside, in a glen or forest glade, in a thatched hut, or even in the shade of a haystack. Naturally, he stayed near a village or town for his alms. His possessions were kept simple and few so that he could travel light, "like a bird, with its wings as its only burden" (D.2). Ideally, he owned only one set of clothing: an under robe, upper robe, outer cloak, and belt. The robes, donated by the laity or made by the monk from thrown-away rags, were dyed reddish brown. He also wore sandals and carried a begging-bowl, a razor, tweezers, nail clippers, some gauze for filtering water, a needle, and a bag of medicines. He was allowed an umbrella against the sun and a fan against the heat. At least once every other month he shaved his head without using a mirror; mirrors were forbidden to him, as were adornments, cosmetics and perfumes, music and song. The ideal Buddhist nun's personal possessions were equally meager.

During the three months of the monsoons (or rainy season)—July to October *(varsa;* in Pali, *vassa)*—open-air living became difficult, and travel impossible, so the Buddha directed that the monks settle for the period in dwellings sufficiently closed-off to protect them from the elements. There they could pursue their spiritual development, learn from one another, and conduct communal business relatively undisturbed. The sites selected for such resting places had to be secluded enough to ensure a proper atmosphere for meditation, but close enough to a village or town for alms-going. The return of the dry season was marked by ceremonies at which the laity presented gifts of cloth and other necessities to the monks, who then set out on their solitary wanderings, leaving only a few of their number behind to maintain the dwellings.

With the passage of time, these temporary dwellings developed into settled monasteries. According to the Vinaya texts, this process began during the Buddha's lifetime, when wealthy donors made permanent gifts of land to the Sangha and erected buildings on them (see Section 2.4). Scholars have debated whether the texts can be believed on this point, the argument boiling down not to any firm evidence but simply to the question of whether such a process could conceivably have occurred during the 45 years of the Buddha's teaching career. Modern experience with the "domestication" of forest monks (see Section 7.5.2) indicates that such a time frame is entirely possible. At any rate, the Vinaya provides detailed rules for the running of such communities on a year-round basis. Although some monks continued their dry-season wanderings, others settled down more or less permanently. This resulted in the distinction between town-dwelling monks and forest-dwelling monks that has continued to the present in modern Theravāda countries.

Town-dwelling monks were involved in the daily routine of the monastery and its service to the people, functioning as scholars, teachers, preachers, administrators, doctors, and even politicians (see Section 6.2). Although they were exhorted to keep their personal possessions to a minimum, none of the monks—contrary to a misperception persistent in the West—took a vow of poverty. The list of possessions forbidden to them was much shorter than the list of possessions allowed. In many cases, gifts that monks were forbidden to accept for their personal use, such as servants, vehicles, and land, were given to monasteries on an institutional basis. Thus some town and city monasteries became lavishly endowed, and the life of their monks quite luxurious. Monasteries also developed along caravan routes, reflecting the symbiotic relationship between the Sangha and the merchant classes, in which the merchants gave financial support to the monasteries, and the monasteries provided a haven for traveling merchants. When merchants established trading enclaves in foreign cities, they would then invite monks to set up monasteries there so that they would not be without the opportunity to make merit (see Section 3.4.4). This relationship helped provide a mechanism for the spread of Buddhism not only throughout India but also to other areas where Indian merchants took their business over land or sea: Southeast Asia, central Asia, and China. Forest-dwelling monks, by contrast, practiced their meditation and stricter asceticism less encumbered with possessions and social entanglements, and were thus freer in their pursuit of their spiritual goals (Strong *EB*, sec. 2.3.3). However, if they developed a reputation for meditative or psychic powers, their hermitages, like the town monasteries, might become laden with donations as well.

As this specialization into two groups developed, a certain tension arose between the two. Although it is easy to paint the town-dwelling monks as the villains of the piece, in actual practice each group acted as a counterweight against the abuses of the other. On the one hand, communal life offered an excellent opportunity for study and memorization of texts, but was a less-than-ideal setting for meditation, as factions split over minor differences in doctrine and practice, and monks in general became less strict in their observance of the rules. For instance, if we can believe the texts, the Second Council was essentially an instance of forest-dwelling monks settling an issue that lax city-dwelling monks had caused. Another incident, reported in both the Sūtras and the Vinaya, contrasts the quarrelsome city monks of Kausambi with the harmony of a small-forest hermitage. On the other hand, the life of forest-dwelling monks lent itself to abuses as well. Later legends that grew up around such charismatic figures as Upagupta (Strong *EB*, sec. 1.2) and Piṇḍola Bhāradvāja suggest that forest meditators might use their psychic powers to attract personal followings, ignoring the strictures of the Vinaya and in effect seceding from the order. In such cases, scholarly monks from the towns might be called in to reassert communal authority. It was perhaps for this reason that the early texts warn of the dangers entailed in displaying one's psychic powers to others. A recurring theme throughout the history of Buddhist monasticism is that the order thrives when town and forest monks find a harmonious balance, and suffers when that harmony breaks down. This pattern derives ultimately from the dynamic of right view that we noted in the preceding chapter (see Section 2.3.2). Study and communal training are needed to recognize what right view is; practice is needed so that right view can be developed to the point of its transcendence. The ideal monk is often pictured as one who successfully combines the meditative prowess of the wandering ascetic with the social concern and communal loyalty of the settled monk. Maudgalyāyana, for instance, was repeatedly praised for devoting his psychic powers not to his own aggrandizement but to the well-being of the monastic community and its followers.

This ideal of isolation combined with social involvement is reflected in the account of the Buddha's daily habits recorded in the commentaries to the Pali Canon. The Buddha, we are told, got up at daybreak and, after attending to his toilet, sat quietly until it was time to go for alms. Then he put on his robes, took his bowl, and entered the village or town, where he was usually received with honor by householders who vied to invite him and his following to the prenoon meal. They would seat him and place food reverently in his bowl. After the meal, he would teach Dharma to his hosts. Returning to the monastery, he sat in the refectory pavilion while the monks who had not been invited to dine in their donors' homes finished their meal. Then he withdrew to his cell—called "the perfumed chamber"—for meditation and rest. In the afternoon, he preached to the laity who came to call on him. Afterward, he went to the bathhouse for a cool bath, then paced back and forth in the courtyard or garden and meditated. He concluded the evening (first watch of night) by instructing monks. During the second watch, he received deities who came for instruction; during the third, he rested and then surveyed the world with his psychic vision to see whom he should seek out to teach the next day. This schedule alternates rest and activity, seclusion and sociability, covering a long and busy day at a leisurely pace. It is with good reason that the tradition has consistently emphasized the daily routine and guarded its observance as a way of harmoniously combining the monk's two roles of meditator and teacher.

3.4.3 Buddhist Nuns

The Buddha is said to have reluctantly instituted the *Bhikṣuṇī Sangha* (Order of Nuns) at the request of his aunt and foster mother, Mahāprajāpatī, and upon the intercession of Ānanda (Strong *EB*, sec. 2.4.1). He conceded that women are able to attain arhantship but formulated eight *garudharma* (vows of respect) for the nuns, strictly subordinating them—institutionally but not spiritually—to the Order of Monks. The vows were as follows: a nun shall honor every monk as her senior, even if she has been ordained for a hundred years, and he one day; during the rainy season retreat she shall not reside in a district where there are no monks; the nuns shall schedule their Observance Day in line with the monks; a nun shall invite criticism at the end of the rainy season retreat from both the nuns' and the monks' assemblies; she shall undergo penance (temporary probation) for a serious offense before both assemblies; a female postulant must undergo a two-year novitiate and then seek ordination from both assemblies; a nun shall not verbally abuse a monk; and whereas monks are allowed formally to reprove nuns, nuns may not reprove monks.

The Buddha is said to have stipulated this strict subordination of the nuns to the monks because "When women retire from household life to the houseless one . . . religion does not long endure" (Cv.X.I.6). He predicted that, because of the admission of women, the True Dharma unadulterated by later "improvements" (S.XVI.13) would last five hundred years, rather than a thousand. (The five-hundred-year mark corresponds to the period when the first Mahāyāna Sūtras and the Theravādin commentaries were being composed, an issue about which both groups were very touchy.) Several years after the founding of the Bhikṣuṇī Sangha, Mahāprajāpatī—arguing that the nuns as a group had achieved institutional maturity—asked the Buddha to allow nuns to mingle their line of seniority with that of the monks. This the Buddha refused to do, as it would cancel the first vow of respect and make it difficult to keep the monks and nuns separate. If the lines of seniority were combined, the boundaries between the two orders would have dissolved, jeopardizing their vows of celibacy. If, however, the orders were so radically separated that all contact between them was precluded, divergences would have been fostered in their interpretation of the teaching. Thus for practical reasons the order founded second was placed under the order founded first so that they could be kept formally separate while at the same time maintaining contact.

The formal subordination of the Order of Nuns to the Order of Monks is best understood in light of general Buddhist views on hierarchy. There is a widespread notion that the Buddha advocated absolute equality for all members of the Sangha, but this was not the case. Although all were regarded as being capable of attaining nirvāṇa, spiritual potential was not translated into organizational structure. Major decisions required unanimous consent of all members, but for the efficient and peaceful day-to-day handling of minor issues within the order, the Buddha recommended a clearly defined hierarchy. When the question of hierarchy first arose in the Sangha, monks advocated that it be based on merit and quickly became embroiled in disputes as to how personal merit was to be measured. They took the question to the Buddha, who decreed a hierarchy based on the neutral criterion of seniority of ordination, making it clear that one's position in the hierarchy was not an indication of one's personal worth. In such a situation, the act of bowing down to one in a higher position is interpreted not as a sign of submission to an individual but as a mark of respect for the customs of the order, much as polite behavior in a civilized society is taken not as a sign that people necessarily like one another, but that they know and respect social norms.

In the case of the nuns, the formal subordination of the Order of Nuns to the Order of Monks was definitely not meant as an indication of spiritual inferiority. The *Verses of the Women Elders* (the Pali Canon's *Therīgāthā)*—an anthology of 73 poems celebrating Awakening, composed by elder nuns and memorized by monks and nuns for many centuries—demonstrates that throughout the Hīnayāna tradition women have been recognized as having attained full arhantship, a state of liberation equal to that of the Master's. As an additional measure to prevent the nuns' position in the hierarchy from being abused or misconstrued, the Buddha formulated rules to keep the monks in check. For instance, monks were forbidden even to request that nuns perform menial tasks for them, and nuns had the right to publicly boycott any monk who treated them in an unseemly manner.

Although the arrangement formalizing relations between the monks and nuns may offend modern sensibilities, it was kinder to womankind than were religious and social arrangements throughout the rest of the ancient and modern world. In all historical civilizations women were largely excluded from religious hierarchies and positions of social power, and relegated to inferior status in the family. The Buddha, however, was careful to provide his female disciples, both nuns and lay women, with opportunities for spiritual advancement. For example, a Pali Sūtra (S.XXXVII.34) encourages education for female lay disciples; this one text may account for the Buddhist countries of Southeast Asia having had the highest female literacy rates in the world for centuries.

Among the illustrious nuns, the canon records Uppalavaṇṇā *Therī* (female elder), one of the Buddha's chief disciples, as being foremost among nuns in psychic powers; Khemā Therī, the other chief nun disciple and a former queen of King Bimbisāra, was ranked foremost among the nuns in terms of her discernment. Kisāgotamī Therī excelled in the frugality of her lifestyle, whereas Dhammadinnā excelled in her ability to teach the Dharma. Bhaddā Kapilānī Therī adopted the renunciant Path when her family arranged a marriage for her to Pippali (Mahākāśyapa, who became one of the Buddha's most eminent disciples), but the pair did not consummate their marriage because both had experienced great compassion after seeing worms and insects killed as a result of plowing. They gave up wealth and family, and after the Order of Nuns was founded Bhaddā Kapilānī Therī became an arhant, declared by the Buddha to be foremost among nuns who could remember past lives. Bhaddā-Kuṇḍalakesā, foremost among nuns in swift intuition, had fallen in love with a handsome but thieving man, whom she pushed off a cliff when she discovered his intentions to steal her jewels and kill her. She joined a sect of extreme ascetics but then left them. Meeting the Buddha, she attained arhantship while hearing him preach, after which she received ordination. As for Mahāprajāpatī, the Buddha's aunt and the most senior of the nuns, she gained Awakening after hearing a short sermon from the Buddha on the basic distinguishing characteristics of Dharma and Vinaya. Upon taking leave of the Buddha before her death at the age of 120, she performed various miracles, second only to those of the Buddha's cremation rites; her five hundred companions died with her. Other Therīs were experts on the Vinaya and meditation, whereas some were known as excellent Dharma preachers with followings of their own.

Less is known about nuns after the Buddha's death and on into Mahāyāna times (see Section 5.2). The texts record few important nun teachers after the first generation, and modern scholars have often assumed that this silence is a sign that the formal subordination of nuns to the monks had undermined their ability to attract material support and large followings of students. However, stone inscriptions list nuns among the major donors to the building of such centers as the great stūpa at Sanchi, which would have been possible only if the nuns had had followings of their own. Thus a more likely cause for the silence of the texts is that the important nun teachers focused primarily on meditation practice and for that reason, as with monk practitioners, they were not recorded in the early Buddhist histories, which tended to focus more on politically influential scholars and missionaries.

Although the Bhikṣuṇī Sangha does not seem to have flourished, it lasted in India for sixteen centuries, a remarkable time span for any human institution. After the demise of Buddhism in India in the thirteenth century C.E., the Buddhist world—with the exception of China, Korea, and Vietnam—gradually lost all valid ordination lineages for nuns as a result of wars and invasions. In Theravāda countries, the nuns' lineages ended near the turn of the first millennium when Coḷa forces laid waste to Sri Lanka. Given the facts that both assemblies were required for ordination and that no quorum of elder nuns was available, an ad hoc arrangement developed whereby women could ordain as lay renunciates following 8 or 10 precepts, but with only minimal formal communal organization. This is the arrangement that still holds in Theravādin countries today.

3.4.4 The Laity

Buddhist adherents who did not opt for the monastic life were taught a level of Dharma appropriate to their duties as married householders. In their search for happiness in this life, they were advised to be diligent in their work, to care for their possessions, to keep their expenditures at a balanced level—avoiding the periodic splurges that normally characterize peasant life—and to associate with good people. For happiness in the next life, they were to develop conviction in the law of karma, generosity, virtue, and discernment. These last four qualities boil down to the three means for acquiring *puṇya* (karmic merit)—generosity, virtue, and meditation—that have formed the basic framework for lay Buddhist practice to the present day.

Although lay people were encouraged to be generous with one another, they were also taught that generosity to the Bhikṣu and Bhikṣuṇī Sanghas paid the highest dividends in terms of the merit earned. Without the generosity of the laity, the monastic orders would not have survived. In return, the monastics instructed the laity in Dharma, both by word and by example, assuring them in part that their generosity would win them an increase of wealth and the love of their fellow living beings both in this life and in the next.

As for virtue, both men and women householders were encouraged to take five *śīla* (precepts) as a constant practice. *Śīla* is defined as abstaining from unskillful conduct of body and speech in line with a personal resolution. The first precept is to refrain from killing living beings, meaning all sorts of animals but not plants. The precept is broken if, knowing that something is a living being and intending to kill it, one attempts to do so and succeeds. Unintentional killing does not break the precept, although it may constitute blamable negligence.

The second precept is to refrain from taking what has not been given; that is, from taking the property of another by force or by stealth. The offense is committed when one knows that the object belongs to another, attempts to steal it, and succeeds in moving it from its place.

The third precept is to refrain from misconduct in sexual matters. Later commentaries state that, for a man, this includes intercourse with a forbidden woman (the wife of another, a woman under the care of a guardian, a betrothed woman, a nun, a woman under a vow of celibacy), as well as intercourse with one's own wife by a "forbidden passage" (the anus), in an unsuitable place (that is, a public place or a shrine), or at an unsuitable time (that is, when she is pregnant, is nursing, or has taken a vow of abstinence). Factors considered here are the rights and obligations of others, the wishes of the woman herself, her health, and that of her child. The commentaries do not consider intercourse with a courtesan forbidden unless she has become betrothed to another. For an unmarried woman under the protection of her family or her religious vows, all men are forbidden under this precept; for a married woman, all men except her husband. For an unmarried woman living independently—a rarity in those days, aside from courtesans—the only men forbidden are those observing religious vows of celibacy.

The fourth precept is to refrain from lying speech. This precept is broken when one intentionally misrepresents the truth to another person, even in jest. The fifth precept is to refrain from drinking liquor. The reasons given are that liquor does the body little good and much harm, and that by weakening mindfulness and self-control it leads to the breaking of the other precepts.

These precepts were to be observed in the context of interpersonal relationships marked by reciprocal duties. For instance, children were to support their parents in old age in return for having been supported during their childhood; they were to help their parents in their work, carry on the family line, behave in such a way as to be deserving of their inheritance, and make meritorious gifts to the religion in their parents' name after the latter's death (Strong *EB*, sec. 2.5.3). In response, parents were to restrain their children from doing evil, encourage them to do good, provide for their education, find them spouses, and in due time turn over their inheritance. A husband was to honor his wife and not disparage her, be faithful to her, give her complete authority in running the household, and provide her with adornments. In return, wives were to organize their work well, be willing and sweet tempered, honor their husbands' relatives and guests, be skillful at homecrafts, manage the servants well, and protect the family belongings. Similar reciprocal patterns governed relations between teacher and student, master and servant, lay person and monastic, friend and friend (D.31).

As a result of their virtue, lay Buddhists were assured a fine reputation, confidence in handling public affairs, a calm and unbewildered death, and rebirth in a heaven. Those desiring to enhance their practice of virtue were encouraged to observe the eight precepts—formulated in such a way as to cover the same ground as the novice monk and nun's first nine precepts (see Section 3.4.1)—either on a constant basis or on the lay Poṣadha: the days of the full moon, new moon, and two half moons. Those who followed this practice would dress in white, to distinguish themselves from the monks and nuns in their ochre robes, and would spend the Poṣadha learning about the Dharma and practicing meditation.

Although lay people were taught the rudiments of meditation (Strong *EB*, sec. 2.5.2), some early texts reveal that they were not usually given instruction on the more advanced aspects of mind training. Abhidharma scholasticism and the more abstruse Sūtras were reserved for the monks and nuns. This is, in part, not the case in modern Buddhist countries, where lay Dharma-study and meditation groups function as important institutions, but it was definitely the norm in ancient times. One ostensible reason is that the ordinary lay person would not have the time to understand, let alone practice, such deep and difficult doctrines. Anyone truly interested in the deeper aspects of the Dharma could at any time opt for the celibate life that was freely available to all.

All the early schools agreed that the laity could attain the first three degrees of sainthood and remain in the household life. Some of them maintained that, although lay people could attain arhantship, lay arhants had to ordain or else die within seven days after their attainment, for the lay state could not support an arhant's purity (Strong *EB*, sec. 2.5.1).

Little research has looked into the life-cycle ceremonies of the Indian Buddhist laity. Various recensions of the Vinaya inform us that monks were regularly invited to teach Dharma at weddings, funerals, and housewarmings, and to dedicate the merit of their teaching to the well being of the sponsors. In fact, if lay Buddhists or the monk's parents invited a monk to such an occasion, he was obliged to go. However, if modern-day Theravāda practice can be taken as a reliable guide, the monk did not officiate at such ceremonies. He simply provided the sponsors the opportunity to gain merit, leaving the remainder of the ceremony up to the sponsors themselves.

Early extracanonical accounts of the lives of the Buddha regularly place his birth, Awakening, and Parinirvāṇa on the full moon night of *Vaiśākha* (May). They also offer elaborate descriptions of how the entire cosmos paid homage at all three events with hymns and floral offerings. Thus it is highly likely that Indian Buddhists celebrated these events in a similar fashion from an early date. At present, this festival is the most important in the Theravāda calendar.

3.4.5 Cult Objects and Forms of Worship

Archaeological evidence indicates that, at the popular level, Buddhism absorbed local religious forms, symbols, and cults from its environment. These had a long ancestry, extending in part back to the Indus civilization and other levels of Indian prehistory, in part deriving from Vedic traditions.

Cults of trees, serpents, and reliquary mounds entered early Buddhism from the preexisting religious tradition, adapted by the Buddhists to suit their own purposes. For example, in the myth of the Buddha, Queen Māyā gave birth to her son under a tree; the Buddha gained Awakening under the Bodhi Tree (a large type of fig, *Ficus religiosa; pippala* or *aśvattha* in Sanskrit) and later entered total nirvāṇa while resting with his head to the north between twin sāla trees. These patterns provided a link with the veneration of trees dating from Indus Valley fertility cults and perhaps earlier. Characteristically, every village had a sacred tree; Buddhists transferred the patterns of worship that had developed around these trees to the cult of the Bodhi Tree. At the base of the sacred tree was an altar, usually surrounded by a fence or railing of wood and stone. These accoutrements were soon set up around the original Bodhi Tree. Saplings from the original tree were planted in various places (trees still standing in Sravasti in India and Anuradhapura in Sri Lanka are claimed to be "children" of the original tree) and were treated with the same veneration. Aśoka, tradition claims, paid such inordinate attention to the tree at Bodhgaya that his jealous queen tried to have it destroyed, but without success. By virtue of Aśoka's devotion, Bodhgaya was improved physically and became a major Buddhist shrine. Instead of an altar in front of the tree, he had built a carved stone seat—the *vajrāsana* (diamond seat, so called because here Gautama achieved stability)—which, though empty, symbolizes the Buddha's presence. This seat, together with stone railings carved during Aśoka's time, still survive.

Nāgas (serpents) had a long association with fertility cults in pre-Buddhist Indian culture, and although Buddhists did not regard them as objects of worship, they came to treat them with respect as protectors of the religion, similar to the respect that Hindu devotees accorded the mounts of their gods. An account in the Vinaya states that, during the third week after his Awakening, the new Buddha was sitting absorbed in the bliss of emancipation when a great storm came up. Mucalinda, the Nāga king, came out of his abode, coiled himself around the Buddha, and protected him with his great hood against the wind and rain for seven days. An early Sūtra (D.20) depicts the Buddha as arranging a truce to protect the nāgas from their archenemies, the half-human, half-bird garuḍas. These stories became the basis for an alliance between Buddhism and protective elements from earlier spirit cults that has lasted through the centuries, as evidenced by art and texts from all areas to which Buddhism has spread.

The two most important sacred Buddhist monuments were the stūpa and the cave temple. Stūpas were erected in the open air over the ashes of holies, as in the case of the Buddha; over relics or personal objects belonging to holies; or to commemorate a miracle, mark a sacred spot, or gain merit from sponsoring the construction. The stūpa's dome rests on a square or circular base. From its top rises a stone umbrella, symbol of the Buddha's spiritual royalty and, in a stylized fashion, of the Bodhi Tree. Unfortunately, the iron pillar supporting the umbrella has served as an unintentional lightning rod, resulting in the destruction of many of these monuments. The symbolism of the stūpa is complex; its abstract form has lent itself to a variety of interpretations. In the largest sense, it represents simultaneously the presence of the Buddha (in his relics) and his absence (as a memorial of his passing away). As a symbol of his absence, the stūpa offers a physical focus for the contemplation of the impermanence of life; as a symbol of his presence, it forms a ritual focus for offerings to the Buddha as a means of gaining merit and guaranteeing a happy destination after death. In this way, the stūpa is both a reminder of the problem of impermanence and an opportunity to store up merit as an interim solution. In performing this dual function, the stūpa cult became one of the few common denominators running through all Asian Buddhist traditions.

Another important structure associated with early Buddhist monastic residences was the *caitya-gṛha* (hall housing a stūpa). The stūpa was placed at the end of a long hall, with a nave in front, where worshipers could gather, and an apse containing the stūpa itself. Outside aisles demarcated by a colonnade made *pradakṣiṇā* (ceremonial clockwise circumambulation) possible. Cave temples repeated this pattern, carved into rock. With the development of the Buddha-image, such images were classed as a form of caitya and in some halls took the place of the more abstract stupa form.

From early Buddhist bas-reliefs we gain some idea of the religion's worship forms. We see people (and even serpents and celestial spirits) gathered around a sacred tree or a stūpa, either standing or kneeling, their hands reverentially folded before their hearts. Often they have placed garlands of flowers on the stūpa, hung them on the tree, or placed them on the shrine before it. Ancient India had a strong tradition of fervent devotionalism, and perhaps the belief that every act, however minor, necessarily led to good or bad consequences encouraged this ardent religiosity among Buddhists as well.

In these early representations of Buddhist worship, many symbols are used instead of actual figures of the Buddha, which came into general use only after 100 B.C.E., probably in response to popular devotionalism (see Section 5.3). The symbols used for worship included an empty throne, a pair of footprints, a wheel, a shrine with a turban on it, a lotus, and a circle under a tree. The empty throne recalled the spot on which the Buddha had attained Awakening; the pair of footprints reminded worshipers that he walked among people and, even though he entered nirvāṇa, left his Path and his continuing influence in the world. They also emphasized the Buddha's transcendence, in that even his feet deserved to be worshiped by the heads of the devotees. The turban symbolized what he had renounced, his royal worldly inheritance; the wheel stood for his first sermon; the circle under the tree, the inexpressibility of his Awakening. The lotus—which appears often, especially in connection with Gautama's birth—has a complex symbolism all its own. It grows from the mud of mundane existence but is transcendent in its purity; its leaves and petals remain untouched by the waters (of becoming). In this, it forms a metaphor for the perfection attainable even in the midst of the human world.

Although Buddha-images are now common throughout the Buddhist world, much of the early cult practice and symbolism still survive in Buddhist religious life today.

4

The Rise and Development of Mahāyāna Buddhism

4.1 THE RISE OF MAHĀYĀNA

During the two centuries from 100 B.C.E. to 100 C.E., as India switched from an oral to a written culture, developments within and without Buddhism caused the religion to undergo one of the most far-reaching splits in its history. On the internal level, the early canons were committed to writing, thus fixing a standardized version of the teachings with a greater finality than ever before. Abhidharma scholars succeeded in getting their texts accepted as part of this established corpus, on a par with the Sūtra and Vinaya Piṭakas, but a backlash gradually developed—centering largely in Andhra, in south India—among those who felt that Abhidharma analysis had missed the point of the teaching. In taking on the Abhidharmists, the members of this backlash found themselves faced with the belief that the Abhidharma was directly or indirectly the word of the Buddha, so they began composing new Sūtras of their own, placing their anti-Abhidharma arguments in the mouths of the Buddha and the great arhants, and claiming that their Sūtras were newly discovered texts that had been hidden since the Buddha's time. The disagreement over whether these new Sūtras could be accepted as normative seems to have been the first rift leading to the major split.

On the external level, Buddhism as a whole was encountering a host of new theistic religious movements in its expanding environment. The cult of Viṣṇu was developing in India, while Hellenistic and Zoroastrian savior cults were spreading into Gandhara in northwestern India and along the major trade routes in central Asia at the same time that Buddhist missionaries were active in these areas. No one knows for sure how and why Buddhism picked up cultic and doctrinal elements from these external sources. Buddhists may have been reacting to external criticisms that they had been orphaned by a dead god who was no longer in a position to offer salvation. They may have also been responding to pressures within their own ranks as the rise of written culture weakened their sense of corporate cohesion and encouraged greater individualism, causing the laity and junior monastics to regard themselves as competent and free to combine elements from various traditions as they saw fit.

At any rate, because Buddhist monastics were wandering the length and breadth of India, the anti-Abhidharma partisans eventually joined forces with the new Buddhist savior cults and other like-minded factions to grow into a widespread movement calling itself the *Mahāyāna* (the Great Course or Great Vehicle—*yāna:* a going, a course, a journey; a vehicle). This was in contrast to the *Hīnayāna* (the Inferior Course), the new movement's pejorative term for those conservatives who did not accept the new doctrines as truly Buddhist. Because the conservatives answered the Mahāyāna propaganda largely with silence, they did not adopt any name for themselves as compared with Mahāyāna. Consequently, modern scholars have given them the name their adversaries gave them, Hīnayāna, although without implying any deprecation. Modern Theravādins do not like being called Hīnayānists—who would?—but there is no other current term that designates the whole set of schools that arose between the first and the fourth centuries after the Parinirvāṇa and continued after the rise of Mahāyāna. The term *Nikāya Buddhism*, for instance, accurately applies to these schools before the rise of Mahāyāna, but not after, as Mahāyāna formed a subgroup within each of them. Continued usage of the name *Hīnayāna* may expunge all derogatory connotations of the term. *Quaker*, *Mormon*, and even *Christian* similarly started out as labels sarcastically attached by outsiders.

It should be noted that Hīnayāna and Mahāyāna groups lived side-by-side between the second and seventh centuries C.E., and that the Hīnayānists remained in the majority throughout most of India. Although differences between the early schools remained, no new Vinaya was created for Mahāyāna monastics. The Chinese pilgrim I-ching in the seventh century numbered the major sects at that time as four—Mahāsanghika, Sthavira, Sarvāstivāda, and Sāṃmatīya—and noted that each sect contained both Mahāyānists and Hīnayānists, often living in the same monasteries. Despite differences in doctrine, there were only minor distinctions between Hīnayāna and Mahāyāna practice (at least until the seventh century C.E. in India), the main difference being one of expressed motivation.

Mahāyāna, the Great Course, claimed its adherents, leads to Buddhahood (supreme, perfect Awakening), whereas the Inferior Course leads only to arhantship. All the early schools recognized three possible goals for Buddhist practice: to become a *śrāvaka* (disciple) arhant, a *pratyeka* Buddha (private, nonteaching Buddha), or a fully Awakened Buddha. All three figures were arhants equally, differing mainly in their ability to attain the goal with or without an established body of doctrine to follow, in their ability to teach others, and in the supramundane powers that did or did not accompany their Awakening. Because the Buddha's teachings were still extant, early schools advocated the śrāvaka Path as the most practical and taught it in the greatest detail. The Mahāyāna also recognized the same three goals but advanced the belief that only the third was truly worthwhile, in that it enabled one to do the most good for the sentient realm as a whole. Rejecting the opportunity to gain Awakening as a śrāvaka here and now, one would develop more extensive virtues—helping a more extensive circle of living beings—so as to realize supreme Buddhahood aeons hence.

Apparently the Mahāyāna originated within the Mahāsanghika sects, which from the first had disparaged the arhant, advocated doctrinal innovations, and championed teachings later typical of the Mahāyāna, such as the claims that the historical Buddha is a mere apparition of the true Buddha, who is transmundane (Strong *EB,* sec. 3.6.3). The Mahāyāna innovation was to advocate the bodhisattva course for all Buddhists; to lay out a detailed Path for aspiring bodhisattvas; and to create a new pantheon and cult of superhuman bodhisattvas and cosmic Buddhas who respond to the pleas of devotees in need.

The hallmark of Mahāyāna is its expanded Sūtra literature rather than any one doctrine or practice. Like its parent Mahāsanghika schools, the movement found its unity in the freedom it gave its followers to be diverse. Written in Sanskrit rather than the Prakrit of the early schools, the new Sūtras claimed to report dialogues of the Buddha. Because they were the product of a written rather than an oral culture, they were much longer and more luxuriant in style than the short, spare discourses of the early schools. In fact, their style is a major defining characteristic of the movement. Their surrealistic locales, measured in mind-boggling dimensions and filled with dazzling apparitions; their immense, all-star casts of characters; and the sheer extravagance of their language all serve to reassert the primacy of the visionary, shamanic side of Buddhism that had been generally neglected by the Abhidharmists. Here, the seeming reality of everyday perception is viewed as a partial, limited way of experiencing a universe filled with multivalent levels so varied and complex that what seems real on one level dissolves into *māyā* (illusion) on another. This has the effect of blurring the line between the real and the illusory, making language seem totally inadequate for describing the truth. In this sense, the style of the expanded Sūtras makes a graphic case for an assumption that underlies the Mahāyāna enterprise: Given the complexity of reality and the limitations of language, teachings can serve, at best, only as skillful means to effect a transformation in the mind of the listener/reader caught in the partiality of a particular view. Once the view has been discarded, the teachings designed to cure it should be discarded as well, to be replaced by other, perhaps seemingly contradictory, teachings appropriate for whatever new view the individual becomes attached to on the next level of practice (see Section 2.3.1). This view of language is so dominant in the Mahāyāna teachings that some texts even assert that the bodhisattva doctrine itself is simply a skillful means.

From the Mahāyānist perspective, the Abhidharmists have erred in advancing a single system for describing all of reality and in holding to teachings that ultimately must be let go. The style of the expanded Sūtras thus serves to proclaim that their authors have access to a heightened mode of perception that places them beyond the reach of scholastic critiques.

In the earliest extant expanded Sūtras—such as *The Small Perfection of Wisdom*—the discussants are well-known figures of early Buddhism and do not disparage the Hīnayānists. Eventually, however, as the Mahāyānists were unable to win over the majority of their brethren, a rift widened between the two courses. For example, the *Vimalakīrti-nirdeśa,* a somewhat later Sūtra, ridicules the arhants, depicting them as helpless losers to Vimalakīrti's talent for one-upmanship. Even the worst sinner still has a chance to become a Buddha, this Sūtra avows, whereas the arhant is at a dead end in an inferior nirvāṇa. The still-later *Lotus (Saddharmapuṇḍarīka) Sūtra* (circa 200 C.E.) is even more blatantly hostile to the Hīnayāna but adopts a seemingly conciliatory, if condescending, posture, affirming that the arhant is not really condemned to an inferior goal because there is in reality just one nirvāṇa, that of a Buddha, which even arhants will reach in due course. Partisan rhetoric reached a peak in the *Mahāyāna Parinirvāṇa Sūtra* (circa 200–400 C.E., known as the *Nirvāṇa Sūtra* for short), which claimed to contain the Buddha's last "secret" teachings before his passing away. According to this Sūtra, whoever maligns the Mahāyāna teachings is destined for severe punishment, even execution. Thus what began as a small rift between the two courses in 100 B.C.E. gradually widened until by 200 C.E. it had become a clear break.

The composition of Mahāyāna Sūtras continued until the eighth century C.E. There are no firsthand historical sources on the circumstances surrounding their composition. The Mahāyāna trend is paralleled, however, by other developments at the time, as Indian culture as a whole was transformed by the widespread adoption of the written word. Splits developed in many traditions between those who tried to restrict written transmission to the modes of oral transmission—that is, set ancient texts with attendant commentaries—and those who championed the creative possibilities of the new, written mode. Hindus were writing new *Upaniṣads, Purāṇas,* and *Āgamas,* attributing them to gods and ancient sages; and Brahmanical philosophy underwent a rift similar to that in Buddhism, between the conservative Mīmāṃsā school and the more innovative Vaiśeṣika school.

In the second century C.E., Mahāyāna authors began publishing *Śāstras* (treatises) in their own names, citing the Sūtras as proofs, to present the Buddhist case to non-Buddhists, and the newer Buddhist doctrine to Hīnayānists who denied the authenticity of the Mahāyāna Sūtras. This new respect for individual human authorship, another result of the shift to written culture, was paralleled by similar trends in secular literature (fiction, poetry, and nonfiction), science, non-Buddhist philosophy, and the techniques of debate and logic.

The first historical glimpses of Mahāyāna are afforded by Chinese reports describing the Serindian missionaries of the second century C.E. At that time, northwest India and adjoining regions of central Asia were under the powerful

Kuṣāṇa dynasty, whose great monarch Kaniṣka (late first or early second century C.E.) is renowned in Buddhist sources as a patron of the Dharma (see Section 4.4). The Kuṣāṇa domain had been a Buddhist stronghold since the second century B.C.E. It included Kashmir and Gandhara, both Sarvāstivādin, and the oasis kingdom of Khotan, a powerful Mahāyāna center where certain texts and other aspects of the movement may have originated. The earliest Mahāyāna texts came to China from Khotan (see Section 8.1.1). Wherever it originated, the Mahāyāna first flourished notably in northwest India, where it reached the height of its strength in 400 C.E., when the Chinese pilgrim Fa-hsien passed through.

4.2 THE TEACHING OF EMPTINESS

The early Mahāyāna texts were intended primarily as therapy for individuals caught in the Abhidharma mind-set. Their authors seem to have drawn their inspiration from passages in the Sūtra Piṭaka listing speculative views as one of the objects of sustenance for becoming (see Section 1.4.3) and advocating right view as a means of abandoning such sustenance. These authors undoubtedly saw Abhidharma views acting more as sustenance for suffering than as means for liberation, and so—to avoid simply replacing one system of views with another—presented their teachings in such a way as to induce the reader to abandon all infatuation with the system-building mind-set to begin with. This abandonment, they felt, would leave the reader freed from attachment to views. The means by which the authors sought to accomplish this therapeutic task varied somewhat from text to text, but all their approaches centered on the notion of *śūnyatā* (emptiness).

Śūnyatā is a concept that appears in the Sūtra Piṭaka but that was generally ignored by the Abhidharma systematizers. In the Sūtra it meant two things: (1) a mode of perception in which nothing is added to or subtracted from the actual data perceived, the highest form of śūnyatā being nirvāṇa as experienced in the present life (M.121); and (2) the lack of self or anything pertaining to a self in the six senses and their objects (S.XXXV.85). In other words, śūnyatā was both a mode of perception and an attribute of the objects perceived. The early Mahāyāna texts adopted both aspects of the concept but combined it with changes in the concept of *śūnya* (empty) that had occurred since the Parinirvāṇa. In the fourth century B.C.E., the grammarian Pāṇini had developed the concept of zero (also *śūnya)* to symbolize empty but functioning positions in his analysis of Sanskrit grammar (he proposed that every word was composed of a root and a suffix, so that words without suffixes actually had the zero suffix). Mathematicians eventually borrowed the concept to supply an essential principle of the decimal notation we use today: that a place in a system may be empty (such as the zeros in 10,000) but can still function in relationship to the rest of the system.

Early Mahāyāna thinkers combined the linguistic and early Buddhist concepts of śūnya to attack the notion, maintained by the Sthaviravādin and

Sarvāstivādin Abhidharmists, among others, that the irreducible dharmas forming the ultimate building blocks of experience were each endowed with svabhāva: their own particular being or nature. Actually, the Mahāyānists claimed, dharmas were empty of svabhāva. Conditional relations functioned as described in the doctrine of dependent co-arising, but there were no "essences" acting as nodes in the relationships, just as mathematical relationships could function among the integers in decimal notation even if they were only zeros. In fact, if dharmas had any essence, the principles of causation and the Four Noble Truths could not operate, for essences by nature cannot change and thus cannot be subject to causal conditions. Whether the Abhidharmists meant the concept of svabhāva to imply an unchanging essence is a moot point, but in time the doctrine of emptiness became a rallying point for the rejection of the entire Abhidharma enterprise.

The Mahāyānists maintained that their interpretation of emptiness was the true meaning of the Buddha's not-self doctrine. From their point of view, the Abhidharmists had understood only the concept that the individual person was empty of self (*pudgala-nairātmya*), whereas in actuality the concept should be expanded to include the realization that dharmas were empty of any own-being or nature *(dharma-nairātmya)* as well. In their eyes, the Abhidharmists were still attached to a subtle notion of "self" in the dharmas, and this attachment prevented them from realizing the true Buddhist goal. Only by viewing experience in truly ultimate terms, as a mathematics of zeros, would one lose all attachments for views of systems and existents, and thereby gain ultimate liberation. Thus this new approach viewed all dharmas as mere conventional truths, whereas the ultimate truth was one: emptiness in both of its modes. Rather than fleeing saṃsāra while still considering it essentially real, as the Abhidharmists recommended, the Mahāyānists summoned their listeners to reevaluate saṃsāra as empty and achieve release right where they were.

The ways in which they used the śūnyatā doctrine to induce this reevaluation varied from text to text. The primary early Mahāyāna discourses—the *Prajñā-pāramitā* (Perfection of Wisdom) *Sūtras*—generally tried to undercut the Abhidharma mind-set by portraying the Buddha and his chief disciples as repudiating the conventional teachings of the Sūtra Piṭaka. This repudiation took the form of paradoxical witticisms that played the conventional level of truth against the ultimate, erasing dualities between subject and object, conditioned and unconditioned, pure and impure, conventional and ultimate, even same and different (or separate, which *different* seems to mean in these texts). Because dharmas have no own-being, there is nothing bound in saṃsāra, nothing freed in nirvāṇa; nothing is observed to arise, nothing is observed to cease. There are no beings to save from saṃsāra, and yet the bodhisattva remains firm in his vow to save all beings. The world is a phantom conjured up by karmic action, the magician, but the phantom maker is itself māyā (a phantom). When one achieves the Perfection of Wisdom by contemplating dependent co-arising, one is without labels or conventions, thus realizing the *tathatā* (suchness) of all things, which is the same as the suchness of the Buddha, one's own suchness, the suchness of nothing at all (Strong *EB*, secs. 4.2.2, 4.2.3).

It is easy to imagine that this type of presentation would have been a great hit with those already disillusioned with Abhidharma scholasticism, but the Abhidharmists themselves—like Queen Victoria on seeing Nijinski performing ballet in tights—were not amused. Thus some proponents of the *Śūnyavāda* (emptiness-teaching) used Abhidharma methods to dismantle the Abhidharma systems from within. The most notable example was Nāgārjuna (circa 150–250 C.E.), who founded the Mādhyamika school, so called because it claimed to maintain emptiness as the *madhyamā pratipad* (Middle Path) between being and non-being. Nāgārjuna's best-known work is the *Mūlamadhyamaka-kārikā*—Middle Stanzas (Strong *EB*, sec. 4.3.1), a polemical treatise of 448 verses in which he uses four basic methods drawn from the Abhidharma enterprise—the assertion of two levels of truth, quotations from the Sūtra Piṭaka, appeals to experience, and a logical method (called *prāsangika)* in which he demonstrates the internal inconsistencies of his opponents' positions—to refute a wide range of wrong views based on the svabhāva thesis.

Nāgārjuna's primary text is a passage from the Sūtra Piṭaka defining right view: "When one sees the arising of the world [sensory phenomena] as it actually is with right wisdom, 'non-being' with reference to the world does not occur to one. When one sees the cessation of the world as it actually is with right wisdom, 'being' with reference to the world does not occur to one" (S.XII.15). Although this passage, in its original context, seems to refer to the phenomenology of the mind-state on the Path, Nāgārjuna cites it to prove that neither *being* nor *non-being* can apply to conditioned phenomena. According to him, the svabhāva thesis—as it deals with discrete essences—is inescapably entwined in concepts of being and non-being. Thus it is an inaccurate description of saṃsāra.

Furthermore, Nāgārjuna uses mostly prāsangika arguments to demonstrate that the svabhāva thesis reduces to logical absurdities when it tries to account for causality, time, motion, and many other basic facts of existence. For instance, he maintains that dharmas with their own inherent nature could not be caused, for if they were caused, their nature would neither be inherent nor theirs. Thus the only alternative is to accept that dharmas are empty of own-being, for only then can causality, and so on, possibly occur. If this is the case, such basic categories as "same" and "separate," "exists," "does not exist," "both exists and does not exist," and "neither exists nor does not exist," cannot apply, for all is empty. There are in ultimate terms no "own-natures" to which these categories could apply. This is true both for saṃsāra and for nirvāṇa. Nāgārjuna equates emptiness in its mode as an attribute with dependent co-arising, the causal pattern underlying the events of saṃsāra; he equates emptiness as a perceptual mode with nirvāṇa. Thus all views, even right views, can have only a provisional use. Right view has the advantage of helping one loosen one's attachments to views, but once it has been used to perform its task it must be abandoned as well, for it too is empty. In ultimate terms, the basic categories from which views are constructed are inadequate to explain the true nature of anything at all.

This last point is a major departure from the position of the Sūtra Piṭaka, for which language is adequate to describe conditioned experience and breaks down only when trying to describe the unconditioned. Still, the therapeutic thrust is similar to that of the Sūtra Piṭaka's when dealing with metaphysical views: to get the listener to abandon attachment to inappropriate modes of thought and to gain the liberation that comes with freedom from clinging. Nāgārjuna insists that those who cling to emptiness as a view are incorrigible. The use of logic in presenting the teaching of emptiness is to short-circuit any pattern of thinking that would provide a basis for clinging through such categories as being and non-being, same and different. In so doing, it brings about the stilling of all preoccupations and mental proliferations. In this mode of perception there is no view of anyone or anything or even of the Buddha teaching at any time. This mode, similar to the tathatā of the *Prajñā-pāramitā Sūtras,* Nāgārjuna simply calls *tattva* (reality); it is the goal of the Buddhist Path, realized not by trying to attain a comprehensive view of reality, but by using right view to abandon the view-making habits of the mind and simply letting reality be.

Scholars have questioned whether Nāgārjuna was a Mahāyānist, largely because none of the writings that are undoubtedly his make any mention of the *Prajñā-pāramitā Sūtras* or of the bodhisattva ideal. Although it is true that many of his ideas do not go beyond what we know of Mahāsanghika doctrines, and that he gives positive expression to many early Buddhist teachings, such as karma and dependent co-arising, his therapeutic use of the emptiness approach so closely parallels that of the Mahāyāna Sūtras that it is difficult not to view him as part of the same movement. Given the task he had set for himself—to convert Abhidharmists from their attachment to views by using their own methods—it would have been unwise for him to refer to any texts that they would have objected to or to denigrate any teachings from the Sūtra Piṭaka.

At any rate, whatever his own orientation, his immediate pupils were quick to claim him for the Mahāyāna fold, and his major influence has been in the Mahāyāna tradition up to this day. Although he did not succeed in putting a stop to Abhidharma scholasticism, he did found a major school of Buddhist thought. His immediate disciple, Āryadeva, carried on the polemic tradition, and Madhyamika became quite popular among academics. Still, it did not make qualitative advances until about 500 C.E., when Bhavaviveka founded the *Svāntantrika* (Independent) subschool by combining the Mādhyamika approach with the epistemology and logic of Dignāga (see Section 6.2) and confronting a host of problems that the school had previously ignored. Candrakīrti (circa seventh century C.E.) then criticized Bhavaviveka's use of logic to arrive at positive truths, maintaining that the only proper "empty" use of logic was to reduce one's opponent's positions to absurdity, without taking a positive position oneself. Candrakīrti's subschool—which took the name of Prāsangika, from the type of argument it espoused—came to dominate Mādhyamika thinking not only in India, but also in Tibet (see Section 11.3.3).

The emptiness doctrine, as taught both in the early Mahāyāna Sūtras and in the Mādhyamika treatises, had far-reaching consequences for Mahāyāna religious life. These consequences were elaborated and expanded especially in later "emptiness" Sūtras, such as the *Vimalakīrti-nirdeśa, Lotus,* and *Śrīmālā Sūtras.* The early *Śūnyavādins*, or proponents of emptiness, referred to the Buddha's teachings as skillful means having only a provisional truth, but the only skillful means they mentioned were traditional ones: the Four Noble Truths, the Noble Eightfold Path, the doctrine of dependent co-arising. However, if all provisional truths are equally empty, it can be argued that almost anything, if intended as a means for sparking realizations, could qualify as a skillful means to the goal.

This argument is actually advanced in the later emptiness Sūtras. For instance, the *Lotus Sūtra* (see Section 5.5.2) explicitly states that lies can be valid "skillful means" (although it avoids calling them lies), which probably explains the Mahāyāna penchant for attributing its Sūtras to the historical Buddha. Vimalakīrti, the lay bodhisattva, also resorts to unconventional means (Strong *EB*, sec. 4.4.5), based on the rationale that "true meditation is to enter into nirvāṇa without cutting off the passions of the world." The bodhisattva can work and play in the secular world without fear of contamination from sense objects, because pure and impure are themselves both ultimately empty of permanent essence. He may associate with merchants, kings, harlots, and drunkards without falling into avarice, arrogance, lust, or dissipation. He may play the role of lay man rather than monastic, and may choose to be born as a woman, to affirm the point that such distinctions as lay and monastic, male and female, are essentially empty. In fact, many statements in the *Vimalakīrti-nirdeśa Sūtra* imply that it is better to lead a life involved in the world than to retreat into the seclusion of the traditional Path, for "only in the swamp of passion are there living creatures to produce the qualities of Buddhahood."

The *Śrīmālā Sūtra* is even more explicit in regards to the relativity of skillful means, stating that of the Four Noble Truths, only one, cessation, is actually true, whereas the rest are fictions, in that all compounded things are fictitious. Thus the Path has no truth status to set it apart from anything else that might be proposed as a skillful means. This teaching, although it was probably intended simply as a mental therapy for closed attitudes, eventually provided the rationale for maintaining that any behavior motivated by compassion, even if it blatantly violated the Noble Eightfold Path, could also qualify as a means to the goal. This opened the way for Buddhist Tantrism in later centuries (see Section 6.3).

As the emptiness approach began to lose its novelty, new Mahāyāna Sūtras began to break from the earlier emptiness Sūtras and treatises by turning emptiness, viewed as a perceptual mode, into a metaphysical absolute, termed the *Dharmakāya* (literally, Dharma-body). In the Hīnayāna texts, the term *Dharmakāya* had simply denoted the body of the Buddha's recorded teachings, but the new Sūtras recast the term to denote both the potential for Awakening and also the source from which all things spring. In contrast to this metaphysical absolute, emptiness as an attribute of dharmas seemed to become more and more akin to nihilism. The resulting dichotomy formed the dialectic that gave rise to a new school in the Mahāyāna, the Yogācāra.

4.3 YOGĀCĀRA

At the beginning of the fourth century C.E. a new series of Sūtras was composed that gathered various metaphysical points from the earlier Mahāyāna Sūtras and organized them into a scheme portraying the role played by consciousness in forming the experience of the universe. These Sūtras included the *Avataṃsaka Sūtra* (Flower Ornament), *Lankāvatāra Sūtra* (Descent into Lanka), and most important, the *Sandhinirmocana Sūtra* (Resolution of Enigmas) (Strong *EB*, sec. 4.3.2). The authors of these Sūtras viewed their work as so momentous that they proclaimed it to be the third turning of the wheel of Dharma. In their view, the first two turnings of the wheel—the teaching of the Four Noble Truths as systematized in the Abhidharma literature, and the founding of the Mādhyamika school—represented the two extremes of being and non-being between which the new thinkers proposed a new Middle Way. According to the *Sandhinirmocana,* the earlier turnings of the wheel were expressed in enigmas that needed their meaning explained. This third turning was devoted to making everything explicit.

Within the century, a number of theoreticians—chiefly Asanga; his teacher, Maitreyanātha; and his brother, Vasubandhu—formed a new school that systematized the views offered in these Sūtras, synthesizing elements from the Sūtra Piṭaka, Abhidharma, and Mādhyamika with the aim of devising a theoretical framework that would have therapeutic use in the practice of meditation along the bodhisattva Path. This school was thus called the *Yogācāra*, or practice of meditation school. Because some of the Sūtras and later theoreticians in the school expressed views that bordered on philosophical idealism—denying the reality of objects outside of the mind—the school developed other names as well: *Vijñānavāda* (Proponents of Consciousness); *Cittamātra* (Mind-Only); *Vijñānamātra* (Consciousness-Only); and *Vijñaptimātra* (Concept-Only).

However, in its original theoretical formulation in the writings of Asanga and Vasubandhu, Yogācāra was not a doctrine of idealism. Rather, it was more a phenomenology of mind, focused primarily on the role that the mind played in forming experience, inasmuch as the mind was the principal factor in giving rise to suffering. Asanga and Vasubandhu were concerned with mapping the creative role of consciousness so that the map could be used to dismantle that role. Because maps of this sort were also creations of the mind, they too would ultimately have to be discarded in the course of the dismantling, but their therapeutic value would have been served in bringing about Awakening. In this, the brothers were following a mode of teaching that dates back through the Buddhist tradition to the Buddha himself (see Section 2.3).

The Yogācārins' approach, as noted previously, combined features of both the Abhidharma and the Mādhyamika extremes between which they were claiming to chart a new course. On the one hand, they accepted the Abhidharmist premise that one needs a systematic diagram of the workings of experience so that one may properly understand the problem of suffering and deal with it effectively. In their view, Mādhyamika dialectics alone are not enough to loosen one's attachments to views; one needs to practice meditation, including dhyāna, as well. Because meditation is primarily a self-administered cure, one needs a comprehensive right view of the causes of suffering to act as a working hypothesis in administering the cure properly. Thus the Yogācārins took over the Abhidharma enterprise, adding new categories and working out advances in formal logic so as to create what they viewed as a more effective presentation of right view.

On the other hand, the Yogācārins accepted the Mādhyamika assertion, which can be traced back to the Sūtra Piṭaka, that views are valuable only to the extent that they induce one to attain a state in which all views are abandoned. In this sense, they retained the doctrine of emptiness, both as a perceptual mode—ultimate freedom from views—and as an attribute of dharmas. They also accepted the Mādhyamika teaching on the role of mind in creating an illusory reality. Here again, there are antecedents in the Sūtra Piṭaka, in particular the first verse of the Dhammapada: "All dharmas are preceded by mind *(manas),* chieftained by mind, made of mind" (Dhp.1). Neither the Abhidharmists nor the Mādhyamikas, however, had ever satisfactorily worked out the mechanics of how the mind gave rise to dharmas, and this was precisely what the Yogācārins proposed to do.

Asanga and Vasubandhu adopted from the *Sandhinirmocana Sūtra* an analysis of reality into three characteristics: the *parinispanna* (perfected or accomplished), the *paratantra* (dependent or relative), and the *parikalpita* (imaginary or mentally constructed). The perfected level is identical with suchness and other characterizations of emptiness as a mode of perception; the dependent level corresponds to dharmas in their Abhidharma sense; and the imaginary level denotes the act of assigning names and concepts, such as the subject/object distinction, to dharmas on the dependent level, thus giving shape to everyday experience. An analogy might be made with a stereogram: The perfected level corresponds to the blank paper on which the stereogram is printed; the dependent level, to the two-dimensional patterns printed on the paper; and the imaginary level, to the three-dimensional image that appears when one focuses one's eyes in front of the pattern or behind it. These levels the Yogācārins called the three svabhāvas, or own-natures, although in actuality they are three levels of emptiness. The perfected level is the ultimate absence of own-nature; dharmas on the dependent level are empty occurrences; and the concepts applied at the imaginary level are empty characteristics. The purpose of the practice is to cleanse the imaginary level from the dependent level so as to leave the perfected. In terms of our analogy, this would be equivalent to focusing direction on the two-dimensional pattern rather than in front or behind it, and then letting the ink fade from the paper when one sees that there is nothing of any substance to it. To accomplish this cleansing, however, one needs an analysis of how the imaginary and dependent levels are created to begin with.

Here the Yogācārin analysis posited eight levels of consciousness: seven active levels—manas (mind) and the six levels of consciousness appropriate to the six senses (see Section 1.4.3)—and an *ālaya-vijñāṇa* (subliminal, passive "store" or "granary" consciousness) that contains the seeds of past karma together with pure seeds that will eventually lead to Awakening. (The notion of seeds here is borrowed from the Sautrāntikas [see Section 3.2.4.]) The store-consciousness accounts for personal continuity through death and other periods when the active consciousnesses are absent, although the Yogācārins deny that it is a self because it is ultimately empty.

According to the *Lankāvatāra Sūtra,* the active levels of consciousness are similar to waves on the ocean of the store-consciousness. Asanga and Vasubandhu described the various levels as interacting in the following way: When a person performs an action, seeds are deposited in the store-consciousness where they are infused ("perfumed") with habitually ingrained attachments to mental constructs. Thus matured, they give rise to a seamless flow of experience on the dependent level in the form of the other levels of consciousness and the objects they represent. Manas then creates the imaginary level by making distinctions of *grasper* and *graspable* (knower and known) and imposing other mental constructs on this flow. The resulting self/other dichotomy sets the stage for craving with regard to the graspables. Craving in turn gives rise to acts of will that deposit new seeds in the store-consciousness, where they keep reproducing themselves from moment to moment until they are matured and ready to begin the round again. Thus the doctrine of karma and dependent co-arising is recast entirely as the workings of consciousness, both in cause and effect.

Were it not for the pure seeds in the store-consciousness, there would be no way out of this round. These pure seeds, however, can be matured by traditional Buddhist meditative practices, such as the foundations of mindfulness (Strong *EB*, sec. 3.5.4), reformulated so as to focus them on dissolving the boundary between self and others. This practice may be combined with other techniques, such as the creation of mental images that then dissolve, to shatter the tendency to hold to any mental constructs at all. Subsequently, other stages of tranquility and insight meditation based on the Four Noble Truths lead further and further into "signless cognition" until a point is reached where defiled dharmas are totally displaced by untainted dharmas and there occurs an *aśraya-parāvṛtti* (reversal of the basis of mind). This reversal is the salvational goal of Yogācāra, constituting a fundamental change of mental orientation. The world remains the same, but the experience of the world is purified to one of total emptiness. Even the analysis of the three svabhāvas and the eight consciousnesses is abandoned at that point, and all experience is left to its suchness (Strong *EB*, sec. 4.3.3).

The early Yogācārin Sūtras added a cosmological dimension to this analysis of consciousness by equating the purified level of the store-consciousness with a term they borrowed from one of the emptiness Sūtras: *tathāgata-garbha* (the womb of Tathāgatahood) (Strong *EB*, sec. 4.3.5). *Garbha* has a twofold general meaning: first, the womb, and, by extension, an inner room, the calyx of a lotus; and second, the womb's contents—that is, an embryo, fetus, child. In the first sense, the purified store-consciousness is the womb where the tathāgata is conceived, nourished, and matured. The *Prajñā-pāramitā Sūtras* had already introduced the uteral metaphor when they declared Prajñā-pāramitā to be the mother of all the Buddhas (Strong *EB*, sec. 4.2.1). The new term *Tathāgata-garbha* makes the concept more explicit. In the second sense, the womb of Tathāgatahood is the embryonic Buddha consisting of the pure dharmas in a person's store-consciousness.

The Yogācārin Sūtras specified that the womb of Tathāgatahood is innate to all living beings, because all beings are irradiated by the pervading power of the Buddha and because they have grown—throughout infinity—a stock of good dharmas under the influence of this radiating grace. This teaching seems to be an outgrowth of the Mahāsanghika doctrine concerning the ability of the Buddha to place inspiration in the mind of others. If this womb did not exist, the Yogācārins maintained, a person could not take religious initiative and could not turn from saṃsāra and aspire to nirvāṇa. This womb is always intrinsically pure and is synonymous with tathatā (suchness), which is identical in everyone. In ordinary beings, it is covered with adventitious defilements; in the bodhisattvas, it is partly pure and partly impure; and in the Buddhas, perfectly pure.

The Sūtras describe the womb of Tathāgatahood in a series of similes: It is analogous to the Buddha in a faded lotus; honey covered by bees; a kernel of grain in the husk; gold in the ore; a treasure hidden in the earth; the fruit in a small seed; a Buddha-image wrapped in rags; a great king in the womb of a low-caste woman; and a precious statue covered with dirt. These similes fall roughly into two classes, organic and mineral. Of the former, two imply growth. The small seed grows into a fruit tree; the fetus grows into a great king. The rest connote an immutable thing that will emerge unstained when it is unwrapped or washed. It is no wonder that the authors of the *Lankāvatāra Sūtra* had to protest that the womb of Tathāgatahood is not the same as the Brahmanical *ātman* (eternal Self). To the ordinary person, gems, gold, and statues are enduring things, as close to eternal immutables as a sensory image can come. The later *Nirvāṇa Sūtra* claimed that the Buddha's "secret" teaching described the innate Buddhahood of all beings as a "great ātman," but this view did not win favor with the Yogācārins.

Because they also equated the womb of Tathāgatahood with the *Dharmakāya*, (Dharma-body of the Buddha), the Yogācārins had to adapt their Buddhology (or theory of Buddhahood) to account not only for the historical Buddha and the transcendent personal Buddha of the Mahāsanghikans, but also for the Awakening potential that is innate in all beings. This they did by advancing the doctrine of the three bodies of the Buddha (Strong *EB*, sec. 4.3.4). The first is *nirmāṇa-kāya* (the apparition-body), which corresponds to *rūpa-kāya* (the form-body) of Siddhārtha of the earlier teachings and to the apparitions of him that may appear to human beings in visions or dreams. The third is the Dharma-body, or nirvāṇa as a perfectly pure reality innate in all. The second is the Yogācārin innovation in this scheme: *saṃbhoga-kāya* (the recompense or enjoyment-body). This is the glorified body that the Buddha attains as a reward for his bodhisattva practices; the transfigured body that the great bodhisattvas apprehend when they see the Buddha. For example, the

Buddha Amitābha in his Pure Land (see Section 5.5.4) is apprehended in his enjoyment-body by the bodhisattvas there, whereas he appears in his apparition body to favored persons in this world.

Archaeological evidence reveals that the Yogācārin theory of the multiple bodies of the Buddha developed at the same time that monasteries throughout India began building "perfumed chambers" (see Section 3.4.2), where Buddha-images were placed and in which the Buddha, in certain senses, was thought to reside. These chambers acted as focal points for devotees, lay and monastic, who wanted to earn the merit that could come from offering gifts directly to the Buddha himself. In light of this evidence, it is possible to view the Yogācārin Buddhology not only as a result of the internal logic of Yogācārin theory, but also as an attempt to explain a sense of "Buddha" that could literally be here, there, and everywhere, residing in monasteries all over the subcontinent.

The grand equation of the purified store-consciousness, the perfected level of experience, the womb of Tathāgatahood, and the Dharmakāya created a number of problems for the Yogācārins. One was the accusation from other Buddhists that this equation was little more than a recasting of the Upaniṣadic equation of the essential self with Brahman, the universal principle underlying the cosmos. Another problem revolved around the question, "If the perfected has been perfected all along, how can it be involved in the creation of suffering?" This is a question the Hīnayāna and Mādhyamika schools had neatly avoided by insisting on the totally transcendent nature of nirvāṇa, by refusing to discuss questions of temporal origins, or both. In the middle of the sixth century C.E., the Yogācārins themselves split over the issue—arguing as to whether the store-consciousness could indeed be equated with the perfected as they became more concerned with their system as a system, rather than as a tool for meditators. The earlier Yogācārins, however, seem to have been unfazed by these issues, perhaps because they viewed their entire theory as a map on the imaginary level of reality that would dissolve, along with the questions it proposed to answer, when the dependent level was cleansed of the imaginary, leaving only the ultimate emptiness of the perfected. Thus the issue could by settled only through meditative practice.

Given the Yogācārin talent for philosophical synthesis, it should come as no surprise that during the succeeding centuries it absorbed and was absorbed by many other trends in its environment. On the Hīnayāna side, it took over the Vaibhāṣika tradition (see Section 4.4) and with it the entire Abhidharma enterprise; pulled together all the classifications, subclassifications, lists, and numbers that appeared in the Sūtras and treatises; and proceeded to invent more. One of the great ironies of the Mahāyāna movement is that it began as a reaction against the Abhidharma and ended up developing the most elaborate Abhidharma tradition of any Buddhist tradition. On the Mahāyāna side, the Yogācāra school entered into a variety of Yogācāra-Mādhyamika syntheses that have preoccupied Mahāyāna scholastics ever since. At the great university of Nalanda (see Section 6.2), Mādhyamika took the dominant role in the syntheses, whereas at the western university at Valabhi, Yogācārin thought was more central. There are a fair number of sticking points in any such synthesis—the Mādhyamikas ridiculed the Yogācārin formulation of the "dependent" nature as a coupling of the real and the unreal, whereas the Yogācārins responded by asking where illusion could have its source except in reality—but these difficulties only served to set combustible intellects on fire with the desire to resolve them. When Buddhist Tantrism developed, it made use of the Yogācārin practice of creating and destroying mental images, together with the concept of meditative reversal, in its radical reformulation of the Path (see Section 6.3.3). Later, the Ch'an and Hua Yen schools in China, and Dzogchen in Tibet, found their textual inspiration largely in Yogācārin works.

4.4 LATER DEVELOPMENTS IN HĪNAYĀNA

It is easy to read histories of Buddhism in India and come away with the impression that, with the founding of the Mahāyāna, Hīnayāna either died out, was consigned to the minority, or at least lost its creative impulse. Actually, nothing could be further from the truth. The accounts of Chinese pilgrims in the seventh century C.E. testify that the Hīnayāna schools then were still in the majority in India; according to Tibetan historians, the schools maintained that position until the demise of Buddhism in northern India in the thirteenth century C.E. They had developed universities of their own well before that point, which were similar to the great university at Nalanda (see Section 6.2). For instance, the Sāṃmatīya school was strong in the western university at Valabhi, which was considered second only to Nalanda itself, whereas the Sarvāstivādins were predominant at two universities in Kashmir. Modern scholarship suggests that the Sautrāntikas were well represented at Nalanda, which was otherwise a Mahāyāna stronghold. Nalanda's successful missionary campaign in Tibet and Southeast Asia ensured that records of the school's intellectual tradition continued to survive after its physical destruction in the early 1200s. The Hīnayāna universities, however, either did not engage in missionary work or were less successful. Thus when their libraries were destroyed, all record of their later teachings was destroyed with them. Nevertheless, it is possible to outline some later trends in Hīnayāna to provide an idea of the creative energy it was still able to maintain in the first millennium of the common era.

In the first century C.E., the great poet Aśvaghoṣa—a member of a Mahāsanghika subschool, the Bahuśrutīyas—composed Sanskrit epics and plays with Buddhist themes, including one of the first epic poems on the complete life of the Buddha, the *Buddhacarita* (which was used as a source for much of Chapters 1 and 2). Aśvaghoṣa made a conscious effort to enlist the sophisticated techniques of *kāvya,* the Indian tradition of fine literature, to the Buddhist cause. His works were something of a tour de force, presenting even the most technical of the early Buddhist doctrines, such as dependent co-arising, in the tightly controlled forms of Sanskrit poetics.

Aśvaghoṣa's use of literary Sanskrit seems to have been part of a general trend, for the rise of kāvya and the fastidious tastes it engendered had a strong effect both on Hīnayāna and on Mahāyāna schools at this time. Many of the early schools translated their canons into Sanskrit during this period so that their doctrines would not seem crude or old-fashioned, whereas the Mahāyānists composed their new Sūtras in Sanskrit, many of them with an eye to the new literary tastes. Several other great Sanskrit Buddhist poets also come from this era, among them Mātṛceṭa, author of what were most probably the most quietly sophisticated Buddhist hymns in India, and Āryaśūra, author of a stylish retelling of a number of the Jātaka tales. Āryaśūra also wrote a Mahāyānist tract on the perfections (Strong *EB*, sec. 4.4.3); Mātṛceṭa's interpretation of Dharmakāya seems to classify him as a Hīnayānist, but he was respected by Buddhists of both courses. A contemporary of Aśvaghoṣa's, Sangharakṣa, composed a Sarvāstivādin counterpart to the *Buddhacarita* that has survived in Chinese translation.

Sangharakṣa, however, was more famous as the teacher of King Kaniṣka, the Kuṣāṇa emperor who ruled much of northern India during the first and second centuries C.E. Kaniṣka sponsored the so-called Fourth Council, either at his capital in Gandhara or in Kashmir, to settle doctrinal differences among the Buddhists in his realm. Given the fact that his monastic advisers were Sarvāstivādins, it is not surprising that Sarvāstivādin views held sway. The Sautrāntikas (see Section 3.2.4), finding themselves outnumbered, split off from the Sarvāstivādins soon afterward. The Council's work resulted in the composition of a number of works, chief among them the *Mahāvibhāṣā,* or the Great Options. This book was a commentary on the first book of the Sarvāstivādin Abhidharma, listing the major views presented on controversial points at the Council and trying to come to a reasoned conclusion on them. Chief among the points was the question of how to explain the Sarvāstivādin views on being and time. The eventual conclusion is interesting in that it shows, like Nāgārjuna's concept of functioning emptiness, the intellectual influence of the decimal notation in mathematics that was becoming widespread at this time: A dharma maintains its own-nature at all times but has different designations depending on its position in past, present, or future, just as a number, such as two, maintains its "twoness" even though it is designated differently depending on whether it is in the units, tens, or hundreds column.

The *Mahāvibhāṣā* attracted a large number of commentators, called Vaibhāṣikas, who tried to settle points left unsettled by the text. Their controversies culminated in the fourth or fifth century C.E. in the work of one Vasubandhu, who may or may not have been the same Vasubandhu as Asanga's brother. This Vasubandhu composed one of the greatest summaries of Buddhist doctrine, the *Abhidharmakośa,* a gigantic work recasting all the issues of the Vaibhāṣika tradition in as logically consistent a form as possible. He then wrote a *Bhāṣya* (autocommentary) on his own work, demolishing it from the Sautrāntika point of view. This commentary was a great turning point in the Abhidharma enterprise. On the one hand, its attacks were so successful that it, rather than the *Mahāvibhāṣā,* became the focus of the ongoing dialogue; on the other hand, it was such an elegant and thorough summary of Abhidharma analysis that it formed the basis for Yogācāra Abhidharma studies for centuries afterward. It has even survived to the present as a cornerstone of the Tibetan monastic curriculum (see Section 11.3.3). Mahāyāna tradition identifies the author of this work as Asanga's brother and states that Asanga converted him to Yogācāra beliefs soon after the work was completed. Modern scholarship has called this point into question, but the conversion of the *Abhidharmakośa* and its commentary to the Yogācāra cause cannot be denied. Dignāga—the foremost pupil of the author of the *Abhidharmakośa*—seems to have remained a Sautrāntikan, and he definitely contributed to another enterprise at which Hīnayāna continued to excel: formal logic and epistemology. In fact, Dignāga's writings revolutionized these subjects and had a long-term effect on philosophical debate in all major Indian traditions for centuries afterward (see Section 6.2).

By and large, Hīnayānists ignored the Mahāyāna polemics except to point out that the Mahāyāna Sūtras were obviously not the teachings of the historical Buddha and that the doctrine of emptiness undercut the truth value of the Path. The Hīnayāna term for the Mahāyānists was *Vaitulika*, which means either Expansionists or Illusionists, referring either to the expanded Mahāyāna Sūtras or to the Mahāyāna teachings on the interpenetration of reality and illusion. One branch of the Sarvāstivādins, the Mūlasarvāstivādins, recast their canon in a literary form similar to the great Mahāyāna Sūtras, but it is impossible to tell whether they did this in response to the Mahāyāna movement or simply to keep up with the literary tastes of the period in general.

The willingness of both the Hīnayāna and Mahāyāna schools to translate the teaching into Sanskrit and to keep abreast of other intellectual trends during this period was obviously an effort to keep the Buddha's message modern and competitive, not only among themselves but also with regard to Hinduism and other religions that were also adapting to those trends. However, this willingness to adapt ultimately provoked a small backlash in later centuries, in that some monks felt that the original teachings had been adulterated and lost. This feeling led them to search out pre-Sanskrit copies of the canon, a quest that in the fifth century C.E. led the south Indian monk Buddhaghosa to Sri Lanka. There he found not only what was apparently an old recension of the Pali Canon, but also the archaic Sinhalese commentaries, which he was led to believe were coeval with the canon. These he translated into Pali, at the same time writing a great summary of the Theravādin position (see Section 7.2). Thus began a renaissance in Theravādin studies that, in a circuitous way, led to Theravāda being the only Hīnayāna school to survive the demise of Buddhism in India relatively intact (see Section 7.3).

5

Soteriology and Pantheon of the Mahāyāna

5.1 THE BODHISATTVA PATH

Mahāyāna is synonymous with the course, *yāna* (vehicle), or *caryā* (career) of the bodhisattva. In the early Mahāyāna Sūtras (composed before the second century C.E.), this is a simple Path that begins with the arousal of the *bodhicitta* (mind-state; that is, aspiration) for supreme, perfect Awakening, and moves on to the practice of the six *pāramitā* (perfections) for the sake of all beings until the goal is reached. Between 100 and 300 C.E., the doctrine of *bhūmi* (the 10 bodhisattva stages) was introduced, and an elaborate schema of paths and stages was devised.

The Mahāyāna Sūtras address their teaching equally to the monastics and laity, exhorting both to recite, copy, and explain the Sūtras, an enterprise that monastic Hīnayāna schools reserved for the monks and nuns. But although the laity and monastics were regarded as equal in some respects, both courses maintained that monastic life was superior to lay life, and the laity still had to pay formal honor to monastics. Only the more libertarian Sūtras authorized the laity to preach Dharma to monastics. The most famous of such Sūtras, the *Vimalakīrti-nirdeśa,* depicts Vimalakīrti, the householder-bodhisattva, encouraging a crowd of young patricians to leave the household life. When they protest that they cannot do so without their parents' consent, Vimalakīrti tells them to arouse the bodhicitta and practice diligently, because that is equivalent to "going forth." Far from diminishing the monastic vocation, this concession is simply second-best for those unable to take the ochre robe.

Although the literature reveals a number of lay preachers, it mentions no organized noncelibate communal life and no householder clergy. Householder-bodhisattvas were welcome to study meditation and philosophy, and probably were allowed to spend protracted periods of retreat in the monasteries. They could teach the doctrine and were encouraged to propagate it. But so far as we know, the Mahāyāna Sūtras were composed by monks, and there is not a single important treatise attributed to any Indian Buddhist lay person.

The bodhisattva Path begins with instruction from a Buddha, a bodhisattva, or some other spiritual friend. This instruction plants seeds of virtue in the mind of the hearers, inducing them to perform good deeds, through which they acquire more and more roots of goodness. After many lives, thanks to the infused grace of the various teacher-saviors and the merit earned by responding to them, a person becomes able to put forth the bodhicitta. Initially there are two motives for this aspiration—the desire for one's own Awakening and compassion for all living beings who suffer in saṃsāra (Strong *EB*, secs. 4.4.1, 4.4.2)—but along the Path one realizes the sameness of self and others, and transcends the duality of purpose. Arousing the bodhicitta is an extremely meritorious deed. It cancels past bad karma, increases merit, wards off bad rebirths, and ensures good ones. In keeping with developing Mahāyāna views of the cosmos—which came more and more to resemble modern holographic theory, in that each part of the cosmos contained the whole—the first arousing of the bodhicitta was said to contain the whole of the Awakened mind-state, albeit in an unstable form.

New bodhisattvas proceed to consolidate their bodhicitta and advance on the Path by cultivating good qualities working for the welfare of living beings, based on a set of vows or *praṇidhāna* (earnest resolutions). Some vows are quite general, stating, "When we have crossed the stream, may we ferry others across. When we are liberated, may we liberate others." Others—such as those of Dharmākara, who later became the Buddha Amitābha—are more specific. Dharmākara made three or four dozen vows in the form, "May I not attain supreme, perfect Awakening until [such-and-such a benefit] is assured beings who are born in my Buddha-land" (where he [Amitābha] would live and teach the Dharma to his devotees). Bodhisattva vows are usually binding until the end of the bodhisattva career, a matter of aeons. Even when the great bodhisattvas have passed beyond dualistic cognitions and intentions, they are motivated, as if on automatic pilot, by the force of their original vows.

Bodhisattvas are supposed to declare their vows in the presence of a Buddha, which means that they must wait until a Buddha appears in the world. The Tathāgata then gives the bodhisattva a prediction that after a certain number of ages he/she will become a Buddha of such-and-such a name, reigning in such-and-such a Buddha-land, which will have such-and-such excellences. Ordinary bodhisattvas who have not yet had the good fortune to be born in the same generation as a Buddha make their vows in the presence of other human bodhisattvas or even with the Buddhas and bodhisattvas of the 10 directions as their witnesses.

The six pāramitā (perfections) are the main course of the bodhisattva career. As we have noted (see Section 3.2.3), the early schools advocated all these qualities and extolled graphic instances of them in the *Jātakas*. Mahāyāna differs from the earlier tradition in making the extremes the model for ordinary devotees (Strong *EB*, sec. 4.4.3).

A quality is practiced to perfection when the most difficult acts are executed with a mind free from discriminatory ideas, without self-consciousness, ulterior motives, or self-congratulation. The perfect giver, for example, does not think "I give" and has no fictive concepts about the gift, the recipient, or the reward that ensues from the act. Thus, *prajñā-pāramitā* (perfection of wisdom) is necessary in order to complete the other five perfections, which in turn form the groundwork for the development of wisdom.

Dāna (perfection of giving) consists of giving material things, knowledge, Dharma-instructions, and one's own body and life to all beings, then in turn transferring or reassigning the ensuing merit to supreme Awakening and the welfare of other beings, rather than aiming it at one's future bliss in saṃsāra. The bodhisattva practices giving and encourages others to do so as well.

Śīla (perfection of morality) consists of following the 10 good paths of action, transferring the merit, and prompting others to do similarly. The 10 paths involve refraining from the following: killing, stealing, engaging in illicit sex, lying, speaking divisively, speaking harshly, chattering frivolously, having covetous thoughts, having hostile thoughts, or believing false views.

Kṣānti (the perfection of patience) is founded on nonanger and nonagitation. It involves patient endurance of hardship and pain, forbearance and forgiveness toward those who injure and abuse the bodhisattva, and patient assent to difficult and uncongenial doctrines, specifically those of the Mahāyāna scriptures.

Vīrya (the perfection of vigor) involves applying persistent energy and zeal in overcoming one's faults and cultivating good qualities, in studying Dharma and the arts and sciences, and in doing good works for the welfare of others. The term *vīrya* is derived from *vīra* (a martial man, a hero). It corresponds to right effort, the sixth factor of the Noble Eightfold Path of early Buddhism, but more explicitly it signifies heroic endeavor to benefit other living beings.

Dhyāna (the perfection of meditation) consists of entering into the meditative absorptions and attainments, yet not accepting rebirth in the paradises to which such states normally destine one in the next life.

Prajñā-pāramitā (the perfection of wisdom) is personified as a goddess, because the word *prajñā* (wisdom, insight, discernment) is grammatically feminine. She is the mother of all Buddhas, for through her they become Awakened Ones. A famous hymn endows her with feminine traits and maternal loving kindness (Strong *EB*, sec. 4.2.1). Wisdom in the *Perfection of Wisdom Sūtras* is defined as full acceptance of the doctrine asserting that phenomena, in the ultimate sense, neither arise nor cease. Only a *mahāsattva* (fearless great being), the Mahāyānists say, can accept this teaching. Three degrees of assent are distinguished. The first is acceptance of the words of the teaching. The second is conforming assent, attained in the sixth bodhisattva-stage and consisting of an intense but not definitive conviction. The third is ultimate acceptance that dharmas are non-arising. This full acceptance, the later texts allege, is to be attained with the eighth stage.

The early theory of stages seems to have recognized only seven bodhisattva-stages, with acceptance that the dharmas are non-arising coming in the seventh. The number of stages was increased from 7 to 10 about 200 C.E. Variant lists of stations and stages circulated for a while, but eventually became standardized as follows (Strong *EB*, sec. 4.4.4):

(a) The stage of the "lineage," where the beginner strives to acquire a stock of merit and knowledge. This extends from the first thought of Awakening until the "experience of heat," the first signpost of success in meditation.

(b) The stage of "practicing with conviction." Here the bodhisattva cultivates four "factors of penetration," namely, "meditative heat," "climax," "patience," and "the highest mundane Dharma." These meditative experiences overcome and expel the antithesis between subject and object, leading to nondiscriminative knowledge. Stages (a) and (b) are preparatory to the actual bodhisattva-stages.

(c) The 10 bodhisattva-stages, namely: (1) the joyful, (2) the stainless, (3) the illuminating, (4) the flaming, (5) the very-hard-to-conquer, (6) the face-to-face, (7) the far-going, (8) the immovable, (9) the good-insight, and (10) the Dharma-cloud. Each stage is practiced in concert with a perfection, with four perfections being added to the early list of six: (7) skill in means, (8) determination, (9) power, and (10) knowledge. The first bodhisattva-stage is the Path of vision, following immediately after "the highest mundane Dharma." Stages 2 to 10 form the Path of meditative cultivation, in which nondual awareness is perfected.

(d) The Buddha-stage follows the diamondlike *samādhi* (concentration), which is the last event on the Path of cultivation. This samādhi plays an important role in Mahāyāna Abhidharma also, where it is realized by bodhisattvas as they sit on the Diamond Throne of Awakening. In it they fulfill the perfections of dhyāna and prajñā in the moment just before attaining bodhi, destroying all the residues of defilement. Mahāyāna doctrine maintains that the ultimate Path consists in awareness that the causes of suffering have been destroyed and will never arise again. In this sense, the bodhisattva's final realization is identical with the arhant's.

There were some differences of opinion concerning the duration of the bodhisattva career, but the prevalent view was that it takes three immeasurable aeons: one to or through the first bodhisattva-stage, one from there through the seventh stage, and one for stages eight to ten. Some later Mahāyānists objected to this elaborate schematization, for a variety of reasons. The correspondence between the stages and perfections conflicts with the earlier teaching that the six perfections are mutually dependent. The spiritual states described are very similar to those in Hīnayāna descriptions of the arhants'

Path, for which no such long ages are deemed necessary. However, the overall progression—from good works and faith through aspiration and training to realization; from deliberate practice to spontaneous exercise; and from mundane knowledge to transcendental wisdom—seems valid. It is an unusually detailed account of the universal path from which people learn and mature, and of the way of holiness in many diverse religions. The 7 or 10 bodhisattva-stages, with their vivid metaphorical names, may have begun with the actual experience of a meditator or a small school of contemplatives for whom the series was a firsthand description, the list then passing into the hands of those who were unfamiliar with the experiences and who produced elaborate theories about them. The doctrine of three immeasurable aeons may have originally been meant metaphorically, in keeping with the deliberately extravagant style of the Mahāyāna Sūtras, but Indian schoolmen took it literally. Later Indian sects tried to find shortcuts in this extended path, and many Chinese Mahāyāna schools rejected the enormous time scale entirely.

5.2 BUDDHIST WOMEN IN THE MAHĀYĀNA

The status of women in the Mahāyāna presents a paradox. In contrast to the prominence of eminent arhant nuns at the time of the Buddha (see Section 3.4.3), the Order of Nuns by the time of Mahāyāna's rise was considerably reduced. At the same time, however, Mahāyāna texts continued to develop literary and mythic images of women as possessors of wisdom and compassion, able to teach men and lay people, similar to the depictions of Sister Dhammadinnā in the earlier texts. The texts proclaimed that at least one lay woman and queen, Śrīmālādevī (Strong *EB*, sec. 4.3.5), might be considered a female Buddha, and that the goddess Prajñāpāramitā (Perfection of Wisdom) is the mother of the Buddhas. The goddess Hārītī, with the guardian deity Mahākāla (Great Dark One), was also included in Mahāyāna worship services. Thus a shift occurred. There is nothing in the Mahāyāna Sūtras comparable to the Pali *Therīgāthā,* which reports the experience of human women attaining Awakening, but there is nothing in the early Sūtras comparable to the new Mahāyāna exaltation of goddesses and female Buddhas.

Apparently, nuns participated little in the elaboration of these Mahāyāna ideas, although the Pali commentaries suggest that Mahāyāna monks actively campaigned for nuns to support their cause. Few Mahāyāna nuns are remembered in history. When the Chinese pilgrim I-ching (635–713 C.E.) visited north India, he found nuns generally poor and undervalued; in his opinion, the status of Chinese nuns was considerably better.

In the Mahāyāna texts, literary portraits of women's role as bearers of insight, compassion, and spiritual attainment existed side by side with strands of androcentrism and misogyny. Some of the new Sūtras, contrary to the earlier teachings, declared that female birth excluded the attainment of nirvāṇa. Asanga wrote that all women are defiled and of little intelligence. Still, some

Mahāyāna texts state that, in ultimate terms, femaleness and maleness are both empty, thus providing an opening for the traditional position of gender neutrality when it comes to the attainment of Awakening. This opening laid the seeds for new roles for Buddhist women both in the Tantric period, which was to follow, and in the Buddhist feminist movement today.

5.3 IMAGES OF THE BUDDHA

The image of the Buddha represents a significant innovation in Buddhist art. As we have already noted, in the earliest Buddhist art the primary image of the deceased Buddha was the stūpa, the reliquary mound intended to function as a locus for pilgrimage and as a reminder of the doctrine of impermanence. Early Buddhology found it inappropriate to represent the Buddha in iconic form because the Buddha had made it clear that he was not to be identified with his body.

Why, then, did this attitude change in the first century B.C.E.? Part of the answer may be found in traditions outside of Buddhism. Some early Indian traditions did not use anthropomorphic images, whereas others, stemming from the pre-Aryan civilization of the Indus, did use a variety of images of male and female individuals and deities. This iconographic tradition reappeared in popular religious art of the third to first centuries B.C.E., concurrent with the development of theism and *bhakti* (devotion) in early popular Hinduism. Buddhists, watching trends in Hinduism, may have wanted a more personal focal point for their worship than the abstract stūpa. A specifically Indian style of Buddha-image was developed in the upper Ganges city of Mathura, which had long specialized in producing images of yakṣas and yakṣiṇīs, male and female deities of superhuman power and size worshiped by devotees seeking worldly protection and benefits. The Mathura Buddha greatly resembled the yakṣa images both in form and function. The earliest sculptors invariably represented him as massive and strong, with his right hand in a gesture of offering protection. Such an image of the Buddha must be considered "popular," that is, a response to the worldly needs of his worshipers.

Greek traditions also seem to have played a role in the development of the Buddha-image. In addition to Mathura, Gandhara in northwest India produced numerous early Buddha-images. This was an area that had experienced many foreign invasions and dynasties, and was thus open to Hellenistic influences. The Gandharan Buddha greatly resembles Apollo and wears a Roman toga, but lacks the warmth of the Mathuran modeling. Unlike Mathuran artisans, Gandharan artisans created narrative sculptures of the Buddha's life, portraying specific incidents in realistic detail, with the Buddha in various poses. In later centuries, the hieratic and narrative modes of Mathuran and Gandharan sculpture gradually combined until in the Gupta period (fourth to seventh century C.E.) the classical meditative, transcendental Buddha-image developed.

Images of the great bodhisattvas appeared concurrently with images of the Buddha in the first century B.C.E. No images were identified with specific bodhisattvas until the following century, when images of Maitreya (see Section 5.4.1) were sculpted. In the second century C.E., differences between the iconography of Buddha and bodhisattva images began to appear, along with the first image of a Cosmic Buddha, Amitābha (see Section 5.5.4), dated 104 C.E. The image of the pensive bodhisattva—his right foot on his left knee, his right hand to his temple—which was to have a long history in Buddhist art, also first appeared at this time. These artistic trends suggest that the late first and early second centuries mark the beginning of independent bodies of bodhisattva and Cosmic Buddha lore. Only later were images of Avalokiteśvara, Mañjuśrī, and Tārā produced. Mahāyāna versions of Śākyamuni—identifiable because they portray him sitting western style on a throne, an attitude common to the Mahāyāna Sūtras but never used in the earlier texts—were not sculpted until the third or fourth century C.E. These images probably reflect the growing tendency among Mahāyānists at that time to view themselves as a distinct group, separate from their Hīnayāna contemporaries and forebears.

5.4 THE COSMIC BODHISATTVAS

Many Mahāyāna Sūtras begin with a catalog of the assembly present on the occasion when the Sūtra was uttered by the Buddha. The *Lotus Sūtra,* for example, opens with Śākyamuni sitting on Mount Gṛdhrakūṭa (Vulture Peak) surrounded by twelve hundred arhant-bhikṣus, eighty thousand nonrelapsing bodhisattvas, Sakra, the Four Great Kings, Śiva, Brahmā, and contingents of spirit beings. This is a literary device that, in addition to cataloging the pantheon, expresses the early Buddhist claim that Śākyamuni is the teacher of gods and men.

The chief innovation in this Mahāyāna pantheon is the class of great bodhisattvas, also called mahāsattvas (great beings). The *Lotus Sūtra* names 23; the *Vimalakīrti,* more than 50. Of these, three became most important: Maitreya, Mañjuśrī, and Avalokiteśvara. All three figure as interlocutors in Mahāyāna Sūtras, where they appear as men and converse with the great disciples and Śākyamuni. These great beings are nonhistorical; there is no evidence that any one of them is an apotheosis of a human hero, as was the case with the Hindu Rāma. Instead, they appear to be unabashed products of the visionary, shamanic mode of perception that is celebrated in these Sutras. Strangely, no Sūtra preaches devotion to a celestial bodhisattva until the third century C.E., a full three centuries after these beings entered the literature.

5.4.1 Maitreya
(Strong *EB,* sec. 1.9)

Maitreya was the earliest cult bodhisattva, mentioned even in the early Hīnayāna Sūtras. A Pali Sutta (D.26) predicts that in the distant future there will arise in the world a Blessed One named Metteyya (Pali for Maitreya), who will be attended by a company of thousands of monks just as Śākyamuni is attended by a company of hundreds. At present, this bodhisattva is residing in the Tuṣita heaven (where future Buddhas traditionally spend their penultimate life), awaiting his last birth. The pious might look forward to that event, dedicating the merit of their current practice to the goal of being reborn as a human being at that time, when all human beings will gain Awakening. In order to pass the interlude happily and to be sure of rebirth along with Maitreya when he comes, they could meanwhile seek rebirth in the Tuṣita paradise. One recommended way of securing a desired rebirth is to concentrate one's thoughts on it at the moment of death. Thus, King Duṭṭhagāmaṇi of Sri Lanka, dying in 80 B.C.E., fixed his last thoughts on Metteyya's heaven where, the chronicles assure us, he was reborn. Similarly, the Chinese pilgrim Hsüan-tsang vowed to be reborn in the Tuṣita heaven with Maitreya. Life in the presence of Maitreya is the Buddhist equivalent of the Christian millennium.

Maitreya, unlike the Buddhas before him, is alive, so he can respond to the prayers of worshipers. Being compassionate, as his name indicates (its Sanskrit root means benevolent), he willingly grants help—being a high god in his present birth, he has the power to do so. His cult thus offers its devotees the advantages of theism and Buddhism combined.

Just as the Buddha had received occasional revelations and inspirations from devas, Mahāyāna masters went into trances and journeyed to the Tuṣita heaven, where Maitreya revealed Dharma-themes to them. On occasion, he also descended to Earth to divulge texts, which makes it exceedingly difficult to decide whether the Yogācārin texts attributed to Maitreyanātha, "Lord Maitreya," are the works of a human author who took that name, or are the outcome of a meditator's visionary experiences.

Beginning from the time that Gandharan art first appeared, Maitreya was frequently represented, perhaps as a result of the messianic expectations—originating probably in present-day Iran—that coursed through India and the Mediterranean world after 200 B.C.E. Many images and paintings of him survive in central Asia. He is often shown sitting on his throne in western fashion. In China, he is also known as "the laughing Buddha," an apocryphal figure who was deemed a preincarnation of Maitreya. Known in Chinese as Pu-tai Ho-shang (Hemp-bag monk; in Japanese, Hotei), his rotund figure is often mistaken by westerners for Śākyamuni Buddha when they find images of him in curio shops. He appears as the savior in the last picture of the ox-taming series of Ch'an and Zen Buddhism.

5.4.2 Mañjuśrī

Mañjuśrī shares with Maitreya preeminence among the bodhisattvas in the Mahāyāna Sūtras up to 300 C.E. In the *Lotus Sūtra* he remembers deeds of former Buddhas that were unknown even to Maitreya. In the *Vimalakīrti* he alone of all Śākyamuni's disciples has wisdom and eloquence enough to stand up to that formidable householder, Vimalakīrti. In the *Gaṇḍavyūha,* the last chapter of the *Avataṃsaka Sūtra*, he counsels the youth Sudhana in his search for Awakening. Many smaller Sūtras are devoted to his legend, attributes, and teachings. Curiously, he is scarcely mentioned in the *Prajñā-pāramitā Sūtras,* and he is absent from the Buddhist art of all schools prior to 400 C.E. When he does appear in art, he is shown as a bodhisattva bhikṣu, with a five-pointed coiffure or tiara, a sword (to cut ignorance) in his right hand, a book (the *Prajñā-pāramitā)* in his left, and a lion for his mount.

The name Mañjuśrī means "gentle or sweet glory." He is also called Mañjughoṣa (Sweet Voice) and Vāgīśvara (Lord of Speech). This last epithet also belongs to Brahmā, whose roles as patron of science, custodian of memory, lord of inspiration, and most ancient of beings Mañjuśrī takes over in the Mahāyāna pantheon. The nuclei around which this bodhisattva-figure grew are a gandharva (youthful celestial being) named Pāñcaśikha (Five-Crest), who appears in the Pali Suttas; and a Brahmā, Sanatkumāra (Forever-a-youth), who in one tale takes on Pāñcaśikha's appearance because his own is too subtle for lower gods to see. Mañjuśrī's connection with these two beings is revealed in his standard epithet, *kumāra-bhūta,* which means "in the form of a youth," or "having become the crown prince." Mañjuśrī is the crown prince of Dharma because, similar to other tenth-stage bodhisattvas, he is on the verge of becoming a King of Dharma, a Buddha.

In due course, devotees endowed Mañjuśrī with a legend of his own. Seventy myriad aeons ago and seventy-two hundred billion Buddha-fields to the east of this world, Mañjuśrī was a pious king who offered worship to a Tathāgata and aroused the bodhicitta. He resolved to pursue an endless but unhurried career toward Awakening, staying in saṃsāra as long as there remained even one being to be saved. Although he has now fulfilled all the virtues of a Buddha, he has not yet considered becoming one, although eventually he will. This implies that there will come a time when the last living being has been saved, a rare eschatological statement in the Buddhist tradition.

Merely hearing his name subtracts many aeons from one's time in saṃsāra. Whoever worships him is born time and again in the Buddha-family and is protected by his power. Those who meditate on his statue will be similarly fortunate and will reach Awakening. If a devotee recites the *Śūraṃgama-samādhi Sūtra* and chants Mañjuśrī's name, then within seven days Mañjuśrī will come to the worshiper, appearing in a dream if bad karma hinders the supplicant from receiving direct vision. Mañjuśrī also takes on the form of a poor man or an orphan to test the kindness of his devotees.

5.4.3 Avalokiteśvara
(Strong *EB*, sec. 5.2.1)

Avalokiteśvara first appears as a mere name in the lists at the beginning of the *Vimalakīrti*, and later, the *Lotus Sūtra.* His first significant role is in the *Sukhāvatī-vyūha Sūtra,* where he and Mahāsthāmaprāpta are Amitābha Buddha's chief attendants. They are the only bodhisattvas in Sukhāvatī whose light is boundless; owing to them, that world-realm is luminous everywhere and always. Both used to be men in this world; on dying they went to Sukhāvatī.

The *Avalokiteśvara Sūtra* was incorporated into the *Lotus Sūtra* as late as the third century C.E. To this day, however, it circulates as an independent work in China and Japan, where it is the main item in the liturgy of the Kuan-yin cult. A few verses at the end describe Sukhāvatī and claim that Avalokiteśvara now stands to the left of the Amitābha and fans him. The rest of the text says nothing about Amitābha but depicts Avalokiteśvara as an omnipresent, omnipotent savior-deity subordinate to no one. He has purified his vows for countless aeons under millions of Buddhas. He possesses all virtues and is especially rich in love and compassion. He rescues those who invoke him from fire, shipwreck, falling off a precipice, missiles, armed robbers and enemies, execution, chains and shackles, witchcraft, demons, wild beasts, snakes, and thunderbolts. His skill in means is infinite: Through it he takes whatever form will help living beings. He adopts the guise of a Buddha, a bodhisattva, a disciple, Brahmā, Indra, and other gods. Like Mañjuśrī, he has played the role of a Buddha and will play it again, without getting "trapped" in nirvāṇa. In this respect the celestial bodhisattvas are said to be superior to the Buddhas.

The origin of this bodhisattva-figure is obscure. The name Avalokiteśvara is composed of *avalokita* (observed; looked down upon or observing; looking down) and *īśvara* (lord). The general idea is that the Bodhisattva observes the world and responds to the cries of living beings. He is also called Lokeśvara, "Lord of the World." A variant name—Avalokitasvara, in which "svara" means sound or voice—underlies the Chinese short name Kuan-yin, "sound-regarder." The longer Chinese name, Kuan-shih-yin, "regarder of the world's sounds," is beautifully clear but does not correspond to any known Sanskrit form of the name. Avalokiteśvara is praised for his voice, which resembles thunder or the tides. He is usually represented in art as a bejeweled lay man wearing a high crown bearing a cross-legged image of Amitābha. He often holds a lotus in his hand. In the Tantric period (600–1200 C.E.), he came to be represented with 11 heads, and with 4, 10, 12, 24, or 1,000 arms ready to help people in trouble. In Tibet, Avalokiteśvara was revered as the country's patron, protector, and founder of the Tibetan race. Tibetans everywhere worshiped him for his compassionate response to the sufferings and trials of life. In China, Avalokiteśvara was eventually represented as a woman. At present she is worshiped as a madonna of gentle compassion throughout east Asia, with the Chinese calling her Kuan-yin; the Japanese, Kannon; the Koreans, Kwanse'ŭm; and the Vietnamese, Quan-âm.

5.4.4 Other Bodhisattva Traditions

Samantabhadra (Universally Auspicious) became popular rather late. He is not mentioned at the beginning of the *Lotus Sūtra,* but in Chapter 26, a late addition, he comes to the world with a fabulous retinue to ask Śākyamuni to expound the *Lotus Sūtra.* He promises to protect the monks who keep this Sūtra, and to avert the menaces of human enemies and demons. Mounted on a white elephant with six tusks, he will accompany the preacher, appearing and reminding him when he forgets any part of the text. If devotees circumambulate for 21 days, Samantabhadra will show his body on the 21st, inspiring the devotees and giving them talismanic spells (Strong *EB*, sec. 5.2.3).

In Buddhist symbolism, Samantabhadra represents daily practice and application, which must proceed by gradual but firm steps, similar to the elephant on which he sits. Samantabhadra is often paired with Mañjuśrī, the personification of wisdom, whose lion leaps and roars with the confidence that comes from experiential understanding. Together the two bodhisattvas thus symbolize twin requisites of spiritual growth: application and wisdom.

Samantabhadra also appears in the *Avataṃsaka* (Flower Ornament) *Sūtra,* as does Mañjuśrī, particularly in its later section called the *Gaṇḍavyūha* (Flower Array) *Sūtra,* where he appears as the greatest of all the bodhisattvas (Strong *EB*, sec. 4.3.6). This textual tradition became very popular in China (Hua-yen) and Japan (Kegon), and was particularly worshiped by women there. It was also portrayed in the top level of bas-reliefs on the great Javanese stūpa Borobudur (see Section 7.2). In Tibet, Samantabhadra came to be regarded as the great Cosmic Buddha who founded the tradition of Dzogchen meditation (see Section 11.3.3).

We have learned how some bodhisattvas, such as Maitreya and Avalokiteśvara, were important throughout the Buddhist world. Others became more important beyond greater India. Tārā (Savioress) became very important in Tibet as the feminine aspect of compassion closely associated with Avalokiteśvara. According to the Tibetan historian Tāranātha, she vowed to work for the salvation of all not as a man, as most do, but as a woman. She first appears in sixth-century Indian art with Avalokiteśvara and, like Prajñāpāramitā, is called the Mother of all the Buddhas; unlike Prajñāpāramitā, however, she became a deity who actively saves her devotees from worldly distress (Strong *EB*, sec. 5.2.2).

5.5 THE COSMIC BUDDHAS

Śākyamuni was the object of adoration even during his lifetime. Although he reproved those who were attached to his person, Buddhists of all schools have glorified his body, ascribing to it the 32 major and 80 minor marks of a superman, extolling its radiant complexion, sweet perfume, and unflagging six-colored aura.

Similarly, from the earliest years Buddhists have regarded Dharma as more than simply a doctrine. It is the constant, the real, the true, the good, the valuable, the harmonious, the normative. The nature of things, *dharmatā* (Dharmaness), is analogous to the Stoic idea of natural law: the fixity, regularity, and necessity in phenomenal occurrences. Perception of Dharma in the moral sphere is the Buddhist version of conscience. Full understanding of the Dharma is Awakening; full experience of the Dharma, nirvāṇa. Thus, Dharma should be not merely respected but also worshiped and sought as a refuge. The Buddha and the Sangha are to be revered because they "have become

Dharma." When the early sects agreed that the Buddha embodied the Dharma, it was not that they were personifying the teaching, but that in their view the Buddha actualized the Dharma, which his teaching then revealed.

From this background it should be clear that the religious fervor the Mahāyānists brought to their worship of the Cosmic Buddhas as the embodiment of the hypostatic Dharma was not entirely unprecedented in the Buddhist tradition. What was new was the cosmology: the landscape in which Awakening is to be pursued, the role of the Buddha and Dharma in relation to the creation of the cosmos, and the ground rules for negotiating one's way through it. No longer was one confined to one's own abilities or to this miserable world as the primary means and arena for the practice. Through faith in the Cosmic Buddhas, combined with a moral life, one could be reborn in an idyllic Buddha-land beyond the realm of saṃsāra, where the great Buddha in charge of the land would provide assistance in the remaining steps along the way to Awakening.

5.5.1 Multiple Bodies of the Buddha and the Buddha-Lands

From the beginning, the Buddha was held to have two types of *kāya* (body): the rūpa-kāya (physical or form-body) and the nirmāṇa-kāya (apparition-bodies) that he could conjure up through his supernormal powers. There was also the sense that he embodied the Dharma, although this concept was not reified (made into a thing) until the rise of the Mahāsanghikas, who held that the true Buddha was transcendent, as was the process of dependent co-arising, which, though not personalized, fulfilled many of the functions of a Creator in its role of giving rise to experienced phenomena. As we noted previously (see Section 4.3), these two concepts eventually fused and led to the identification of the true Buddha with the *Dharmakāya* (Dharma-body) at the same time that the concept of the true Dharma was being converted to a metaphysical absolute, the basic creative principle operative throughout the cosmos and immanent in all things. Because this doctrine also held that all conditioned phenomena were illusory, it reduced the status of the Buddha's physical body to an apparition body (Strong *EB*, sec. 5.1). Because the early texts maintained that the Buddha could create many apparition-bodies at once, it stood to reason that there should be apparition-bodies in all times and places; that benevolent omnipotence should respond to the needs of all suffering beings. Thus Buddhas must currently be elsewhere in the universe, as well as in the past and future of this world-realm.

Early Buddhist cosmology had posited only one *lokadhātu* (world system), consisting of four continents on Earth together with assorted hells below and heavens above. Later the belief arose that a universe in which a Buddha acts consists of one billion such worlds (a so-called great chiliocosm). In the 10 directions (east, southeast, south, southwest, west, northwest, north, northeast, nadir, and zenith), there are universes "as numerous as the sands of the Ganges." Some but not all of these universes are Buddha-lands, in each of which a Tathāgata lives and teaches the Dharma.

The *Buddha-kṣetra* (Buddha-lands, also Buddha-fields) differ from the heavens of the gods in that they are presided over by a Buddha so that the inhabitants can practice the Way, earn merit, and gain wisdom. Thus devotees practice to be reborn in these lands—calling upon a Buddha's name, worshiping him, expressing faith in him, and living a pure life—so that once they attain their desired Buddha-lands, their Buddhas will help them to mature further in the spiritual Paths. Although the Cosmic Buddha-lands are fully separate from saṃsāra, and residence there results in the full Awakening of the supreme Buddhas, they are very similar to the heavens of the gods in earlier Buddhism in a number of respects. The inhabitants are freed from labor, and the necessities of life come to them for the mere wishing. Sex is attenuated or entirely eliminated, as in the earlier Brahmā-worlds, and birth takes place without coitus or gestation. However, not all the Buddha-lands are the same, as the different Buddhas who preside over them made different vows, as bodhisattvas, concerning the features they would create in their Buddha-lands.

Certain features of these Mahāyāna paradises deserve comment. Their many jewels, jewel-trees, and diamond bodies indicate a low opinion of organic matter as perishable and impure. In this penchant they follow an aesthetic that first appears in the Sūtra Piṭaka (D.17). Jewels, moreover, are visionary substances, believed to possess occult properties and radiate spiritual forces. Concentrating on them induces trances fostering visions of paradise that tend to be bright, with gemlike colors and shapes.

This Mahāyāna space myth expressed a radical expansion of worldview and a corresponding change in values from the earlier Buddhist texts. The drama of salvation was no longer confined to this physical world-realm, and help from outside might be expected. Śākyamuni's followers were not spiritual orphans, for extraterrestrial friends stood always ready to protect them: not only gods such as Sakra, Brahmā, and the Four Great Kings, but also great bodhisattvas and Buddhas. This vision of endless space populated by spiritual beings corresponds to the general worldview of classical Hinduism, which was also developing at this time.

5.5.2 Śākyamuni According to the *Lotus Sūtra*

Śākyamuni remained the foremost of the Cosmic Buddhas until Tantrism transformed the Indian Buddhist pantheon. The *Lotus* ranks among the most worshiped of the Mahāyāna Sūtras not because of profound technical philosophy, of which it contains only a few fragments, but because of its assertion in graphic parables and concrete religious language that the historical Gautama is in reality an everlasting, ever-present cosmic father. As the Sūtra opens, Śākyamuni enters samādhi, the earth quakes, and a ray shoots forth from the tuft of hair between his brows, illuminating myriad Buddha-fields in the eastern direction and revealing their inhabitants, from denizens of the hells up to the Buddhas and their assemblies. This extraordinary apparition serves to establish the Buddha's stupendous power and knowledge, and to set the scale for his saving activities.

The Buddha then tells Śāriputra that only a Tathāgata knows all the dharmas as they really are. As the Dharma is exceedingly difficult to fathom, the Buddhas employ their supreme skill in good means to accommodate the doctrine to the varying capacities of living beings. Śāriputra pleads with the Buddha to reveal the True Dharma. The Buddha consents and declares: "It is for a single aim that the Tathāgata appears in the world, namely to impart to living beings the knowledge and vision of a Tathāgata." The Buddhas, furthermore, preach the Dharma by means of only One Vehicle, the *Buddha-yāna* (Buddha-vehicle). But when a Buddha appears in a degenerate epoch, among beings who are corrupt and lacking in merit, he uses the expedient device of the Three Vehicles (arhant, private-buddha, and bodhisattva). Śāriputra rejoices to hear the Buddha say that the arhants are not condemned to an inferior nirvāṇa; that they too will reach supreme, perfect Awakening. Śākyamuni then predicts that Śāriputra will become a Buddha in the distant future.

Śāriputra asks the Buddha to dispel the perplexity that the idea of the One Vehicle has occasioned among sincere Hīnayānists in the assembly. Śākyamuni responds with the parable of the burning house. A rich householder had a vast and decrepit mansion inhabited by hundreds of living beings. A fire broke out, and the man devised a stratagem to get his 20 young sons out of the house. They did not come when he called them, because they were too engrossed in their playing to notice the flames. So he told them that toy carts—bullock carts, goat carts, and deer carts—awaited them outside. The boys came out and found that there was only one kind of cart, a magnificent bullock cart.

Śāriputra agrees that the father was not guilty of telling a falsehood as his aim was to save his children. Śākyamuni says that the Buddha, being the father of the world, is not guilty of falsehood either, because he was employing *upāya* (skillful means) when he announced that there are three vehicles. Just as the rich man gave each of his sons the best of carts, so the Buddha leads all beings to the same supreme Awakening (Strong *EB*, sec. 4.1).

Śākyamuni states, "Many trillions of aeons ago, I realized supreme perfect Awakening." When a Tathāgata who so long ago reached perfect Awakening goes through a semblance of attainment, he does so in order to lead beings to maturity. Without becoming extinguished, he makes a show of it so that weak beings will not take his continuing presence for granted. When these people are convinced that the apparition of Tathāgatas is rare, they become more zealous. Śākyamuni declares that he resides forever on Mount Gṛdhrakūṭa, preaching the Dharma, and that when the unawakened imagine that this ordinary world is engulfed in flames at the end of an aeon, it is really a paradise with gardens, palaces, and aerial cars, teeming with gods and human beings.

The *Lotus Sūtra* is obviously an attempt to provide Śākyamuni with a resplendent Buddha-land in no way inferior to that of the mythic Cosmic Buddhas described in other Sūtras. However, the "this world" portrayed in the *Lotus* bears little if any resemblance to the human world; and as the Sūtra replaces the historical Buddha, Dharma, and Sangha with a mythic, supernatural version of all three, it actually devalues the human condition and the potential for Awakening here and now. The career of the historical Buddha is said to be simply a show; any comprehensible expression of the Dharma inherently inadequate; and the great human disciples as-yet-unawakened. Faith is no longer directed to a teaching that can be tested in practice. Rather, it is directed to the hope that one will have the opportunity to see the Tathāgata and hear his teaching in a transfigured realm. As with the cult of Maitreya, valid efforts at practice in this lifetime are thus limited to acts of faith, making vows, and affirmations of commitment in the hope of hearing the Dharma at the end of the aeon. Many later Mahāyāna teachers found that they had to counteract this implication of the *Lotus Sūtra*—and cults of other Cosmic Buddhas as well—as when the Japanese Zen master Hakuin (see Section 10.7) said, "This very place is the Lotus Land, and this very body is the Buddha," in order to spur his students on to the higher practice in this lifetime.

5.5.3 Akṣobhya

Akṣobhya was the earliest of the nonhistorical Cosmic Buddhas. In the *Vimalakīrti-nirdeśa* Śākyamuni says to the assembly, "There is a land named Abhirati and a Buddha named Akṣobhya. This Vimalakīrti died in that land and came to birth here." To satisfy the assembly's longing to see the land, Vimalakīrti enters samādhi, grasps Abhirati, and sets it down in this world to be seen. Afterward it returns to its proper place in the East. In the *Small Perfection of Wisdom,* Śākyamuni exerts his wonder-working power and enables his assembly to see Akṣobhya and his retinue. Neither Sūtra advocates devotion to Akṣobhya. Apparently, however, rebirth in Abhirati was sought by some people (Strong *EB*, sec. 5.4.3). It could be attained through moral acts or even through hearing Akṣobhya's name. This Buddha became moderately popular in Tantrism. In art he is represented as blue, with a *vajra* (diamond) in his right hand, his left hand in *bhūmi-sparśa-mudrā* (the earth-witness gesture), and a blue elephant for his mount. The name Akṣobhya means "immovable" or "imperturbable." Legend holds that while he was still a bodhisattva he made a vow to practice deeds without anger. The bodhisattva who does similarly will go to birth in Abhirati. Paradoxically, Akṣobhya's expressions in the systems of Unexcelled Yoga Tantras (see Section 6.3.3) are all wrathful forms of Śiva, expressing the Tantric concept that awakened forms of wrath are ultimately based on nonanger.

5.5.4 Amitābha (Amita)

Amitābha (Unlimited Light) and Amitāyus (Unlimited Life Span) are alternate names for the same Buddha. Chinese A-mi-t'o and Japanese Amida are rendered from the short form, Amita. The cult of this Buddha dates back at least to 100 C.E.

Although the origin legends of the cosmic bodhisattvas are vague and subject to conflicting versions, the Amitābha legend is specific, furnished with history-like detail, and unified. Successive translations of the *Sukhāvatī-vyūha Sūtra,* and a related surviving late Sanskrit text, reveal—in spite of significant variations—a consistent pattern of development. The later the version, the more Amitābha is glorified over Śākyamuni, and the fewer the restrictions on his power.

The spiritual development of Amita begins with a bhikṣu named Dharmākara (Mine or Treasury of Dharma), who countless aeons ago heard a sermon from the Buddha Lokeśvararāja and expressed a fervent desire to become a Buddha like him. He implored the Buddha to teach him the way to supreme perfect Awakening and the qualities of a pure Buddha-field. The Tathāgata then taught him the excellences and amenities of innumerable Buddha-lands for ten million years. Dharmākara took these good qualities, concentrated them all in one Buddha-land, and meditated on them for five aeons. Then he went to his future Buddha-land, *Sukhāvatī*, the Land of Bliss (Strong *EB*, sec. 5.4.1).

In his Buddha-land, said Dharmākara, there would be no evil destinies (hell, animals, ghosts). There would be only a nominal difference between human beings and gods. All beings born there would almost, but not quite, be arhants destined for nirvāṇa. Unless their bodhisattva vows bound them to further rebirths, they would be reborn only once. Nevertheless, their life span in Sukhāvatī would be unlimited. Evil would not be known there even by name. All beings would be able automatically to hear whatever Dharma-theme they wished, yet there would be neither teaching nor learning because all would be capable of direct cognition and would be able to recite the Dharma informed by omniscience.

The most crucial question concerning a Buddha-land is how to attain rebirth there. Dharmākara's vows provide a specific answer, although different versions of the *Sukhāvatī-vyūha Sūtra* vary somewhat. In the (fifth-century?) Chinese version adopted as orthodox by the Chinese and Japanese Pure Land sects, Amida's 18th vow states that all living beings in the 10 directions who with sincere faith desire rebirth in his land will attain it by calling this desire to mind only 10 times. Only those who have committed atrocities or slandered the True Dharma are excluded. The 19th vow states that all living beings in the 10 directions who arouse the thought of bodhi, cultivate all the virtues, and wholeheartedly vow to be reborn in Amita's land will, when they die, see Amita and a large retinue before them. The 20th vow states that if living beings in the 10 directions hear Amita's name, fix their thoughts on his land (that is, meditate on it), plant the roots of virtue, and wholeheartedly dedicate the resulting merit to rebirth there, their desire will be fulfilled.

Although the Pure Land doctrine that developed around this Sūtra can be characterized as one of salvation by faith, the actual conditions for salvation specified in these vows qualify as a doctrine of faith and works. Salvation is not affected by Amita's power alone. The candidate must also make an effort by living a virtuous life. From the point of view of earlier Buddhism, however, it is obvious that the work requirements for rebirth in this streamwinner land (see Section 2.3.2) have been considerably relaxed from what they were in the Sūtra Piṭaka. Wisdom, in particular, is conspicuous by its absence.

Having proclaimed his vows, Dharmākara practiced the bodhisattva course for a trillion years until finally, 10 aeons ago, he became the Tathāgata

Amitābha, presiding over the world-realm Sukhāvatī a trillion Buddha-fields away to the west, a realm endowed with all the virtues he had vowed that it would have.

In India, Amitābha never became as popular as Śākyamuni. He is not very frequently represented in Indian art. Chinese pilgrims in the seventh century, however, reported that the worship of Amitābha was widespread in India. In the *Lotus Sūtra* and in Tantrism, Amitābha figures as one of the Five Tathāgatas who rule the four cardinal points and the center, but there is no separate Amitābha sect in Tibet. The Far East was where the Buddha of the Western paradise became a dominant focus of reverence.

5.5.5 Vairocana

Vairocana (Shining Out) is an epithet of the sun. Originally it was simply an epithet of Śākyamuni, but in due course the name acquired separate identity as a celestial Buddha. In the Tantric set of the Five Tathāgatas, he occupies the center, which is Śākyamuni's position in the exoteric Mahāyāna *maṇḍala* (sacred circle, cosmoplan). The Chinese Hua-yen (see Section 8.5.2) view that Vairocana is the Dharma-body of Śākyamuni thus reaffirms the identity from which Vairocana was historically derived.

The *Mahāvairocana Sūtra*, a Yoga Tantra (see Section 6.3.2) composed in about the seventh century, consists of Vairocana's revelations to the Tantric equivalents of bodhisattvas. Vairocana did not become popular either in art or in cult until the seventh century, when his role as Śākyamuni's transcendental counterpart gave him preeminence in the Tantric cosmoplans and their associated rites.

Mahāvairocana (Great Resplendent One)—a form equated with the cosmos as a whole—appears both in the Hua-yen school of China and the Shingon school of Japan (see Section 10.4). Called Dainichi (Great Sun) in Japanese, he is conceived of as the "Cosmos as Buddha," whose body, speech, and mind make up the universe.

5.5.6 Bhaiṣajyaguru—The Healing Buddha (Strong *EB*, sec. 5.4.2)

The healing Buddha, Bhaiṣajyaguru (Master of Healing), or Bhaiṣajyarājā (King of Healing), appeared late in the Mahāyāna pantheon. Other bodhisattvas and Buddhas were concerned with healing also, but this Buddha's prime focus was on all aspects of the art; in Tibet he was the patron of medicine and monastic physicians. Two Sūtras were written establishing his cult: the *Bhaiṣajyaguru Sūtra*, of which a Sanskrit version exists, and the *Saptabuddha Sūtra*. Both Sūtras exist in Chinese and Tibetan translations, but in India no images of Bhaiṣajyaguru predate the *Bhaiṣajyaguru Sūtra's* transmission to China by the fourth century C.E. This suggests a central Asian origin of his cult that later spread to India to be noticed by Śāntideva (circa 650–750 C.E.) of Nalanda University.

When represented in art, Bhaiṣajyaguru sits in the lotus position; his body is either gold or the blue color of lapis lazuli, emanating blue rays, with his left hand on his lap holding a lapis bowl of medicine, and his right hand upheld, holding a medicinal plant. He benefits worshipers particularly in this world. In addition to bestowing great longevity, wealth, and position, he was also able to help kings avert disasters. The recitation of his mantra (incantation) could confer many benefits. His cult was important in east Asia as missionaries spread his promises of health, longevity, prosperity, and protection of the state. In Japan he was regarded as particularly important in averting national disasters, such as droughts and epidemics, and was even called upon to help turn back the Mongol invasions.

The cult of Bhaiṣajyaguru represents the culmination of a long-term development in the Buddhist tradition. As we have noticed throughout this book, the theme of healing has been central to Buddhism from the earliest of times. The Buddha is the supreme physician; the Dharma is his means of healing; the Sangha, his attendants. However, the only true health recognized by the Buddha in the early Sutras was the spiritual health of nirvāṇa (M.75). His monks were instructed to learn medicine so that they could treat one another's illnesses, but were forbidden to act as doctors to the laity as this would distract them from their pursuit of true health. The Vinaya records an incident in which a nun known to be an excellent healer was practicing medicine, an action that prompted the Buddha to forbid making one's livelihood in this manner. Nevertheless, the Vinaya itself, in its discussion of allowable medicines, acted somewhat as a *materia medica* that monks memorized and took with them as they spread Buddhism to lands where medicine was less advanced than in India. Evidence abounds revealing that monks of all schools have used their medical knowledge as an aid in spreading the teaching, but it was not until the Mahāyāna texts that they were actively encouraged to do so. Because of the Mahāyānist belief that nirvāṇa is immanent in saṃsāra, the boundary line between physical and spiritual health was blurred. Bodhisattvas, as physicians, were instructed to treat both corporeal and spiritual aspects of disease as part of the perfection of giving, under the rationale that disease can be an obstacle to spiritual progress.

By the beginning of the Common Era, monastic centers not only provided medical help for sick monastics and lay devotees, but also taught medicine along with other arts and sciences. In the seventh century C.E. the Chinese pilgrim Hsüan Tsang noticed that medicine was included in the curriculum of the monastic universities (see Section 6.2), and by the fourteenth century the Tibetan historian Butön noted its transmission to Tibetan monasteries, where it was flourishing under Bhaiṣajyaguru's patronage.

6

Vajrayāna and Later Indian Buddhism

6.1 SYNCRETISM AND SURVIVAL

Throughout its history in India, Buddhism interacted with the other religions in its environment, both influencing and being influenced by them. We have already seen this process at work in the development of Abhidharma philosophy and in the rise of the bodhisattva cults. Such changes always raise the question as to how much any one religion can absorb from others without being absorbed by them. Even when a religion does successfully maintain its identity, there is the question of how much it becomes altered by the process of defining and defending itself in relation to its rivals. These questions became especially acute for Buddhism in India during the latter half of the first millennium C.E. as Hinduism grew stronger in all levels of society.

The contest between Buddhism and Hinduism was conducted on two fronts: doctrine and practice. Because these two fronts were for a period almost totally separate, those who specialized in defending Buddhism against doctrinal attacks became so focused on their immediate task that they lost touch with the original therapeutic thrust of the teaching. For them, Buddhism was a philosophical position to be defended in debate against Hindu and Jain philosophers, so they reformulated many of the teachings to conform with the new criteria of logic and epistemology that formed the ground rules for the debate. Divorced from their therapeutic context, the major points of the doctrine became little more than abstract concepts. Even the Prāsangika

Mādhyamika school, which refused to defend any position, maintained that the practical expression of the Buddhist doctrine of emptiness lay in a debating stance: the use of logic to demolish the theories of others without proposing a positive theory of one's own. We might wonder how successful the debaters were in maintaining the essential features of Buddhist doctrine, but the debaters themselves were always conscious of their identity as Buddhists, and of the need to protect what they viewed as Buddhism from outside encroachments.

However, the view of Buddhism the debaters were defending became less and less related to the area of practice, its depiction of the goal more and more remote from the realm of human possibility. Thus it was of little help in defending the religion on the popular level. At the same time, because the basic concepts of the doctrine had become divorced from their original practical matrix, they could be freely reinterpreted in light of other practices, some of which might be quite alien to the original teachings. This is precisely what happened as Buddhism encountered what was perhaps the major event in the history of Indian popular religion during the first millennium C.E.: the rise of Śaivism, the traditions surrounding the god Śiva. (All dates from this point onward are common era unless otherwise noted.) Śaivism had an almost inexhaustible capacity to absorb elements in its cultural environment and convert them to its own purposes. Because it had such a strong influence on Buddhism during this period, it is worth going into some detail on the Śaivite practices that proved most influential.

Śaivism seems to have originated as a pre-Aryan, Indus Valley fertility religion (see Section 1.1), centered on a yogin god, which for a while was driven underground by the Aryan invasions but which then witnessed a resurgence after Brahmanism had been weakened by Buddhism and other śramaṇa movements. As Śaivism came to the fore, it absorbed Vedic ritual patterns, Sāṃkhya philosophy, and the cults of many local gods and goddesses. The gods became different expressions of Śiva's personality, whereas the goddesses became his consorts, although—in keeping with the Indian view that the female principle is active and the male passive—they maintained their role as sources of spiritual power. Śaivism also absorbed and developed various types of yoga (meditative practice), including *haṭha yoga*, which involved elaborate physical postures and breath control, and *kuṇḍalinī yoga*, which involved the manipulation of the subtle flow of energy through channels in the body. As the religion grew, Śiva took on the form of the Lord of the Dance, a god from whom emanated all the beings in the great dance of the cosmos, simply for the purpose of his own entertainment, and into whom all beings would eventually return. Because the cosmos was an expression of the power of Śiva's dance, whatever pleasure a person found in the cosmos was part of the pleasure experienced by Śiva himself in union with his power (which in Sanskrit is a female form). From this perspective, sensual pleasure and spiritual bliss were directly related in the vibratory hum of a blissful heart. The way to reunion with Śiva thus lay through the deliberate cultivation of heightened sensual bliss through the arts. Śaivite temples were designed in line with the latest advances in painting, sculpture, and architecture. In them, stories from the Śaivite mythical cycle were performed utilizing all the arts—music, poetry, theater, the erotic arts, and dance especially—to bring the faithful into contact with Śiva's presence by creating an intense taste of aesthetic/sensual/spiritual bliss.

In this doctrinal and physical setting there developed the most striking Śaivite rite, *deva-yoga*, a ritual form through which temple dancers, prior to their performances, would imitate the body, speech, and mind of the gods and goddesses they were to portray so as to assume their identity and thus receive direct divine inspiration during the performance. Even today, Indian classical dancers undergo a simplified version of this rite before performing and are convinced that the god or goddess actually enters into them as they perform. In addition to this aboveground form of deva-yoga, however, there were underground forms as well, most notably in the radical Śaivite Kāpālika (Skull-Bearer) sect. Initiates in this sect imitated Śiva in his most demeaned role, as a penitent for having cut off one of the heads of the god Brahmā, in hopes that through the devotion they showed by taking on this lowly form they would be rewarded with the highest yogic powers. They conducted their deva-yoga rituals in cemeteries, deliberately violating sexual and other taboos, complying with the principle of transgressive sacrality, or the deliberate inversion of social norms as a means of harnessing hidden powers in the psyche. Their yoga culminated with ritual intercourse, in which the male and female initiates would imitate Śiva and his consort in union as a means of taking on their identities and receiving their powers, which the initiates hoped to use for various ends. Female initiates, or yoginīs, enjoyed an exalted status in this cult inasmuch as they embodied the goddess—usually Kālī—who was the ultimate source of power. Although the Kāpālikas were reviled by the mainstream even within Śaivism itself, they developed an underground charisma that exerted a strong influence on the popular imagination and, in northeastern India during the seventh century C.E., even began to receive royal support.

The question for Buddhism was how to react to this new movement, inasmuch as its traditional rituals had nothing nearly so viscerally appealing to offer the public. The Hīnayāna schools seem, for the most part, to have distanced themselves from these developments. However, the four classes of Buddhist Tantras, or esoteric ritual texts, dating from the sixth century onward, show three basic ways in which Śaivite practices were absorbed by the Mahāyāna: *Kriyā* (Action) and *Caryā* (Performance) Tantras use simple ritual forms for the purpose of making merit in the classic Mahāyāna context; Yoga Tantras teach, for the most part, a nonsexual deva-yoga centered on Śākyamuni in a cosmic form called Mahāvairocana; and *Anuttarayoga* (Unexcelled Yoga) Tantras teach a sexual deva-yoga, often using symbols from the Kāpālika sect, centered in wrathful Buddhas derived from wrathful forms of Śiva, identified as a family of Buddhas higher than Śākyamuni and Mahāvairocana.

These last two sets of Tantras appear to be primarily the work of lay yoga practitioners operating outside of traditional Buddhist institutions. However, beginning in the eighth century, monastic scholars tried to reunite doctrine and practice by bringing the Yoga Tantras into the mainstream of the Buddhist university curriculum. In the tenth century, they began admitting even the Unexcelled Yoga Tantras as well, writing elaborate commentaries teaching that the yoga should be visualized rather than physically practiced, and identifying the more scandalous parts of the ritual as code symbols for standard Mādhyamika doctrines. Meditation retreats were built as adjuncts to the universities so that scholar-monks could practice their visualizations in an orthodox monastic setting. Lay practitioners, however, continued their physical practice of Unexcelled Yoga, denouncing the monastics for being bound to small-minded rules. The monastics, in turn, called the lay practitioners fools for ignoring the doctrine of karma.

Despite their differences, the lay and monastic practitioners together created a radically new development in the Buddhist tradition that took on the status of a separate vehicle, as different from the Mahāyāna as the Mahāyāna was from the Hīnayāna. The new vehicle acquired several names. Most prominent among them was *Vajrayāna*, the Adamantine Vehicle, named after *Vajradhātu* (the Adamantine Realm), the new vehicle's term for the ground of Buddhahood. In adopting the symbolism of the vajra (diamond/thunderbolt), the new vehicle was laying claim to a tradition with deep roots in Indian religion, as the vajra was the weapon wielded by the Vedic storm god Indra (see Section 1.4.2). As both a diamond and a thunderbolt, the vajra stands for two aspects of supreme power: total invincibility and unfettered spontaneity. Another term for the new vehicle was *Mantrayāna*, the Incantation Vehicle, derived from its extensive use of mantras. The new vehicle took an essentially Śaivite view of the religious life—in which sexual union is the paradigm for the highest religious state, and the coalescing of all dualities in an adamantine union of light, emptiness, and bliss is the practitioner's goal—and gave it a Buddhist expression. Scholars will probably never agree as to whether this final chapter in the development of Indian Buddhism should be viewed as a sign of creative strength, in that Buddhists were able to recast their doctrines in imaginative ways to meet the Śaivite challenge, or as a sign of weakness in their being unable to resist the passionate intensity of their rivals. Because survival is typically a matter of both appropriating from and adapting to one's environment, both interpretations probably contain their measure of truth.

6.2 BUDDHIST DIALECTICS AND THE MONASTIC UNIVERSITIES

A Pali Sutta (Sn.IV.8-9) quotes the Buddha as warning his followers against becoming involved in the public debates, descended from Vedic ritual contests, that by his time had become one of the hallmarks of Indian intellectual life. According to the Buddha, the debates served no purpose aside from fostering such mental defilements as pride and dejection. In the early years after his Parinirvāṇa, however, scholars engaged in the development of Abhidharma found it necessary to defend their views against those of their opponents, both Buddhist and non-Buddhist, in the public arena. This resulted in Abhidharma texts designed to function as handbooks for debaters, offering advice on the precise definition of terms, the proper use of negation, and other issues in dialectics (the science of logical argument). The institution of the public debate continued unabated until the destruction of the universities. After a brief hiatus, it was revived in Tibet and continues today in the Tibetan tradition. The debates played a major role in shaping the development of Buddhist thought. Nāgārjuna, for instance, presented his views in the form of answers to a debater's criticisms; Asanga and Vasubandhu, in the course of their writings, rewrote the rules for a deductive proof.

As the volume of philosophical literature grew, both in Buddhist and in non-Buddhist traditions, the training of debaters increasingly became a full-time job. Training centers were required, equipped with vast libraries and offering organized courses of instruction, and it was thus that some of the major Buddhist monasteries became the world's first universities. The one at Nalanda—home of Śāriputra, the reputed father of Abhidharma studies—seems to have been the first. Although other universities developed in various parts of India, most notably Valabhi in western India, Nalanda remained the most renowned and influential. The first records mentioning it as a center of studies date from the second century C.E. By the end of the Gupta period in the sixth century C.E., Nalanda was a major university enjoying the patronage even of Hindu monarchs. Nāgārjuna is said to have taught there in the second century, followed by Asanga in the fourth and Dignāga in the fifth.

Dignāga's main fields of interest were logic and dialectics. His works in these fields were so revolutionary that they rewrote the ground rules for debate and had a wide influence even on non-Buddhist philosophers. More important historically, however, was his contribution to epistemology, the theory of knowledge. Prior to his time, epistemology had been taught in Buddhist circles as an adjunct to logic, and logic as an adjunct to the study of the Sūtra and Abhidharma. Dignāga's writings, however, endowed epistemology with foremost importance, stating that the pursuit of true knowledge first requires familiarity with the criteria or means of knowledge. Thus the study of these criteria should come first so that the texts could be judged against them. This program, which was generally accepted, helped to universalize and secularize the curriculum at the university, making it a place where the texts of all traditions could be studied on an equal footing, subject to the overarching discipline of dialectics. Even the schools that consciously rejected Dignāga's thinking were influenced by him. In the seventh century, Dharmakīrti—who, like Dignāga, appears to have been a Sautrāntika—wrote commentaries on Dignāga's thought, defending it against critics and reworking it so skillfully that he came to eclipse Dignāga as the major authority in the field of epistemology.

After the fall of the Guptas, the Pāla dynasty (eighth–twelfth centuries C.E.) continued sponsoring the university at Nalanda, which enjoyed its heyday during its rule, becoming internationally renowned. Missionaries were trained to spread Buddhism outside of India, students came from all over the Buddhist world in search of texts and teachers, and royal patronage came from as far away as Java. The curriculum broadened to cover, in addition to Buddhism, the Vedas, grammar, linguistics, logic, philology, medicine, music, belles lettres, literary criticism, art, architecture, sculpture, astronomy, and the

Sāṃkhya system of philosophy. Scholars produced new texts as well as introductions, critiques, and commentaries on the works inherited from earlier writers, refining and synthesizing the teachings of the various schools. The Chinese pilgrim Hsüan-tsang reported that Nalanda was a vast educational complex, with lavishly decorated buildings, three multistory libraries, rigorous admissions standards, one hundred lectures a day, and a schedule of debates lasting from dawn until late at night.

Nalanda and other universities in the Pāla period played a paradoxical role in the rise of Vajrayāna and its integration with earlier Buddhist thought. The initial spread of Vajrayāna may be attributed in part to the increasing remoteness of the monks in the universities from the spiritual life of the people in general. When Dignāga wrote his masterpiece on epistemology, he dedicated it to the Buddha who, in his words, embodied the criteria of epistemology. Such a conception of the Buddha was unlikely to speak to the religious needs of the general populace, and yet it came to typify the concerns of the monastic scholars. The growing reputation of the universities also siphoned some of the best minds in Buddhism away from meditation and ordinary teaching duties. Chinese travelers report that many monastics used their university education as a stepping-stone toward social advancement, disrobing after establishing their reputations so as to pursue political careers. Famous scholars who remained monks might receive lavish honors and patronage, including gifts of land. All of this opened the door to political corruption within the university, which must have severely affected the spiritual side of university life and the public view of the Sangha as a whole.

Many causes have been cited for the growth of Vajrayāna, but one of them is surely the universities' neglect of the spiritual concerns of ordinary people. In particular, for all the sophistication of their teachings, the university scholars lacked the essential prerequisite for the continued vitality of the tradition: living exemplars who had followed their teachings to the promised goal. As a result, lay Buddhists in general, from royalty to the common populace, began to look beyond the Buddhist tradition and its elite monastic universities for guidance. The universities were at this time paralleling a general movement in Indian society toward rigid stratification and a widening gulf between the general population and the political and intellectual elites. Part of Vajrayāna's appeal was that it cut across class and caste lines—actually enfranchising the lower classes, allowing outsiders to be insiders—and could also point to living examples of the ideals it taught.

Once the Vajrayāna movement had begun to grow and receive royal support, however, the universities—realizing that their continued existence depended on pleasing the tastes of their royal patrons—were among the first to adopt it and bring it into the mainstream of the Buddhist tradition. In doing so, they were near the forefront of the movement. A glance at the list of major writings produced by scholars in this period gives the impression that the entire society had become consumed with enthusiasm for Tantrism, yet the Tibetan historian Tāranātha admits that by far the majority of Indian Buddhists throughout the Pāla period belonged to the Hīnayāna schools. The original

Tantric adepts, who had resisted social conventions from the start, denounced the influence of university scholars in their movement and devised ways of re-expressing their teachings so as not to be co-opted by the intellectual elite.

The monks at the Buddhist universities, however, were not the only elite to espouse the new movement. Members of other political and religious elites—Hindu and Jain, as well as Buddhist—also came to include Tantrism in their religious practices. One possible explanation for the seeming paradox of an anti-elite cult practice being embraced by the elites lies in social psychology. The Gupta and Pāla periods mark a rigid period in the history of the Indian caste system. When a society becomes increasingly specialized and stratified, its members on all levels find large areas of their personalities being denied expression. As a result, they begin to feel alienated not only from one another but also from themselves. A monk engaged full-time in the study of logic and epistemology—as with any other member of society, male or female, forced into a confining role—may well feel that he is neglecting important religious needs. Tantrism, which offers a fast-track approach to spirituality through the ritual harnessing of powers from the repressed parts of the psyche, would thus naturally have had an appeal.

6.3 BUDDHIST TANTRISM

Vajrayāna is often referred to as Buddhist Tantrism, after the Tantras that form its primary body of texts. However, it is important to bear in mind that not all Buddhist Tantras originated with Vajrayāna. Most of the Action and Performance Tantras (see Section 6.1) appear to have been composed for use in a typical Mahayana setting; the Buddhas and bodhisattvas they invoke come from the standard Mahāyāna pantheon, and the doctrines and concepts they espouse fit well with standard Mahāyāna thought. Only with the Yoga and Unexcelled Yoga Tantras do we enter a distinctively new phase of Buddhist thought and practice.

Because the Tantras were originally intended to be secret doctrines, requiring initiation into their mysteries, it is impossible to date their initial composition with any certainty. However, they were not the earliest Buddhist ritual or incantation texts. The Pali Canon contains texts for Buddhists to recite for protection against evil spirits and dangerous animals. Unlike the Tantras, however, these early texts do not claim that their words have the power of coercion. Most of them, such as the Metta Sutta (Sn.I.8), derive their power from the compassion in the reciter's mind; the good karma produced by thoughts of goodwill is what protects the reciter from danger. In another discourse, the Āṭānāṭiya Sutta (D.32), the deva Vaiśravaṇa (see Section 1.4.2) promises that if any practicing Buddhists are being harassed by spirits under his jurisdiction, they need only chant his mantra and he will deal with the offenders. In this case, the power comes from Vaiśravaṇa's voluntary offer to fellow Buddhists; this is the pattern followed in the ritual passages of the early Mahāyāna texts.

With the Tantras, however, the words themselves are said to have the power to coerce deities and other forces to do one's bidding. In this respect, they are closer to Brahmanical linguistic theory—according to which, sacred words are identical with Brahmā, embodying a level of being and power prior to that of the material cosmos—than they are to Buddhist linguistic theory, in which words are simply social conventions.

There is evidence that Tantras were developed and handed down orally quite early in the Buddhist tradition. The Sinhalese commentaries to the Pali Canon, whose composition ended in the second century C.E., mention secret texts passed on from teacher to student, which may or may not have included Tantric elements. The commentators were careful to recommend that only those texts compatible with the Buddha's teachings be passed on. In the early Mahāyāna, mantras (incantations) associated with Bhaiṣajyaguru and Avalokiteśvara were used for healing and for protection against enemies. The Chinese Canon contains a Sūtra composed largely of mantras translated from an Indian original in 230 C.E.

The largest extant collection of Tantric texts is contained in the Tibetan Canon (see Section 11.3.2), which follows an Indian scholastic tradition in dividing them into the four categories mentioned previously: Action, Performance, Yoga, and Unexcelled Yoga. There is little agreement as to whether the four categories represent the sequential development of Buddhist Tantrism, or if they were composed at roughly the same time by different groups presenting different approaches to the question of how to integrate Tantric and Buddhist practice. However, the four categories seem to offer a fairly logical progression in terms of practices, pantheons, and doctrines; and although history rarely operates in a smooth progression, it is convenient for purposes of explanation to present the four categories as a historical sequence.

6.3.1 Action and Performance Tantras (Strong *EB*, sec. 5.5.3)

The two categories of Action and Performance are virtually identical, although later tradition maintains that the Action Tantras were to be used as a prelude to the student's *abhiṣeka* (initiation and consecration) as a full-fledged Tantric practitioner, whereas the Performance Tantras were to be used after that event. For purposes of discussion, they may be treated together.

The rituals in these categories follow patterns common to all Tantras. Of primary importance is the guru, or teacher, who initiates the student into the details of the ritual. The student is to have absolute faith in the guru and obey all the vows and requirements the guru demands. Initiation takes place in a maṇḍala, a circle delineated by chalk, powder, or string, separating the ritual arena from the mundane world outside; in this sense, a maṇḍala is the Indian version of the power circles used in occult traditions throughout the world. In some cases, the maṇḍala is decorated with drawings and diagrams, which the initiate is told to memorize and then visualize as being imposed on the surrounding world each time he/she performs the rite. In this manner, the realm of ritual power is transferred from the small circle on the ground into the initiate's mind, and then from the mind to the entire world on which the ritual is to exert its influence.

In the course of the initiation, the student is taught the words of the mantra, some of which are standard Sanskrit or Prakrit words, others of which are *dhāraṇīs,* strings of syllables abbreviated from longer passages or strung together for psychological effect. However, the purpose of the mantra is not to convey a message as an ordinary sentence, but to provoke a spontaneous reaction in the mind of the initiate and to effect a change in the sonic substructure of reality. The student is also taught *mudrās,* or gestures—some of which involve the manipulation of ritual objects such as vajras and bells—to accompany the recitation of the mantra. Many of the mudrās are identical with the gestures of classical Indian dance, which is hardly surprising, considering that the dance and ritual have a common source.

With the visualization of the maṇḍala, the repetition of the mantra, and the performance of the mudrās, Tantric ritual demanded the total involvement of the initiate's body, speech, and mind. The effect it had on the microcosm of the initiate's being was thus said to alter the macrocosm that he/she wanted to manipulate.

Action and Performance Tantras were aimed at acquiring *siddhi* (success) that could be put to three sorts of uses: pacifying (such things as illness and dangers); fostering (prosperity and merit making through acts such as worshiping relics and building stūpas); and destroying (enemies, dangers). These three classes correspond, in order, to the three families of deities that were said to enter the maṇḍala under the coercion of the mantra: the Tathāgata family of Buddhas, the Lotus family headed by Avalokiteśvara, and the Vajra family headed by Vajrapāṇi. These families fall into a distinct hierarchy, with the Tathāgatas at top and the Vajras on the bottom, forming an interesting contrast with the Unexcelled Yoga Tantras in which all the families coalesce into one, headed by Vajrapāṇi.

The Action and Performance Tantras differ from earlier Buddhist ritual texts on two important counts, reflected in the Lotus and Vajra rites: (1) the belief that merit depends on knowing the right verbal formula to accompany the act of merit making, rather than on the quality of the intention motivating the act; and (2) the inclusion of rituals that are avowedly harmful. However, all of these Tantras are similar to early ritual texts in that they deal only with subsidiary goals. None of them claim to bring about Awakening.

6.3.2 Yoga Tantras

With the Yoga Tantras, however, we enter the realm of the true Vajrayāna, in which Awakening was to be attained not through the arduous means of the Noble Eightfold Path or the bodhisattva Path of the pāramitās, but through an empowerment ritual performed in the Great Maṇḍala of the Vajra (Adamantine) Realm. To justify this vision of the Buddhist Path, the *Sarva-tathāgata-tattva-saṃgraha* (Reality of All Buddhas Symposium Tantra) retells the story of Gautama's life, stating that at the crucial juncture of the night of his Awakening, the Buddhas of the Ten Directions, headed by Samantabhadra (see Section

5.4.4), aroused him from his concentration and conducted his mind-made body to the highest heaven. There they gave him a preliminary consecration followed by five mantras of self-consecration. Each of these mantras spontaneously gave rise to visions in his heart that he developed in stages until he was able to visualize himself as Vajrasattva, the personal aspect of the Vajra Realm, the principle underlying all Buddhahood. At that point, he requested all the Buddhas to empower him. They complied with his request, and as they entered him, he gained complete Awakening to the wisdom of the essential sameness of all Buddhas. Thus he became Mahāvairocana, The Great Resplendent One (see Section 5.5.5), the central Buddha of the Vajra Realm maṇḍala. After attaining his goal, he preached the Yoga Tantras on Mount Meru, the mythological mountain at the center of the cosmos, and then returned to the Bodhi Tree to do battle with Māra, essentially as a show for beings with inferior powers of understanding.

As this story indicates, the Yoga Tantras introduced a new account not only of the means to Awakening, but also of the nature and content of the Awakening itself. Following the pattern of the Śaivite dance rituals, Awakening is viewed as a performing art, vivified by direct access to the underlying source of all Buddhahood. Rather than the three knowledges reported in the earlier texts (see Section 1.4), the wisdom of Awakening here consists of realizing one's identity with all the Buddhas of the Vajra Realm. The actual consecration rituals dictated by the various Yoga Tantras vary from text to text, but the preceding story demonstrates the basic dynamic, a combination of coercion and supplication, in which the initiate assumes identity with the Buddhas and then asks for their empowerment to seal the identity. Once both sides have participated, the initiate gains access to the wisdom of all Buddhas and may view the identity as permanent.

The theory underlying this ritual is virtually the same as the emanation theory underlying the Śaivite practice of deva-yoga. Through the sound of the mantra, the motion of the mudrās, and the power of visualizations, one establishes a direct conduit to the unmanifest reality—here called the Vajra Realm—from which all beings come. This conduit enables one to attain identity with all other beings emanating from that element, at the same time enabling them to enter into oneself. This theory is reflected in the standard Vajra Realm maṇḍala, which postulates five families of Buddhas, all of which are emanations of Vajrasattva, headed by Mahāvairocana in the center, Akṣobhya (see Section 5.5.3) of the Vajra family in the east, Ratnaketu (Gem Headdress) of the Gem family in the south, Amitābha (see Section 5.5.4) of the Dharma/Lotus family in the west, and Amoghasiddhi (Infallible Success) of the Karma family in the north. (For a variant form of these families, see Strong *EB*, sec. 5.5.5.) Each of these Buddhas, in addition to representing aspects of Vajrasattva, also supervises specific classes of subsidiary rituals. Ratnaketu, for instance, is responsible for rituals dealing with material wealth and prosperity. From these Buddhas emanate 4 Buddha goddesses, 16 Bodhisattvas, 8 Vajra offering goddesses, and 4 Vajra door guardians, filling the maṇḍala with a symmetrical array of 37 beings in all, apparently meant to represent the 37 Wings to Awakening (see Section 2.5). From the maṇḍala, in turn, come all beings in the cosmos.

Despite their adoption of a Śaivite pattern of ritual practice, the Yoga Tantras by and large reflect a celibate Buddhist sensibility. As with the earlier Mahāyāna Sūtras, they include transformed Śaivite gods and their consorts in their maṇḍalas, but in a distinctly subservient capacity. The *Sarva-tathāgata-tattva-saṃgraha* even relates an extended story of Śiva's defeat by the Buddha, who then frees the Hindu god after placing a moon mark on the latter's forehead with his toe. Although the non-Buddhist deities in the maṇḍala are provided with consorts, the Buddhas are portrayed as celibate, accompanied by celibate Buddha-goddesses.

6.3.3 Unexcelled Yoga Tantras (Strong *EB*, secs. 5.5.2, 5.5.4)

With the fourth class of Tantras, however, we enter a different world. Unlike the earlier Tantras, which are set in a recognizably Mahāyāna locale, many of the Tantras of this class begin with a statement to the effect that, "Thus have I heard. At one time the Blessed One was reposing in the vagina of the Lady of the Vajra Realm." These Tantras, similar to the Yoga Tantras, teach deva-yoga for the sake of Awakening, but the yoga here centers on ritualized sexual union in which the innate state of intensified bliss attained during controlled orgasm is equated with the Vajra Realm.

To justify this revisioning of the Path, these Tantras followed the example of the Yoga Tantras by rewriting the story of Siddhārtha Gautama's Awakening. According to the *Caṇḍamahāroṣana Tantra,* Gautama actually attained Buddhahood while still living in his palace, engaged in ritual sexual intercourse with his wife Gopā. Afterward he followed the ascetic quest, doing battle with Māra simply for the benefit of those who would be inspired by such an example.

The theory underlying the practice of sexual yoga is that the impediments to union with the Vajra Realm are actually psychophysical *granthi* (knots) in the subtle energy channels flowing through the body. On the physical level, these knots are blocks in the energy flow that can be overcome only through the energy aroused by the great passion and bliss "churned" through skillful sexual union. Thus, in this view, the arresting of passion is a sin, for it only adds further knots to the channels. Instead, the practitioner is to use energetic passion and wrath, consciously channeled, to work through the knots caused by lesser defilements (Strong *EB*, sec. 5.5.1).

However, in addition to their physical side, these knots have their emotional and intellectual sides as well. Emotionally, they correspond to inhibitions; intellectually, to dualistic thinking. Thus the texts also advocate a psychological program for attacking them. To eradicate inhibitions, they adopt many of the symbols and practices of the Kāpālikas, whose sexual yoga embodied the principle of transgressive sacrality, or the ritual inversion of social taboos, as a way of laying claim to psychological and physical powers repressed by social convention. The *Hevajra* and *Guyhasamāja* Tantras, among others, advocate the violation of sexual, dietary, and sanitary taboos. In particular, all the major Tantras of this class advocate that the best form of sexual union for the purpose of empowerment is that with a partner from another caste, in defiance of one of the strongest Hindu social conventions. In addition, some of them violate specifically Buddhist taboos. For example, the *Guyhasamāja* recommends visualizing Buddhas and then either smashing them or verbally abusing them.

Later commentators maintained that the objectionable elements in these Tantras were not to be physically practiced, but were only to be imagined, as a way of overcoming dualistic thinking in terms of pure and impure, sacred and profane. However, a large body of evidence indicates that at least the original authors of these Tantras were writing from the experience of physical practice.

To eradicate dualistic thinking, these Tantras advocate a regimen of mental training to accompany the sexual rite. The yogin and yoginī are to stare unblinkingly into each other's eyes, as would a god and goddess, creating a sense of intersubjectivity in which the sense of "I" and "other" dissolves. The male organ—usually equated with compassion as the "means"—is to be regarded as the vajra, thus erasing the distinction between means and end. The union of the male organ with the female—symbolized as a lotus—is to be viewed as the union of compassion and wisdom; the bliss that arises from the union is to be stripped of all limiting particulars until it becomes Great Bliss, which is then understood as being identical with the emptiness of the Vajra Realm.

An important part of this antidualistic training is the playful attitude these Tantras take toward language and concepts in general (see Sections 1.4.3, 2.3.1). Scholars have frequently commented on the mixture of ungrammatical Sanskrit and local vernaculars of which these Tantras are composed, and have attributed this linguistic hodgepodge to a lack of elite education on the part of the authors. This may be a factor, but because it would have been easy for later commentators to clean up the mistakes in grammar, it is more likely that the language is intentionally unconventional. Similar to Lewis Carroll's *Jabberwocky,* the Tantras seek to tap inchoate meanings on a prelinguistic level of the mind. In addition, the terminology makes use of *sandhyābhāṣā* ("twilight" language), in which key terms are used as a code with several levels of meaning, any of which may be valid depending on the context. In some cases, symbolism is deliberately reversed. Thus the *Cakrasaṃvara Tantra* turns the basic symbolism of the rite around by equating the vajra with understanding, and the lotus with compassion. All of this is to help loosen the student's attachment to the idea that words have "right" and "wrong" meanings, or that any one interpretation can encompass reality.

This sense of playfulness is also reflected in the ease with which these Tantras mix Buddhist doctrines with Brahmanical and Śaivite doctrines of a Creator God, a Universal Self, a Great Breath (Mahāprāṇa) of which the cosmos is made, and so forth. Furthermore, their maṇḍalas mix Buddhist and Śaivite iconography so thoroughly that it is difficult to distinguish which of the two traditions is dominant. Akṣobhya, as the chief Buddha of the family of Wrath, takes the center of the maṇḍala, with Vairocana/Śākyamuni moved off to the eastern side. Akṣobhya, in turn, never appears in his own form, but instead expresses himself in personalities derived from wrathful forms of Śiva: Bhairava, Cakrasambhava, Kālacakra, Heruka, and so on. Furthermore, all the Buddhas in the maṇḍala are depicted in sexual union with their consorts. The essential message here is that all distinctions, even between Buddhist and non-Buddhist systems, are ultimately irrelevant.

Thus the language and doctrines of the Tantras are part of the student's mental training in helping to loosen attachment to dualities and conceptual precision, in preparation for the coalescing of all concepts in the moment of great bliss and emptiness at the culmination of the ritual. In short, this is a language meant to perform rather than inform, to help loosen the intellectual aspect of the knots in the students' internal energy flow. Once the energy flow is cleared of knots, one undergoes a reversal of the personality (see Section 4.3) and attains union with the Vajra Realm. From this point on, one has little need for further verbal instruction, as one's every spontaneous thought expresses wisdom; one's every spontaneous act embodies compassion.

One of the most interesting aspects of Unexcelled Yoga, from the point of view of the psychology of religion, is its use of transgressive sacrality. This principle was not only a sign of the rite's defiant countercultural status but also a source of its psychological power. It broke taboos, renounced practices that the dominant society regarded as pure and good, and in their place exalted things that society said were impure and bad. It denied distinctions that society considered meaningful, made use of a secret code to give new "twilight" or deliberately ambiguous implications to ordinary statements, and conferred significance to gestures, words, and actions that society said were meaningless or even evil. It used cemeteries, places avoided by society as ritually impure, for its ritual venues, and drew its power from elements of body, speech, and mind disavowed by social conventions. In short, the ritual claimed as its own a psychological and physical territory unclaimed and uncharted by the social sphere. In doing so, it forced the ritual participants to confront and overcome the fears that kept uncharted parts of the psyche repressed, with the aim of releasing those repressed forces and harnessing them for power and knowledge to be used in accomplishing specific ends.

Any rite that unleashes these forces is obviously dangerous. The more repressed the person, the uglier the repressed forces when they are released. This fact is reflected in the Tantras themselves, which warn that their teachings are suitable only for those whose compassion and mental control are most stable and secure. Nevertheless, despite the perils inherent in this practice, the Tantras managed to attract a determined following in search of the powers they promised to harness.

As with other religious groups in history that practiced transgressive sacrality—such as the Druids during the Christian Middle Ages in Europe—the members of the original Tantric circles formed tightly run countersocieties adopting taboos that were, if anything, even more restrictive than those they were rebelling against. In particular, the members of these circles held to two refuges that even transgressive sacrality was not allowed to touch: the guru and the yoginī goddess. The guru was to be regarded as being identical to a Primordial Buddha transcending even the five families of Buddhas; one was never to speak ill of the guru for fear of falling into hell. As for the goddess, the yoginī was to take refuge in her simply by taking on her identity. The yogin was taught, literally, to take refuge in the vagina of his partner; he was to do her every bidding, to worship her, and to never offend any woman's feelings or else he would lose all possibility of making spiritual progress in this lifetime.

Thus we have the taboos of a circle of practitioners who set themselves apart from established religious institutions and demanded total devotion from their followers, establishing their own institutions defined by what they were rebelling against. This fact is reflected in another taboo that the Tantrics developed: The initiate was not to associate with Hīnayānists on threat of losing his/her empowerment for life.

6.3.4 Lay Vajrayāna Practitioners: Siddhas and Yoginīs

From the point of view of the sociology of religion, perhaps the most striking aspect of Tantrism was the prominent role played by women, both as founders and as innovators in the movement. The earliest attested Buddhist Tantric circle was an eighth-century group of lay yogins and yoginīs led by Princess Lakṣmīnkarā of Uddiyana, in what is now the Swat Valley of northern Pakistan. According to a biography compiled in the eleventh century, Princess Lakṣmīnkarā had been promised in her youth to a prince of Sri Lanka, a common symbol for saṃsāra. Upon arriving at the island with a rich dowry, she found that her betrothed enjoyed hunting, which offended her good Buddhist instincts. Experiencing a severe mental crisis, she gave her dowry away and renounced the world by feigning insanity. Finally she escaped to a cremation ground where she meditated, clothed in ashes. There she experienced visions of Buddhas and bodhisattvas, gaining instruction from them. Ultimately she returned to Uddiyana to teach her new vision of the Buddhist path.

Her group of students, which included men and women from all castes, is credited by Tibetan tradition with composing the seven root texts of the Tantric movement. Among these texts is a short piece by Sahajayoginīcintā, a wine seller, who claimed that sensual pleasure is essentially no different from religious bliss. She thus advocated the use of the erotic arts in sexual yoga as a way of creating an experience of pleasure so intense that one's sense of a separate self dissolves and one can be mindful of nothing else.

Within a few generations, Princess Lakṣmīnkarā's students established contact with similar-minded groups, forming a network throughout India. The *Hevajra* and *Cakrasaṃvara Tantras* list places sacred to the movement, located mostly in northwestern India, but also in the south (Andhra), the northeast (Orissa, the Pāla empire), and as far away as the Srivijayan empire in Southeast Asia (see Section 7.2). Buddhist *siddhas* (accomplished, fulfilled persons who had achieved the highest spiritual success) wandered across India, living outside the regular monastic communities as itinerant yoga practitioners and teachers of their personal vision of Awakening. Success depended on the teacher's ability to identify the students' problems and understand their karmic source; manipulate them through personal, often striking interaction; and use charisma to overcome blocks that students could not surmount themselves. Thus they embodied the Vajrayāna vision of the union of wisdom and compassion.

By the late eleventh century, the center of the movement seems to have shifted to the Pāla empire. Abhayadatta, writing at that time, recorded the hagiographies of 84 of the siddhas called *The Legends of the Eighty-four Mahāsiddhas,* most of whom were natives of the northeast (Strong *EB*, sec. 5.5.7). These individuals came from all stations of life, much as in earlier Buddhist times. Among them were former kings, princes, monks, and brahmins; the wealthy and poor; the handsome, ugly, young, and aged. Many came from such despised occupations as clothes washer, rag scavenger, beggar, cowherd, weaver, cobbler, fisherman, pearl diver, rope maker, bird catcher, hunter, and smith. Some were even thieves. Those who came from higher castes were usually required to take on low-caste occupations as a way of subduing their caste pride.

Typically in these legends, the potential siddha faces a personal crisis, becoming aware of the tedium of saṃsāra. Troubled, he/she may go to a cremation ground for respite or, during a visit by a wandering mendicant-yogin or ḍākinī, request teaching. The teacher directly addresses the karmic knot causing the person's distress and sings a verse stating the appropriate counteractive. When the person responds appropriately to the song, the teacher gives initiation into a *sādhana* (Vajrayāna practice). Some students attain realization immediately, but most practice from 6 months to 12 years to erase their defilements. Their attainment is termed *mahāmudrā* (the great seal or stance). In Unexcelled Yoga, this stands for the state of innate bliss attained at the climax of the practice; in the context of these hagiographies it includes both the Awakening to the state of nonduality and the gaining of mundane psychic powers, which the initiates then use during their long careers as siddhas. They spend the rest of their lives (sometimes up to seven hundred years or more) in selfless service to untold numbers of beings. Finally, they usually are said to rise, often in bodily form and with their disciples, to the Paradise of the Ḍākinīs, a Pure Land presided over by a female Buddha. These ḍākinīs and their Paradise are a Vajrayāna innovation, but they may have their origins in pre-Aryan traditions.

An interesting study in contrasts is offered by the story of Nāropa (1016–1100), whom the Tibetan Kagyü sects (see Section 11.2.2) recognize as the source of their lineage. In their version of his life, he is a Bengali brahmin of towering intellectual gifts who becomes the abbot of Nalanda university, only to be chastised by a ḍākinī in a vision for knowing nothing of what he taught. As a result of the vision, he leaves his monastic position and finds his guru only after enduring visions that undermine such conventional attitudes as honesty, humanity, and purity. As part of his training, he suffers further acts of humiliation, including being forced to steal delicacies from a wedding feast and getting caught for the theft, for which he is subsequently beaten to within an inch of his life. These humiliations form his initiation, putting his mind in the proper state to receive his teacher's more subtle instructions. In Abhayadatta's version of the story, however, Nāropa is a simple Kashmiri woodcutter who attends to his guru for many years, receiving instruction only after having proven his full devotion to the guru by a successful theft from the wedding feast. These two versions of the story demonstrate how the content of hagiographical literature can be shaped by the purposes of the authors and the expectations of their intended audiences.

Although most of the siddha legends center on men, a closer look reveals that many of the male siddhas had female teachers or received transmissions of texts and practices innovated by women. Without the formal restrictions of monastic Buddhism, women were free to practice on their own and innovated many new forms, including female Buddhas, female yoga practices, yoginī maṇḍalas, and Vajrayānic feasts led by women for women. Only those men who knew the secret etiquette for approaching such secret female practitioners could apprentice themselves to them and join in their rituals.

In the ninth or tenth century, Saraha, Kāṇha, and Tilopa, natives of northeastern India, took the process of inversion inherent in the Tantric movement one step further by denouncing the use of Tantras in favor of completely spontaneous action. This movement is sometimes called the *Sahajayāna* (natural or spontaneous vehicle). *Sahaja* denotes the world of freedom naturally born *(ja)* with every moment *(saha),* thus indicating that every moment offers the opportunity to realize the absolute (Strong *EB*, sec. 5.5.6). Their songs, using allusive "twilight language" sung to folk tunes, couched spiritual messages in a form that spoke deeply to people on all levels of society. Recorded in the Indian literary vernacular Apabhraṃśa, these songs became very popular.

Saraha originally had been a Hindu brahmin priest, but became a Buddhist monk with a propensity to drink. Once, while he was in a drunken stupor, a bodhisattva appeared to him, directing him to seek out a low-caste female arrow maker. At their first meeting, she presented him with the image of her humble craft: making arrows that had to be perfectly straight. Using two eyes (dualistic vision), she could not straighten the shaft, but using one eye (nonduality), she could. Saraha immediately intuited her message, abandoned his monastic status, and became her disciple and companion, taking on her low caste and occupation as a way of expressing his transcendence of dualism. In one of his songs, he declared: "Here there's no beginning, no middle, no end, no saṃsāra, no nirvāṇa. In this state of supreme bliss, there's no self and no other." For him, the Awakened person was beyond good and evil, Path and attainment.

6.3.5 Mainstream Monastic Vajrayāna

The question of how these antinomian movements related to the mainstream Buddhist tradition was controversial right from their inception. Most Buddhists reportedly rejected these practices, whereas a minority found justification for them in the teachings of Mādhyamika and Yogācāra. The issue revolved around whether the earliest formulations of the Buddhist Path were to be regarded as absolute, unchanging truths. Hīnayāna schools cited the fact that the Noble Eightfold Path is a noble truth on par with the truth of the goal. Even though the Sūtra Piṭaka maintains that the spiritual impact of an action is determined by the state of mind in which it is committed, it also notes that certain actions are inherently unskillful, in that they invariably involve subtle levels of unskillful motivation. Thus the Hīnayānists rejected any means not in accord with the Path. For them, Awakening by any other means—and divorced from any reference to the Buddha's original insights concerning karma—was self-deception, and not true Awakening; thus, the Tantric taboo against associating with Hīnayānists, and the general lack of syncretism between Hīnayāna and Tantrism. The only extant Hīnayāna Tantras fit into the Action and Performance classes; none of them claim to bring about Awakening.

The Mahāyāna schools, even if they did not all embrace the new movement, did provide room in their doctrines for placing the means of the Path on a lower level of truth as compared with the absolute truth of the goal (see Section 4.2). If everything is śūnya (empty), as Mādhyamika says, and if distinctions exist only on the imaginary level, as Yogācāra claims, nothing should be disallowed as a means of realization for properly motivated and trained practitioners of Unexcelled Yoga. Vices could be used to overcome vices, because both vice and nonvice were essentially empty (Strong *EB*, sec. 5.5.1). From this point of view, the pattern of inversion and denial of distinctions could be interpreted as being analogous to the overcoming of the limits of conventional truth and the arrival at the ultimate truth of emptiness: the identification of saṃsāra with nirvāṇa; the vision of the imaginary as simply a wave on the ocean of the perfected. Given this rationale, it was only a short step to accepting the unkempt siddhas and yoginīs into the tradition. Thus was born mainstream Vajrayāna.

Before the adepts of Unexcelled Yoga could enter the mainstream, however, they had to be laundered somewhat so as not to offend monastic sensibilities. Beginning in the tenth century, monastic scholars from the great universities began writing voluminous commentaries on the Unexcelled Yoga Tantras, interpreting even their most scandalous passages in terms of traditional Buddhist doctrine, primarily Mādhyamika.

The basic assumption in adopting these texts into the mainstream was that the ritual of sexual yoga could be re-created in the imagination, arousing the male and female energies within each meditator, thus becoming a practice that even a celibate monk or nun could practice (see Section 11.5 for a detailed description of deva-yoga in a monastic setting). Ritual implements—a stylized thunderbolt and a bell—were manipulated in place of the male and female organs in the course of imagining the rite. One issue that remained unsettled was whether the imagined or the performed rite was superior. Some claimed that the imagined rite was perfectly adequate for gaining Awakening, and was actually superior in that it avoided the pitfalls inherent in the performed rite. Others maintained that the imagined rite was simply a mental exercise in preparation for the time when one would be sufficiently skilled and mature to take on a live partner. This controversy has continued throughout the Vajrayāna tradition up to the present.

Through the missionary activity of the university scholars, mainstream Vajrayāna spread outside of India. In the eighth century, three monks separately took Yoga Tantra texts to China, translating them and founding the Chen-yen school, which won favor at the court of the T'ang emperors but did not last more than a century (see Section 8.5). At the beginning of the ninth century, Kūkai introduced Chen-yen into Japan as the Shingon school. It first became popular among the nobility and has continued to the present day (see Section 10.4). In the eleventh century, the missionary Atiśa, from Nalanda's neighboring university at Vikramasila, took scholastic Tantrism to Tibet at the invitation of the Tibetan king, establishing what was to become the orthodox Buddhism of that country until this century (see Section 11.2.2). Lay Tantrism was also established in Tibet by Tibetans who sought out initiations in India and Kashmir. Scholarly Tantrism was exported, along with some lay Tantrism, throughout Southeast Asia, from Sri Lanka and Burma to Indonesia, where it found its greatest success (see Section 7.2). Scattered remnants of the school are found in Buddhist Southeast Asia even today (Strong *EB*, sec. 6.6).

Mainstream Vajrayāna was prolific in art as well. Buddhist centers of pilgrimage and learning attracted artists, together with scholars and seekers, adopting the Pāla style: elaborate, forceful, elegant, but somewhat harsh compared to the graceful strength of earlier Gupta art. Temples were patterned after maṇḍalas, utilizing all the arts so as to engage all the senses in the quest for spiritual empowerment. Architectural remains found at Khajuraho, famous for the erotic bas-reliefs on its Śaivite temples, reveal that the Buddhist temples that once stood there were only slightly subdued versions of their more exuberant Śaivite neighbors.

Much of the mainstream blossoming of Indian Vajrayāna perished in the Muslim invasions, but not before it had sent out shoots to other parts of Asia. Not only the teachings had spread—Pāla art had a long-lasting influence on the art of Tibet and Southeast Asia. In India itself, the Tantric movement went back underground, although the songs of the Sahajayāna maintained wide popularity. Hindu remnants of Tantrism survive today, especially in the northeast, in secret Tantric circles devoid of any traces of their past mainstream connections, and in the Vaiṣṇava Sahajiyā sect still extant in Bengal.

6.4 THE DISAPPEARANCE OF INDIAN BUDDHISM

Despite its attempts to meet the challenge of Hinduism, Indian Buddhism went into a slow decline beginning around the seventh century. The Chinese pilgrim Hsüan-tsang, who traveled throughout India at that time (see Section 8.5), found numerous monastic centers in the area from the Sindh east through the Gangetic Plain, but the religion was already losing ground in the south and the northwest. In the south, devotional Hinduism, spread by the Tamil minstrel saints, was coming to the fore, at the same time that Śankara was revitalizing Advaita Vedānta. Hindu temples were being built, but no new Buddhist ones. In Andhra, Hsüan-tsang found only 20 monasteries, with a total of 3,000 residents. Many monasteries were already deserted.

Far northwest of India, the Ephthalite Huns had devastated the monasteries of Gandhara in the sixth century; Hsüan-tsang found one thousand monasteries in ruins, stūpas destroyed, and Hindu temples flourishing. Buddhist institutions in Uddiyana prospered in the fifth and part of the sixth centuries, but were later devastated by natural disasters.

Muslim Turks began attacking western and northwestern India in the eighth century, destroying the great university at Valabhi (see Section 4.4). Through a long series of bitterly fought battles, they encroached further and further into Indian territory until they sacked Mathura in the eleventh century. There they were held in check for 150 years. The utter destruction caused by this Turkish warfare was something totally new to the Indians, who were more familiar with war as a chivalrous spectator sport among kings. The Turks followed a scorched-earth policy, looting and destroying thousands of temples and putting the populace to the sword. Huge numbers of refugees, lay and monastic, fled east to the Buddhist homeland in the Gangetic Plain, where the Pāla empire offered them shelter.

As we have noted, the main centers of Buddhist strength in its homeland were its great universities, which won support even from the Hindu Pāla dynasty for their role in producing educated civil servants. These high-profile institutions, however, required high maintenance. Because the local population could not support all the student-monks through alms, there was a constant need to finance the students' and professors' material needs. Evidence suggests that by the eleventh century, the Buddhist universities were in a precarious financial position. Atīśa, the great missionary to Sumatra and Tibet, for example, had to charge for his services, the money being sent to his home university. It is a matter of conjecture why the universities were placed in this position. The Pālas themselves may have been weakened financially, or they may have decided that the universities were no longer worth their support, or both. We do know that university monks were involved in politics; this may have cast an unfavorable light on their institutions. We also know that the Pālas themselves were declining politically, for the Senas seized power in 1162, and the empire fragmented into small states.

The Pālas' decline opened the way for the Muslim Turks to come sweeping though the Gangetic Plain at the end of the twelfth century. The small states were unable to put up any resistance, and the universities were left defenseless: their wealth plundered, their inhabitants massacred, their buildings and libraries put to the torch. Because the universities had been the repositories not only of Buddhist traditions but also of secular arts and sciences, their annihilation was a devastating blow to Indian culture as a whole. Indian Buddhism never recovered, although it continued to subsist in isolated pockets, such as in Andhra and Orissa until the sixteenth century, and in the Nepal Valley and eastern Bengal until the present. The Tibetan historian Tāranātha reports that Buddhist refugees also fled to Southeast Asia and Tibet. A few monks remained in the ruins of the monasteries into the next century, but repeated raids by the Turks made their position untenable.

Miraculously, the great temple at Bodhgaya survived unscathed, as did holy sites in more out-of-the-way places, such as Sanchi and Ajanta. Mostly, though, Buddhist shrines were demolished. What the Turks did not destroy, centuries of scavenging has in most cases leveled to the ground. Brick buildings were dismantled, the bricks used to build homes and line wells. Even today, bricks from the ancient monasteries, stamped with Buddhist symbols, can be found in village buildings near where the great Buddhist centers used to be.

Scholars are divided in their opinions as to why Buddhism succumbed to the Muslim invasion when it had survived previous ones, such as the Kuṣāṇa annexation of the northwest and the Hun attacks on the Gupta empire. Part of the answer lies in the nature of the invaders. The Turks, unlike the Kuṣāṇas, were not open to conversion; unlike the Huns, they settled down to rule and pursued a policy of religious suppression to boot. For them, the Buddhists were idolators; the Muslim word for idol, *but/budh,* actually derives from "Buddha." Thus, they viewed the destruction of Buddhism as a religious duty. Furthermore, their own beliefs glorified the warrior's life they led. A religion that taught peace and denounced war obviously would have no appeal for them.

Other reasons for the demise of the Indian Sangha as an institution, however, relate more to the nature of Buddhism itself during this period. The development of large established monasteries and universities had deprived the Sangha of the fluid, grassroots character that had enabled it to survive earlier social upheavals. Perhaps if its earlier forms had been maintained, the Sangha would have been less vulnerable to attack. This point is suggested by Hinduism's having survived the Muslim invasions, albeit in a truncated form. As had happened to the Buddhist universities, Hindu philosophical schools and monastic orders were wiped out, but grassroots devotionalism survived. Indian social structure during this time was essentially Hindu: a caste system revolving around the patronage of a local feudatory "king." Because the Muslims allowed the local kings to hold power in their fiefdoms as long as they paid tribute, this was one social structure that was in a position to survive. Buddhism, however, focused on the monastic Sangha, and the monastic Sangha had by then come to revolve around the universities. Without the presence of educated monks, the devotionalism of the laity could easily become assimilated into Hindu devotionalism, as the Buddha became regarded as an avatar of Viṣṇu.

Still, there remains the question of why surviving Buddhist monks were unable to persuade any of the local kings to sponsor a revival of the Sangha. Several reasons for this have been proposed: The university monks may have become so removed from the local population that they were regarded with suspicion; the remnants of the Sangha may have been so lax in their conduct that they did not inspire support; or it may be that Buddhist teachings could not provide the nationalist ideology that the local kings desired as they attempted to throw off the Muslim yoke. Because it took the Hindus from the thirteenth to the eighteenth century to unite their forces in an attempt to drive the Muslims from power, Indian society throughout this period was too unstable to support a thriving Sangha. Ultimately, the British rather than the Indians were the ones who united the country, and the return to stability did bring about modest attempts at a Buddhist revival.

The demise of the Sangha, however, did not mean that Buddhist doctrines disappeared from India without trace. We have noted how Buddhism was influenced by Hinduism during their many centuries of coexistence; influences went the other way as well. The Buddhist doctrine of harmlessness had inspired the brahmins to do the Buddhists one better by becoming vegetarians; the Buddhist ideal of the renunciate life had been incorporated into the Hindu life cycle as the fourth and final stage of life. Specific Buddhist groups had also had an effect. The Advaita Vedānta school founded by Gauḍapāda and Śankara in the sixth and seventh centuries applied Yogācāra ideas to the interpretation of Vedic texts. The Sahajayāna movement of Saraha and Kaṇha influenced the Bengali minstrel saints, including the fifteenth-century mystic Kabir, and the Bengali Bauls. In a more pervasive manner, the Buddhist notion of karma as a moral rather than a ritual force had permeated Indian thought, as had the notion of Dharma as rectitude of the mind rather than Vedic orthopraxy. The measure of how quietly pervasive these Buddhist ideas became in Indian society is indicated by what happened when the Aśokan edicts were deciphered and translated in the late nineteenth century (see Section 3.3). According to many Indians, there was nothing particularly Buddhist about Aśoka's message, for it conveyed what they regarded as the basic ideals of Indian morality as a whole. Perhaps the best symbol of the continuing Buddhist influence on Indian life is the Dharma wheel that the Indians placed in the middle of their flag on gaining independence from the British. It was the only symbol that all segments of Indian society would accept as a sign of what united them.

6.4.1 Buddhism in Nepal

The Nepal Valley contains some of the few surviving remnants of medieval Indian Buddhism. In the material sense, these remnants fall into two areas: texts and the arts. Unlike the Tibetans, the Nepalese have continued to use Sanskrit texts for their studies and rituals; thus their libraries have preserved the Sanskrit originals for many Indian Buddhist texts that were otherwise lost. In terms of art, the monastic buildings still surviving in Patan seem to be faithful replicas of the great Indian universities, whereas Nepalese painting and statuary preserve the medieval Pāla style. In the social sense, however, the picture is more complex, as the Nepalese have evolved new patterns to replace the monastic Sangha and have developed their own distinctive way of defining Buddhist religious identity.

Inscriptions reveal that Buddhist monasteries were present in the valley in the fifth century C.E.; in the seventh century, I-ching heard reports that the valley was home both to Hīnayāna and to Mahāyāna adherents. Vajrayāna later became predominant at an unknown date and absorbed all other forms of Buddhism into its fold. From the 1200s to 1768, the Hindu Malla dynasty controlled the valley and, like many preconquest Hindu dynasties in India, provided support to Buddhist institutions. Gradually, however, the economic base for the monasteries began to shrink. This dwindling economic base, together with the influence of lay Buddhist Tantric adepts, led to a process whereby the Sangha began to adopt the Hindu model of a married, hereditary priesthood. This process was already under way by the end of the fourteenth century, when King Jayasthiti Malla (r. 1382–95) established a caste system for his Buddhist subjects, in which upper-class Buddhist lay people were classified as the *u-dai* caste, and married Buddhist priests were divided into two subcastes: *vajrācārya,* descended from Tantric adepts, and *śākya-bhikṣu,* descended from married Buddhist monks. This adoption of the Hindu pattern apparently took several centuries, for as late as the seventeenth century the city of Patan boasted more than 20 celibate monasteries in its immediate vicinity.

In 1768, the Mallas were ousted by the Gurkhas, a militant Hindu clan descended from Rajasthani refugees. The Gurkhas established their own dynasty, which has lasted to the present, and set about to transform the local Newari culture. As part of this program, they withdrew support from Buddhist institutions and promoted Hinduism as an element of Nepalese political identity. This policy formally ended in 1951, when Nepal was opened to the outside world, but there are reports that it has died hard. Theravāda Buddhism has been reintroduced from Sri Lanka and Thailand, and the influx of refugees from Tibet has brought about the establishment of Tibetan monasteries in the valley. These newly imported forms of Buddhism remain a small minority, with native Nepalese Buddhism largely impervious to their influence.

As in Hindu practice, the center of Nepalese Buddhism is the act of homage. This begins in the home, to one's parents and elders, and extends beyond the home in acts of homage to priests and deities. Religion is thus less a matter of beliefs than of proper etiquette in knowing how to show respect to others on the human and celestial planes. We have already noticed how Vajrayāna absorbed elements from Śaivism, and this tendency has continued in Nepal. Buddhist and Hindu groups have each found ways of including the deities of the other in their own pantheons. Hindus regard Śākyamuni as a form of Viṣṇu, whereas Buddhists see Śiva and Viṣṇu as bodhisattvas. Forms of ritual and worship are also similar, with the care and feeding of Buddhist icons following the Hindu pattern. This means that the act of homage is somewhat noncommittal, as the same deity may be worshiped in either his/her Buddhist or Hindu identity. Some members of the priestly castes, secure in their command of ritual knowledge, declare themselves to be exclusively Hindu or Buddhist in their allegiance, but most Nepalese are loathe to define their acts of homage in such an exclusive way. They feel it wiser to stay on good terms with all the powers that be, in case they ever need to ask or negotiate with a particular power for help. As is frequently the case in matters of etiquette, they consider it poor form to be too inquisitive about the personal preferences that may lie behind another person's good behavior, or too explicit about their own.

Nepalese Hindus and Buddhists are both conscious of the Buddhists as a separate group, with their own distinct identity, but this identity is primarily a matter of caste. Buddhists observe the obligatory rights of homage traditional to their caste, but in terms of optional acts of homage they are free to offer respect to any deity they please. As we shall see in the following chapters (Sections 7.5.1, 8.7), a fluid sense of religious identity is common throughout Buddhist countries, but the Nepalese pattern of determining religious identity by birth is Hindu in origin. Buddhists assume their caste identity not only in their dealings with Hindus but also among themselves. Only members of the vajrācārya and śākya-bhikṣu castes, for instance, are allowed to live in temple compounds. Vajrācāryas form the elite, as ritual specialists and scholars, whereas the śākya-bhikṣus hold a more limited ritual role, many of the men earning their livelihood working in precious metals. Young boys from both castes are ordained for a period of four days, after which they renounce their vows and return to lay life. Vajrācāryas then undergo secret Tantric initiation as well. Vajrācāryas can give Tantric initiations to members of other Buddhist castes, but the new initiates from those castes do not then become Vajrācāryas themselves. Thus, not only is one's identity as a Buddhist a function of caste, but so is one's role within the religion. Nepalese Buddhists justify this development by saying that it was necessary for their survival in the context of a Hindu society, but there is no denying that the price of survival has been a radical departure from the earlier Buddhist attitude toward caste.

6.4.2 The Buddhist Revival

Since the latter part of the nineteenth century, when the British consolidated their hold over India and instituted a policy of religious tolerance, there have been several attempts at fostering a rebirth of Buddhism in its original home. In the 1890s, a group of Sri Lankans led by Anagarika Dharmapala (see Section 7.4.1) started the Maha Bodhi Society with the express purpose of reintroducing Buddhism to India. Although the society was able to establish centers in cities and at ancient Buddhist sites, and to petition the British Raj to give Buddhists control over the great temple at Bodhgaya, it has had little success in winning converts.

The European "discovery" of Buddhism in the nineteenth and twentieth centuries helped revive interest in the religion among India's educated classes as they were trying to recover their national heritage as part of their move toward independence. Again, this trend won no converts to the religion, although it did influence the Bengali author Rabindranath Tagore and others in their interpretation of Hinduism. It also established Buddhism as a part of the curriculum in Indian universities. Indian researchers have since contributed much original work to the field of Buddhist studies.

In 1956, Bhimrao Ramji Ambedkar, the late leader of Maharashtra's outcaste untouchables, led 600,000 of his followers into the Buddhist fold in a mass conversion. The primary motivation was political, and few of the converts knew anything of the religion they were embracing aside from its not demeaning their caste. Although India now has far more nominal Buddhists than it did prior to the conversion, the movement is not likely to spread to other castes, for it has identified Buddhism as the religion of the untouchables, which is hardly a selling point in a society that is still caste-conscious. The few native Indian temples set up in various parts of the country have followed the example of the Christian missionaries and are engaged primarily in charitable work. Standards of practice and discipline are quite low.

In 1959, Tibetan Buddhists fleeing the Chinese invasion of their homeland began to establish themselves in India, both in the north (Dharamsala) and in the south (Mysore). They have succeeded in establishing monasteries and are fighting valiantly to preserve their scholastic curriculum, but they are losing many of their young to the attractions of modern materialism. Buddhists from many other Asian countries have flocked to Buddhist pilgrimage centers in India, setting up temples representative of their cultures and bringing Buddhist devotionalism back to the land of its origin. It is doubtful, however, that any of these movements will inspire a large-scale return to Buddhism among Indians.

Fortunately for Buddhism, it was able to establish firm roots in other countries long before its demise in India, and in many of those countries it is still strong. The story of how Buddhism developed from an Indian to a world religion will be the subject of the remainder of this text.

7

Buddhism in Sri Lanka and Southeast Asia

7.1 ORTHODOXY AND SYNCRETISM, HISTORY AND STRUCTURE

As cultural areas, Sri Lanka and Southeast Asia are vastly different. What they have in common is that, beginning from the eleventh century, Buddhists in Sri Lanka have worked together with those on mainland Southeast Asia to maintain Theravāda as their dominant religious tradition. Prior to then, Theravāda had been merely one among many forms of Buddhism—including Sanskrit Hīnayāna, Mahāyāna, and Tantrism—practiced in this region along with Hinduism and indigenous animist cults. Although Theravāda is essentially a conservative tradition, its rise to prominence involved adopting many elements from the other traditions in its environment. This borrowing shaped even what eventually developed as Theravādin orthodoxy.

Buddhists in this region, however, have not been unaware of this process of syncretism, nor have they all resigned themselves to it. Those with little sense of history have tended to accept the situation and see no problem with it. Those with a historical sense have tended to reject many if not all of the syncretic elements and have tried to recover and put into practice what they view as the pure orthodox tradition. The history of Theravāda—the only element in the syncretic mix that has not lost its living history—is the story of this quest for purity.

On one level, this quest has been expressed through reforms sponsored by royal patrons, who have sent missions to foreign lands in search of Pali texts and pedigreed ordination lineages, and who have encouraged strict practice and Pali studies in the monasteries they have supported. On another level, the quest has been expressed in a return to the forest by meditators trying to rediscover the roots of their tradition in an environment similar to that in which the Buddha found the Dharma in the first place. These two expressions of the quest have nurtured each other over the centuries and together have managed to keep not only Theravāda but also the entire syncretic Buddhist tradition alive. With one small exception—the island of Bali in Indonesia—the mixture of Buddhism and Hinduism that once characterized the entire region has now survived only under the protective umbrella of Theravādin orthodoxy.

The split between historical and ahistorical attitudes has characterized not only the Buddhists in this region, but also the modern scholarship devoted to studying them. Historians' trend analyses have focused on specific events in the ups and downs over the course of time in the quest for orthodoxy. Anthropologists' structural analyses of religion as a social phenomenon have tended to focus on how orthodox and heterodox elements typically interact at a particular point in time. Recent studies paralleling the combination of present and past factors in the doctrine of dependent co-arising (see Section 1.4.3) have attempted to capture more of the tradition by combining these two approaches, but even together they cannot depict the entire tradition as it is actually practiced. There is more to the past than an intelligible narrative can contain; there is more to the present than a neat model can hope to encompass. Nevertheless, there seems to be no better way to capture at least something of the complex world of Buddhism in the region than through combining these two approaches. Thus this chapter will follow the same dual pattern, providing both a narrative account of the tradition over the centuries as it can be pieced together from chronicles and archaeological sources, and a structural model of one part of the tradition—the syncretic Buddhism of a central Thai village—at a recent cross section in time.

7.2 BUDDHISM IN "FURTHER INDIA"

A. *Southeast Asia.* A Sri Lankan narrative tradition maintains that King Aśoka in 247 B.C.E. sent missionaries to Suvannabhuma, which has been identified with the Mon country in Lower Burma (Myanmar) and central Thailand, but otherwise there is no written or archaeological evidence indicating that Buddhism was practiced in the area at that early date. Indian records dating from the first century B.C.E. indicate that Indian traders were familiar with the region, and within a short period of time the traders had begun importing Indian culture to its people. By the first century C.E., the region's first Indianized Southeast Asian states—ones whose rulers accepted Indian culture, including Brahmanical and Buddhist beliefs—appeared.

Once Brahmanism and Buddhism were established in the courts and began spreading to the populace, the religious history of the region up until the eleventh century C.E. differed little from that of India itself. Various forms of Buddhism—primarily Theravāda, Sarvāstivāda, Mahāyāna, and Vajrayāna—coexisted with Hinduism and indigenous animist beliefs. The question of which element in the mix was dominant where and at what time was largely a matter of the vagaries of royal patronage. There are only a few discernible patterns to this patronage. Buddhism tended to enjoy more consistent support in the areas closest to India—Burma, Thailand, and the Sri Vijaya empire centered on Sumatra and the Malay Peninsula—and, ironically, the largest and most enduring Buddhist monuments, Borobudur in central Java and the Bayon in Cambodia, were built in kingdoms where Buddhism was only briefly the main recipient of royal patronage.

In the late eighth century, much of Southeast Asia came under the rule of the Śailendra dynasty of central Java. Although central Javanese religion during this period was a mixture of indigenous elements, Mahāyāna, and Śaivism—with Tantrism linking the three–the Śailendras were primarily Buddhist. Their rule was brief—they had taken over from a Śaivite dynasty in central Java in 780, and their last queen married a Śaivite prince in 832—but in the period around 800, one of their rulers built at Borobudur the greatest and most glorious of all Buddhist stūpas. This is a giant maṇḍala in stone, its bas-reliefs representing the pilgrim's search for Awakening along the 10 stages of the bodhisattva's Path and perhaps the 4 levels of Tantra as well. The circumambulation path up the monument leads through walled corridors past more than two thousand reliefs depicting scenes from Śākyamuni's life, the Jātaka tales, and the *Gaṇḍavyūha Sūtra*, finally reaching a broad open summit covered with 72 small stūpas containing Buddha images surrounding a large central stūpa. The ascent is a symbolic journey through the material world, out of saṃsāra and into nirvāṇa.

While Borobudur was being built, Jayavarman, a Cambodian prince whom the Śailendras had taken hostage, returned to his homeland and proclaimed it independent, founding a Khmer empire that eventually covered much of what is now Cambodia, Laos, Thailand, and Vietnam. This empire lasted until its capital, Yasodharapura, fell to the Thais in 1431. Its greatest architectural achievement was a series of temples and mausoleums built at the capital, known today as Angkor. Jayavarman brought with him from Java the cult of the god-king (the belief that the ruler of the country was an incarnation of Śiva), and most of the Angkor complex is dedicated to this cult. Not until the last great builder of Angkor, Jayavarman VII, ascended the throne in 1181 did Buddhist elements begin to appear in the royal temples.

Jayavarman VII was a follower of the Mahāyāna cult of Avalokiteśvara and, in a Buddhist adaptation of his predecessors' beliefs, conceived of himself as a bodhisattva king, a concept that was to have a long life in

Cambodian and Thai politics. Modeling himself on the bodhisattva of compassion, he stated in his inscriptions that he was as sensitive to the sufferings of his people as if they were his own. His greatest architectural project, the Bayon, is a maze of towers covered on all sides with enormous masks of the bodhisattva—or perhaps the king himself—watching out over the populace. The bas-reliefs on the walls of the Bayon are unique in Angkorian art in that they depict the daily life of the common people and were perhaps intended as a sign of the king's compassion for his subjects. His building program, however, seems to have overextended the empire's resources, for it was left unfinished, and no new temples were added to Angkor after his reign.

B. *Sri Lanka.* Prior to Aśoka's missions to Sri Lanka in the third century B.C.E., Indo-Aryan clansmen had come to the island from the Gangetic Plain, bringing with them Brahmanical customs along with a north Indian language and political institutions. The Sinhala clan founded a royal dynasty and maintained ties with northern India. According to tradition, King Aśoka sent a group of missionaries, headed by his own son, Mahinda, from the Theravādin center at Sanchi to convert the Sinhala king, Tissa, in approximately 247 B.C.E. The king accepted the faith quickly (Strong *EB*, sec. 6.1.1), built a large monastery—the Mahāvihāra—for the monks in his capital at Anuradhapura, and provided patronage for them to spread their teachings throughout the island. Within a few years, Mahinda's sister, Sanghamittā, brought a shoot of the Bodhi Tree from Bodhgaya and founded the Sri Lankan branch of the Bhikkhuṇī Sangha.

Thus, from the beginning, the Sangha maintained close relations with the royal court, and Buddhism became the state religion. Even in the court, however, Buddhist practices were combined with Brahmanical rituals. When the general populace converted to Buddhism, they simply mixed it with their previous Brahmanical and animist beliefs and practices.

Nevertheless, a strain of purism developed, as events during the early centuries of Buddhism on the island gave the monks of the Mahāvihāra a strong sense that their tradition was both precious and very fragile. Although they maintained contact with the Buddhist homeland via Indian ports on the western coast and continually added to a body of commentarial literature brought over from India, they came to see themselves as the sole custodians of a static tradition threatened not only by non-Buddhist elements on the island but also by foreign invaders and heterodox Buddhist traditions developing in India. In the first century B.C.E., an invasion by south Indian Coḷa forces, followed by a famine, was so devastating that the canon, which was being preserved solely through oral transmission, was nearly lost. Soon after Sri Lankan forces regained control of the island, the Mahāvihāra underwent a split over a point of discipline, with the less conservative group breaking off and establishing a new monastery, the Abhayagiri Vihāra, with the support of the new king. The Mahāvihārans, feeling threatened on several fronts, sent their best scholars to a cave in central Sri Lanka to commit the canon and its commentaries to writing. Not long afterward, they regained royal patronage.

The split between the Mahāvihāra and the Abhayagiri Vihāra, which came to call itself the Dharmaruci sect, continued until the twelfth century C.E., with royal support alternating between the two. Soon after the initial split, the Dharmaruci began accepting Mahāsanghika teachings, and later became the exponent of Mahāyāna and Tantrism as these were exported from India. As for the Mahāvihārans, they continued adding to their commentaries until the second century C.E., when their fear that any new additions might obscure the original teachings inspired them to close the commentaries for good. Their reputation for conservatism spread back to the Indian mainland; by the fourth and fifth centuries C.E., mainland Buddhists reacting to the Mahāyāna movement became interested in the traditions that the Mahāvihāra had preserved. Monks from the Mahāvihāra were invited to teach on the mainland, a group of bhikkhuṇīs was invited to help establish the Bhikkhuṇī Sangha in China (see Section 8.4), and Indian monks came to Sri Lanka to study.

One of these monks, Buddhaghosa, came from the Theravādin center in Kancipuram and asked permission to translate the commentaries from Sinhala into Pali so as to make them available to an international audience. According to tradition, the elders of the Mahāvihāra asked him first to compose a treatise on Buddhist practice to test his understanding of the Dharma. The massive treatise he composed in response, the *Visuddhimagga (The Path to Purification),* so impressed them that they willingly provided him with the commentaries together with all the scribes and other assistance he might need. Eventually, he collated the various Sinhalese commentaries and prepared Pali commentaries to most of the books in the canon. They, together with *The Path to Purification,* have since come to define Theravādin orthodoxy up to the present, and in Sri Lanka and Burma are regarded as even more authoritative than the canon itself.

Buddhaghosa's works demonstrate how much even the most conservative Theravādins in his time had acquired from other elements in the prevailing Buddhist–Brahmanical milieu. For example, they contain views on the supernatural quality of the Buddha that were apparently adopted from the Mahāsanghikas. They also refer to "secret doctrines" that the elders would teach only to certain students. More importantly, they drop the canon's emphasis on whole-body breath awareness as the prime form of concentration practice (see Section 2.3.2) in favor of trance states acquired by staring at objects of various colors, a technique that plays only a peripheral role in the canon (Strong *EB*, sec. 3.5.6). They then define dhyāna in terms of these trance states, which by their own admission are virtually impossible to attain through breath awareness. This shift in the definition of what constitutes dhyāna led to the controversy, still alive in the Theravāda tradition, concerning the relationship between dhyāna and mindfulness, and the question of how necessary dhyāna is for the attainment of liberating insight.

After Buddhaghosa made the commentaries accessible to scholars in south India, Kancipuram came to eclipse the Mahāvihāra as the main center of Theravādin studies. New scholars there provided commentaries to the texts that Buddhaghosa did not live to finish, and subcommentaries to the texts he did. I-ching reports that when he visited Sri Lanka in the seventh century, the members of the Dharmaruci sect outnumbered the Mahāvihārans considerably. Wars and rebellions began to ravage the island, and some kings, made desperate by the political situation, robbed the monasteries to support their military campaigns. Eventually, in 1017, Anuradhapura fell to Coḷa forces, and in the ensuing half-century of political chaos the Bhikkhu and Bhikkhuṇī Sanghas died out.

7.3 THE THERAVĀDA CONNECTION

After the fall of Anuradhapura, a series of events in Burma and Sri Lanka set the stage for Theravāda to become the predominant form of Buddhism in these areas. In the middle part of the eleventh century, King Aniruddha (Anawrahta) (r. 1040–77) had brought most of present-day Burma, together with Nanchao in southern China, under the control of his kingdom centered in Pagan. With his base of power expanded, he embarked Pagan on a program of temple building that over the course of the next two centuries made it one of the architectural glories of Southeast Asia. He is credited with bringing the Pali Canon to Pagan from Thaton in Lower Burma and with converting Burma to Theravāda, but archaeological evidence indicates that whatever it was he brought from Thaton, it was not pure Theravāda. Still, Theravāda must have been a conspicuous part of the religious scene in Pagan at this time, for in 1065 King Aniruddha received a request from King Vijayabahu I of Sri Lanka for help in reinstating a proper Theravādin ordination line on that island, and Pagan had the monks to send him.

King Vijayabahu had just succeeded, with Pagan's help, in driving the Coḷa forces from Sri Lanka and was in the process of establishing a new capital, not at Anuradhapura, but further inland at Polonnaruwa. Part of his program was to build a new home for the Mahāvihāra sect, but as there were not enough monks left on the island to conduct ordinations, he had to send abroad for new monks to reinstate a proper ordination line. The main Theravādin center of the time was the Coḷa port of Kancipuram, but for obvious reasons King Vijayabahu was not about to send an embassy to the Coḷas asking for monks, so he ended up sending the embassy to his allies in Pagan instead. This is the first recorded instance of Sri Lanka switching its religious focus away from India and to mainland Southeast Asia, and it was to establish a precedent that served both sides of the new connection well in the following centuries, when India began exporting Islam instead of Buddhism and Brahmanism.

King Aniruddha complied with the Sri Lankan request by sending a contingent of monks together with Pali texts, and this opened a line of communication between the two kingdoms—involving not only religious texts, but also artistic and architectural styles—that was to last on and off for two centuries. The connection strengthened the Theravāda tradition in both countries. Ironically, although Sri Lanka was originally on the receiving end of the help, it came to dominate the exchange of texts. Elements of Sri Lankan history and mythology, together with the Sri Lankan recension of the Pali Canon, came more and more to dominate the murals in Pagan.

Sri Lankan dominance further increased under the reign of King Parākramabāhu I (1153–86). By his time, remnants of the Dharmaruci sect had surfaced in the ordination lineage founded at the time of King Vijayabahu and had begun another split. Taking as his adviser a Venerable Mahākassapa—an elder dwelling in a forest monastery outside of Polonnaruwa—and consciously following King Aśoka's example, King Parākramabāhu forcibly united all the monks in Sri Lanka into the Mahāvihāra sect. Recalcitrant Mahāyānists were persuaded to change their views, voluntarily disrobe, or be forcibly expelled from the monkhood. All remaining monks were subjected to a stringent code of conduct, based on the Pali Vinaya, but with a few interesting modifications (Strong *EB*, sec. 6.4).

These developments were interrupted in the early thirteenth century when a foreign invasion destroyed Polonnaruwa, but they resumed under the rule of Parākramabāhu II, who took the throne in 1236, again reviving the Theravādin ordination line—this time by importing monks from Kancipuram, which was the last time a "Further Indian" state obtained help from India in Buddhist matters. He also established a system for governing the Bhikkhu Sangha, divided into village dwellers and forest dwellers, that was to provide the norm for monastic governance in Southeast Asia up to the early twentieth century.

The thirteenth century also saw the beginning of Pagan's political decline, which was accelerated when Mongol forces looted the capital in 1287. By the beginning of the following century, a Mon kingdom in Lower Burma had split away, and by the middle of the century, Pagan was no longer an important power. Nevertheless, the connection between Sri Lanka and Burma remained, and the events of the eleventh to thirteenth centuries—the forging of this connection concurrent with the demise of Buddhism in India—shaped perceptions in Southeast Asia in a way that influenced events up to the recent past: (1) The connection established Sri Lanka as a prime center of Theravādin orthodoxy and Pali scholarship, so the destruction of the Buddhist homeland in northern India was less damaging for Southeast Asian Buddhists than it otherwise might have been; (2) the connection kept the traditions surrounding the Pali Canon alive, so the canon and its commentaries became prime sources of inspiration, not only for the religious life of the area, but also for such aspects of secular culture as law and popular literature; and (3) in tying the example of King Aśoka firmly to the furtherance of Pali studies and the maintenance of orthodox Theravādin ordination lines, the connection created a model that rulers in Burma, Sri Lanka, and Thailand (which joined the connection in the fourteenth century after winning independence from the Khmers) followed up through the twentieth century. Kings in these countries who founded new dynasties or expanded their empires often came to see the reestablishment of Theravādin orthodoxy in their kingdoms as one of their means of making personal merit and stabilizing their political achievements. This perception was reinforced by the cautionary tale that many of them read in the fall of the great Indian universities after the rise of Tantrism, the moral of the tale being that dominant Tantrism, with its deprecation of social convention, leads to political disaster. Whatever the truth of this perception, it spurred the ruling elite to take a serious interest in the state of Buddhist practice in their kingdoms. This interest was a major factor in ensuring that enclaves of Buddhism survived in the face of mounting Islamic pressure throughout the medieval period.

In the early fourteenth century, a forest-based version of the ordination line established by Parākramabāhu II was welcomed into Lower Burma by a Mon king, and into Thailand by the kings of Sukhothai and Chieng Mai, whose countries had recently gained their independence from the Khmers. Sukhothai abandoned Khmer architectural styles in favor of the style developed jointly by Pagan and Polonnaruwa, and quickly went beyond imitation to become a major center of Buddhist art. Its bronze Buddha images in particular are among the most graceful ever produced. Theravāda also spread to Laos, where it quickly became the state religion.

In the fifteenth century, another forest-based Sri Lankan line was established in Ayudhaya (by then the new capital of central Thailand) and, at the invitation of King Tilokarāja, in Chieng Mai, where it reformed the now-degenerate remnants of the previous century's Sri Lankan reform movement. In the latter part of the same century, King Dhammazedi of Pegu (Burma) requested a new ordination line from Sri Lanka that he used to reform the Burmese Sangha. At about this time, Theravāda was also brought to the Dai tribes in southern Yunnan. Southern Vietnam, however, came under the control of the Chinese-dominated court from the North, which brought the entire country into the sphere of Chinese Mahāyāna. Thus from this point on, the religious history of Vietnam properly belongs with that of China (see Section 9.9), although a few pockets of Theravāda still exist near Cambodia.

In the mid-eighteenth century, tables were turned when—after the complete degeneracy of the Sri Lankan Sangha—King Kīrti Śrī Rājasinha obtained help from the Thai court at Ayudhaya, sent him Pali texts and reinstated a proper ordination line in his kingdom. Later in the same century the Burmese destroyed Ayudhaya, burning its libraries and even melting its Buddha images down for their gold. When King Rāma I finally established a new capital at Bangkok, he began an active campaign to destroy all remnants of Tantric practices and beliefs—which he blamed for the fall of Ayudhaya—and sent emissaries to Sri Lanka for reliable editions of the Pali Canon. His grandson, Rāma IV, instituted a reform movement in the Thai Sangha by sponsoring a spread of the ordination line King Dhammazedi of Pegu had brought from Sri Lanka four centuries earlier.

Modern scholarship has revealed that the chroniclers of these reform movements tended to exaggerate the purity and success of the reforms. For example, in terms of purity, King Parākramabāhu I's edict on the cleansing of the Sangha contains a number of rules that are not in line with the Pali Canon, including one allowing the chanting of magical formulae for the sake of others, a practice the canon specifically forbids (Strong *EB*, sec. 6.5.3). Rāma IV, during his 20-plus years as a monk, was an avid student of astrology, an activity also forbidden by the canon. Pali dhāraṇīs and visualization chants, evidently written by Pali scholars to compete with Sanskrit Tantric dhāraṇīs in the fourteenth and fifteenth centuries, are still widely memorized and chanted throughout Theravādin countries today, a sign that the reformers were not above taking on the methods of their competitors in an effort to win converts.

As for their success, there is ample evidence that the reforms existed as little more than a veneer on top of the syncretic mix of popular beliefs that had been established before the eleventh century. For example, European travelers to Ayudhaya in the seventeenth century left behind reports disclosing that the old Cambodian notion of god-king dominated the court, and that Tantric visualization exercises dominated the practice of meditation in the monasteries. Modern-day anthropologists have discovered Tantric and animistic practices not only in the rural areas of Theravādin countries but also in the modernizing cities.

These findings, however, should not be allowed to obscure the fact that this consistent pattern of Theravādin reforms for nine centuries succeeded in keeping the traditions of Pali scholarship alive and in establishing Theravādin beliefs as the orthodoxy in Sri Lanka, Burma, Thailand, and other areas in their sphere of influence. Theravāda thus remained the standard to which other elements in the syncretic mix of Southeast Asia Buddhism had to either bend or pay lip service, or else go underground (sometimes literally— see Strong *EB*, sec. 6.6). This Theravādin standard created a sense of cultural unity and continuity in these countries that outlasted the rise and fall of many political dynasties and may in part explain why Buddhists in these kingdoms were the only ones in the Indianized states of the region able to resist the Islamic influences emanating from India through most of this period (unlike Buddhists in Malaysia and Indonesia, who did not join the Theravāda connection).

Thus it is difficult to disagree with the kings who felt that, in fostering what they viewed as Theravādin orthodoxy within their borders, they were furthering both the religion and the stability of their societies, and quite simply keeping Buddhism—whether pure or impure—alive.

7.4 THE COLONIAL PERIOD

Given that the survival of this Theravāda-dominated syncretism depended to a large extent on royal patronage, it should come as no surprise that the colonial period (sixteenth century through to the twentieth century) had an enormous impact on the status of Buddhism in this region. Even in Thailand, the only country in the region that did not become a European colony, the political situation strongly affected the government's religious policy. Throughout the area, the spread of Western education and medicine deprived city and village monks of their traditional roles as teachers and doctors, reducing them to a social role composed of ritual functions based on a worldview that westerners, and Christian missionaries in particular, began attacking as ignorant and superstitious.

7.4.1 Sri Lanka

Of the three focal countries under discussion, Sri Lanka suffered most from the colonial period. The Portuguese (1505–1658) were the first Europeans to take power, seizing the lowlands, destroying monasteries, persecuting Buddhists, and forcibly converting them to Catholicism. Under this onslaught, the Sinhala kings withdrew to Kandy in the mountains, where they ruled from 1592 until 1815, supporting Buddhism insofar as their circumstances and resources would allow. When the Dutch and later the British replaced the Portuguese as the dominant powers in the lowlands, their religious policy was somewhat more benign, but the schools and printing presses that the Protestant missionaries established under their rule mounted an active campaign to disparage Buddhism as the superstitious faith of ignorant masses. After the British took over the entire island in 1815, the level of scholarship and practice in the Sri Lankan Sangha—now deprived of government support—steadily degenerated. Stripped of their traditional role as teachers, their medical knowledge discredited, monks found their social role increasingly curtailed.

Finally, in the 1860s, Mohottiwatte Guṇānanda, a Buddhist novice who had received his education in Christian schools, responded to the Christian attack by wandering throughout the country, engaging Christian missionaries in open debates. His campaign climaxed with a week-long debate in 1873 at which he was declared the winner. As a result, Guṇānanda's cause attracted large-scale support not only from fellow Sri Lankans, but also from Helena Blavatsky and Henry Steel Olcott, founders of the Theosophical Society. Blavatsky and Olcott came to Sri Lanka from America, declared themselves Buddhists, and campaigned to free Sri Lankan Buddhism both from the oppression of the colonial Christian regime and from the syncretic spirit cults that had been a part of the Buddhist tradition from its earliest days on the island.

The Theosophists encouraged Sri Lankan lay people to play an active role in the revival of Buddhism, giving rise to what has been called Protestant Buddhism, both in the sense that it was a protest against Christianity and in the sense that it adopted many of the techniques and traditions of the Christian missionaries. As was the case with Protestant Christianity, Protestant Buddhism was spearheaded by educated lay people who took over the role of religious teacher from the monks and tried to strip away from the tradition any elements that had no basis in the early texts. As in any confrontation, Protestant Buddhists—led by a Sri Lankan protégé of Olcott and Blavatsky, Anagarika Dharmapala (Strong *EB*, sec. 9.1)—tended to define themselves in terms of the enemy. On the one hand, they stressed the scientific, rationalist side of Buddhism to counteract the charge that the religion was superstitious; on the other hand, they defined Buddhist doctrines as repudiations of Christian doctrines. In their eyes, for instance, the not-self teaching (see Section 2.3.1) was a metaphysical doctrine that denied the Christian concept of soul.

In some ways, Protestant Buddhism was simply the means by which lay organizations took over the old role of the Theravādin kings in trying to support the return of Buddhism to its original tenets. However, because monks were now no longer doctors and teachers, the movement had to expand the concept of Buddhist revival not only to cover the reform of the monastic Sangha, but also to deal directly with the education and uplifting of the Buddhist laity in general. This expansion provided a model for Sri Lankan Buddhist movements throughout the twentieth century.

Because it was directed against European culture, the Buddhist cause became the rallying point for the nationalist, anticolonial cause as well. This had the effect of politicizing not only the lay Buddhist organizations but also the monastic Sangha. By the time independence was finally won after World War II, the monks had become so thoroughly involved in political activities that one faction actually planned and executed a political assassination in the early years of independence (Strong *EB*, sec. 6.8.3). This act sent a shock through the country just as it was looking to Buddhism as a guide for the definition of national identity after more than four centuries of European rule.

7.4.2 Burma

The Burmese Sangha fared somewhat better than the Sri Lankan Sangha under British rule (1886–1948), perhaps because the British had learned from their mistakes in Sri Lanka, perhaps simply because colonial rule was shorter here. Although the British refused to take up the king's role as watchdog of the Sangha, they arranged for the monks to elect their own ecclesiastical leaders and allowed ecclesiastical examinations to be given on a regular basis. As a result, Pali studies—including the Burmese specialty, the Abhidhamma analysis of mind-states—continued unabated. However, the lack of any outside authority taking an interest in the state of the practice led to a deterioration in the discipline within the monasteries.

Despite its rather benign religious policy, British rule had the effect of politicizing the Burmese Sangha, as it had the Sri Lankan. Unlike Sri Lanka, Burma had a tradition of easily obtained temporary ordination. When the British banned political gatherings, many nationalists took advantage of the opportunity to ordain and preach their political ideas to the laity who would gather at the monasteries for religious purposes. These politico-monks played a prominent part in the early days of the independence movement, later faded into the background, and then reemerged as an ecclesiastical lobby after independence was won following World War II.

7.4.3 Thailand

As mentioned previously, Thailand did not come under colonial rule, although this is not to say that the survival of the Thai monarchy during the colonial period was a foregone conclusion. With pressure from the British in the west and south, and from the French in the north and east, Thai monarchs had to follow a skillful campaign of external diplomacy and internal reform to remain in power. Religious reform was an important part of this campaign.

King Rāma IV (r. 1851–68) had been ordained as a monk for nearly 30 years before his ascent to the throne, and during that time had begun his own personal reform from within the Thai Sangha. The reform was called the Dhammayut (In Accordance with the Dhamma) movement, and entailed an unusual combination of strict adherence to the Vinaya and a more rationalist, critical attitude toward the Pali Suttas, Abhidhamma, and commentarial literature in particular. It is difficult to ascertain whether Rāma IV's historical perspective on the relative authority of the commentaries resulted from his contact with westerners—he was an avid fan of Western science—or from a more traditional Thai skepticism toward the commentaries, which were primarily a Sri Lankan and Burmese enterprise. But at any rate, his view set the tone for Thai Pali studies up to the present time.

The reign of King Rāma V (r. 1868–1910) was marked by a drive for centralization that weakened the Sangha in some respects but strengthened it in others. On the one hand, a secular educational system was established, taking the traditional role of teacher from the monks and placing it in the hands of lay teachers who received their orders from the central government. Thus, even though the Thais, unlike the Sri Lankans and Burmese, were not saddled with a Christian educational system, Thai monks were stripped of one of their most important social roles. When Western medicine began its spread through Thailand in the latter part of the 1800s, monks were deprived of yet another important social role, which began to make them seem superfluous in the eyes of many educated Thais.

On the other hand, Rāma V, together with his half-brother, the Prince-Patriarch Vajirañāṇa, succeeded in creating a national organization for the Thai Sangha, uniting all the various regional groupings except one—ironically, their father's Dhammayut movement—into a single sect, called the Mahānikāya (Great Sect). The Dhammayut was formally declared a separate sect, although both sects were placed under a single ecclesiastical authority. The Prince-Patriarch wrote a series of new textbooks, reflecting a rationalist approach to the Dharma and the legends surrounding the Buddha. These textbooks became the basis for nationally administered ecclesiastical exams that were meant not only to standardize knowledge of the Dharma throughout the country, but also to form the prerequisite for advancement through the system of ecclesiastical rank instituted by the government.

These reforms had their onerous side as well. Ancient, noncanonical texts from outlying parts of the country were brought into Bangkok for evaluation. If they were found to conflict with the new curriculum, they were burned, and sets of the new textbooks were sent back as replacements to the monasteries from which they had been brought. An important rule in the Vinaya was changed to the effect that monks were forbidden to hold ordinations unless authorized by the central authorities. Monks from outlying areas who posed a potential political threat to central power were brought into Bangkok for questioning and sometimes placed under household arrest (Strong *EB*, sec. 6.9).

On the whole, however, the reforms succeeded in raising the general level of practice and study among the majority of monks, in managing to keep Buddhism respectable in the eyes of the more educated members of the society, and in countering the charges made by Christian missionaries that Buddhism was a religion of the ignorant and superstitious. At the same time, the central government's newfound strength enabled it to keep the Thai Sangha from becoming politicized like the Sanghas in Sri Lanka and Burma. Thus, the reforms followed the traditional pattern of the Theravāda connection whereby kings kept their societies together by making efforts to standardize the study and practice of the religion. Still, the reforms were unable to provide the village and city monks with new social roles to replace the ones they had lost to Western education and technology. In this respect the Thai Sangha was placed in the same quandary as its brethren in Sri Lanka and Burma.

7.5 THE POSTCOLONIAL PERIOD

In the heady days following independence after World War II, lay organizations in Sri Lanka and Burma began a conscious policy of sponsoring Buddhism, following with the traditional pattern of the Theravādin connection. In Burma, the most active organization in this regard was the government. From 1954–56, the Burmese government sponsored a Sixth Buddhist Council, inviting religious leaders from all the Theravādin countries to reestablish contact and reedit their texts. Prior to that, the prime minister of Burma, U Nu, founded a government-sponsored meditation center in Rangoon and persuaded Mahasi Sayadaw—a scholar/meditating monk from Mandalay who traced his meditation heritage back two generations to a monk living in a cave in Upper Burma—to become the center's chief teacher. Mahasi's method of meditation equated mindfulness with a precise noting of fleeting mental and physical events, pursued relentlessly until it produced certain physiological and psychological reactions that were identified with the stages of insight knowledge as set out in *The Path of Purification*. U Nu's plan was to make the center the starting point for a reform of the entire Burmese Sangha, but he fell from power before he could achieve his aim. Still, the center spawned many offshoots not only in Burma, but also in Sri Lanka, Thailand, Malaysia, and the West, making the Mahasi method one of the more prominent meditation methods in present-day Theravāda. U Ba Khin, Burma's accountant general in its first decade of independence, also established his own personal meditation center in Rangoon, with himself as teacher, and his method of practice has spawned centers abroad as well. The military junta that replaced U Nu originally espoused a purely secular ideology, but in more recent years it has turned to advertising its support for the Sangha as a way of shoring up its crumbling popularity.

As for Sri Lanka, the government established a World Buddhist Fellowship in 1950 and began sponsoring an Encyclopedia of Buddhism, an ongoing project that has won international respect for its high level of scholarship. Monks were sent to study meditation at the Mahasi center in Burma in order to revive the almost moribund state of meditation on the island. The most active role in the postcolonial Buddhist revival on the island, however, has been played by nongovernmental lay organizations. These include the Sarvodaya Shramadāna (Donation of Labor for the Uplift of the Masses) movement, founded in 1958, which has been attempting to bring Buddhist ideals to bear on the material, social, and spiritual development of the Sri Lankan poor; the numerous lay meditation centers scattered throughout the island; and the Buddhist Publication Society, founded in 1958 for the dissemination of Buddhist literature in English and Sinhala, which has since established a membership throughout the world. Unfortunately, the attempts to build a national Sri Lankan identity around Buddhism have exacerbated relations between the Sinhala Buddhist majority and the Tamil Hindu/Islamic minority, resulting in civil war.

The most important factors determining the postwar fortunes of Buddhism in Sri Lanka and Southeast Asia, however, were forces beyond the control of any one government or organization: overpopulation, industrialization, and urbanization. These had the effect of rendering popular Buddhism, with its strong ties to the needs of the rural agrarian class, increasingly irrelevant to an increasing proportion of the populace. Even more radical social changes came with the cold war. Communist takeovers in Laos and Cambodia destroyed organized religion in those countries, but in a strange spin-off of geopolitics, the cold war resulted in a windfall of knowledge concerning Buddhist syncretism in this area, especially with regard to Buddhism in rural Thailand.

American military and political advisers were concerned with stabilizing Thai society in an effort to keep the country from falling to the communists, and the realization came that the most unstable societies in Asia were those where Christian missionaries had been most successful in winning converts. As a result, anthropologists received government grants to study the role of Buddhism in Thai society in hopes that knowledge of Thai peasant beliefs and of the monks' role would assist in using the monks to mold public opinion. It is difficult to gauge what impact these studies played in the conduct of the cold war. Still, the anthropologists were working in the interests of science and their professional reputations, and their studies have left us with a remarkably detailed picture of Theravādin Buddhist syncretism and its social role at a unique point in history.

One of the anthropologists' most important discoveries was that the traditional distinction between village-dwelling and forest-dwelling monks is as valid as ever. Thus, in the following sections, which present a short summary of some anthropological findings concerning Thai Buddhism, we will divide the discussion into two parts, the first on domesticated Buddhism, and the second on Buddhism in the forest. Bear in mind that the situation in Sri Lanka and Burma, although differing in details, follows the same general patterns.

7.5.1 Domesticated (Popular) Buddhism

In the symbolism of the Pali Canon, leaving saṃsāra for the freedom of nirvāṇa is likened to the act of leaving home for the freedom of the outside world. Domesticated Buddhism earns its name not only because it is located in the villages, but also because it is not yet ready to leave home. It aims at nirvāṇa by a circuitous route. Its main concern is with proximate ends (better conditions in this lifetime, a more fortunate rebirth), the goal of nirvāṇa being put off to a distant future lifetime after one has tasted the pleasures that good karma has to offer in this world and the next.

Although the Buddha's main concern was that his listeners attain the bliss of nirvāṇa as quickly as possible, he recognized that not all of them were ready to commit themselves immediately to the goal. Thus he offered advice for those who are more concerned with using the doctrine of karma to earn the *puñña* (Pali for merit) that will entitle them to a more pleasurable journey through saṃsāra than with attaining nirvāṇa. As noted in Section 3.4.4, the main means of acquiring merit are generosity, virtue, and meditation; these three categories shape the practice of popular Buddhism, both for monks and laity, on all levels of Thai society. Here we will take as our example Buddhism as practiced in a typical central Thai peasant community to show how the domesticated Buddhism of a village *wat,* or temple/monastery, interacts with the other elements in the syncretic mix of Thai popular Buddhism in the quest for merit.

The wat serves as the primary institution for facilitating the making of merit. For the typical Thai peasant, a community is not civilized, an area is not settled, until a wat has been built and monks have taken up residence. The translation chosen for the word *wat*—temple/monastery—provides an idea of the dual function the institution plays. It is both a ritual arena for merit-making ceremonies and a place where monks may devote themselves to the meritorious activities of following the monastic code, studying the Buddha's teachings, and meditating as much as the circumstances of the village location will allow. Thais themselves recognize the dual function of the wat by dividing it into two areas, the *Buddhavāsa,* or dwelling of the Buddha, and the *Sanghavāsa,* or dwelling of the community of monks. In wealthier wats the two areas are clearly defined, sometimes separated by walls; in poorer wats they are not so clearly separated, but the concepts still apply to a more intuitively felt sense of sacred space and dwelling space.

The Buddhavāsa contains the main meeting hall of the wat, which invariably houses a Buddha image and the altars devoted to it. Other elements may include a library housing old texts, and a *chedi* (cetiya), or stūpa, which ideally will enshrine a relic of the Buddha or, failing that, copies of the Pali Canon together with consecrated objects. The Buddhavāsa is the ritual arena of the wat, and the central ritual arena of the village as a whole. It is here that villagers gather to participate in communal merit-making ceremonies, such as making donations, taking the precepts, and listening to the Dharma.

Because monks play a crucial role in these communal merit-making ceremonies, the Sanghavāsa is a necessary adjunct to the Buddhavāsa. The moral purity the monks gain by observing the monastic code makes them the ideal recipients of the gifts of the laity. Their celibate lifestyle frees them to devote their time to studying the Dharma and other subjects that the laity have little time to pursue on their own. Thus the monks function both as the repository of merit that the laity can tap into by giving the monks support, and as the custodians of the knowledge valued in the smooth functioning of the community. In this respect, the monks form a ritual and, relatively speaking, literate elite, although it should be remembered that monkhood is open to males regardless of social background, and most of the monks in a given village monastery are close relatives of the villagers. As noted previously, the past century has seen the monks' role as the custodians of knowledge limited to a certain extent, but they are still the prime repository of many forms of traditional knowledge not taught in the government schools. They are also the primary counselors for problems on the personal, family, and communal levels.

Despite its avowed purpose, the Sanghavāsa of a village wat is not the ideal place for a monk to practice the teaching. The wat functions as the social center of the village, and thus there is plenty of activity to distract the monks from their meditation. Also, the observance of the Vinaya rules may not be especially strict (Strong *EB*, sec. 6.8.1). This laxness naturally affects the strength of the merit that the monks are developing and into which the villagers hope to tap. Still, except for major lapses, villagers rarely take issue with the monks over the level of their practice, both because the monks are their own relatives and because they fear the demerit that is said to come from criticizing monks. Those villagers who are dissatisfied with the amount of merit their monks are producing will simply go to another nearby village wat or to a forest wat where the level of practice is stronger and offers better returns on their investment. This last statement, although it may sound crass, accurately reflects how the Thais themselves describe their motivation.

A third element in the wat—which, in legal terms, makes it a wat—is the *sīmā* (sacred boundary) containing the ordination hall. The sīmā is considered so sacred that no political authority, not even the king, has jurisdiction over it. If a criminal takes refuge in the sīmā, the police have to ask permission of the wat's abbot before they can enter the area to catch him. In wats that make a clear delineation between the Buddhavāsa and Sanghavāsa, there is some disagreement over which area the sīmā belongs to, but actually it belongs to both. Being the most sacred spot in the wat, it is where their functions merge on the highest level. The ordination hall is where the monks meet to conduct their communal business, such as the fortnightly recitation of the Pāṭimokkha, yet it is also where very important merit-making rituals are held, such as Buddha-image consecrations and—the most important merit-making ritual, in which the dual functions of the entire wat as ritual center and monastic dwelling unite—the ordination ceremony through which a member of the community, with the support of his relatives and friends, offers himself up to become a monk to further his own pursuit of merit and to aid the community in theirs.

The high value placed on the monks as a repository of merit can be best understood by making a structural model of the Thai peasant's view of the forces working on his or her life. On the first level are the empirical forces: the peasant's position in society, the weather's influence over the success of the crops, and the cycle of life itself—a process of birth, aging, illness, and death. Because one is virtually powerless against these forces on the empirical level, one must tap into the power of the invisible forces that have control over them.

The invisible forces begin with the spirits believed to inhabit the world, among them the deities guarding particular locations such as one's house or fields, wandering ghosts of the newly dead, ancestor spirits, fertility goddesses, and others. According to animist beliefs, these spirits have the power to affect the course of one's fortunes. They may work invisibly or else enter one's dreams, take possession of members of one's family, or communicate with spirit mediums to indicate their pleasure or displeasure with one's conduct. In dealing with them, one may try to tap into their power by promising to perform a certain action if their help is forthcoming; one may appease their anger with offerings or, failing that, try to control them through occult rituals, spells, or talismans.

Invisible forces taught by Brahmanism make up the second layer. The Brahmanical gods are generally viewed as a higher level of spirits, to be handled with a higher level of offerings and rituals, but except on very important occasions they are rarely thought to be concerned with the affairs of peasants, as they have more important business to attend to. The Brahmanical forces that weigh most heavily on a peasant's mind are astrology and numerology. The planets, which govern both systems, are conceived as gods more predictable and less capricious than the spirits, but at the same time less susceptible to offerings and rituals. Their beneficent influences may be tapped into by the proper scheduling of events. Their malevolent influences can be counteracted only by means of good luck, which may be fostered by such things as talismans, good-luck rituals, lucky numbers, and auspicious colors.

Buddhism adds another set of gods and spirits to the invisible world, and—with the remnants of Tantrism—another element to the ritualists' repertoire. Its most important contribution, however, is a layer of force overarching all others: the principle of karma, the belief that one meets with events determined by the intentional quality of one's past and present thoughts, words, and deeds. Even gods, according to Buddhist teachings, are subject to this law. From the orthodox point of view, this law invalidates the influence of the planets and lowers the status of the spirit world. However, from the syncretist point of view, karma does not abrogate the lower levels of force; it simply provides another method for explaining and influencing them. For example, one's social position, the success of one's crops, and the vicissitudes of life in general can be attributed to one's accumulated good and bad karma. The extent to which spirits meddle in one's life can be attributed either to one's general stock of karma or to particular actions by which one has harmed or helped a particular spirit in this life or the past. One's birth chart is essentially a diagram displaying the strengths and weaknesses of one's karma inherited from past lives. Therefore, an entire host of problems may be dealt with by adding to one's stock of merit in general or, in cases when a particular spirit is looking for repayment for past wrongs, by making merit and dedicating it to the spirit. Thus, merit is power, a means for controlling the forces of the world on all levels so as to gain happiness in this life and the next. The role of this power explains the importance of merit in the eyes of the typical peasant, and the need in human society for a place where merit can be most effectively made.

Simply because the doctrine of karma blankets all other forms of power, however, does not mean that merit making entirely supplants other means of trying to acquire power, such as occult rituals or propitiatory offerings. The drawback of merit is that it tends to be of a general, rather than a specific, nature, and there is no control over how quickly its results will be felt. It is the most invisible and impersonal of the invisible powers. Thus there are occasions—as when a spirit enters one's dreams and makes a specific demand—when the typical peasant, instead of making merit, will turn for help to a ritual specialist, either a lay person who has acquired the appropriate knowledge, or a monk who has learned some occult rituals on the side.

General familiarity with rituals, both animistic and Brahmanical, has also influenced the typical peasant's view of karma in that merit is often seen as lying not in the quality of the intent behind an action but in the proper ritualized performance of acts that are defined as meritorious. This ritualization of karma is one of the great ironies of syncretic Buddhism. As we learned in Chapter 1, one of the Buddha's primary achievements was to divorce the doctrine of karma from its purely ritual role in the Vedic worldview and to apply it to morality in general. Typical Thai peasants, however, confess that the quality of their intentions is very difficult to control, and thus they find a sense of security in returning karma to the more tractable and well-defined area of ritually prescribed action.

The ritualization of merit may be illustrated with a typical merit-making ritual on the morning of the Uposatha, which occurs on the days of the full, new, and half moons. The primary function of the ritual is to make merit by presenting food to the monks and listening to a sermon. Monks and villagers gather in separate zones of the main meeting hall. Before the food is presented, the villagers pay respect to the Buddha-image and request the Triple Refuge and Five Precepts from the chief monk. The reason for requesting the Triple Refuge is that if any of the villagers have had recourse to animist or Brahmanical practices since the last Uposatha service, their allegiance to the Buddha, Dharma, and Sangha has been tarnished. This is their chance to renew allegiance with no questions asked. The reason for requesting the Five Precepts is that a donation is said to bear the greatest fruit if both the donor and the recipient live by the precepts. A typical villager finds it very difficult to abide by the precepts in the course of daily life, and may have little intention of trying to observe the precepts after leaving the monastery, but by taking the precepts he/she is said to be "in possession of" the precepts at least for the period of time when the donation is being given. Thus the preliminaries to the actual donation function as a ritual empowerment.

Once the preliminaries are completed, the villagers as a group make a formal declaration of donating their offerings to the Sangha, because the act of making a donation to the general Sangha is said to entail more merit than simply donating it to individual monks. The declaration may be relatively short or may last several minutes, making specific mention of the various benefits the donors hope to gain from their donation, as well as the various animist, Brahmanical, and Buddhist deities and spirits they hope will rejoice in the merit of the act, and ending with the wish that the generosity of the donation will someday lead to nirvāṇa. Only then is the food formally handed to the monks, who chant blessings rejoicing in the merit the villagers have made. The monks then eat the food there in the meeting hall while the villagers look on, chatting informally about the events of the past week.

When the monks are finished eating, one of them delivers a sermon. The villagers then have their meal, and many of them return home at this point. Others stay on for the morning chanting service. The texts of the service, compiled by Rāma IV while he was ordained, are a reflection on the virtues of the Triple Gem and a contemplation of the Three Characteristics. Some of the villagers are aware of the meaning, others are not, but all are convinced that by repeating and listening to the Pali phrases they are gaining merit by calming their minds and listening to the Dharma. This act would qualify as a ritualized form of meditation. Combined with the ritualized donation and precepts of the earlier part of the service, this ritualized meditation makes the morning ritual, in the eyes of the villagers, a complete expression of the three major forms of making merit.

A great variety of other merit-making rituals can take place in the wat, in the villagers' homes, or in their fields (see Strong *EB*, secs. 6.2, 6.5.3, for examples from Laos and Sri Lanka). However, the ritualization of merit making is most striking in the prime event drawing the villagers and monks together: the ordination of a new monk. In the Buddha's time, ordination was a renunciation of family life and was expected to be a lifelong commitment. Disrobing, the Buddha said, was a disgrace. In Thai popular Buddhism, however, temporary ordination—usually lasting three months—is the norm rather than the exception, functioning as a rite of passage for young men and preparing them, ironically, for marriage. By ordaining, they repay the debt they owe to their parents for all the troubles and hardships involved in raising them; during their time as monks they prepare for adulthood by gaining the knowledge and strength of character they will need as they take on wife and children.

Parents are said to acquire a vast store of merit by allowing a son to ordain. They become "relatives of the religion" and are guaranteed to meet with Buddhism again in future lifetimes. Because ordination usually takes place during the three months of the rainy season when their crops are growing, they hope that the merit of doing without their son's labor will bring them even more merit, at least enough to influence the crop. As for the sons, they are given the time to study Buddhist doctrine from the curriculum established by Prince Vajirañāṇa, which concludes with a section on Dharma appropriate for householders. They also must develop the patience, propriety, and self-reliance that adherence to the monastic code requires. Thus, at the end of the three months, after they have gone through a simple disrobing ceremony (Strong *EB*, sec. 6.5.1), they are considered "ripe"—knowledgeable and responsible enough to be eligible for marriage. They have also gained familiarity with the monks' life, which prepares them for their future role as supporters of the wat.

Of course, not all monks disrobe after three months. A small number stay on for longer periods, even for life, during which time they find a number of vocations open to them. To begin with, monkhood is one of the few avenues of social mobility open to a Thai peasant. A monk may acquire an education from the school system set up especially for monks, which leads all the way to university degrees. Once he receives his degrees, he may disrobe and use them to find a job in the fast-expanding economy, or he may stay on in the monkhood and work his way up the hierarchy. A number of the recent Supreme Patriarchs of the Thai Sangha have been sons of peasants.

Alternatively, rather than taking the route of education—termed *gandhadhura,* the duty of books—a monk may seek out a meditation teacher and devote himself to *vipassanādhura,* the duty of insight. Fear of the dangers and hardships associated with a meditative life in the forest, however, usually leads the monk's relatives to discourage him from such a course.

A third course open to a monk is to stay on at his village wat, acquiring what merit he can and picking up whatever Buddhist or ritual knowledge he feels will be helpful to his fellow villagers. Thais in general, especially now that their society is undergoing rapid change, have a certain nostalgia for the folk figure of Luang Taa, the elderly village monk who may not have much of an education or a position in the ecclesiastical hierarchy, but who is, through the accumulated experience of his years in the monkhood, a source of consolation and wisdom for all those who seek his advice. However accurate this nostalgic picture may be, it provides a good indication of the affection that Thais in general feel for the domesticated village monks who are partners with them in acquiring the merit that will lead to their long-term happiness and well-being.

Because the last vestiges of the Theravāda Bhikkhuṇī Sangha died out with the Mongol sacking of Pagan in 1287, women do not now have the opportunity for ordination that men do. There are communities of eight-precept nuns, either independent or attached to monasteries, but young women, unlike young men, are actively discouraged from ordaining. For a peasant economy that until only recently viewed itself as underpopulated, young women's fertility is too valuable. However, there are ways that a woman determined to devote herself to a religious life can circumvent her parents' objections. A common way is, when faced with illness, to promise to a guardian deity that she will ordain; if she recovers, she has her opening. Failing this, a woman may put off ordaining until after her children are grown.

Once she becomes a nun, she will find her role very different from that of a monk. Nuns play a very small part in the community's pursuit of merit. They may be invited to chant at funerals, but that is the extent of their ritual role. This limited role has both its drawbacks and its advantages. On the one hand, nuns usually draw their support from their immediate families. If no support is forthcoming, they must undertake work of various kinds to maintain themselves. If, on the other hand, the nun can obtain adequate material support, she will find that she has more free time than the typical village monk to devote to meditation and her own personal pursuit of merit.

For a woman who does not ordain, the center of her religious life is in the home. She may donate to the monks a share of the food she prepares, adding a religious dimension to her role in the kitchen. She may also use part of her share of the family income to sponsor merit-making ceremonies, construction of religious edifices, and so forth. If she has been initiated by a female ritual specialist, she may practice private rituals for the prosperity or safety of herself or her family. Most important of all, she may train her children to live by the Dharma. Thai peasants have not been taught a great deal of political history, and thus are not infected with the mind-set that tends to glorify the male role in public affairs at the expense of the female role in the family. Buddhism places a high importance on the role that parents play in the lives of their children. Children are to regard their mother and father as their foremost teachers, and to treat them with the same respect due an arhant. Thus her role as a foremost teacher is where a Thai peasant woman will find her greatest source of merit, free from the ritualized forms that the men have devised.

When death comes to a Thai village, all elements of the popular religion come into play in the ensuing funeral. From the animist point of view, the main concern is to keep the spirit of the deceased from disrupting the life of the community. Because the spirit is thought to hover around the dead body, cremation is the preferred means of disposing of the corpse. Once the body has been cremated, the spirit has its locus removed and is more likely to go on to its next life. To keep the spirit under control before the cremation, the feet, wrists, and neck of the corpse are bound, a hex sign and other charms are placed on the chest before the coffin is closed, and people who attend the funeral will often repeat a silent charm to themselves as protection against the spirit. Although financial considerations often determine how long the funeral will last, animist considerations can also play a role, the general rule being that if the deceased died from violent or sudden causes, the funeral should be held as quickly as possible, for the spirits of such people are especially troublesome. Wakes are held to keep the body company at night, so that the spirit will not feel neglected and start prowling around the village.

Brahmanical elements enter into the funeral arrangements primarily through numerology. Monks are invited in even numbers, rather than the odd numbers used for auspicious occasions, and the number four—the most inauspicious of all, as it is associated with death—is heavily used. Aside from the numerology, the main role Brahmanism plays at this time is in coloring the attitudes of people attending the funeral. Funeral rites, even the merit-making ceremonies connected with them, are classified by the official Thai Sangha text on rituals as *avamangala* (inauspicious). This is purely a Brahmanical concept, for there is nothing inauspicious about death from a Buddhist point of view. Contemplation of death and even of corpses is one of the original Buddhist meditation themes for counteracting lust and complacency. However, from a Brahmanical point of view, any involvement with a corpse is polluting and a cause for bad luck. Thus there are a variety of taboos observed by those who attend funerals. They may repeat charms to themselves—similar to the animist charms mentioned previously—to ward off ritual pollution; they are careful not to visit sick people on the way home from the funeral; and they may leave a small bowl of lustral water next to the door of their home compound before leaving for the funeral, using it to sprinkle their heads before entering the compound on their return.

Merit making is the main component of the funeral rites, although here the merit making serves a dual purpose: to comfort the living and to dedicate the merit to the deceased so as to improve his/her chances for a good rebirth. Donations are presented to monks, sermons are given, and, in particular, the monks chant. The chants they use are an entirely different set from that used on auspicious occasions. Here, so soon after a death, chants referring to good fortune are judged inappropriate, so the Pali passages deal with the Three Characteristics, the ineffectiveness of spells and other human powers in the face of death, and the efficacy of good karma in leading to a happy rebirth—topics that are consoling for those who have been devoting their life to the pursuit of merit. Passages from the Abhidhamma are also chanted, on the grounds that they are the highest level of Dharma and that listening to them will produce the highest level of merit, which is then passed on to the deceased.

Their inauspiciousness aside, funerals are among the main social occasions in the life of Thai peasants. If the deceased was well loved or highly respected, the body may be kept for several months in a temporary mausoleum until the family—or the community as a whole, if the deceased was a monk—has been able to save up enough money for a lavish funeral ceremony that will fittingly express its regard for the person who has passed away. When this is the case, the funeral is a remarkably cheerful affair. The bereaved have had time to get over their loss and can take satisfaction in the conviction that they are helping the deceased to a favorable rebirth. The communal nature of the bereaved's merit making guarantees that even their own upcoming death is domesticated somewhat, as they are assured of enjoying the fruits of their good karma together with friends and family in the next life.

7.5.2 Buddhism in the Forest

The question arises as to whether this domesticated mix of Buddhism, animism, and Brahmanism is really Buddhism. The answer for an anthropologist is yes: Anything that Buddhists do or believe counts as Buddhism; orthodoxy carries no more weight than do the heterodox elements that coexist with it. But for many Buddhists, the answer is no, or at best a yes that is heavily qualified: This mix is the bark that may help keep the tree alive by ensuring popular support, but it is not the heartwood; at times it may even be a parasite that strangles the tree and brings it down. A glance at the canon will reveal that the life of a ritual specialist is not what the Buddha envisaged for his monks.

But if the popular practice of Buddhism is not the true Dharma, then where—outside of the texts—is the Dharma to be found? The answer is, in the forest. King Parākramabāhu I's edict (Strong *EB*, sec. 6.4) shows that he looked to a forest monk for guidance in his reforms, and the same was true of King Parākramabāhu II; the kings of fourteenth and fifteenth century Chieng Mai and Sukhothai; and, in the postcolonial period, U Nu of Burma and the ruling elite of Thailand. Some rulers looked without finding anything. Rāma V, before embarking on his program to standardize the curriculum for Buddhist monks, had his Dharma department conduct a survey of the known forest monasteries throughout his kingdom in hopes that a meditation tradition worthy of royal patronage could be found, but the survey turned up nothing but Tantric and occult practices. This convinced him that the Path to nirvāṇa was no longer being pursued, and that the only avenue open to him was to support the study of the texts. Still, the important point in all of these cases is that the forest was the first place to which these rulers turned.

Like in the American frontier, the forest has played an important, if ambivalent, role in the societies of south and Southeast Asia. On the one hand, it is a place of danger: wild animals, disease, outlaws, malevolent spirits, and treacherous temptations. On the other hand, it is where the Buddha attained Awakening, a place where truths transcending social conventions may be found and brought back to reform the social order.

Throughout the Theravādin tradition, the concept of forest Buddhism has carried the same ambivalence. True, the forest is a place of heterodoxy, where hermits and strange cults go to escape societal norms, and from which messianic movements arise to challenge the political order. One example of this aspect of forest Buddhism can be found in the Ari sect (founded in the latter years of Pagan), whose members claimed to be monks and nuns, but who reportedly engaged in a wide variety of practices in flagrant violation of the Vinaya rules, such as slaughtering animals for meat, drinking alcohol, and deflowering virgins. Another example is the elusive Sacca Lokuttara (Transcendent Truth) movement, a group of recluses who refuse to bind themselves by the precepts and today maintain a very low-profile existence in the border regions of northeast Thailand.

However, the forest has also been the home of movements that outdo the social norm in terms of their adherence to the texts: groups of lay or ordained practitioners who reject syncretic elements, leave the bustle of domesticated Buddhism, and devote themselves fully to scholarship, meditation, or both, pursuing a life in keeping with their beliefs about what the texts actually taught.

The uncertainty as to whether one will find orthodoxy or heterodoxy when going into the forest explains why the ruling elite tends not to look there for its inspiration in times of relative social stability. But in times of instability, it has no choice but to take the risk. Given the enormous forces for change that have swept over Asia in the postcolonial period, it should come as no surprise that forest movements have had a major voice in modern Thai Buddhism. Three examples will provide some idea of the range of messages this voice has conveyed.

The oldest of the three movements is the Forest or *Kammaṭṭhāna* (meditation) tradition founded by Phra Ajaan Sao Kantasīlo (1861–1941) and Phra Ajaan Mun Bhūridatto (1870–1949) in the forests of northeastern Thailand. Members of this movement—mostly belonging to the Dhammayut sect, although there is also a Mahānikāya offshoot—are renowned for their asceticism, their strict adherence to the Vinaya, and their meditative powers. The movement took its original inspiration from a handful of texts resulting from missions to Sri Lanka sponsored by Rāma IV, but aside from questions of Vinaya, the movement has a strong antischolastic bent. Many of its members insist that their prime teacher has been the forest itself. The movement kept to the forests of north and northeastern Thailand during the early years of its existence, to seek the solitude needed for serious meditation and also to avoid the dragnet of the government's unifying reforms at the turn of the twentieth century. In the 1950s, however, it began to emerge from the forests and to attract a sizable following in central Thailand. Soon it numbered among its supporters members of the ruling elite, including the royal family.

Another forest movement was started by Buddhadāsa Bhikkhu (1906–93) in the 1930s, shortly after the fall of the absolute monarchy. In 1932, Buddhadāsa quit his studies in Bangkok, acquired a complete edition of the Pali Canon, and returned to an old abandoned monastery near his hometown in southern Thailand. There he studied and meditated in seclusion; after a few years he began publishing books and giving public talks, eventually producing a body of literature that has come to fill an entire room in the Thai National Library. He also founded a meditation hermitage, Suan Mokh (the Garden of Liberation). He is best known for his attacks on animist and Brahmanical elements in Thai Buddhist practice and his original teachings on the doctrine of dependent co-arising. Karma, according to his view, bears fruit only instantaneously, and not over time; the Buddhist doctrine of rebirth applies only to the arising of the sense of "me and mine" within the mind; and the question of rebirth after death is irrelevant to the Buddha's teachings. Buddhadāsa attracted a following primarily among the nonruling, educated elite.

A third forest movement is Khao Suan Luang (Royal Park Mountain), a women's practice center founded in western Thailand in 1945 by Upāsikā Kee Nanayon (1901–79). Upāsikā Kee was best known for her austere lifestyle and for her teachings that recommended restraint of the senses, a strong concentration based on the breath, and insight gained through direct contemplation of the arising and passing away of mental states within the mind. She began publishing transcripts of her talks for free distribution in 1954, and her books have attracted a wide following.

All three of these movements agree that modern Thailand would benefit from abandoning the astrology, the animist beliefs, and the ritualized approach to karma present in popular Buddhism; from adhering more closely to the Five Precepts; and from engaging in more meditation, both for the monastics and the laity. They also agree that the way to nirvāṇa is still open, in contrast with the view that became common after King Rāma V's survey, which maintained that nirvāṇa was no longer a realistic possibility. Nevertheless, their prescriptions for modern Thai Buddhism differ considerably from one another.

The Kammaṭṭhāna tradition maintains that a monk's primary duty is to devote his life entirely to meditation so as to abandon the defilements that bind him to saṃsāra; he should then worry about helping society only when he has put his own house in order. On a practical level, teachers in this tradition have advised their supporters among the ruling elite to eschew corruption and to work for a more equal distribution of economic opportunity throughout the Thai countryside, but by and large they espouse no particular social or political program.

Buddhadāsa, however, was very vocal and confrontational regarding social matters. Because selfishness lies at the essence of suffering, he taught, monks and laity alike should meditate to reduce the sense of "I," but they cannot truly comprehend "not-self" unless they devote themselves at the same time to a life of selfless social service aimed at returning society to the moral principles inherent in nature.

Upāsikā Kee's following has remained firmly apolitical, on the grounds that political confrontations would involve them in fruitless entanglements (see Strong *EB*, sec. 6.7), but their mere existence as an active, highly visible community is in itself a repudiation of the limited role that mainstream Thai Buddhism has traditionally assigned to women.

These voices have in the past few decades found a significant hearing throughout Thai Buddhism and have begun to spark a renewed interest in meditation among monks, nuns, and lay people in rural and urban areas. At the same time, however, the message from these voices has been compromised somewhat as the forest movements become increasingly co-opted and domesticated as they grow more popular. This pattern has occurred repeatedly in the past, when reform movements have degenerated to the point where they needed reforming themselves. The traditional recourse was to look for new movements from the forest. At present, however, the forests are rapidly disappearing and are being replaced by the urban concrete jungle as the center of lawlessness, diseases, treacherous temptations, and heterodox teachings (Strong *EB*, sec. 6.8.2). It remains to be seen whether the concrete jungle will also be able to provide sources of inspiration for the continued survival of Theravādin orthodoxy in the face of the massive social changes continuing to sweep through this part of the world.

8

Buddhism in Central Asia and China

CENTRAL ASIA

8.1 THE DHARMA TRAVELS THE SILK ROAD

Central Asia's contribution to the history of Buddhism lies largely in its role as an intermediary in the spread of the Dharma to east Asia and Tibet. However, for more than a millennium, beginning with the third century B.C.E. and lasting in some areas until the eleventh century C.E., people in the area practiced the religion for their own benefit, created Buddhist art for their own enjoyment and edification, and spread the Dharma not because it was an outside force flowing through their territory, but because it had made such an important contribution to their own lives. Unfortunately, the ravages of weather and the many military invasions that have swept through the area have left few remnants of Buddhism's former presence, but those few remnants attest to a vibrant and sophisticated culture of a high order. Undoubtedly, there are traces of a specifically central Asian Buddhism still alive in east Asian Buddhist culture, but barring any major archaeological finds in the future, it is difficult to know precisely what those traces are.

8.1.1 From the Mauryan to the Kuṣāṇa Empire

The Buddhist history of central Asia can be divided roughly into three periods. The first begins in the time of King Aśoka (see Section 3.3) and lasts until the fall of the Kuṣāṇa empire in the third century C.E. Two extant Aśokan inscriptions in Afghanistan serve as evidence of Aśoka's efforts in spreading the Dharma to this area. Aśoka's son, Kustana, is said to have founded the kingdom of Khotan, now located in the southern portion of eastern Turkestan, in 240 B.C.E. Aśoka's great grandson, Vijayasabhāva, is traditionally credited with championing Buddhism in the kingdom. The first Buddhist monastery there was constructed in 211 B.C.E.

In the first century C.E., a group of nomadic Indo-Scythians swept down from the north and gained control of northern India, Afghanistan, and a large part of central Asia from the Aral Sea east to the border of China, founding the Kuṣāṇa (Kushan) dynasty. A member of the dynasty, Kaniṣka I (see Section 4.4), converted to Buddhism and played an influential role in the development of the religion not only in central Asia but also in India itself.

During its three centuries of rule, the Kuṣāṇa empire ranked among the four major powers of the world, alongside Parthia, Rome, and China. In terms of cultural sophistication, it was the greatest empire central Asia has ever seen. The stability it brought to the region facilitated the movement of goods and ideas along the major trade routes, including the north–south route from India into Bactria and Sogdia, and the east–west route from Persia into China, called the Silk Road after the most prized commodity that traveled west along the road. The location of the Kuṣāṇa empire gave it control over a most lucrative part of the Silk Road, at the same time opening it to cultural influences from all directions. The range of these influences is reflected in Kuṣāṇa coins, which were imprinted with Buddhist, Greek, Roman, Iranian, and Hindu figures. This cosmopolitan mix can be seen in Kuṣāṇa Buddhist art as well. The Kuṣāṇas developed a synthesis of Greco-Roman, Persian (Sasanian), and Indian styles in what appear to be among the first sculptures of the Buddha in human form (see Section 5.3). They also seem to be responsible for introducing the towering form of the Buddhist stūpa to India, topped by a tall, tapering spire, replacing the earlier hemispherical form. The Kuṣāṇa taste in stūpa architecture has continued to influence stūpa design throughout Asia, from the tall spires of Thai and Burmese cetiyas to the multistoried pagodas of China, Korea, and Japan.

Central Asians were not only on the receiving end of outside influences during this period. They also were active in exporting Buddhist ideas to other areas, most notably to China. The first translator of Buddhist texts into Chinese was a Parthian, and throughout the early centuries of Chinese Buddhism the most active missionaries were central Asians.

8.1.2 Between Two Empires

The second period in central Asian Buddhist history extends from the fall of the Kuṣāṇas in the middle of the third century to the rise of the Tibetan empire in the middle of the eighth. Although the region was fragmented politically and subject to occasional invasions by the Ephthalite Huns, the movement of ideas and goods along the Silk Road continually increased. Originating in what is now western Iran and continuing south of the Caspian Sea, the Silk Road divided into a northern route through Samarkand and a southern one along the Amu River. The two routes were reunited in northwest China at the city of Tun-huang, in Kansu province. Along this route, Buddhism acquired many powerful and wealthy patrons among those who had profited from the trade in goods. Eager to demonstrate their devotion, kings and merchants financed towering statues, lavish temples, as well as the work of missionaries and translators.

Unfortunately, we have only fragmentary evidence for the development of Buddhism in central Asia during this time, so it is virtually impossible to tell how much the central Asians added of their own to the religion, and how much they simply accepted and transmitted it in its Indian form. There is the possibility that the bodhisattva Kṣitigarbha (Earth Womb)—who later took the form of Jizo, the bodhisattva of children and aborted fetuses in Japan—was originally a central Asian figure. Bhaiṣajyaguru (see Section 5.5.6) may also have been a central Asian invention. It is likely that parts of the *Avataṃsaka Sūtra* (see Section 4.3), which mentions central Asian place-names, were composed in Khotan. Central Asians were known to have a fervent interest in the practice of meditation and the development of psychic powers, an interest that may have stemmed from the strong shamanic traditions in the area.

Reports from Chinese travelers tell us that the city-states of Kucha, Turfan, and others along the northern route of the Silk Road belonged primarily to the Sarvāstivādin school, whereas Khotan and others along the southern route were strongholds of Mahāyāna. Khotan in particular seems to have been the major center of Buddhist activity in central Asia until the eleventh century. Chinese travelers left detailed reports of the Buddhist festivals celebrated there and had high praise for the decorum and discipline of Khotanese monks. One of the few Buddhist texts undoubtedly composed in central Asia—the *Book of Zambasta*—was written in Khotan. It contains an eclectic mix of Indian Buddhist myths and an idealist version of Yogācāra philosophy, maintaining that all dharmas, including ignorance and wisdom, are ultimately unreal. Fragmentary murals found in Khotan depicting maṇḍalas centered on Mahāvairocana suggest that the Yoga Tantras also were practiced there.

During this period Chinese pilgrims, convinced of the need to learn Buddhism in its homeland rather than through central Asian intermediaries, began making the long, arduous journey overland to India. First among these pilgrims was the Chinese monk Fa-hsien, who reached India in 400 C.E. The last pilgrims were also the most famous: Hsüan-tsang and I-ching, who made separate journeys in the seventh century shortly before the Tibetans closed the route. This period also marks the high point in the history of the major translation center at Tun-huang. First settled by the Chinese during the Han dynasty (202 B.C.E.–220 C.E.), Tun-huang had for centuries been home to a cosmopolitan population. As the Chinese demand for Buddhist texts grew, monk-scholars of many nationalities formed translation teams to meet the demand. Prominent among these teams was the group of Indians and Chinese who gathered around Dharmarakṣa (b. 230), a native of Tun-huang born of Indo-Scythian parents.

Tun-huang became not only a translation center but also a center of Buddhist art, known especially for its cave temples. The largest of these is the Cave of a Thousand Buddhas (Ch'ien-fo Tung), dating from 366. Today 492 caves still exist, with elaborately painted frescoes accompanied by statues ranging from barely 1 inch to 109 feet in height. More than six hundred additional caves are located in the surrounding region.

8.1.3 The Tibetan Empire and Afterward

The seventh century was the beginning of a new period in central Asian Buddhist history as Tibet suddenly rose to become the major power in the area. Originally the destroyers of the Buddhist monasteries and libraries they encountered in their conquests, the Tibetans quickly converted to the religion and became its avid protectors. Their first contact with Buddhism was in Khotan, but they also learned a great deal from the many central Asian monks who fled to Lhasa, their capital, for haven from the destruction the Tibetans themselves were causing. Taking advantage of the An Lu-shan rebellion in China (see Section 8.5), Tibetans occupied the Chinese capital in 763 and captured Tun-huang in 787. The Tibetan king at the time, an avid Buddhist, arranged for the skilled translation teams at Tun-huang to translate Buddhist texts into Tibetan and to answer his questions on the Dharma. Murals in the Tun-huang caves attest to the Tibetan kings' having also sponsored Buddhist art at the center.

Tibetan control of the Silk Road shut off all traffic between China and India during this period. The influx of Indian Buddhist texts that had provided a constant stimulus to the development of east Asian Buddhism thus ended. From this point onward, east Asian Buddhism was shaped primarily by internal forces.

The Tibetan empire collapsed in the middle of the ninth century, with much of its central Asian territory taken over by the Uighir Turks. Meanwhile, Islam had begun making mass conversions in western–central Asia in the eighth century, and by the eleventh had swept throughout the region. Only the Uighirs, who had converted to Buddhism from Manichaeism and had settled in Turfan, resisted Islamic influence. The Chinese recaptured Tun-huang in the eleventh century, but danger from marauding Mongol attackers forced them to seal a library in one of the caves. This was to have great consequences for the study of Buddhism in the twentieth century.

In the thirteenth and fourteenth centuries, the Mongols under Genghis Khan conquered the region, destroying whatever religious culture they found. Although they eventually converted to the Gelug sect of Tibetan Buddhism (see Section 11.4), they made no effort to impose their religion on their subjects. Thus central Asia remained Muslim. The Silk Road was reopened, with the Mongol chieftains boasting that a solitary virgin with a hoard of gold could travel from one end of the road to the other and arrive with both her virginity and her gold intact. India, however, was no longer exporting Buddhism, so the Dharma no longer traveled the road. After the fall of the Mongol empire, the Silk Road fell into disuse as newly opened sea routes offered a passage that was both quicker and less hazardous.

This, however, was not the end of central Asian Buddhist history. In 1907–1908, the sealed cave at Tun-huang was discovered and reopened, yielding an invaluable treasure of twenty thousand drawings and manuscripts dating from the fifth through the eleventh centuries. Among them was the world's oldest printed book, a Chinese translation of the *Diamond Sūtra* dated to 868 C.E. The collection contained manuscripts in a variety of languages, both living and dead, ranging from translations, historical documents, contracts, and financial statements to songs, poems, and Sūtras. These texts have been extremely helpful for filling in gaps in Buddhist history, especially concerning the development of the early Ch'an school in China (see Section 8.5.5), and the first centuries of Tibetan Buddhism (see Section 11.2.1). More than any other archaeological find thus far, the Tun-huang manuscripts have demonstrated the significance of the now-extinct Buddhist culture of central Asia in shaping the living Buddhist cultures of east Asia and Tibet.

CHINA

8.2 A GRAND ASSIMILATION

Buddhism's encounter with Chinese civilization is one of the most momentous stories of intercultural assimilation in human history. The two traditions blended so thoroughly that it is easy to forget that Buddhism was a very foreign import when it was first brought to China, and that five centuries passed before the Chinese felt that they had a full picture of what it had to offer. Of all the Asian civilizations that Buddhism encountered outside of India, China's was by far the most sophisticated, complex, and ethnocentric, with its own thoroughly developed system of social organization, religious ideology, and speculative thought. Nevertheless, Buddhism had a great deal to offer that the Chinese lacked, and this offering came at a troubled point in Chinese history, when many Chinese were ready to learn from people whom they otherwise considered barbarians.

Buddhism's contribution comprised four levels, dealing with institutions, devotion, doctrine, and meditation techniques. On the institutional level, the monastic Sangha offered something totally new to China: a chance for men and women from all levels of society to devote their lives fully to a religious vocation. This was particularly important during the wars of the late third and early fourth centuries, when the basic units of the Chinese social and religious framework—the family and the state—were falling apart. On the devotional level, Buddhism provided a pantheon of bodhisattvas and cosmic Buddhas who were more approachable than the Taoist gods, and more powerful and compassionate than the local spirits of Chinese folk religion. As for doctrine, the Buddhist teachings on karma, rebirth, and dependent co-arising provided a consistent explanation for the individual sufferings experienced on all levels of society, at the same time addressing the central issue of Chinese speculative philosophy: how the governance of society might best be brought into harmony with the metaphysical principles underlying nature. As for meditation practice, Buddhism taught a system of mind training that supplemented the techniques taught by the native shamanic Taoist tradition, giving new meaning to the pursuit of Deathlessness and placing it more within reach of a wider range of men and women.

Of these four aspects, the institutional was the most controversial. Chinese society had operated on the assumption that all social institutions should be subsumed under the emperor, who functioned as the mediator between heaven and Earth. The Sangha, however, insisted on its independence from the sociopolitical realm, a status symbolized by Buddhist monastics refusing to kowtow to the emperor. This issue was hotly debated for several centuries, with the Confucian defenders of traditional Chinese ways attacking the Sangha on four grounds: moral, economic, political, and ethnocentric. The Sangha was immoral in that the monastics practiced celibacy, which violated the traditional canons of filial piety, in which a person's prime duty to his/her ancestors was to produce children. Also, the monks and nuns shaved their heads and cremated their dead, which were abominations against the body that had been received from one's parents. The Sangha was economically detrimental in that it siphoned off the donations of gullible believers and produced no concrete results in the world: "They eat but do not farm, wear clothes but do not weave," charged the Confucian bureaucrats, who themselves neither farmed nor wove. The Sangha was a threat to social stability in that it did not recognize the superiority of the state. Finally, the institution as a whole was a foreign invention, and therefore inherently inferior.

Buddhists had encountered the first three arguments in India and so were generally well prepared to respond. Monks and nuns, by teaching the religion to their parents, were repaying their filial debt in the highest possible manner (Strong *EB*, sec. 8.2.1). The fruit of their practice was not to be measured in this world, although the merit earned by supporting the Sangha helped guarantee economic prosperity. Their instructions in morality and the principle of karma actually helped the emperor in his work of bringing order to society; they deserved their independence in that the goal they sought pertained to life after death, an area over which no emperor could claim power. As for the argument that the Sangha was foreign, some pointed out that foreign things were not necessarily inferior. Others who were more inventive argued that the Sangha had actually existed on Chinese soil since the time of King Aśoka, thus giving the religion a fairly long Chinese pedigree.

Both sides of these arguments were repeated with little variation throughout the period of assimilation, and for the most part an uneasy truce prevailed. Buddhist monastics ultimately were not required to kowtow before the emperor, but the Sangha as a whole was placed under a government overseer (sometimes a monk, sometimes a lay man, sometimes sympathetic, sometimes not), with government permission required before any man or woman could be ordained. Occasionally the truce broke down, most disastrously in 842–45, when a Taoist emperor ordered the destruction of almost the entire institution. Eventually, however, the Sangha became accepted as an established part of Chinese society.

The assimilation of Buddhist doctrine was complicated by Buddhism's having come to China in scattered bits and pieces—a random mixture of Hīnayāna and Mahāyāna texts, all claiming to originate from the Buddha—rather than as a coherent whole. At the same time, the doctrine was undergoing major changes in its Indian homeland. The Chinese had no way of knowing the historical and cultural background for these texts, so they had to not only master the basic concepts but also devise a framework in which to place the variety of conflicting teachings that seemed to grow ever more complex with each new wave of translations. The process of assimilation occurred in four stages. The first stage, in which Buddhist ideas and practices were viewed simply as an extension of preexisting Taoist beliefs, lasted from the time of the first Buddhist missionaries from central Asia to approximately the beginning of the fourth century C.E. In the second stage, which lasted until the beginning of the fifth century C.E., Chinese intellectuals began incorporating Buddhist ideas into a Chinese framework. In the third stage, lasting roughly until the end of the sixth century C.E., a more concerted effort was made to understand individual Buddhist philosophical schools and scholastic treatises on their own terms. The fourth stage, lasting until the ninth century C.E., was a period of doctrinal synthesis in which various schemes using Chinese philosophical categories were proposed for organizing the entire corpus of Buddhist doctrine and practice around a constellation of themes drawn from Mahāyāna Sūtras.

The eighth and ninth centuries C.E. were especially fertile in terms of the creative attempts at making sense of Buddhism as a totality, but they were also among the most politically unstable times in Chinese history. A series of rebellions and persecutions succeeded not only in decimating the population of the empire, but also in cutting short many of the great syntheses just as they were taking shape. Many issues remained unsettled—among them, the relationship between doctrine and practice, and the attitude of the Awakened mind toward morality and social convention—but the devastation of the period forced a settlement. The school of practice that survived the period most nearly intact was one of the more iconoclastic of the *Ch'an* (dhyāna) meditation traditions, which presented its masters in the guise of spontaneous Taoist sages. Its texts thus became the norm for the entire Buddhist tradition, and the spontaneous master, unfettered by social conventions, became the paradigm for the goal of Buddhist practice.

Ironically, it was just at this time that the government was looking for an ideology to form the basis of a bureaucracy that would provide China with a more stable, centralized form of administration. Iconoclasm, even though it performed a necessary function in preventing the meditative tradition from being overcome with formalism and routine, could not act as a state ideology. Confucian scholars thus took the initiative in presenting a reformed version of their doctrine—known in the West as neo-Confucianism—as the new ideology. Interestingly enough, the Buddhist doctrine of karma and the belief in the primacy of the mind had become so embedded in Chinese thought that the neo-Confucians adopted these as among their basic principles. At the same time, they quoted some of the more iconoclastic Ch'an texts to prove that Buddhism was an amoral practice whose goal was to strip the mind down to its most basic animal functions, instead of raising it to a higher moral plane. The Buddhists countered with attempts to show that Buddhism, Taoism, and Confucianism were three aspects of a single teaching—the "three legs that supported the bronze vessel," with Buddhism at least equal to the other two—but the neo-Confucians won the day. Neo-Confucian ideology became the dominant intellectual standard from the fourteenth to the early twentieth century, whereas Buddhism became more and more the religion of the untutored masses. Thus, in a sense, Buddhism found itself under attack by a doctrine of its own that had become basic to all Chinese thought, and it suffered a major defeat partly because it had projected a Chinese image all too well.

Nevertheless, despite its defeat on the doctrinal level, Buddhism maintained its strength as an institution, a devotional religion, and a system of meditation training still open to all. Ch'an retained some of its intellectual currency, serving as an individualistic alternative to the often stifling orthodoxy of the neo-Confucian ideology. As a result, Buddhism came to play a role that it was best equipped to play, standing somewhat outside the social order, offering haven to those who found that order restrictive or repressive, but in no way threatening the peace and well-being of society.

8.3 BUDDHISM ON THE FRINGES OF SOCIETY

Chinese Buddhists preserved a story effectively stating that their religion was first brought to China at the instigation of an emperor of the Later Han dynasty, Ming Ti (r. 58–75 C.E.), whose curiosity about Buddhism had been piqued by a portentous dream (Strong *EB*, sec. 8.1.1). Historical records, however, indicate that the religion was more likely brought into Han China by central Asian merchants, who set up monasteries in their enclaves in the major Chinese cities and invited central Asian monks to staff them. The first reference to Buddhism in imperial historical records, nevertheless, does date from the reign of Ming Ti. The records tell of a Chinese nobleman who combined the "gentle Buddhist rites and fasts" with Taoist practices aimed at physical immortality. For several centuries this was Buddhism's basic role as a subculture in China: a set of rites and practices augmenting Taoism. The first reference to the appearance of Buddhist statues in the imperial court, dating from the second century C.E., follows the same pattern. A Taoist adept added Buddhist rituals to a program of Taoist rites to bless the emperor. The connection between Buddhism and Taoism was justified by a story that began circulating in China during this period that claimed that the Buddha was actually the

Taoist sage Lao-tzu, who had gone west at one point in his career to teach the barbarians. The Buddhists may have originally welcomed this story, for it made their religion seem less of a foreign import. Eventually, as they began asserting their own separate identity, they found the story more and more objectionable, but not until the thirteenth century were they able to establish once and for all that it was a fabrication.

The first reference to a Buddhist monastery in China, dating from the middle of the second century C.E., also contains the first explicit description of one of the Buddhist rites practiced during these first centuries: the washing of a Buddha-image, a rite that was to enjoy long-term popularity in east Asia (see Section 8.7.2). The second century was also when the first Buddhist texts were translated into Chinese. The Parthian monk An Shih-kao reached the Chinese capital of Loyang in 148 and began translating a set of texts dealing with meditation practices, such as breath awareness, and numerical lists of Dharma topics, including the Wings to Awakening. An Shih-kao was not himself fluent in Chinese, so a strategy was devised whereby he would recite the text to a bilingual interpreter, who would then transmit it to a group of Chinese, who would then discuss points of interpretation and produce a polished final copy. This was the procedure that similar teams of translators were to follow until the seventh century. Another translator, Lokakṣema, was the first known Mahāyāna missionary. Working in Loyang between 168 and 188, he effected the first translation of a Prajñā-pāramitā text into Chinese and recruited the first Chinese monk.

The quality of the first few generations of translations was rather poor, partly due to the inherent difficulty of translating into a sophisticated language such as Chinese, whose technical terms already packed a heavy load of connotations picked up from native philosophical traditions. For instance, in the early years, nirvāṇa and *asaṃskṛta* (the Unconditioned) were rendered as *wu-wei,* literally nonaction, which in Taoism referred to the effortless spontaneous action of the Sage in harmony with the essence of nature. *Tao,* the Way, which in Taoism meant the underlying essence of all things, was used to translate *bodhi, yoga, Dharma,* and *mārga* (path). Other inaccuracies in translation were products of simple misunderstanding: Skandha (aggregate) was rendered as *yin,* the passive or receptive principle of nature; right exertion was rendered as idea-severance, foundation of mindfulness as idea-stop. Many of these mistakes remained unrectified until the early fifth century. We can only conjecture as to what the early Chinese Buddhists made of these texts in the meantime.

Because no Vinaya texts were translated for well over a century, the Chinese Sangha was hampered in its organization and development. Not until the early fifth century were complete Vinaya texts made available through the efforts of Tao-an and Kumārajīva in the north, and Fa-hsien, Guṇavarman, and Sanghavarman in the south.

The Later Han regime fell apart during the latter half of the second century and ended in 220, to be followed by a period in which three kingdoms vied unsuccessfully to reunite the empire. During this period, Buddhism began gaining converts among the peasants, the petty bureaucrats, and even from the courts, as people suffering from political unrest sought refuge in supernatural powers. Central Asian Buddhist monks claiming psychic abilities won many converts. Images of Buddhas and bodhisattvas—especially Maitreya, Amitābha, and Avalokiteśvara—played a central role both in devotion and in meditation practice. (The meditator would stare at the image to create a psychic connection with the supernatural being who would then, it was hoped, grant knowledge or protection.) This cult of the Buddha-image was responsible for some of the royal converts to Buddhism during this period. For instance, Sun Hao (r. 264–80), ruler of the kingdom of Wu, was originally anti-Buddhist. When a Buddha-image was found in the park of his harem, he had it moved to his urinal where he performed his own version of the rite of washing the image, much to the amusement of his courtiers. Immediately stricken with a painful and mysterious disease, he had to submit to the power of the Buddha and accept the Five Precepts.

The work of translation and evangelizing continued through the third century and came to fruition in the period when the empire was briefly reunited under the western Chin dynasty (265–316). Dharmarakṣa (see Section 8.1.2), "the bodhisattva from Tun-huang," worked in north China from 266 to 308, completing a large number of translations, including the first Chinese versions of the *Lotus Sūtra* and the *Large Perfection of Wisdom*. In addition, he gave extensive lectures, attracted numerous converts, ordained monks, and founded monasteries. His disciples proselytized vigorously. The sacking of the capitals at Loyang and Chang'an at the end of the western Chin period served to disperse Dharmarakṣa's school to other parts of the country, thus disseminating a new vigorous and intellectual style of Buddhism. This process was repeated often during the centuries of political division. Monasteries and libraries were often burned, but what the Sangha lost in security it gained in mobility and communication.

8.4 BUDDHISM ENTERS THE MAINSTREAM OF CHINESE CULTURE

In 318 the western Chin dynasty fell as non-Chinese tribes living in Chinese territory conquered the northern half of the empire, driving the ruling elites south to the area of the Yangtze River. This event ushered in the period of the northern and southern dynasties (318–589), during which the southern half of the empire was ruled by a series of native dynasties, whereas the north fell under a succession of sinicized "barbarian" rulers. The political division of the empire was reflected in a cultural division. The south tended to follow more traditional modes of Chinese culture; the north, however, was more open to outside influences.

Buddhism made enormous advances in gaining adherents in both the north and south. The institution of the Sangha provided a haven for men and women from all levels of society, including those orphaned by the sporadic warfare as well as those whose general exposure to hardship inspired them with the desire for a religious vocation. The Dharma offered solace for those seeking release from suffering. The sense of dislocation suffered by the elites at this time resembled that felt in India at the time of the Buddha. Many began questioning their cultural ideology and found that Buddhism had satisfactory answers for their questions. As a result, Buddhism was more and more accepted into mainstream Chinese culture and began to have an important impact on the life and values of society as a whole.

The period was remarkable for two major developments. One was the institution of a Buddhist nuns' order. In 317, Chu Ching-chien (Pure Example; circa 292–361) was the first Chinese woman to take the novice's precepts. When joined by 24 other like-minded women, she founded a convent in Ch'ang-an. Soon other convents were founded in both north and south China. Not until 434, however, was the Bhikṣuṇī Sangha established on Chinese soil, when a group of Sri Lankan bhikṣuṇīs came specifically for that purpose. This ordination line has lasted in Chinese communities in Taiwan, Hong Kong, and Singapore up to the present day.

The founding of the Bhikṣuṇī Sangha was a momentous event in the history of China, for it opened up the possibility of a religious vocation to women who, up until that point in time, had to lead their entire lives under the supervision of their "Three Masters": father, husband, and son. Women with literary or religious talents could now devote their time to study, meditation, and devotion. Many nuns came to prominence as teachers known for their mastery of classical Chinese literature as well as Buddhist texts. Unfortunately, the rules of their order required that their convents be built within city walls; they thus incurred all the disadvantages of being close to the centers of political power. Open to charges of corruption when they were perceived as wielding too much influence in the imperial courts, they were among the first to bear the brunt of any imperial crackdowns on Buddhist monastic orders.

The other remarkable development during this period was the widespread conversion of the ruling elites to Buddhism, beginning in the early decades of the fourth century. Particularly in the south, sons and daughters of noble families, many of whom had been orphaned during the warfare at the end of the western Chin, entered the monastic orders. Already versed in the Chinese classics, their urbanity and erudition proved to be of great assistance in spreading the religion among their fellow members of the nobility, as they brought home the point that a Buddhist could be "one of us." Although many of the elite monks took ordination because of a true sense of spiritual need, some of them were attracted to the monastic life as a new version of the traditional life of the retired scholar, who chose a lifestyle of rustic simplicity to devote himself fully to art, literature, and philosophical conversation. As a result, Buddhist themes began appearing in the traditional scholar's domains of painting and literature during the fourth century.

The conversion of the elites, together with the continued spread of Buddhist devotion among the lower classes, brought about a three-way split in the modes of Sangha life: large monastic estates patronized by the ruling elites, smaller village monasteries, and forest hermitages for monks who focused on ch'an (dhyāna) practice. In principle, the Sangha, in contrast to Chinese society in general, was relatively free of class distinctions. People from the lower classes who showed intellectual promise could find in the monastic orders an opportunity for a literary education that was otherwise closed to them. However, there was a general tendency for members of the smaller village monasteries to remain illiterate, their Buddhism an amalgam of devotional practices and local spirit cults. Similarly, in the forest hermitages there was little concern for the Vinaya, and the monks tended to combine the methods of Buddhist meditation with traditional Taoist practices aimed at immortality. Unlike the great monastic estates, the smaller monasteries and hermitages remained outside the pale of government control. These tendencies characterized Buddhism for many centuries in both the north and south.

On the level of elite Buddhism, however, the northern and southern kingdoms differed widely. In the south, the monks and nuns who frequented the court were members of the Chinese elite, moving naturally among their own kind, speaking the same language and inhabiting the same intellectual universe as the members of the court. The sense of fellow identity they were able to cultivate enabled them to succeed in exerting the independence of the Sangha from the political realm without giving rise to any sense of threat. In 340 and again in 402, the question arose as to whether monastics should pay deference to the emperor, and on both occasions the ultimate decision was no. Occasionally the sense of easy familiarity between rulers and the aristocratic monks backfired. Po Yüan, the first Chinese monk known to have developed a personal friendship with a member of the imperial house, so impressed his host that he was asked to leave the Sangha and join the court. When he refused, he was whipped to death. The same fate befell his brother. On the whole, though, the relationship between the Sangha and the southern rulers was stable and secure.

Not so in the north. Northern elite Buddhism was largely a continuation of the earlier pattern, in which missionary monks were of foreign extraction and depended largely on their psychic powers to gain favor with the court. A prime example was the brave and righteous old Kuchean wonder-worker Fo-t'u-teng, who arrived in north China around 310. He served as court advisor for more than 20 years, performing magic, forecasting the future, mitigating the excesses of the barbarian rulers, and training a cadre of disciplined and enterprising Chinese monks. Fo-t'u-teng had no pretensions to being a scholar. The Buddhism that grew under his influence stressed devotion and meditation, rather than intellectual sophistication. The lack of class and racial fellowship between monks and rulers, however, meant that the relationship in the north was more volatile than in the south, with the government alternating between lavish support for and severe repression of the Sangha. Twice—in 446 and 574—edicts were issued for the total suppression of Buddhism, in response to complaints from government officials that the Sangha was growing too strong. However, because none of the rulers involved controlled all of

China, the monastics could escape with copies of their scriptures to other parts of the empire. In both cases the repression was short-lived, as Buddhism had acquired widespread popular support, and in both cases the ruling dynasties did their best to make up for the harm that had been done. In 460, for example, the ruler of the northern Wei dynasty (386–534) undertook the creation of one of the world's great religious monuments, the cave temples of Yiin-kang, as an act of expiation for the earlier persecution.

Another long-lasting contribution to Chinese Buddhism had been made earlier by the founder of the northern Wei dynasty, who appointed a moral and learned monk to the civil service post of Sangha-director, thus establishing government jurisdiction over the monasteries in his realm. This arrangement was followed by all succeeding dynasties up to the twentieth century. Unlike the monks in the south, the appointed monk did not fight for the Sangha's independence from the state but paid deference to the emperor, justifying his action by identifying the emperor with the Tathāgata.

However, the most important development of this period, in both the north and south, was that Buddhism came to take center stage in Chinese intellectual life. The first step in this process, begun by the elite monks of the south during the fourth century, was to apply Buddhist ideas to issues that had been raised in Confucian and Taoist intellectual circles during the third century. Ultimately, proponents of this "Buddho-Taoism" began to realize that they were distorting the Buddha's message and so began efforts to understand Buddhism on its own terms. This prepared the way for the great monk-translator Kumārajīva, who arrived in Ch'ang-an and inaugurated a period in which scholars focused on mastering Indian scholastic treatises and attempted to create order from the much more extensive picture of Buddhism that resulted.

8.4.1 The Era of Buddho-Taoism

To understand Buddho-Taoism and its impact on the subsequent centuries of Buddhist thought in east Asia, it is necessary to backtrack and deal in some detail with the issues of third-century intellectual life in China. The third century had been a period of great philosophical activity in China, one that was to determine the vocabulary and values the Chinese used in trying to make Buddhism intelligible to themselves for many centuries afterward. Trained bureaucrats focused on what was, for them, the central issue of philosophy: the art of government. Because they felt that any successful government had to harmonize with the principles underlying nature, their discussions modulated quickly from social philosophy to metaphysics and back. The event that sparked their philosophizing—termed *hsüan hsüeh* (Arcane Learning)—was the fall of the Han dynasty: Why had the dynasty failed even though it had been run in accordance with the *I Ching*, the traditional book of divination, and the Confucian classics? Was there something wrong with these classics, or had they simply been misapplied?

The masters of Arcane Learning decided that the problem lay primarily in the interpretation of the classics and not so much in the classics themselves.

They made a distinction between the basic principles underlying the insights of the classic thinkers and the way in which those principles had been expressed. The more an expression took into account the particulars of the situation it addressed, the farther it was from the basic principle. Thus the masters of Arcane Learning developed a preference for what later generations came to call "sudden" expressions—those that expressed in most immediate terms the basic principles—over "gradual" expressions, which in some cases were a necessary bridge from the principle to a particular situation, but in other situations might prove misleading. This preference carried over into the study of Buddhism and explains why many Buddhist thinkers and meditators tried so hard to avoid any indication that their teachings were "gradual."

Once the principle underlying the text was separated from its expression, the question arose as to how the principle was to be grasped. Here Wang Pi (226–49) and other members of the first generation of masters of Arcane Learning (called the proponents of 'nonbeing') borrowed a concept from the Taoist texts: that the realm of differentiated and nameable phenomena, which they termed 'being,' came from a common principle that was undifferentiated and unnameable, which they termed 'nonbeing.' 'Nonbeing' was the essence of all phenomena, whereas 'being' was the function of 'nonbeing.' Words were adequate for expressing phenomena, but not for their underlying principle. Again, this distinction between essence and function, and the strong sense that words were incapable of expressing underlying essences, were to play a large role in Chinese Buddhist thought.

Because 'nonbeing' was the ultimate principle underlying not only the universe but also any form of government that attempted to harmonize with nature, the way to intuit this principle was for the Ruler to attain a frame of mind in touch with the undifferentiated and unnamed. Thus attuned, he would be able to make spontaneous decisions that, in a natural pattern of stimulus and response between Ruler and heaven, would lead to the harmony of society and the world of phenomena in general.

This line of thinking sparked a reaction from a coterie of Taoist intellectuals, led by Juan Chi (210–63), who insisted that if the same principle underlay all beings and could be touched by a completely natural mind, everyone had the ability to touch it and the right to do whatever came spontaneously. These thinkers practiced what they taught and became known for flouting almost every social convention imaginable. Although their position was never widely adopted, it remained as an undercurrent in Chinese society in the belief that people who behave unconventionally are either insane or else directly in touch with a higher principle. This belief also had an effect on attitudes toward unconventional Buddhist meditation masters in later centuries.

However, solid pillars of society, such as Hsiang Hsiu (circa 221–300), could not countenance this call for anarchy, so they reformulated the basic principles of Arcane Learning in retaliation. Because they used these new principles to interpret Taoist classics as a way of undercutting their opponents, their thought has been termed neo-Taoism. In their day, however, the neo-Taoists were termed the proponents of 'being'. Their basic position was that there is no single underlying principle of the universe, and no difference between essence and function. Words are thus perfectly adequate for expressing the essence of things. Each individual thing or living being arises spontaneously, uncaused, with its own allotted place in the totality of things, its spontaneous nature being to function in its allotted way. Good and evil for each being are thus relative to how well they follow their individual function. Only the Sage (Ruler) has the allotment to know the allotment of all beings under heaven, and to lie above their relative norms of good and evil. Thus only he has the right to be in a natural relationship of stimulus and response with the forces of heaven.

This reformulation succeeded in closing the door on anarchy and defending the status quo. However, it could not account for the source of the allotment of things and made the basic structure of the universe seem arbitrary and amoral. It was on this point that many Chinese thinkers at the beginning of the fourth century realized that Buddhism had much to offer to their ongoing discussion. The doctrine of karma and rebirth offered a moral structure to the universe and to the pattern of stimulus and response between humanity and its environment, at the same time accounting for the allotment of all phenomena. Chinese monks—such as Chi Tun (314–66)—also realized that the Prajñā-pāramitā doctrines of emptiness and the two levels of truth were relevant to the discussion. Some of them discerned that the doctrine of emptiness agreed with the teachings that claimed that things had no underlying essence—although nothing arose spontaneously—in that all things were part of an interdependent causal web. Others viewed emptiness as the essence from which all things came—like the Tao—and to which they would all return. These views resurfaced several centuries later and formed the basis for the great doctrinal syntheses of the sixth to ninth centuries.

The important development in the fourth century, however, was that Buddhism gained recognition as a potential solution for issues that had been plaguing Chinese thought. The contribution of Chinese monks to these issues was also momentous in sociological terms. It ended the bureaucratic monopoly on metaphysical speculation, bringing it into the religious cloister, where the goal of speculation was more personal than political. In principle it also opened the role of Sage—the wise person who could attain a state of mind that was in touch with the basic essence of the universe, which had long been the Ruler's monopoly—to men and women from all levels of society. At the same time, this opening up of roles did not pose the threat of anarchy, because the nature of that essence was thoroughly moral.

In the course of making this drastic shift in Chinese intellectual life, some of the monks responsible for Buddho-Taoism began to realize how little they actually understood Buddhism. Chief among them were Tao-an (312–85) and his disciple, Hui-yüan (334–circa 416). Tao-an was the most illustrious of Fo-t'u-teng's disciples. Driven from Ch'ang-an by civil war, he established a center in the south and joined the Buddho-Taoist discussions. As he collected and cataloged copies of the scriptures to aid in his work, he was struck by the gaps and inconsistencies in the various translations then available. When in 379 he was captured by northern forces and taken back to Ch'ang-an at the request of the new emperor, a Tibetan, he went back with a plan. He opened the first translation bureau granted imperial support and succeeded in attracting not only Indian monks knowledgeable in Buddhist texts but also a high-caliber team of Chinese scribes. Monks were dispatched to Khotan to bring back reliable texts. In the few years before his death, the bureau was able to translate an important body of literature, mostly Sarvāstivādin. In this it laid the groundwork for the major accomplishments of Kumārajīva, the monk-scholar from Kucha who was to change the face of Chinese Buddhist doctrine.

8.4.2 The Rise of Buddhist Scholasticism

Kumārajīva (344–413) was brought to Ch'ang-an in 401 as the bounty from a military conquest. The son of an Indian nobleman and a Kuchean princess, he had ordained as a novice at an early age and traveled to India, together with his mother, who had been ordained as a nun, where he was converted to the Mādhyamika school. Famous in China for his command of Buddhist doctrine even before his capture, Kumārajīva was able to inaugurate an extensive translation project in cooperation with hundreds of monks. The quality of their work far surpassed that of previous translators in terms of accuracy, intelligibility, and elegance. Even though their translations were still flawed on technical points, many of these texts are regarded even today as standards of the old translation style, in preference to the later and more accurate new translation style developed in the seventh century by Hsüan-tsang (circa 596–664). Kumārajīva's lyrical version of the *Lotus Sūtra,* for example, has been chanted daily by millions of Buddhists throughout east Asia for centuries.

Kumārajīva's contributions to Chinese Buddhism, however, went beyond the translation of texts. He lectured his translation team and other audiences on the importance of understanding Buddhist ideas in their original doctrinal context. Although he translated a variety of Mahāyāna and—at the request of his hosts—Hīnayāna texts, his specialty was Madhyamika. In his commentaries, prefaces, and lectures, he gave his Chinese disciples a thorough grounding in the subject. Although his school of disciples was scattered by an invasion of Ch'ang-an in 420, this disbanding had the long-term effect of disseminating his ideas throughout China, inaugurating a new era in Chinese Buddhist studies. During the fifth and sixth centuries, monks formed study groups specializing in particular texts: Mādhyamika treatises, Vinaya texts (Sarvāstivādin and Dharmaguptaka), Yogācāra treatises, the *Lotus Sūtra,* and the *Nirvāṇa Sūtra,* among others. Even two Hīnayāna texts—the *Abhidharmakośa* and the *Satyasiddhi* (a text of the Bahuśrutīya offshoot of the Mahāsanghikas)—attracted followings, although these were eventually absorbed into Mahāyāna schools. Of these study groups, the one devoted to three basic Mādhyamika treatises (San-lun) came the closest to becoming a distinct school, although interest in Mādhyamika gradually waned during this period, as its doctrine was felt to be too nihilistic. Yogācāra, with its more positive doctrine of the Dharmakāya, and tathāgata-garbha, which the Chinese interpreted as *fo-hsing* (Buddha-nature), became more and more prominent. Some monks specialized in single texts; others traveled from group to group to broaden their learning. Eventually these study groups either died out in China or else were absorbed into the multisystem schools of later centuries. A few of them were exported to Korea and Japan, where they have maintained a separate existence up to the present day.

Paradoxically, this respect for Buddhist texts spawned a number of apocryphal translations—texts composed in Chinese that claimed to be translations from Sanskrit—as individual thinkers tried to bestow the authority of scripture on their own understanding of Buddhist doctrine. Foremost among these texts was *The Awakening of Faith*, attributed to Aśvaghoṣa (see Section 4.4), which gave a Taoist tinge to the notion of the Buddha-nature as the One Mind from which all things came. This text was to play a major role in shaping the Ch'an and Hua-yen schools.

As Chinese scholars gained greater familiarity with Buddhist texts during this period, they were confronted with a variety of doctrinal issues. Some of the issues, such as the question as to whether some beings were ineligible for Buddhahood (Strong *EB*, sec. 8.3.1), were hotly debated. This particular issue was sparked by an incomplete translation of the *Nirvāṇa Sūtra* and was settled only after a more complete translation of the text came to light. This incident underscored the point that not all available translations were totally reliable, and that there was a continued need for efforts to get back to the source. However, even in the more trustworthy translations there were many points of contradiction. The fact that all the Sūtras claimed to come from the Buddha led many thinkers to seek a comprehensive system for resolving the differences among them. They ended up turning from the scholastic treatises to the Mahāyāna Sūtras, which furnished the rudiments of an explanation: The Buddha used skillful means and preached different doctrines to suit the conditions of his various audiences at different points in his career. This interpretation struck a responsive chord, as it fit in with the Arcane Learning theme of distinguishing basic principles from their expression. That the Mahāyāna Sūtras were the ones offering this explanation is one of the factors that assured the ascendancy of Mahāyāna over Hīnayāna in Chinese thought.

One of the first proposals for ordering Buddhist doctrines based on this insight was offered by Hui Kuang (468–537). According to him, the Buddha taught four essential doctrines, in ascending order of sophistication: (1) the Abhidharma doctrine that claims that phenomena arise in accordance with causes and conditions, a doctrine taught to counteract the view of spontaneous origination; (2) the Satyasiddhi doctrine that claims that phenomena are no more than mere names, as they cannot exist independently of causes and conditions; (3) the Mādhyamika doctrine that claims that even names are empty because there are no substantial phenomena underlying them; and (4) the doctrine of the ever-abiding Buddha-nature that constitutes the ultimate reality, taught by the *Nirvāṇa* and *Avataṃsaka Sūtras,* among others. This attempt to provide a comprehensive framework for all Buddhist teachings laid the groundwork for the great doctrinal syntheses of the Sui and T'ang dynasties.

8.5 THE SUI AND T'ANG DYNASTIES (581–907)

In 581, an avowed Buddhist—Wen-ti (r. 581–604)—succeeded in reuniting the empire, partly through a conscious policy of promoting Buddhism combined with Confucianism as a unifying ideology. Although the Sui dynasty he founded fell in 617, the T'ang dynasty that replaced it lasted for almost three centuries. Thus Buddhism was faced with a new situation: For the first time since it had entered the mainstream of Chinese civilization, the empire was united. This proved to be a mixed blessing. In the area of doctrine and meditation practice, the Chinese during these centuries finally mastered the Buddhist tradition and made it their own. Many of the great scholars and meditators whose reputations were to assume legendary proportions in Chinese Buddhism—Hsüan-tsang, Chih-i, Fa-tsang, Hui-neng, and Lin-chi, among others—flourished during this time. In the institutional area, however, because political power was concentrated in a single ruling house with authority over the entire empire, the Sangha was more exposed to the whims and preferences of a small handful of people. This was ultimately to prove disastrous.

Although Wen-ti had enforced throughout the empire the southern principle that monastics need not kowtow to government officials, the general pattern of relations between the Sangha and the state followed the northern tradition of volatile ups and downs. The T'ang ruling house claimed to be descended from the Taoist sage Lao-tzu, so their general sentiments were not pro-Buddhist. A few of the rulers converted to Buddhism and lavished enormous donations on the Sangha, only to be followed by successors who felt called upon to undo their predecessors' excesses and bring the religion back in line. In the first two centuries of the dynasty, however, anti-Buddhist measures were fairly circumscribed. The religion had broad support outside of the court, and rulers feared that excessively harsh measures would backfire.

One of the highlights of the first century of the T'ang occurred in 645, when the pilgrim-monk Hsüan-tsang (596–664) returned from his long overland journey to India with a collection of more than 675 Buddhist texts. The story of his journey fired the imagination of the Chinese people, and they gave him a hero's welcome on his arrival at Ch'ang-an. Gaining imperial support for a translation team to render his collection of texts into Chinese, he ultimately converted the Taoist emperor, T'ai-tsung (r. 626–49), to Buddhism. Sadly, he lived to translate only a small portion of the texts he had brought back. His translation team was undoubtedly the most talented ever assembled on Chinese soil, and he himself was one of the few Chinese ever to master Sanskrit. He and his coworkers developed a new, more accurate vocabulary for rendering Buddhist ideas into Chinese, but only one text using this vocabulary—the apocryphal *Heart Sūtra*—ever gained popularity. At his death, the reigning emperor—whose personal admiration for Hsüan-tsang did not extend to Buddhism—ordered the translation team disbanded and the remaining untranslated texts placed in an imperial library. They were never translated. The Yogācāra school founded by Hsüan-tsang—called Fa-hsiang (Dharma Characteristic)—survived no more than a century in China. This was due partly to its assertion that not all beings were eligible for Buddhahood, and partly to concerted attacks from the Hua-yen school, its major competitor for imperial patronage. However, the school did continue in Korea and Japan. Hsüan-tsang's influence on Chinese Buddhism lived on less in his scholarship than in the tales that developed around his journey, which provided the model for the classic novel *Journey to the West* (see Section 8.7).

Another landmark in the Buddhist history of the T'ang was the reign of Empress Wu (circa 625–706). Beginning her life in court as a concubine of Emperor T'ai-tsung and continuing as the major wife of his son, Wu Chao skillfully maneuvered herself into a position of power before her husband's death by eliminating her rivals. Not content to rule as regent for her son, she declared herself emperor and established a new dynasty. Unable to gain support from Taoists or Confucians, she sought to solidify her precarious position as a woman ruler by claiming to be the incarnation of Maitreya and actively cultivating the support of the Sangha, who obliged her by reporting omens and "discovering" texts that justified her rule. Although much of this activity was of dubious benefit to the religion, she sponsored important translation teams—on occasion working as a scribe herself—and actively patronized the Ch'an and Hua-yen schools.

After Empress Wu was driven from the throne in 705, a descendent of the original T'ang line, Hsüan-tsung (r. 712–56), came to power, determined to correct what he viewed as the Sangha's abuse of its privileged position. Although many imperially supported monasteries had used their wealth for charitable purposes, such as alms houses for the poor, there were genuine abuses that needed correcting. Many monks and nuns had become ordained, not with a desire to practice the religion, but simply to evade taxation and live comfortably off the generosity of lay donors. Some monasteries were blatant business enterprises, occupying prime commercial locations near markets (Strong *EB*, sec. 8.8.2). Others, called "merit cloisters," were tax havens for the aristocrats who had built them and who were still receiving proceeds from the land. One of Hsüan-tsung's first moves to suppress Buddhism was a "sifting and weeding" of the monastics on imperial rosters. More than thirty thousand monks and nuns were defrocked, approximately one-fourth of the registered monastics in the empire. Although he planned further moves against the Sangha, Hsüan-tsung was prevented by political developments. Ironically, during this selective purge he had begun to patronize Tantric Buddhist missionaries, Indian initiates into the Yoga Tantras (see Section 6.3.2). Chinese Tantrism, called Chen-yen, or Truth-Word, flourished at the court for a little less than a century, providing spells for producing rain and protecting the state. Upon the death of the last Tantric advisor to the court, Amoghavajra (705–74), Chen-yen died out as a separate school in China, although some of its practices were incorporated into popular Taoism, where they still exist today.

Hsüan-tsung's reign is regarded as the peak of T'ang art, poetry, and culture, but it also marked the beginning of the end of the dynasty. The debilitating An Lu-shan Rebellion (755–64), together with widespread famine, cut the population of the empire from 53 to 17 million. The rebellion did both short-term and long-term damage to the Sangha. The short-term damage lay in the destruction of many monasteries and the total demise of Hsüan-tsung's Fa-hsiang school. The long-term damage was caused by a government policy devised to raise money for the financially strapped imperial treasury. Official certificates, allowing the bearer to become ordained as a Buddhist monastic, were offered to anyone who would pay a flat fee. This reversed a centuries-long practice of tight state controls over ordinations, and huge numbers of people responded. Although the policy worked admirably in the short run, raising the needed funds, it continued unchecked for decades after the rebellion, decimating the tax rolls and filling the monasteries with tax dodgers. In 830 it was estimated that there were twice as many monks and nuns as there had been in 730. Even Buddhists were saying that the policy was destroying their religion.

Clearly, something had to be done, but no ruler had either the desire or the will to effect any major restrictions until Emperor Wu-tsung (r. 840–46) came to the throne. A rabid Taoist, Wu-tsung was driven more by religious zeal than by political considerations. When his Taoist priests convinced him that their efforts to make him immortal were being foiled by the preponderance of "black" in the empire—black being the color of the Buddhist monastic robes—he determined to wipe Buddhism from the face of China. In a series of edicts dating from 842 to 845, he succeeded in destroying more than 4,600 temples and 40,000 shrines across the empire, and forcing 260,500 monks and nuns back to lay life. The Japanese monk Ennin happened to be studying in China at the time and left behind a graphic account of the sufferings incurred not only by the Sangha but also by those who had come to depend on it. Slave families that had been assigned to monasteries were separated, and the poor were evicted from the alms houses. Military governors in a few regions refused to obey the edicts, and lay Buddhists did their best to shelter some of the monks and nuns, but by and large the purge was as thorough as any a premodern state could inflict on its citizens.

Shortly after issuing his most strident anti-Buddhist edicts, Wu-tsung began suffering from the effects of his Taoist "immortality pills." He issued demands that live sea otters and the hearts and livers of fifteen-year-old youths and maidens be brought to the palace for his potions. Within a few months he was dead, poisoned by his quest for immortality, at age 32. Buddhists immediately interpreted his death as karmic retribution for his persecution of the religion.

Whatever scorn later emperors may have felt for Buddhism, this perception may account for the fact that there were no more purges of the Sangha until the twentieth century.

Wu-tsung's successor, Hsuen-tsung (r. 846–59), made attempts to reinstate the religion, although he had to proceed cautiously in the face of continued anti-Buddhist feeling in the court. Nonetheless, he and his successors had managed to reopen monasteries and reordain large numbers of monastics when a second blow came in the form of the Huang Ch'ao Rebellion (875–84). Although this rebellion was not directed against Buddhist institutions per se, the wanton destruction it caused lay many monasteries to waste. After the rebellion, the power of the imperial house was so sapped that little could be done to help the Sangha. The dynasty fell in 907, and not until 970 was the empire reunited.

The double blow of persecution and rebellion at the end of the T'ang had a telling effect on the development of Chinese Buddhism. In particular, the destruction of monastic libraries meant that the great scholastic schools, which depended on written commentaries for their continued existence, were damaged almost beyond repair. T'ien-t'ai and Hua-yen, the most important of the schools, revived somewhat in the Sung dynasty only because Korean monks were able to provide the Chinese with texts that had been sequestered in Korea. Even the traditions that depended more on oral transmission, Ch'an and Ching-te (Pure Land), were damaged as well. Of the nine Ch'an meditation lineages existing before the persecution, only two survived the end of the dynasty, largely because they were located in areas where local governors resisted the purge. The texts that had formed the theoretical basis for Pure Land practice were mostly destroyed. Nevertheless, even in their truncated form, these innovative schools continued to have an influence in later centuries. We can only conjecture what might have developed if more of their breadth and variety had been allowed to survive the end of the dynasty that had spawned them.

8.5.1 T'ien-t'ai

T'ien-t'ai (Heavenly Terrace), the first of the great multisystem schools, took its name from the mountain in Chekiang where its principal center was located. Although Hui-ssu (515–76) is honored as the school's founder, the first true architect of the T'ien-t'ai system was his student Chih-i (538–97). As mentioned previously (see Section 8.4.2), the major issue facing Chinese Buddhist thinkers in the fifth and sixth centuries was how to find a comprehensive framework to encompass and explain the great variety of Buddhist texts emanating from India. Chih-i offered a solution to this problem by borrowing a concept, consciously or unconsciously, from the Arcane Learning proponents of 'nonbeing' (see Section 8.4.1): the idea that the *li* (principle) underlying all *shih* (phenomena) lies beyond words. From this it follows that all true statements describing that principle can at best be only partially adequate; their opposites may also be partially true. Thus the statements that come closest to expressing the truth of principle are the middle ones that encompass seeming contradictions, pointing out how both sides of the contradiction are true although neither is fully true. From this principle, Chih-i was able to build a system of great complexity and subtlety for comprehending the entire range of Buddhist doctrines and practice.

Chih-i applied this approach to what he called the three views of Buddhism: the provisional view of existing dharmas, represented by the Abhidharmists; the ultimate view of emptiness, represented by Mādhyamika; and the middle or complete view of the Buddha-nature, taught in the *Lotus, Avataṃsaka,* and *Nirvāṇa Sūtras.* This last view points directly at the highest principle underlying the cosmos, while at the same time comprehending the truth and limitations of the provisional and ultimate views. Chih-i was sophisticated enough to realize that even the complete view was not an entirely adequate expression of Buddha-nature; it was simply as close as language could get. Hence his insistence that study be paired with practice, for only then could absolute identity with Buddha-nature be fully realized.

Chih-i classified both doctrinal teachings and meditational practices into three categories: sudden, those that pointed directly to Buddha-nature; gradual, those that used expedient means; and variable, those that mixed sudden and gradual approaches in a variety of ways. Encompassing all these approaches was the complete approach, which Chih-i tried to provide in his two great works: *The Profound Meaning of the Lotus Sūtra (Fa-hua hsüan-i),* dealing with doctrine; and *The Great Calming and Contemplation (Mo-ho chih-kuan),* dealing with meditation practice.

Chih-i followed a passage in the *Nirvāṇa Sūtra,* classifying the Buddha's teachings into five flavors corresponding to five dairy products. The first flavor, corresponding to milk, includes the very earliest Buddhist texts; the second flavor, the cream, includes the Sūtra Piṭaka; the third flavor, the curds, corresponds to the great Mahāyāna Sūtras, such as the *Śrīmālā* and the *Vimalakīrti-nirdeśa;* the fourth flavor, the butter, corresponds to the *Prajñāpāramita Sūtras;* and the fifth flavor, the ghee, corresponds to the *Nirvāṇa Sūtra* itself. Just as cream comes from milk, and curds from cream, and so forth, the later Sūtras come from the earlier ones, being neither identical with nor different from them. Chih-i, following traditions that had developed within China during his time, made two changes in this lineup. The first flavor, he said, was the sudden flavor of the *Avataṃsaka Sūtra,* which the Chinese believed was the first sermon the Buddha delivered immediately after his Awakening; it was called sudden both because it was as direct expression of Buddha-nature as possible, and also because it made no concessions to the capacities of its listeners. Most who heard it were bewildered. Thus the Buddha retraced his steps and began formulating the body of gradual teachings that make up the Sūtra Piṭaka.

Chih-i's second main change in the lineup was to include the *Lotus Sūtra* under the fifth flavor as the most perfect expression of the Buddha's teachings. This was because it had the same "sudden" message as the *Avataṃsaka Sūtra,* but illustrated the message with expedient similes and explanations that made its meaning perfectly clear to all its listeners. Thus it represents Buddhist doctrine at its most complete.

As with all categories in Chih-i's thought, these flavors are relative: Because no words can adequately express Buddha-nature, all teachings are gradual to some extent; because all the teachings come from an Awakened mind, they are all partially sudden. This relativity is what gives Chih-i's categories, which otherwise would have become little more than sorting boxes, nuance and complexity. Because they are relative, they are also interpenetrating. The realization of this point constitutes the highest teaching: that principle cannot be found apart from phenomena. Even though distinctions are made between shallow and profound, and so forth, all truths are universally coextensive. The entire cosmos is immanent in a moment of thought and is perceived simultaneously by the Awakened mind as empty, substantial, both, and neither.

To show the way to this realization, Chih-i wrote the most extensive and comprehensive meditation guide that had ever appeared in China. Again, he made a distinction between sudden, gradual, and variable methods. "Sudden," in the context of practice, means that the method focuses immediately on Buddha-nature as its object from the moment that bodhicitta occurs. In gradual methods, one makes use of various expedient objects, such as the breath, *nien-fo* (the repetition of the Buddha's name), or contemplation of the *Lotus Sūtra* (the method that had given rise to Chih-i's own first experience of great samādhi). Here again, the distinctions are relative. Buddha-nature is present in all mental moments; thus all meditation methods are in a sense sudden. Because in the ultimate sense Buddha-nature transcends the subject/object dichotomy, it cannot be an object. Thus all methods are to some extent gradual. The complete method entailed contemplating the mind in all postures, simply viewing its passing states as partial expressions of Buddha-nature. However, Chih-i advised that contemplation of mind be practiced in conjunction with the more gradual methods; otherwise, simply viewing good and bad states coming and going, one might be misled into believing that there was no practical need to distinguish right and wrong. In this manner, his view of the total practice encompassed the particulars without denying their validity.

Issues of sudden and gradual, verbal doctrine and practice, and principle and phenomena coalesce in Chih-i's analysis of the question of the identity between the mind and Buddha-nature. In the course of one's practice, one proceeds step-by-step through six levels of identity, beginning with identity in principle—the identity that adheres between principle and phenomena in general, even before acquaintance with the Buddha's teaching—moving on to verbal identity, that is, the intellectual understanding that the mind and Buddha-nature are identical, and then developing through three stages of practice until culminating in ultimate identity, the full attainment of Buddhahood. One had to understand these six levels at the outset, Chih-i maintained, for otherwise one would be led either to the arrogance of thinking that one was already fully identical with Buddha-nature before the practice, or into discouragement in thinking that one had nothing in common with the goal. Again, the complete view overcomes the limitations inherent in an either/or dichotomy, encompassing and transcending the partial truth and falsity of one-sided views.

Chih-i's thought had a far-reaching influence on east Asian Buddhism. Even those who did not read his work came to assume that he had proven the internal coherence of Buddhism once and for all, so they could get on to other work. He established the doctrine of the Buddha-nature as the ultimate Buddhist teaching, a position that was accepted by all east Asian schools of doctrine and practice. His writings on meditation, in particular, formed the matrix in which the Ch'an schools developed. Many later Ch'an meditation guides, even into the eleventh century, repeated large portions of *The Great Calming and Contemplation* verbatim. Unlike the later Ch'an schools, however, Chih-i did not deprecate gradual methods of teaching or practice. According to him, Buddhism was similar to a complete course of medical science. A person with a limited view might not see the necessity for certain medicines or techniques, but a truly skilled doctor knows the variety of illnesses that can occur and the need for a full panoply of techniques for dealing with them. However, the strength of the T'ien-t'ai system, its comprehensiveness, was also its weakness in that it required its followers to diffuse their energies in an effort to master all areas of doctrine and practice. This may be one of the reasons why, in the seventh century, many T'ien-t'ai monks went over to the newly developing Ch'an schools.

During the sixth century, however, Chih-i and T'ien-t'ai in general received strong support from the ruling house of the Sui dynasty, which felt that the school's integration of southern scholarship with northern meditation and devotional methods paralleled its policy of political integration. The connection with the Sui ruling house, however, meant that the school was eclipsed during the early T'ang dynasty. In the eighth century, Chan-jan (711–82) revived the school in response to what he saw as the mistaken views of Hua-yen. Chan-jan was responsible for reformulating Chih-i's views into a matrix that came to be the school's slogan: the five periods and the eight teachings. The five periods corresponded to the five flavors; the eight teachings were actually two lists of four categories. The first list consisted of four methods of teachings: sudden, gradual, secret (one teaching that meant different things to different groups), and variable (one teaching that gave sudden results to one group and gradual results to another). The second list consisted of four doctrines: *tripiṭaka* (doctrines particular to the Hīnayāna, such as the Wings to Awakening); shared (common to both the Hīnayāna and the Mahāyāna); distinctive (exclusive to Mahāyāna); and complete (totally comprehensive). In this manner Chan-jan sorted out three separate ways of classifying the Buddha's teachings—in terms of chronology, method, and doctrine—while at the same time tracing the complex relations among the three. Thus he managed to clear up an issue that the Hua-yen patriarch Fa-tsang had confused.

T'ien-t'ai was practically wiped out during the troubled years of the ninth century. Texts were destroyed, and it was not until the latter part of the Five Dynasty period (907–60) that the ruler of Chekiang was able to send to Korea for copies of T'ien-t'ai texts to be brought back to China. The Korean monk Chegwan (d. 971) not only brought the texts but also composed a short summary of T'ien-t'ai doctrines (mistakenly attributing Chan-jan's innovations to

Chih-i), which became one of the standard texts of the school. Beginning in the eleventh century, T'ien-t'ai was established as the main surviving doctrinal school, but its earlier preeminence in meditation was totally eclipsed by Ch'an. The school's Japanese offshoot, Tendai (see Section 10.4), proved to be institutionally much stronger than the parent stock.

8.5.2 Hua-yen

Hua-yen, the second great multisystem school, took its name from the *Avataṃsaka* (Flower Ornament = Hua-yen) *Sūtra,* whose teachings formed the basis for many of the school's doctrines. It is a difficult school to define, not only because of the inherent complexity of its teachings, but also because those teachings changed so radically over the course of the three centuries from the school's first patriarch to its last. To convey a sense of this change, we will discuss the teachings of two patriarchs: the third, Fa-tsang (643–712), who was the school's first great architect; and the fifth, Tsung-mi (779–840), a Ch'an patriarch who recast Hua-yen thought in a way that made it relevant to Ch'an practice.

The first four patriarchs of the Hua-yen school differed with the T'ien-t'ai school on the issue of the One Vehicle taught in the *Lotus Sūtra* (see Section 5.5.2). According to T'ien-t'ai, the *One Vehicle* was a blanket term for the three vehicles of śrāvaka, pratyeka-buddha, and bodhisattva. According to the Hua-yen patriarchs, the One Vehicle was actually a separate vehicle, superior to all the others. Although it shared some common points with standard Mahāyāna, it also possessed special doctrines of its own. This point was made most succinctly by the fourth Hua-yen patriarch, Ch'eng-kuan (738–839), in his theory of the fourfold *dharmadhātu,* or Dharma-realm, which lists four different ways of viewing reality. The first view, that of the Hīnayāna Abhidharma, sees reality in terms of shih (differentiated phenomena). The second view, that of Mādhyamika and Yogācāra, sees reality in terms of the nature (hsing) underlying all phenomena. The third view, that of such Sūtras as the *Lotus* and *The Awakening of Faith,* sees reality in terms of the unimpeded interpenetration of principle and phenomena (li), whereas the fourth view, expounded in the *Avataṃsaka Sūtra* and exclusive to the One Vehicle, sees reality in terms of the unimpeded interpenetration of phenomena with all other phenomena in the cosmos. The image illustrating this view is that of Indra's net: a net of fine filaments stretching in all directions with a jewel at each interstice of the net. Each jewel reflects all the other jewels in the net, which means that each reflects the reflections in all the other jewels, and so on to infinity. This viewpoint is said to be that of a Buddha. Thus, much of Hua-yen metaphysics is concerned with the phenomenology of Awakening: what the cosmos looks like to an Awakened one.

Although this fourth viewpoint is supposed to be entirely separate from the others, it depends logically on the third, that of the unimpeded interpenetration of principle and phenomena. This dependence is brought out even in the writings of Fa-tsang, who of all the Hua-yen patriarchs lay the most stress on the absolute separateness of the One Vehicle. Fa-tsang's analysis begins with the teaching from *The Awakening of Faith* that describes how the entire cosmos comes from the Buddha-nature, which is One Mind with two aspects: principle and phenomena. "Principle" here means the law of dependent co-arising; "phenomena" means all things that co-arise dependently. Each aspect has two sides: Principle is characterized both by immutability (it is an unalterable law) and conditionedness (it finds expression in conditioned things); phenomena are characterized by quasi existence (they function in a causal network) and emptiness (they have no separate essence of their own). Fa-tsang then goes on to establish that principle cannot exist separately from phenomena. In fact, principle and phenomena are two sides of one thing. The quasi existence of phenomena is nothing other than the conditionedness of principle. Following Nāgārjuna's identification of emptiness with the law of dependent co-arising, the emptiness of phenomena is nothing other than the immutability of principle. Thus there cannot be one without the other.

From this equation, Fa-tsang goes on to claim that the entire cosmos is identical with the mind and body of the Buddha Mahāvairocana (see Section 5.5), for Buddha-nature is nothing other than the principle of dependent co-arising. It is important to keep this point in mind in order to see how Fa-tsang builds a conceptual model for moving from the third view of the dharmadhātu to the fourth—what he called simply "the dependent co-arising of the dharmadhātu." Mahāvairocana means Great Illuminator. The nature of the mind, from which the cosmos is made, is to reflect all that appears to it. Thus Fa-tsang's basic metaphor for the process of mutually dependent co-arising is that of light and mirrors. Causes penetrate their effects, just as light penetrates a mirror. Effects embrace their causes, just as mirrors contain all the light that penetrates them. From this conception of causality, Fa-tsang makes three assertions about the dependent co-arising of the dharmadhātu: (1) All phenomena interpenetrate one another. In other words, because each phenomenon is empty—that is, a result of the combined effects of all other phenomena—it is penetrated by all other phenomena and embraces them all. Because each has quasi existence, participating in the conditioning of all other phenomena, each phenomenon penetrates them all and is embraced by them all. Thus, (2) all phenomena are identical, in that each phenomenon functions in the same way. (3) Because the totality of each part already contains that part, interpenetration is repeated infinitely, as in the image of Indra's net.

Fa-tsang actively courted and won imperial patronage. According to his biography he explained the dependent co-arising of the dharmadhātu to Empress Wu with a concrete image. In the middle of a room he placed a Buddha-image and a lamp, representing the Buddha Mahāvairocana and the principle of dependent co-arising. He then placed mirrors in the 10 directions surrounding the Buddha-image: the 8 major directions plus above and below the Buddha-image. He then walked her around the room to show that each mirror (phenomenon) contained not only the Buddha-image (principle) but also all the other mirrors (phenomena), and that their mutual interpenetration repeated infinitely.

Fa-tsang worked out other implications of the dependent co-arising of the dharmadhātu in terms of three pairs of characteristics: totality and particularity, identity and difference, and unity and individuality. With regard to the totality of all phenomena, each phenomenon is both a particular within the totality and equivalent to the totality itself. One interesting result is that because each part depends on the whole, it is also the sole cause of the whole. This is because the lack of any one part means that the whole is lacking. However, each part is simply a part, because a whole has to be made up of parts. Thus, Fa-tsang says, particularity and totality are equivalent in this view of reality. With regard to the relationship between particular phenomena, because the existence of each phenomenon is its function—and because the function of each is to act as a cause of the whole—each phenomenon is identical with every other single phenomenon. But because the cosmos as we know it has to be made up of different parts, each phenomenon has to be different from others. Thus their identity comes from their differences. With regard to all other particular phenomena, each phenomenon unites with the others in forming the whole, and yet each maintains its individuality. Otherwise there would be nothing to keep up the process of continually forming the whole. Thus their unity comes from their individuality.

It should be obvious from these assertions that Fa-tsang did not shrink from paradoxes. In fact, when we turn to see how these teachings function in the practice of meditation, we find that their primary role is to short-circuit ordinary discursive thinking and to dazzle the mind into acceptance. Fa-tsang saw the bodhisattva Path as consisting of 53 stages, but for him the 10th stage, accepting the dependent co-arising of the dharmadhātu on faith, was the crucial one. As with the original Buddhist teachings (see Section 1.4.3), his view of the principle of interpenetration worked not only in the immediate present, but also across time. However, because he viewed the cosmos as already being identical with the mind and body of the Buddha Mahāvairocana, he regarded cause and effect as operating in both directions of time, forward as well as back: Because existence is function, the result is what makes the cause a cause, for without the result, the cause would not function as a cause, and thus would not exist as such. In this view, the attainment of the 10th stage already includes all the subsequent stages. On attaining this stage, one is already a bodhisattva and a Buddha. All that remains is to continue contemplating the emptiness and functioning of phenomena. Tranquility meditation, according to Fa-tsang, means viewing phenomena as empty. This gives rise to wisdom, so that the mind does not dwell in saṃsāra. Insight meditation means to view emptiness functioning in the form of phenomena. This gives rise to compassion, in that all phenomena are identical, so that there is no dwelling in nirvāṇa. With a mind dwelling neither in saṃsāra nor nirvāṇa, one remains in the cosmos, acting out of wisdom and compassion, which is a Buddha's true function.

Like most Mahāyānists, Fa-tsang viewed it an act of selfishness for a bodhisattva to enter nirvāṇa. However, he went further than most Mahāyānists in decreeing an unconditioned nirvāṇa a theoretical impossibility. According to him, there is no Unconditioned separate from the Conditioned. The universe already is the body and mind of the Buddha Mahāvairocana. Even if there were an unconditioned realm to go to, no one would be able to go until the entire universe went, grass and insects included. Because every part is interpenetrated by, identical with, and in union with every other part, all parts would have to go together. Thus Fa-tsang replaces the two parts of the early Buddhist view of Awakening—knowledge of the law of dependent co-arising and knowledge of nirvāṇa (see Section 1.4.3)—with only the first of the two. Additionally, according to him, that knowledge does not come from trying to deconstruct the process of dependent co-arising, but simply from appreciating its marvelous ramifications. In his vision, the cosmos is a dazzling place. One does not try to gain release from it, but instead tries, as the Taoists and Confucians, to live in harmony with it. One attains Buddhahood by appreciating its wonder; and one continues to live in it for infinity, acting out of wisdom and compassion, attuned to its infinitely repeating ramifications.

These, at least, were the intended implications of Fa-tsang's teachings. Chan-jan (see Section 8.5.1), however, saw other implications. Placed against Chih-i's doctrine of the six identities, Fa-tsang's assertion—that Buddhahood was implicitly attained at the stage of accepting the right view of the universe—equated the second stage of identity with the sixth. This, Chan-jan said, would lead to the danger of arrogance. One would feel that because one was already Awakened, there was no need to practice morality or any other stages of the Path. This point is borne out by Empress Wu's reported reaction to Fa-tsang's lesson in dependent co-arising. After touring the mirrored room, she had an identical room made for entertaining her paramours. According to her reasoning, if the cosmos already was identical with the Buddha Mahāvairocana, there was no way to say that things should be any better than they already were, and one was justified in acting in whatever way one liked. For her, the best thing to do in an infinitely repeating cosmos was to make love.

This issue—the place of Buddhist moral values on the Path—later formed the basis for Tsung-mi's recasting of Hua-yen doctrine. Tsung-mi was a master of the Ho-tse school of southern Ch'an, founded by Shen-hui (see Section 8.5.5). All southern Ch'an schools taught a doctrine of sudden Awakening, according to which gradual practice could not give rise to a true understanding of the Buddha-nature. Because Awakening was an all-or-nothing affair, gradual approaches to the immediacy of full understanding only got in the way. Thus some of the more radical Ch'an schools advocated the abandoning of moral norms and formal meditation practice altogether. Recognizing the danger in this approach, Tsung-mi sought a doctrinal justification for his conviction that sudden Awakening had to be followed by gradual cultivation—including observance of moral principles and formal meditation—in order to integrate that Awakening fully into one's life.

He found the justification he was looking for in the writings of Ch'eng-kuan, the fourth Hua-yen patriarch, and so went to study with him. In the course of his studies, he learned much that suited his purposes, but the doctrines that were the hallmarks of the Hua-yen school—the separateness of the

One Vehicle, the superiority of the *Avataṃsaka Sūtra,* the interpenetration of phenomena with phenomena—struck him as irrelevant. Thus he ended up abandoning or downplaying them in his own writings. Nevertheless, later generations counted him as the fifth patriarch of the school, largely because of the extensive use he made of the writings of the earlier patriarchs even while putting them in a new framework. In this sense, Tsung-mi is an object lesson in how the schools of T'ang Buddhism cannot be pigeonholed with a few neat slogans, for they developed in response to the concerns of their individual members.

Like Fa-tsang, Tsung-mi began with the theory, derived from *The Awakening of Faith Sūtra,* of the One Mind already intrinsically Awakened at the basis of reality. Unlike Fa-tsang, however, he did not dwell on the interpenetration of phenomena, but instead closely followed the evolutionary scheme discussed in the Sūtra in order to show how this One Mind gives rise to deluded experience. The process unfolds in 10 stages, analogous to what happens when a person falls asleep and dreams. In the first two stages, the purity of the tathāgata-garbha splits into two aspects: Awakened and unawakened. The unawakened aspect, the ālaya-vijñāṇa, is similar to a person simply falling asleep. In the next four stages, thought arises, followed by a perceived subject, perceived objects, and attachment to the basic elements (dharmas) of existence. This is analogous to the arising of dreams, along with dreaming consciousness, the perception of objects in the dream, and clinging to the things seen in the dream as real. In the next two stages there arises attachment to self, followed by such defilements as greed, anger, and delusion. This is similar to the dreaming person identifying with the person in the dream and feeling like and dislike for the objects in the dream. In the last two stages, karma is generated and one experiences the consequences. This is similar to the person in the dream acting in accordance with likes and dislikes, experiencing pleasure and pain.

Throughout this process, called natural origination, Tsung-mi follows *The Awakening of Faith* in asserting that the mind is still intrinsically Awakened in spite of the arising of delusion. The basic image is of an ocean: The water of the ocean is still intrinsically water even though wind makes it form into waves. Tsung-mi then develops this image to show how Buddhist practice reverses the process of delusion and brings the mind full circle back to the attainment of full Awakening. One learns the Dharma from one already Awakened and so realizes the true nature of the mind as being identical with the tathāgata-garbha. This is called sudden Awakening and is similar to the stopping of the wind. However, the inertia of the water continues forming waves. To calm down the waves, one must continue with gradual cultivation of one's sudden realization to bring it to completion.

Here Tsung-mi introduces a fivefold classification of Buddhist teachings designed to reverse the stages in the origination of delusion: (1) The teachings of human and divine beings, consisting essentially of the doctrine of karma and morality, overturn the process of generating karma and experiencing the consequences. (2) The Hīnayāna teachings then undercut one of the basic assumptions of the first category—the existence of a self taking rebirth—by analyzing the self into impersonal dharmas. This overturns the stages of defilement and attachment to self. (3) The Fa-hsiang/Yogācāra teachings of the three natures then serve to correct an assumption of the Hīnayāna teachings—that dharmas exist in an ultimate sense—by showing that they are simply projections of the ālaya-vijñāṇa. This overturns the stages of perceived subject, perceived objects, and attachment to dharmas. (4) The emptiness teachings then show that the projecting ālaya-vijñāṇa is just as unreal as the projected subject/object dichotomy. Although this stage succeeds in establishing that the ālaya-vijñāṇa is not the ultimate reality, it does not show what that reality is. Thus the need for the fifth class of teachings: (5) the revelation of the (Buddha) nature in such texts as *The Awakening of Faith,* the *Avataṃsaka Sūtra,* and the *Lotus Sūtra.*

Tsung-mi maintains that classes (2) to (4) express their teachings in negative terms in order to rid the mind of its attachment to concepts. Only when the mind has completed its training in these classes is it ready for the positive language of class (5), which—following Shen-hui—he says is ultimately expressed in a single word: awareness. Thus a full return to the awareness that constitutes the tathāgata-garbha can be attained only after a complete course of gradual cultivation, including training in morality and formal meditation. Tsung-mi treats the interpenetration of phenomena as little more than a footnote to the teaching of awareness, showing that he regarded it as an inappropriate teaching for people in lower stages of the Path and as ultimately irrelevant as a guide even to the advanced stage. The person who fathoms awareness on his/her own will realize this aspect of reality without having to be told.

In this way, Tsung-mi was able to preserve the components of the traditional Buddhist Path even in the light of the doctrine of sudden Awakening. However, he left a few of the basic difficulties in the doctrine of the tathāgata-garbha untouched. To borrow the image of the ocean and the wind: If everything is initially ocean, where does the wind come from? And if it is possible for initial Awakening to become defiled, what is to prevent the Awakening attained at the end of the Path from becoming defiled again? Unfortunately the creative dialogue on these issues in China ended with Tsung-mi, largely because of the general turmoil of the latter ninth century, so we can only guess as to how the dialogue might have addressed these issues had it been allowed to continue.

The events of 845 effectively put an end to the Hua-yen school, destroying its texts and dispersing its followers. The Korean monk Ŭich'ŏn (see Section 9.4.1) brought Hua-yen texts from Korea in the eleventh century, and a number of Ch'an monks wrote commentaries on them during the Sung and later dynasties. The lineage of patriarchs, however, was never revived. Hua-yen played a more influential role in Japan and Korea. In Japan, Fa-tsang's thought survived both in the Kegon school (see Section 10.3), which was a direct offshoot of Hua-yen, and in the more important Shingon sect, which combined Hua-yen theory with the practice of Yoga Tantras (see Section

10.4). In Korea, Tsung-mi's thought provided the basis for Chinul's integration of Sŏn (Ch'an) and standard doctrinal schools (see Section 9.4.2). This integration has shaped Korean Buddhism up to the present day.

8.5.3 Pure Land (Ching-te)

Pure Land was only briefly a formal school in China, from the sixth to the ninth century, but it has had a long career as the most popular movement in Chinese Buddhism. The roots of the movement date back to the Later Han dynasty. A text translated in the second century C.E. advocated concentrating on or visualizing the Buddhas of the 10 directions. Prominent among these Buddhas was Amitābha (see Section 5.5.4), whose paradise was located in the West.

The first acknowledged patriarch of a Pure Land lineage was a northerner, T'an-luan (476–542). T'an-luan received his religious vocation when, convalescing from a grave illness, he saw a vision of a heavenly gate opening before him. He turned first to Taoism and its recipes for attaining immortality; a treatise he composed describing a Taoist meditation technique is still extant. He then met the Indian monk Bodhiruci, who arrived in Loyang in 508. Bodhiruci convinced him that Buddhism had a superior method for gaining everlasting life and taught him the Amitābha texts. T'an-luan was converted and burned his Taoist books.

Like many meditation masters of the time, Bodhiruci advocated the use of *dhāraṇī* (spells) for concentration. T'an-luan's practice gradually developed into the nien-fo (recitation of the Buddha's name). The term *nien-fo* in T'an-luan's earliest writings referred to the practice of meditation. There are three possible meanings for the word *nien:* (1) concentration or meditation; (2) a length of time equal to one thought; hence, the expression *shih-nien* (10 *nien)* meant the length of time consisting of 10 thought-moments. This led eventually to a reinterpretation, as *nien* also means (3) vocal recitation, with the phrase *shih-nien* seen as meaning 10 recitations of the Buddha's name.

T'an-luan organized societies for recitation of Amitābha's name and propagated the Pure Land cult with great success. He also lay the foundations for its doctrine, declaring that even those who have committed evil deeds and atrocities are eligible for rebirth in the Western paradise if they sincerely desire it. However, those who revile the Dharma are excluded, he said, because blasphemy is not conducive to aspiration and because the karmic retribution for blasphemy is repeated rebirth in the lowest hell. Eventually, he came to advocate dependence on *t'a-li* ("other power") rather than on *tzu-li* (one's own power), asserting that even the merit one seems to earn for oneself through nien-fo is facilitated by the overarching power of Amita's vows. Rebirth in the Pure Land and attainment of Buddhahood there are a result of this power. Thus, instead of meditation, the prime requisites of Pure Land practice became faith coupled with recitation of Amitābha's name.

These two points—recitation rather than meditation, and the inclusion of sinners with those who can benefit from Amitābha's vow—were the main Chinese departures from Indian Amitābha doctrines. T'an-luan's motive in explaining away the *Sukhāvatī-vyūha Sūtra's* statement claiming that grave sinners are excluded from the effect of Amita's vow was his conviction that all living beings possess Buddha-nature. This conviction may account for the popularity of Pure Land in China, for no native Chinese philosophy (except Mohism, which became extinct before Buddhism was widely accepted in the country) preached universal love and the worth of every person regardless of family or class.

Times were hard in the sixth century, and many Buddhists had become obsessed with the notion, derived from the *Lotus Sūtra,* that the latter days of Buddhism had arrived. Indian texts distinguished three Dharma periods: (1) True Dharma (0–500 after the Parinirvāṇa [A.P.]); (2) Counterfeit Dharma (501–1000 or 501–1500 A.P., depending on the source); and (3) Latter-day or Degenerate Dharma (expected to last ten thousand years after the end of the age of Counterfeit Dharma). Sixth-century Chinese dated the Parinirvāṇa at 949 B.C.E., so the Latter-day Dharma would begin about 550 C.E. Thus there was a ready market for easy and efficacious practices appropriate for a degenerate age, promising rewards in a better world. This was precisely what T'ai-luan's Pure Land offered. It placed few intellectual or financial demands on its followers, and made no pretense that life in this world, even that which was in harmony with nature, could in any way be ideal. On these points it differed radically from thinkers such as the early Hua-yen patriarchs, and came closer than they did to the early Buddhist valuation of life in the human world.

The next great Pure Land masters were Tao-ch'o (562–645) and his disciple Shan-tao (613–81), who gave to Chinese Pure Land its definitive shape. Shan-tao was the first Pure Land master to settle in the capital and was remarkably successful in spreading the faith there. Nien-fo was still the crucial religious act in his teaching—in fact, he recommended that it be repeated at all times, as a mantra—but he included other practices in addition to the recitation: meditation, morality, and scholarship. As a result, Pure Land became independent, no longer a mere appendage to other schools.

The last two great masters of this formative period were Tz'u-min (680–748) and Fa-chao (late eighth century). Fa-chao was the first Pure Land master to teach the faith in the T'ang imperial court. The courtiers' attraction to such a "common" faith demonstrates how shaken they were by the An Lu-shan Rebellion. Fa-chao's ecstatic method of reciting Amitābha's name in five rhythms, which he equated with the five wonderful sounds to be heard in Sukhāvatī, proved very popular.

The Pure Land patriarchs developed a large body of texts, not only to spread their teachings among the common folk but also to defend their practice from the attacks of the more philosophical schools. Pure Land philosophy adopted the distinction between principle and phenomena to explain the need for the nien-fo. Just as principle cannot be perceived without recourse to phenomena, they said, true Buddha-nature cannot be grasped without recourse to simple expedient means. What was originally a strong antipathy between Ch'an and Pure Land, reflected in the arguments between Tz'u-min and members of the Southern School, gradually became more conciliatory. Tsung-mi, for instance, commented that the Ch'an approach of contemplating Buddha-nature and the gradual means of nien-fo were complementary aspects of a single practice. Thus by the ninth century, the groundwork was being laid for the later fusion of the two schools.

Pure Land by that time was so fully formed and so widely diffused a movement that it ceased to need great masters. Although the texts of its early patriarchs were destroyed in the turmoil of 845, the nature of the faith was such that it had little need for texts. Thus, aside from Ch'an, it was the only movement to survive the suppression relatively intact. Despite T'ang emperors' having followed it, neo-Confucian gentlemen, beginning with the twelfth century, disdained to participate in a cult that was both "vulgar" (because the common people adhered to it) and "foreign." Their wives, however, continued to recite *"na-mo a-mi-t'o-fo"* ("Homage to Amita Buddha") and taught it to their children. To this day, a shortened version of the phrase *"O-mi-t'o-fo"* is a common greeting and exclamation among older Chinese. No native Chinese god has ever commanded the universal worship that Amita has received. His popularity was so pervasive that by the sixteenth century it had permeated Ch'an. Even today, the faith is still strong among the vast majority of Chinese Buddhists, and *"na-mo a-mi-t'o-fo"* is chanted regularly in the daily liturgy of Ch'an monasteries.

8.5.4 The Third Period Sect (San-chieh-chiao)

A related development during this time was the establishment of the Third Period Sect (San-chieh-chiao). Similar to the Pure Land sect, this movement assumed the existence of three periods in the survival of Dharma after the Buddha's Parinirvāṇa, and decided that the age of Degenerate Dharma, when even superficial rituals were no longer observed, had arrived. The school's founder, Hsin-hsing (540–93), taught that all beings were possessed of the Buddha-nature, and that all were thus worthy of compassion and respect, regardless of class, sex, or species. Because of the degeneracy of the times, he and his followers felt that monastic isolation was an obstacle to the practice of compassion, so their implementation of the Dharma took the form of lavish donations for the well-being of others. In 620 an "Inexhaustible Treasury," patterned after a model in the *Vimalakīrti-nirdeśa Sūtra,* was established in Ch'ang-an. Although other Buddhist lay groups in China and Japan had organized similar credit unions and mutual financing societies, the Third Period Sect's project assumed enormous proportions. Capital accumulated at a rate defying the ability of accountants to keep track of it. Funds were dispersed for such projects as temple repair, relief for the sick and homeless, and religious rituals throughout the empire. According to accounts of the time, loans were always repaid when due, even though no interest was charged and no legal contracts were required of the borrowers.

The sect's appeal to the oppressed common people is obvious. But for those in power, it was a seditious threat because of its teaching that no government in a time of decay was worthy of respect. Various T'ang emperors initiated actions against it, until in 725 Hsüan-tsung succeeded in dissolving all of its monasteries, having closed the Inexhaustible Treasury in 721 after it had marked a century of altruistic work.

8.5.5 Ch'an

The most enduring—and for many, the most appealing—of the indigenous Chinese sects was Ch'an (Dhyāna), better known in the West by its Japanese name, Zen. Much of Ch'an's appeal lies in the legends it produced, graphic depictions of sudden Awakening gained through dramatic encounters between master and student. Recent scholarship, based on manuscripts found at Tun-huang, has shown that many of the legends are myths, and that the actual history of the Ch'an school is much more complex than the school's own records indicate. The dust raised by this modern revisionism has yet to settle, but a general outline of the doctrinal and social forces that shaped the school's distinctive literature has begun to emerge.

We have already noted (see Sections 3.4.2, 7.5) the tendency for Buddhist monasticism to split into two specialized vocations: scholarly and meditative. Ch'an is a classic case of a specialized meditative tradition, and it left by far the most extensive records of any such tradition. Before detailed knowledge of the meditative traditions in India and Southeast Asia became available to the West in the past few decades, Ch'an was widely assumed to be the only instance of a strictly meditative Buddhist tradition. As a result, many scholars, Eastern and Western, liked to speculate on the distinctive differences between the Indian and Chinese national character that brought about such an unprecedented tradition on Chinese soil. Now that we have more extensive knowledge of such traditions in other Buddhist countries, especially the Kammaṭṭhāna tradition in Thailand (see Section 7.5.2), we can see that what makes Ch'an distinctive is not that its masters rejected textual authority in favor of immediate meditative experience, or that they used unusual and outrageous methods to spark intuitive realizations in their students' minds. Rather, Ch'an is distinctive in that it systematized records of such teachings and methods into a course of study for later generations so as to prevent the practice from ossifying as it became established in the social mainstream.

We have noted that there is a tendency among Buddhist meditative traditions to become domesticated as the attainments of their teachers become widely known. In most cases, the traditions then die out within a few generations as material prosperity smothers the authenticity of the practice. Most extant early Ch'an writings date from the two main periods during which the tradition became domesticated: the period from the mid-eighth to the mid-ninth century, and then again from the late tenth to the early twelfth. This may simply be a historical accident, in that writings from other periods may have been destroyed, but comparison with the Kammaṭṭhāna tradition suggests that this may not be an accident after all. A meditative tradition would tend not to leave written records until it became so famous that it felt compelled to propagate and defend its teachings beyond the immediate circle of person-to-person contact.

Further comparison with the Kammaṭṭhāna tradition reveals another point in common: an ambivalent attitude toward established scholarly traditions. Meditative traditions must use the terminology established by the scholarly tradition to discuss their teachings, but they may find that the fashions of scholarship are inimical to their approach. Scholars may champion spurious texts or mistaken interpretations of legitimate texts. On a more subtle level, even when scholarly theories are essentially correct, the tendency to focus on theory may obscure the direct experience of what the theory purports to describe. These two concerns—to defend the school's doctrines and practices from outside attack, and to prevent later generations from focusing on theory to the exclusion of seeing into their own minds—account for much of the form and content of Ch'an literature.

The literature produced during the two periods of the school's domestication exhibits two approaches to these concerns. In the long run, the literature produced during the second period was far more successful than that produced during the first. In fact, not until the second period did Ch'an actually become a unified school with an established body of doctrine and legendary tradition. Prior to that, the "school" was more a loose family of lineages, each with its own fluid amalgam of teachings and traditions, scattered through mountainous regions in central and southwestern China. Even after its establishment as a distinct school, Ch'an continued to split over several recurrent issues, the most prominent of them being the question of whether Ch'an practice was in harmony with traditional scriptural doctrines or was something entirely separate and unique.

A. *Ch'an in the Tang Dynasty.* The first Ch'an masters to gain widespread popular attention were members of the East Mountain School of Hupeh province, Hung-jen (circa 600–674) and his student Shen-hsiu (circa 606–706). Hung-jen attracted a large following of monks, but not until 700, when Empress Wu invited Shen-hsiu to teach in the imperial palace, did the school attain national prominence. Shen-hsiu seems to have been a member of the royal family himself, and he wrote a number of texts describing the doctrines and practices of his school. Other students of Hung-jen also wrote texts, recording Hung-jen's teachings and those of his predecessors, establishing a lineage that went back several generations. Some of them claimed that this lineage was connected with Bodhidharma, a fifth-century central Asian monk famous for his meditative prowess. In an attempt to compensate for the school's lack of any clear basis in a particular Buddhist text, they also connected Bodhidharma with the *Lankāvatāra Sūtra* (see Section 4.3). Although modern scholarship indicates that the school's connections with Bodhidharma, and his with the Lankāvatāra, were tenuous at best, later legends surrounding Bodhidharma claiming him as the First Patriarch of the school played a central role in the developing Ch'an mythology. According to the reckoning of the East Mountain School, Hung-jen was the Fifth Patriarch of the school, and Shen-hsiu the Sixth.

Shen-hsiu and his contemporaries adopted much of the meditative terminology used by Chih-i, the great T'ien-tai systematizer, but gave new meanings to many of the terms. The most important doctrine for the school was the teaching of the Buddha-nature immanent in all things. Different members of the school dealt in different ways with the practical implications of this teaching, and in particular with the question of how to regard the defilements of the mind in light of the Buddha-nature's supposedly being intrinsically pure. Shen-hsiu approached the problem from two angles. When describing the practice from the outside, he stated that the pure mind and the defiled mind, though conjoined, were essentially separate, each with its own intrinsic reality. Neither generated the other. Thus the goal of the practice was to rid the mirrorlike pure mind of any impurities. When describing the techniques used to rid the mind of its impurities, however, he recommended that the meditator regard the impurities as essentially unreal. Some of the practices he taught implied a sudden approach to Awakening; others, a more gradual approach.

Shen-hsiu's school remained popular in the capital for several generations, but its popularity attracted controversy. In 730, a monk named Shen-hui (684–758)—a former student of Shen-hsiu and of Hui-neng, another student of Hung-jen—mounted a campaign in the capital, attacking Shen-hsiu and his followers for teaching a limited gradualistic and dualistic approach to the practice. Shen-hui insisted that the doctrine of the essential purity of the Buddha-nature meant that mental impurities were nonexistent, and that Awakening was an all-or-nothing proposition that could not be approached in stepwise fashion. Shen-hui produced new and more dramatic stories of Bodhidharma to support his campaign, and insisted that Hui-neng, about whom almost nothing is known, was Ch'an's actual Sixth Patriarch.

There seems to be general agreement, both in later Ch'an schools and among modern scholars, that Shen-hui's unfair campaign against what he called the Northern School of Shen-hsiu was essentially self-serving. Active during the period when documents permitting ordination were easily bought, he seemed to be more interested in attracting new ordinands to his cause than in training meditators. Although the emperor in 796 posthumously declared him the true Seventh Patriarch, he maintained this title only in the Ho-tse school he founded, which did not last beyond the persecutions of 845.

Shen-hui's attack on gradualism, however, had a lasting effect on Ch'an rhetoric. No Ch'an school after his time gave expression to any doctrines or practices that might be labeled "gradual." The term *Southern School* came to stand for any Ch'an lineage that taught sudden Awakening, although records from Tun-huang show that the Northern School taught sudden Awakening as well. All the schools that lasted into the Sung dynasty claimed to be southern, accepting Hui-neng—who was provided with an attractive mythology in a later work called the *Platform Sūtra*—as the Sixth Patriarch, and passing over Shen-hui in almost total silence. As for the Northern School, it continued until the tenth century, when it died out with the end of the T'ang.

The *Platform Sūtra,* despite its shaky historical foundations, became one of the most influential texts in the development of southern Ch'an. It gave a Chinese flavor to a teaching from the *Nirvāṇa Sūtra* concerning the identity of concentration and wisdom, defining concentration as the essence of wisdom, and wisdom as the function of concentration. This identity is reflected in its definition of *tso-ch'an* (sitting meditation). Sitting (corresponding to concentration) means not a physical posture, but a state of not activating thought in any and all circumstances; meditation (corresponding to wisdom) is the state of seeing one's original nature without confusion. This definition is reminiscent of Chih-i's sudden method of practice, but the Sūtra offers no details as to whether, as in Chih-i's teachings, this approach was to be combined with formal meditation techniques, or if it implied a rejection of such techniques altogether. Various southern schools took up different sides on this question, but the mainstream position retained formal techniques as the backbone of the practice, using the sudden perspective as a corrective to the pitfalls that formalism might entail.

The early sectarian Ch'an battles continued until the persecutions of 845. Although a number of newly ascendant Ch'an lineages joined in the fray, other lineages did their best to stay in the mountains and avoid the controversy. Realizing that elaborate doctrinal explanations could only deliver a meditator into the hands of his scholarly opponents, they developed a new teaching style that made heavy use of paradox, cryptic statements, shouts, and beatings to jolt their students out of the verbalizing mind-set that led to doctrinal controversies in the first place. Although these methods were borrowed from the methods of old Taoist sages, they were also bolstered by the teaching in the *Vimalakīrti-nirdeśa Sūtra* concerning the inability of language to express nonduality. Prominent among this new style of teacher were Ma-tsu (709–88), Huang-po (d. 850), Lin-chi (d. 866), and Tung-shan (807–69). Four of the later Five Houses of Ch'an in the Sung dynasty traced their lineage back to Ma-tsu; the most prominent among them descended from Lin-chi, one of Ma-tsu's Dharma descendants, whose predilection for shouts and beatings became their house style. The remaining house, Ts'ao-tung, traced itself back to Tung-shan, whose methods—though unorthodox as well—placed more of an emphasis on quiet sitting. During the Sung dynasty, the Five Houses eventually became institutionally quite distinct from one another, but historical records indicate that during the late T'ang they were fairly fluid, with students from one lineage often studying under masters from other lineages and going off into the mountains to meditate alone.

Because these schools avoided the capital, they were best positioned to survive the persecutions of 845. Few contemporary documents survive from this period, so it is difficult to tell what role the unorthodox methods of these lineages played in the schools' meditative and communal life as a whole. The suspicion is that many of the stories attributed to them are later creations, as these figures became literary types that took on a life of their own in the following centuries as new stories accreted around them in response to issues that developed within the various Ch'an lineages.

B. *Ch'an during the Five Dynasties.* The T'ang-Sung interregnum, called the Five Dynasties period (907–60), marked an important watershed in the history of Ch'an. To escape the turmoil that was engulfing most of the empire, thousands of monks from the southern Ch'an lineages took refuge in present-day Fukien, a relatively peaceful enclave in southern China. Forced into close proximity, they began to view themselves as a unified school. Threatened with the potential for total political chaos, they began writing down their oral traditions as a way of preserving them for future generations. Their writings focused on tales exemplifying unorthodox teaching methods: unusual discourses and tales of encounters between masters and their students, showing how Awakening could be sparked in a variety of ways and later expressed in a variety of forms. Although their initial impetus may have been simply to preserve these teachings, they soon put the encounter dialogues to other uses as well. One was to flesh out the Ch'an lineage accounts, called lamp records, to demonstrate in detail the various ways in which the light of Awakening had been passed from generation to generation. In doing so, these writers succeeded in turning the entire lineage—from the time of the Buddha through the T'ang dynasty—into a "sudden" lineage. The earliest extant example of this style of lamp record was *The Collection of the Patriarchal Hall,* compiled in 952 by Ching-hsiu Wen-teng.

Another use of encounter dialogues, pioneered by Yün-men Wen-yen (d. 949), was to assign the dialogues as *k'ung-an* ("public cases"; in Japanese, *kōan*) to meditators as central topics of meditation. Dialogues for this purpose were chosen for their ability to baffle the ordinary rational and verbal processes of the mind, using language for its ability not to inform, but to perform: to shake up the mind and point to the principle, the Buddha-nature, that could shine through only when the mind was in a spontaneous, nonverbal state (see Section 8.4.1; compare Section 6.3.3). This practice was to help counteract the tendency of adhering to the words of the texts or to the methods of formal sitting meditation as ends in them selves. To continue a metaphor we have used frequently in this text—that Buddhist teachings are to be regarded primarily as a form of therapy—k'ung-an meditation takes as its means of therapy case records of successful cures.

A typical example of a k'ung-an is this: A monk asked Tung-shan, "Where can we go to escape hot and cold?" Tung-shan answered, "Why not go where there is neither hot nor cold?" "What sort of place is neither hot nor cold?" "When cold, let it freeze you to death. When hot, let it burn you to death." The apparent message here is that the suffering caused by hot and cold come from the mental labels of "hot" and "cold" applied to sensations. If one were simply to allow the sensation to take place without the label, one would touch a principle freed from any suffering related to the sensation. To know this message, however, was not to solve the riddle of the k'ung-an. The solution lay in actually being able to attain that ability in one's meditation.

The encounter with the k'ung-an, however, did not end there. One was expected to convey one's realization to one's teacher in live words or actions, liberated from context, that were supposed to embody one's new perspective. This use of the "rhetoric of embodiment" was a new solution to the dilemma that many Chinese Buddhist schools had found themselves in when they adopted tenets of the proponents of 'nonbeing' (see Section 8.4.1). Buddhist texts taught that there was such a thing as wrong release; thus there was the need to validate any spontaneous realizations attained in meditation. The proponents of 'nonbeing', however, taught that ultimate principles lay beyond words; thus there should be no verbal content to any ultimate realizations by which they could be validated. The k'ung-an masters thus looked to the rhetoric of embodiment—in which the style of one's words and actions was supposed to express the nonverbal level of mind from which they sprang—as the new way of gauging the authenticity of one's realizations. In other words, one's level of attainment was judged not by what one said, but by how one said it. The assumption behind this faith in the rhetoric of embodiment was that if the immediacy of Awakening in the present moment was the same as that experienced by the great masters of the past, it should find its expression in a similarly live style of communication. Thus, although k'ung-an practice placed a high value on the present moment, it did so by establishing present moments of the past, together with their rhetorical expressions, as its paradigms.

C. *Ch'an in the Early Sung.* The founding of the Sung dynasty brought renewed official support for Buddhist monasticism. The Sung rulers took an interest in regulating monastic life, and Ch'an advocates campaigned to have Ch'an masters appointed as abbots of the large monasteries under imperial sponsorship. New lamp records—far more extensive in content than those of the interregnum, and written in a far more literary style—were composed to promote the school's good reputation in the eyes of the court. The first of the new lamp records was *The Transmission of the Lamp* (1004), compiled by Yung-an Tao-yüan for the edification of the Ching-te emperor. This codified the Ch'an lineage in a form that was to become standard throughout the remaining history of the school, tracing the transmission back not only to Bodhidharma, but through Mahākāśyapa all the way to the Buddha.

The campaign was successful, but success had its price. The communities over which Ch'an masters were placed were highly regulated, with elaborate ritual cycles and rigid daily schedules for study, work, and meditation. There is no way of knowing the extent to which the descendants of the uncouth Ch'an meditators of the ninth century had already become domesticated by the end of the T'ang, but within the first few generations of the Sung the process of domestication was complete.

To deal with this situation, Ch'an writers took the records made during the Five Dynasties period and adapted them into tools for keeping the practice from being stifled out of existence. They coined a slogan to define what was distinctive about the Ch'an school, making a virtue out of the fact that they did not give pride of place to any one Sūtra: "A special transmission outside the [written] teachings; not setting up the scriptures; pointing directly at a person's mind; seeing into its nature and attaining Buddhahood." The first extensive compilation of k'ung-ans to demonstrate this principle in action was the *Record* of Fen-yang Shan-chao (947–1024), who appended explanatory verses and commentaries to two hundred old cases and one hundred new cases of his own invention. This was the format later followed by the great compilations, such as the *Blue Cliff Record,* compiled by Yüan-wu K'o-ch'in (1063–1135), and the *Gateless Barrier,* by Wu-men Hui-k'ai (1183–1260), which superseded Fen-yang's *Record* as the school's classic texts.

It will come as something of a surprise to readers familiar with the spontaneous and iconoclastic side of Ch'an encounter dialogues to learn that the lamp records were primarily political documents designed to win imperial patronage, and that most of the dialogues were composed as ritual texts for use in formal meetings when the abbot would ascend the high sermon seat to address the assembled residents of the monastery in full regalia. In this context, the dialogues served as reminders that although discipline and etiquette were the rule in the monastery, they were not an end in themselves. Furthermore, they served as notice that the Ch'an tradition comprehended both the realm of ritual and the realm beyond. Thus, although the lamp records had used the old stories as a means for the school to gain institutional power, the k'ung-an records served both to counterbalance and to give spiritual legitimacy to the institutionalization once that power was gained. Used together, these two forms of Ch'an literature helped secure the school in its position as the dominant form of Chinese Buddhism.

Some have argued that the early Sung dynasty was Ch'an's true golden age, in terms of literary activity, popular support, and social prestige, but such things historically have been the death knoll of meditation lineages. Ch'an has gone through many fallow periods since the early Sung. For instance, Dōgen, a Japanese monk who studied in China in the early thirteenth century (see Section 10.5.1), reported that most Ch'an monks at that time were more interested in formulating doctrinal syntheses between Ch'an, Confucianism, and Taoism than they were in the pursuit of Awakening. An inherent weakness in the rhetoric of embodiment was that the style could be mistaken for the substance, fostering the view that Awakening was simply a cheeky rhetorical stance, or the sectarian belief that one style of embodiment was more Awakened than another. Even Ch'an practitioners complained that many of their fellows misunderstood the intent of the encounter dialogues, using them as an excuse for the arrogant flouting of social conventions and moral norms. But the existence of the dialogues as graphic case histories of successful goads to Awakening has laid the seeds for the school's periodic revival throughout the millennium since they were written down. This in itself entitles Ch'an to a distinctive place in Buddhist history.

D. *Ch'an and the Arts.* Another distinctive feature of the school has been its relationship to Chinese aesthetics. Here again, however, there is a tendency to overrate Ch'an's uniqueness. Many Ch'an monks, especially in the Sung, composed poetry using a Taoist aesthetic that valued spontaneity and concrete visual imagery. Like the doctrine of the Tao, the doctrine of the Buddha-nature inherent in all things—to be realized by direct intuition—made metaphor an ideal mode for expressing Ch'an messages. For instance, Han Shan, a seventh-century (?) Ch'an hermit, described the experience of Awakening to one's already-Awakened nature in these terms: "At noon, I sit in my hut / And realize: The sun is already up."

Gradually, writers who discussed aesthetics in general began noticing parallels between their topic and Ch'an meditation in two important areas: (1) the relationship between study and originality in artistic expression, and (2) the nature of the creative process itself. It is difficult to determine, however, whether this tendency should be regarded as a Ch'an influence on Chinese aesthetic theory, or as simply the use of Ch'an analogies to make preexisting aesthetic ideas respectable in terms of new intellectual fashions. Many of the theories justified by analogy to Ch'an were also justified by analogy to Taoist practice, often by the same writers. For instance, some writers in the Sung dynasty used Ch'an parallels to justify complete spontaneity in poetic expression. Others made reference to the Ch'an concept of standardized k'ung-an practice and orthodox lineages to maintain that one should develop one's aesthetic sensibilities (analogous, they said, to the Dharma-eye) by heavily reading only the best models (patriarchs) of T'ang poetry until their style became one's own second nature. One's spontaneous expressions would then effortlessly embody the formal rules of poetry. This they called the "live method," analogous to the "live utterances" (see Section 8.6) of Ch'an masters. In earlier centuries, however, these same ideas had been taken from analogy to a practice in Taoist alchemy whereby one took elixirs, gradually changing the chemistry of one's body until one's bones were suddenly transformed.

The same uncertainty as to their ultimate provenance surrounds these writers' views of the creative process. The creative moment, they said, was akin to Ch'an meditation in that by stilling and emptying the mind, one was able to "enter the spirit," that is, intuitively apprehend the inner nature of the things about which one was painting or writing, at the same time attaining an inner mental realm of surpassing freedom that charged one's works with special meaning. This experience was called a "marvelous Awakening" and was said to parallel the marvelous Awakening of Ch'an. Still, similar ideas were also being advanced with analogies to Taoist practice; it is interesting to note that many of the poets and painters who were held up as ideal models of marvelous Awakening had little if any connection to Buddhism, much less to Ch'an. Also, their artistic styles were often quite elaborate, unlike the style of spontaneous force and cultivated simplicity that has since become associated—chiefly through the example of Japanese art—with Ch'an and Zen in the West.

Not all Chinese writers on aesthetics accepted the analogy between Ch'an and artistic or poetic creativity. One late Sung poet, Liu K'o-chuang (1187–1269), pointed out that Ch'an is essentially a message that transcends words, whereas poetry is nothing if not verbal expression. Also, he said, using Ch'an meditation to explain the creative process is like using something subtle and far away to describe something concrete and near at hand. Writers after Liu fell into two camps, defending and attacking the validity of the analogy between Ch'an and the creative process, but only in their most effusive moments did proponents of the theory forget that creative expression was merely an analogue for Ch'an Awakening and was in no way identical to it. Han Shan had made the point centuries earlier:

No one knows I sit here alone.
A solitary moon glimmers in the spring.
That's not the moon in the spring,
The moon's in the sky where it always is.
This little song that I sing:
There is no Ch'an in the song.

Nevertheless, it is interesting to note how Ch'an gradually replaced Taoism as the model used by poets and artists to make the point that artistic inspiration is analogous to religious inspiration and can lead to truths of similar profundity. In later centuries, neo-Confucianism gradually took over this role from Ch'an. Only when Ch'an spread to Japan—a culture that from early times had blurred the line between aesthetic and religious experience (see Section 10.1)—was the Ch'an/art analogy seriously treated as an equation, giving rise to a spare, forceful artistic style that was considered quintessentially Zen.

8.6 THE SUNG DYNASTY (970–1279)

The Sung dynasty witnessed a major restructuring of Chinese society, as the agrarian feudal economy of previous dynasties developed into an urban economy administered by a centralized bureaucracy. The major intellectual concern of the times was to recast Chinese culture into a comprehensive, harmonious form that could serve as a unifying ideology for the newly consolidated state. To ease the sense of alienation that such a major social shift might cause, writers of this period harkened back to the golden age of Chinese civilization during the T'ang, which they claimed to be preserving even as they molded it into a radically new form.

These trends influenced Buddhism on many levels. On the level of popular devotion, the various pantheons of Taoist immortals, Buddhist bodhisattvas, and local spirits were organized in the popular imagination into a bureaucratic hierarchy, mirroring the political process occurring on Earth. On the institutional and doctrinal levels, the early Sung rulers were concerned with placing the Sangha on a more stable, rational basis. The Chinese Buddhist Canon was printed for the first time, at state expense. This massive undertaking required 11 years and 130,000 wood-printing blocks, and yet was only one among many such public printings of Buddhist texts intended to standardize the teaching. Large monastic estates were created, with government support balanced by standardized discipline and strict government controls over ordinations. A small number of these monasteries were designated as Vinaya monasteries, the only places where ordinations could be conducted. These functioned more or less as boot camps for new monks who would then take up residence in the other monasteries (Strong *EB*, sec. 8.5.1). To provide a standard code for these centers, the Vinaya expert Yüan-chao (1048–1116) eventually devised a Vinaya (Lü) school, based on the commentaries that the T'ang scholar Tao-hsüan (596–667) had written on the Dharmaguptaka Vinaya. This established the Dharmaguptaka Vinaya as standard in Chinese monasteries, a position it has held up to the present.

The question of who would be put in charge of the remaining monasteries led to intense political jockeying between the two main surviving T'ang schools: Ch'an and T'ien-t'ai. Ch'an prevailed for several reasons. To begin with, it could produce records to show that its lineage, unlike T'ien-t'ai's, had not lapsed during the persecution of 845. Also, the lineage of masters portrayed in these records was, in effect, a line of native Chinese Buddhas, which satisfied nationalist sentiments. The nonverbal nature of the transmission made it a convenient rallying point, in that all were free to intuit the nonverbal level in their own terms; and it satisfied the conviction, dating back to the time of Arcane Learning, that nonverbal intuition characterized the clearest understanding of the highest principles.

As a result, the vast majority of imperial monasteries were designated Ch'an monasteries, with only a small minority left as teaching monasteries, headed by members of the T'ien-t'ai school. In a large sense, however, this was a hollow victory for the Ch'an monks. Life at the two types of monasteries differed little, in that both were run on the same tight schedule of study and meditation. The only differences were that k'ung-ans were read at the formal meetings in the Ch'an monasteries, whereas Sūtras and scholastic treatises were read at similar meetings in teaching monasteries; and the designation of the monastery was what determined the lineage from which the abbot would come. Only a small cadre of monks actually studied with the abbot, the remaining monks being free to come and go. Many of them actually spent their time traveling among Ch'an and teaching monasteries to broaden their education. This gave rise to the system of the three *men* (traditions) that identified a monk's affiliation: *lü-men* (the disciplinary tradition in which he had been ordained); *tsung-men* (his lineal tradition, that is, the Ch'an lineage under which he first received tonsure and meditation training); and *chiao-men* (his doctrinal lineage, that is, the school of formal doctrine under which he had studied).

Even in Ch'an monasteries, many monks devoted a good amount of their time to the study of formal doctrine, such as Hua-yen texts, as well as to non-Buddhist topics, such as Confucianism, literature, and painting. (No scholarly study has been made of convents during the Sung, but we can assume that similar developments were taking place among the nuns as well.) This was, in part, a continuation of the fourth-century view of monastic life as a Buddhist version of the life of the retired scholar. It was also an effort to stay current with the interests of the monasteries' elite patrons.

After centuries during which Buddhism had virtually monopolized Chinese intellectual life, Confucianism was coming to the fore as the strongest contender to dominate the standard ideology for the new bureaucracy. In part, this was because Buddhism was no longer a growing force. No new texts were being translated, so there was no challenge to create new multisystem syntheses. Buddhism, Taoism, and Confucianism were viewed as static traditions, and the question of the day was how to integrate them into a single ideology that would prevent the sectarian conflicts that had proven so divisive in the past. This boiled down to the question of which tradition among the three would be paramount.

Confucianism had the advantage. Even during the periods of strongest government support for Buddhism, Confucianism had provided the ideology for the day-to-day running of the empire. Of the three traditions, it gave the highest priority to the maintenance of family and state. The Confucians were also able to point out aspects of Buddhism that made it untrustworthy as a guide for bureaucrats. They cited k'ung-ans to show that Ch'an was amoral; they pointed out instances in history when the fervor of Buddhist popular devotion had been detrimental to the economic interests of the state. In particular, a memorial written during the T'ang dynasty by a Confucian scholar, scathingly critical of the excesses that surrounded the public worship of a Buddha relic in 819, became required reading for all potential government officials.

Perhaps the most successful strategy adopted by the neo-Confucians was to take attractive and useful elements of Buddhist doctrine and graft them onto their own. For instance, they implemented government-sponsored social programs—from public clinics and cemeteries to housing for the aged, infirm, and orphans—to embody the Buddhist principle of compassion unlimited by social barriers. The most important of the neo-Confucians during the Sung was Chu Hsi (1130–1200), who drew on the writings of Chan-jan and Tsung-mi to offer a moralistic, practical philosophy integrating the Buddhist doctrine of karma and self-cultivation with the worldly wisdom and humanistic values that had been Confucianism's major strengths. Thus, although Buddhism lost the battle to become the dominant ideology of the new bureaucracy, certain Buddhist doctrines helped shape the ideology, where they were enshrined as basic principles in the inherited wisdom of Chinese civilization.

Despite its declining political position, the Sangha maintained its stability as an organization with solid support from the laity. Buddhist doctrinal studies no longer attracted high-caliber intellects, but the Ch'an school continued to produce innovative practitioners. The early twelfth century in particular stands out in this regard. Hung-chih Cheng-chüeh (1091–1157) formulated the distinctive *mo-chao* (silent illumination) practice of the Ts'ao-tung lineage, whereas his rival, Ta-hui Tsung-kao (1089–1163), popularized a distinctively new approach to Lin-chi k'ung-an practice. Ta-hui, a dharma-heir of Yüan-wu K'o-ch'in (see Section 8.5.5), insisted that the proper approach to the k'ung-an entailed focusing on *hua-t'ou* (crucial phrases) in the dialogues and converting them from *ssu chu* (dead utterances) to *huo chu* (live utterances). This was accomplished by investigating the dialogues, not in terms of their meaning in context, but simply as decontextualized acts of verbalizing in and of themselves. Only then could one break through the process of verbalization to the Buddha-nature behind it. Yüan-wu, Hung-chih, and Ta-hui were also notable for being the earliest known Ch'an masters to have left numerous female dharma-heirs, chief among them being Ta-hui's first student, the nun Ting-kuang, who became a successful teacher in her own right.

Modern scholars often refer to the Sung dynasty as the beginning of the ossification of Buddhism in China, but this is largely a perception inherited from texts composed during the Sung period itself. The monks who drew up the anecdotal lamp records, codified the k'ung-ans, and perfected the crucial phrase approach were doing something very creative and new, never before attempted in the history of Buddhism, and yet they tried their best to disguise their creativity. The main impression they wanted to convey was that they were simply preserving a valuable tradition. In this, they were following the general pattern of Sung intellectual life that we noted previously: a strategy of trying to ease the shift to a totally new form of society by disguising innovations as mere clarifications of past traditions. Much of the common perception of the T'ang as the golden age of Chinese Buddhism stems from the skill with which Sung writers self-effacingly presented what they viewed as most valuable in their past, even as they recast it in radically new forms.

8.7 THE RELIGION OF THE MASSES (1279–1949)

Except for the brief interlude of the Yüan dynasty (1279–1368), when Mongol forces ruled China, the government bureaucracy and monastic system devised during the Sung proved remarkably stable and secure. The major long-term effect of the Mongol rule on Buddhism was that it drove a number of Ch'an monks into exile in Japan, thus establishing the Lin-chi (Rinzai) lineage there. Otherwise, the development of Buddhism in China from the thirteenth to the twentieth century was largely an uninterrupted process characterized by several long-term trends. Lay organizations became more prominent in Buddhist circles, engaging largely in charitable work. Pure Land became overwhelmingly the religion of the uneducated masses: the poor, women, children, and merchants without a Confucian education. Any young man who underwent training as a Confucian bureaucrat had to unlearn the simple faith he had learned at his mother's knee. Pure Land even came to pervade the Ch'an monasteries during the Ming dynasty (1368–1644), when the nien-fo was combined with k'ung-an practice, and monastics adopted the slogan that Ch'an and Pure Land were essentially one. The union of Ch'an and Pure Land is perhaps best symbolized by the k'ung-an that became most popular at this time: Who in the mind is reciting the nien-fo? Ch'an retained some of its intellectual respectability among the educated elite, primarily as a lively alternative to the staid bureaucratic orthodoxy. A gentleman might be a Confucian in the way he conducted government and family affairs, but a "Channist" in his private moments as a poet or artist. In this way Buddhism functioned as an unthreatening counterbalance to the institutions and ideology of the Confucian state.

The peaceful coexistence of Buddhism and Confucianism during the Ming dynasty—and the use of Buddhist themes by Confucians to inculcate their ideals among the Buddhist public—is best illustrated by the great novel that appeared at this time, *The Journey to the West.* Although the novel is loosely based on the story of Hsüan-tsang's pilgrimage to India and contains many figures from the Buddhist pantheon and Chinese folklore, the author, Wu Ch'eng-en (1500–82), was a Confucian. The Buddhist virtues he teaches in the novel are essentially those where Buddhism and Confucianism concur. The monk Yuan Chuang (Hsüan-tsang) and his companions are allegorical figures. The monk represents moral conscience; the resourceful yet mischievous magical monkey-king, Sun Hou-tzu, is human nature with all of its weaknesses and potentials; the pig fairy, Chu Pa-hsieh, reflects greed and other base motives. In the course of the adventures, the monkey-king learns self-discipline, loosely defined so as to fit either the Buddhist or neo-Confucian mode, in order to tame his wayward tendencies. In this manner, the Buddhist reader is taught Confucian ideals in a palatable way—a fine example of a Confucian turning the Mahāyāna strategy of skillful means to his own uses.

As the religion of the masses, Buddhism also became the religion of the disaffected. Some of the lay Buddhist organizations—such as the White Lotus Society, loosely connected with the T'ien-t'ai school—actually staged insurrections against the Mongol and Manchu rulers. The White Lotus rebellion at the end of the eighteenth century (1796–1804) took the ruling Manchus 10 years to suppress. A few notorious temples, such as the center at Shao-lin, trained monks in the martial arts, but the Sangha as a whole remained aloof from such affairs.

Modern historians tend to write disparagingly of the lack of dynamism and creativity in Chinese Buddhism from the late fourteenth to early nineteenth century, but we must remember that stability, silence, and lack of innovation in a monastic tradition are not necessarily bad. Although they may induce a life of ritualism and complacency, they also afford the opportunity for sincere monastics to devote themselves fully to a life of practice undisturbed by violent social or sectarian upheavals. The purpose of monasteries and convents is to create a peaceful environment for practice, sheltered from affairs of the world so that affairs of the mind can take on prominence. In the eyes of the Sangha, the great doctrinal syntheses had already been achieved; effective meditation techniques had already been pioneered. Thus all that remained was to follow a path already blazed. We have no way of knowing how many people actually followed the path, because such pursuits offer few external signs and little of interest to outside observers. To borrow a phrase from the proverbial Chinese curse, Buddhism during this period was blest in that it was not living in interesting times.

There were, however, occasional attempts at revitalization, during both the Ming and the Manchu Ch'ing dynasty (1644–1912). The Pure Land/Ch'an synthesis during the Ming not only produced figures famous in China, but also spawned new schools of "Ming Ch'an" in Japan and Vietnam. Perhaps the most wide-ranging reform during these centuries was the one initiated in the late nineteenth century, stimulated by the need to rebuild monasteries and reprint scriptures destroyed in central China during the T'ai-p'ing rebellion (1850–64). The rebels, fervid Christians, had looted and burned most of the great monasteries in the areas they occupied. This shocked both monastics and laity into forming scripture-printing societies and study clubs. Some young monks who acquired modern ideas through lay-initiated schools agitated for social revolution (Strong *EB*, sec. 8.7.2) and participated in the overthrow of the Manchu dynasty in 1911. However, these radicals were not approved of by the majority of the Sangha, who believed that monastics should stay out of politics and study the scriptures rather than modern secular subjects.

The most famous of these radicals was the modernist monk T'ai-hsii (1890–1947), who set up schools, introduced Western-style classroom instruction, taught secular subjects and foreign languages (including Tibetan and Pali), and revived the study of scholastic treatises, especially those of the Fa-hsiang school. T'ai-hsii was never accepted by the abbots of the great Ch'an monasteries of central and south China, who held the real power in the Sangha and who were carrying out their own extensive reforms along traditional lines. However, he opened relations with coreligionists abroad and promoted the idea of a world fellowship of Buddhists.

The Nationalist regime in mainland China (1912–49) fluctuated between mild hostility and mild support for Buddhism, but by and large allowed Buddhists a freedom they had not enjoyed during two and a half centuries of Manchu rule, when all private associations were under suspicion of treason. In 1930 there were said to be 738,000 monastics and 267,000 Buddhist temples in China. This was by far the largest clergy in China, or in any national church in the world. The majority did not live in strictly run monasteries, but at least fifty thousand did. Although Buddhism was not a prominent force in national life, Republican China—insofar as it was religious—was more Buddhist than anything else. Despite the changes sweeping over the country, Buddhist religious life followed many of the same patterns as it had for centuries.

8.7.1 Religious Life: Monastic

Buddhist religious life had taken some unusual directions in China, influenced by indigenous and Taoist ideas and practices. Taoism and Buddhism both contained shamanic elements in practice and thus had certain similarities that eased the introduction of Buddhist practice during the Han dynasty. Meditation guides were the first Buddhist texts sought after by the Chinese, who hoped for the psychic or supernatural powers that meditation might provide.

Devotionalism was less pronounced in Taoism than in Buddhism, however. Buddhist devotional cults grew rapidly from the time of the fall of Han through the Three Kingdoms and Six Dynasties period (220–584). The most popular objects of devotion were Kuan-yin (= Avalokiteśvara, who eventually metamorphosed from male to female during the Sung dynasty—see Strong *EB*, sec. 8.7.1), Amitābha, and Maitreya. Kuan-yin saved one from dangers here on Earth, whereas Amitābha and Maitreya welcomed one to happiness after death. There was also a cult of the Hīnayāna saint Piṇḍola Bhāradvāja (see Section 3.4.2). According to Sarvāstivādin tradition, the Buddha had assigned him the duty of looking after the religion as punishment for having exhibited his psychic powers to lay people. He and other arhants were often portrayed in the *lohan* (arhant) halls that were built in monasteries even after Mahāyāna was established as the dominant form of Chinese Buddhism. By the fifth century the belief developed that Mañjuśrī (see Section 5.4.2) had made his home on Mount Wu-t'ai, which by the eighth century was attracting pilgrims from as far away as India.

Members of the Chinese Sangha did not, as a rule, beg for their food. Instead, they were supported by income from monastic landholdings or by gifts from lay donors. Having a choice in their food, some monastics followed Taoist diets. The practice of eating nothing but pine needles was borrowed directly from the Taoists. A diet of fragrant oil was observed by the few monastics who practiced self-immolation in the early centuries of Chinese Buddhism. This practice was inspired by a passage from Chapter 23 in the *Lotus Sūtra,* describing bodhisattvas who set fire to their bodies as an offering to the Triple Gem. Although there is good reason to believe that the compilers of the *Lotus Sutra* meant the passage to be taken figuratively, a small number of monastics took it literally and practiced self-immolation at night, making their bodies into lamps as a way of offering light to others and demonstrating their total commitment to the Dharma. The Taoists also accepted transformation by fire, although it is not certain whether any Taoists actually set fire to themselves; at any rate, the notion was not utterly foreign to the Chinese. So far as is known, this suicide by fire was practiced only in China or areas within the Chinese cultural sphere, such as Vietnam (see Section 9.12). An attenuated form of this practice, still common today, is that of monastics using incense to burn marks on their heads when they ordain, as a sign of dedicating their bodies to the Triple Gem.

Another dietary practice was vegetarianism. The Vinaya does not forbid the eating of meat, although it does forbid monastics from eating the flesh of animals killed specifically to feed them. Strict vegetarianism for monks and nuns is a practice peculiar to east Asian Buddhism, and again (in addition to Buddhist sources such as the *Nirvāṇa Sūtra)*, Taoist precedents are probably responsible.

The Sangha in China eventually developed a family and clan system parallel to the secular clans of blood lineages, with an elaborate hierarchy of relationships based upon tonsure, the first act required of one leaving the household life. The newly tonsured individual moved from secular to Buddhist family complete with "father," "uncles," "brothers," and "cousins" (these male terms were used among both monks and nuns). This practice had both Chinese and Indian precedents, as the newly ordained monks and nuns in India were also told to regard their preceptors as their parents.

Relic worship is an interesting Buddhist cult practice in China. The relic may be the famous finger bone of the Buddha presented to an emperor of the T'ang dynasty, or it may be an entire mummified body of an especially holy monk or nun. Many of these mummies still exist, the one with the longest known continuous history dating back to 713 C.E. This is the mummy of Hui-neng, the Sixth Ch'an Patriarch, whose body did not decay after death. It was eventually covered with lacquer and exists to this day in a special grotto built for it in south China. In the early biographies of monks and nuns, dating from the Later Han dynasty to the Liang dynasty (150–519), we frequently read that a certain monk or nun, known to be especially holy, did not decay after death. Eventually it became part of a test of a revered monastic's holiness. The body would be placed in a large urn and checked after a certain length of time. If it had not decayed, he/she was truly a saint.

8.7.2 Religious Life: Lay

Lay practices attested to in early times and continuing to modern days include the Lantern Festival, which has no Indian counterpart; the Buddha's birthday; All Souls' Day; vegetarian feasts; image processions; and the release of living beings.

The Lantern Festival takes place on the fifteenth day of the first lunar month. Buddhist festivals in general occur on days of the changing phases of the moon, whereas native Chinese festivals more often occur during months and days consisting of double numbers—as, for example, the fifth day of the fifth month. The legend behind the Lantern Festival alleges that, in order to determine whose doctrine was true and whose false, three altars were once set up: one for Buddhist scriptures, one for Taoist scriptures, and one for local gods. These were set on fire, and only the Buddhist scriptures did not burn. The reigning emperor then ordered that to commemorate the day of the trial by fire, lamps were to be lit symbolizing the great light of Buddhism. This day also marks the conclusion of festivities celebrating the New Year.

The Buddha's birthday is celebrated on the eighth day of the fourth month. It is also known as the day for bathing the Buddha, in commemoration of the gods' having bathed him immediately after his birth. A tiny image of the baby Buddha is placed in a basin of fragrant water, often with flower petals in it.

The baby Buddha stands with his right arm upraised as he announces that this is his final birth. Worshipers ladle three dippers full of water or tea over the image, pay reverence three times, then ladle three dippers more.

Vegetarian feasts are meals donated by a lay person to accomplish a karmic purpose or to fulfill a vow. Donors invite a certain number of monks or nuns to these meals for a certain number of days in a row, often seven. Lay societies also hold communal vegetarian meals, which take on the aspect of a church potluck supper. Image procession is simply the parading of an image of the Buddha or a bodhisattva either around a temple or monastery grounds, or through the streets of a village or town. The occasion can be the Buddha's birthday or any other special event.

All Souls' Day is the fifteenth day of the seventh lunar month. Patterned on the *Ullambana Sūtra* (a text composed in China), it commemorates the arhant Maudgalyāyana's (in Chinese, Mulien) search in hell for his mother. Lanterns are lit, placed on little boats, and set adrift on a river to float where they will. If there are no rivers, lanterns are made for the occasion and lit for everyone's enjoyment. The festival, although still a commemoration of the dead, is a happy get-together. It is the one festival in the year when Buddhists can express in a Buddhist way their Confucian filial duties by aiding the dead in their proper journey, keeping them from becoming malevolent and thereby dangerous to the living. The dead are even taught the Dharma, to give them proper direction in their interlife sojourn.

Releasing living beings is an ancient practice. Monastic compounds had ponds in which the laity put fish, turtles, eels, and other aquatic creatures originally destined for the cooking pot. Caged birds were also released, the pious lay person buying them from a vendor and then setting them free.

One notable feature of these public festivals is that, with the exception of funeral services, all are very joyful, with the feeling of a neighborhood party—which, indeed, many are. The laughter and chatter do not indicate lack of respect for the religion but rather its genuine integration into one's life and outlook.

The keeping of merit books was a practice that developed somewhat later, especially during the Ming dynasty. Detailed lists of good and bad deeds were evaluated in terms of relative merits and demerits so as to help the faithful keep track of their spiritual progress. This practice reflects the bureaucratization of the Chinese view of the afterlife. Yama, the Buddhist king of the underworld, was portrayed as a mandarin; his minions kept the sort of detailed, petty record books that bureaucrats are famous for keeping. Thus Chinese Buddhists wanted clear information on the official standards against which they were to be judged after death.

In the worldview of a typical Chinese lay Buddhist, like that of a Thai (see Section 7.5.1), karma is not necessarily the primary explanation for the vicissitudes of life. There are also the forces of *yin* and *yang*—the cosmic principles of receptivity and activity—as well as the world of spirits and of one's ancestors. If a person is taken ill, his/her family might resort to a spirit medium to see which variety of force is causing the particular illness, and then take appropriate action: making merit to improve a poor stock of karma, making offerings to spirits or ancestors, resorting to a geomancer to bring the yin and yang forces in the environment back into balance, or seeking out a doctor to deal with the physical causes of the disease. Thus a person who participates in a Buddhist ritual is not necessarily a committed Buddhist; by the same token, a committed Buddhist might find it advisable at times to hire the services of a non-Buddhist ritual specialist. The Buddhist techniques for dealing with the invisible forces acting on life, then, are simply one set of alternatives among many that an individual may choose to follow on an ad hoc basis, much as he/she might choose to take Western or Chinese medicine depending on the nature of a particular disease. This ad hoc approach to religion in dealing with mundane issues is especially noticeable in China because the traditional alternatives to Buddhism are also organized religions, but it is typical of the relationship between Buddhism and spirit cults throughout the Asian Buddhist world (see Sections 9.5, 10.4, 11.5).

8.8 MODERN CHINESE BUDDHISM

When the Communists took control of the mainland in 1949, monks and nuns were treated as social parasites. The new regime confiscated Buddhist properties in 1951, depriving monastics of the livelihood they had previously earned by providing services for the lay community. Young monastics were returned to lay status. Older ones were put to work farming, weaving, running vegetarian restaurants, or teaching school. Ordination was discouraged, and the Sangha became an institution of the aged.

In 1953 the government established a Chinese Buddhist Association to impose direct control over Buddhist institutions and their contacts with international Buddhist organizations. Famous and beautiful old temples were maintained at government expense, Buddhist art works were safeguarded, and sites such as the Yiin-kang caves were designated national treasures. However, the Cultural Revolution (1966–76) signaled an abrupt and destructive change in policy. Rampaging Red Guards targeted Buddhist sites as remnants of the feudalistic past that stood in the way of their new order. Many monks and nuns fled China for Hong Kong and Taiwan.

Currently, however, the government is gradually easing its policies of religious repression. A turning point occurred in 1989, when a Buddhist delegation from Taiwan undertook a tour of Buddhist sites with the official sanction of the Communist regime. Temples and shrines ransacked during the Cultural Revolution are being rebuilt, often with the help of outside sources in Taiwan, Hong Kong, North America, and Japan. Defrocked nuns and monks, no longer routinely denounced as "parasites," are being allowed to resume their monastic lives. The motivations here are both spiritual and economic. Those who persisted in their Buddhist faith despite official denunciations welcome an increasing sense of individual freedom. Government bureaucrats, however, have an eye on the lucrative tourist trade.

The island of Taiwan was not occupied by the Communists after the revolution, and so it experienced no abrupt severing of Buddhist or other Chinese traditions. The old guard of the Nationalist party, although primarily Christian, portrayed itself as the caretaker of China's cultural heritage, using Confucian propaganda to maintain solid popular support for its policy of constant preparedness for war. Buddhism was treated as largely irrelevant to the needs of the times. Now, however, a number of factors—the changing of the guard, the relaxing of military policy, and the fast-growing economy—have contributed to a modest Buddhist revival. The growth of the economy in particular has provided a surplus of funds that can be devoted to religious projects, while at the same time leading to a sense of spiritual alienation from the increasingly materialistic society. This sense of alienation has led many to search for the solace offered by a variety of lay and monastic Buddhist organizations.

Buddhism has proven to be particularly attractive to women in Taiwan, who have been swelling the ranks of the Sangha to an unprecedented degree. In a society that does not espouse equality of the sexes as an ideal, much less a reality, the life of a nun offers an autonomy otherwise unavailable to women. Buddhist groups also attract many lay women who view Buddhism as a spiritual refuge and enthusiastically devote their services to its advancement.

Chinese communities scattered throughout Southeast Asia are also experiencing a Buddhist revival. Greater access to books, both in Chinese and English, has disseminated knowledge not only of previously obscure aspects of Chinese Buddhism, but also of non-Chinese Buddhist traditions. As a result, lay organizations devoted to Theravādin or Tibetan practice have sprung up in Singapore, Malaysia, and Hong Kong, as well as Taiwan, and Chinese natives of these countries have ordained in Theravādin and Tibetan orders.

Whether these developments will spread back to the mainland depends on political and cultural developments that are difficult to foretell. But at least the seeds are there, and, unlike the aftermath of the persecution of 845, Chinese Buddhism may very well recover from the Cultural Revolution with greater, not less, vitality and range.

8.9 A BUDDHIST CHARITABLE ORGANIZATION

One of China's most distinctive contributions to Buddhism has been its tradition of Buddhist charitable organizations, which we have already noted in Sections 8.5.4 and 8.7. At present, the most notable example of this tradition is the Buddhist Compassion Relief Love and Mercy Foundation, founded in Taiwan in 1966 by a nun, Dharma Master Cheng Yen.

Born in 1937, Cheng Yen's early life was blighted by her having inadvertently contributed to the death of her father. She sought solace in the teachings of various religions, but only the Buddhist teaching of responsibility for one's own karma gave her any satisfaction. Still, there was much in the general practice of Chinese Buddhism, with its appeals to Buddhas and bodhisattvas for divine help, that struck her as superstitious. In the dichotomy of Paths offered by Mahāyāna doctrine—to either beseech a bodhisattva for help or to become a bodhisattva oneself—she resolved to follow the latter course. In 1962 she ran away from home in hopes of ordaining, yet resolved that she would not become a nun until she found a Dharma-master who shared her views. Traveling throughout the island, she did not meet a master who met her standards until, shortly before a mass ordination in Taipei the following year, a famous scholar agreed to sponsor her.

Shortly thereafter, she retreated to a small temple, isolated in the mountains, near the east coast city of Hwalien. Her style of teaching, using simple, modern language to explain abstract concepts, and her personal determination to work for her own livelihood rather than live idly on the donations of others, soon attracted a small but dedicated following. In 1966, struck by the sufferings of the poor aborigines in her area—and in particular by their inability to gain admission to the local hospital for medical care—she resolved to establish a charitable fund to help them. Asking advice from a group of Catholic nuns, she was told that Buddhism was a poor basis for charitable work, as it was a passive religion that ignored the needs of others. Stung by this remark, she gathered her five disciples and thirty supporters and had them join in a resolution that they would become "Kuan-yin's watchful eyes and useful hands," so that the world would never call Buddhists a passive group again.

From these small beginnings, the foundation has overcome many obstacles to become an organization numbering three million followers in Taiwan alone, plus many thousands of Chinese around the world. Coinciding with the phenomenal economic growth of the worldwide Chinese community, the foundation has provided many Chinese with a philanthropic outlet for their newfound wealth. In Taiwan, the active work of the foundation is carried out by three thousand "commissioners," volunteers who collect donations, propose and personally carry out specific projects, and conduct follow-up studies on the results of their efforts. Their projects include modern hospitals that charge no admission fees (a novelty in Taiwan) and offer free care for those who cannot afford to pay, a nursing college, and a medical school and research center. They also offer food and housing assistance to Taiwan's poor and needy as well as disaster relief throughout the world. Their activities have recently spread to America, where they have provided aid for the inner-city poor and relief to Californians made homeless by the fires of 1993. In addition—in response to what many Asians view as the greatest crime in American society—they have provided companionship for neglected patients in old-age homes.

The stated aims of the foundation are Platonic—Truth, Beauty, and Goodness—but in more practical terms it hopes to benefit both the recipients and the donors of the aid. For the recipients, the aim is to make them self-reliant, if possible, and in a position to become charitable themselves. For the donors, the aims are more complex and are related to Master Cheng Yen's view of the function of the "Love and Mercy" in the foundation's title. Using the classical symbol of the dusty mirror, she says that the purity of Buddha-nature within each person is clouded by the dust of petty, selfish defilements. The relative density of these defilements is a function of one's karma from past lives together with the positive or negative cultivation of personal qualities through action in this life—a view similar to the early Buddhist teachings on the interaction of past and present influences on one's state of mind (see Section 1.4.3). Positive cultivation means washing the defilements away with merciful conscience and selfless love. When the dust is gone, the inherent love and mercy of the Buddha-nature will be able to shine through. Thus love and mercy are both a means of self-cleansing and a natural expression of one's inner nature once it is cleansed.

In this sense, the opportunity to give aid is a chance to cleanse one's own heart, and for this reason the members of the foundation are exhorted to honor and be grateful to those they are able to help. Volunteers who assist in the hospitals and other activities of the foundation are taught to do their work with an absorbed, observant state of mind, reflecting on the range of suffering inherent in the human condition, so that they will be able to abandon their own petty greed, aversion, and delusion, thus feeling greater appreciation for their own families. In a pattern of mutual reinforcement, this creates a healthier family environment, which in turn makes it easier for one to contribute further to aiding the greater family of the entire sentient realm.

Master Cheng Yen and her followers tend to regard many of the ritual traditions of Chinese Buddhism with some disfavor. As one of her followers has said, "We don't believe in burning incense or in similar rituals, since good deeds mean much more than creating smoke." Some Taiwanese have objected to this aspect of the foundation, saying that Master Cheng Yen is founding a new school of Buddhism, but she claims simply to be bringing Buddhism back to its original form, plain and down-to-earth. This view is reflected in the foundation's buildings, which replace the ornate intricacy of traditional Chinese temple architecture with clean, unadorned lines and spacious, well-lit rooms. For many Chinese, this is the new face of Buddhism as it approaches the twenty-first century.

9

Buddhism in Korea and Vietnam

9.1 AN INDIAN IMPORT VIA CHINA

The cultures of both Korea and Vietnam have long existed in an organic relationship with that of their dominant neighbor, China. Both countries adopted the Chinese form of writing, which enabled them to participate fully in Chinese literary culture. China's centralized form of government bureaucracy served as a model for Korean and Vietnamese rulers, with Confucianism providing the underlying ideology. Chinese models also influenced their arts and technology.

Within this organic relationship, Buddhism played a paradoxical role, both contributing to the sense of cultural unity and providing a focal point for differences. Buddhism came to both countries largely—although not exclusively—through China. As a result, Chinese schools such as Ch'an and Pure Land, and cults such as the worship of Kuan-yin, became dominant. The influence was not entirely one-sided, however. One of the early Buddhist missionaries in China, K'ang Seng-hui (d. 280), was born in an Indian trading community located at Chiáo-chih, near present-day Hanoi, and received his initial training in a Buddhist monastery established by Indians there. During the fourth century, Chinese monks unable to go to India for Buddhist training and texts would study in Chiáo-chih instead. Korean monks wrote some of the earliest Ch'an texts, and one, Musang (694?–762), even headed a Ch'an school in Szechuan. Korean scholars played a prominent role in formulating

Hua-yen and Fa-hsiang doctrine. We have already noted how Chegwan (see Section 8.5.1), a Korean, helped revive the T'ien-t'ai school in China during the Five Dynasties period.

Despite these connections, however, the fact that Buddhism's roots lay outside of China allowed it to serve as a rallying point for Korean and Vietnamese nationalists reacting against foreign military and cultural incursions. Temples in Korea were dedicated to the protection of the military and were assumed to ward off attacks. During the sixth century, Korean Buddhists came to believe that their country had been Śākyamuni's home in a previous lifetime. Thus they claimed a special connection with Buddhism; the Chinese, in their eyes, did not transmit a new doctrine to them, but simply reminded them of their own heritage. To emphasize the connection, members of the Silla royal house were named after Śākyamuni's relatives, and many Korean kings consciously followed the model of the Universal Monarch (see Section 2.2) as a way of securing the loyalty of their subjects. In a similar pattern, the Vietnamese dedicated Buddhist stūpas to national heroes and heroines who had fought off foreign invaders.

Both countries differed from China in another important respect: size. Neither was able to sustain the diversity of schools that had flourished in the much larger Chinese context. As a result, Buddhism in both countries has had an active tendency toward ecumenicism, with the local forms of Ch'an and Pure Land providing the overall framework.

KOREA

9.2 THE THREE KINGDOMS PERIOD (18 B.C.E.–688 C.E.)

The history of Korea as a distinct cultural entity began in the first century B.C.E. as rival clans led by warrior aristocracies competed for control of the Korean Peninsula. Eventually three clans emerged victorious, establishing the separate kingdoms of Koguryo, Paekche, and Silla.

Each kingdom had its own unique responses to the entrance of Buddhism, but with certain patterns in common. Like the northern Chinese courts with whom they had close connections, the royalty of each kingdom viewed Buddhism as a cult offering supernatural protection for the nation through its connections with powerful Buddhas and bodhisattvas. Each viewed Buddhism as a potential force for internal unification and pacification as well, because it offered a moral ideology that could supersede the more divisive mythologies associated with rival aristocratic clans. Kings and other members of the royal families entered the Sangha as monks and nuns, and actively disseminated the religion to the general populace, where it integrated with native shamanic beliefs. Symbolic of this integration was the tendency to build Buddhist temples on secluded mountaintops. Like many native traditions, Korean shamanism placed great faith in the power of mountain spirits, who often took the form of demonic tigers. By laying claim to the homes of these spirits, the Buddhists hoped to appropriate their powers for the protection of the nation.

A. *Koguryŏ (37 B.C.E.–668 C.E.):* The territory of the Koguryŏ kingdom covered the northern portion of the Korean Peninsula, overlapping modern China. Traditionally, Buddhism's entry into the kingdom is placed in the year 372, the second year in the reign of King Sosurim. A monk from China, Sundo (Shun-tao), is credited with introducing Mahāyāna at the behest of the Chinese king Fu Chien. There is evidence, however, that a native Koguryŏ Sangha had developed prior to this date. Scholars have speculated as to whether this Sangha received its Buddhism directly from central Asia rather than through China, but the evidence is inconclusive. At any rate, Sundo's mission does seem to represent the introduction of the religion to the Koguryŏ court. Within twenty years after his mission, nine temples were established in the capital of Kuknaesŏng (Tong'gou, China). Shortly before the kingdom fell, Buddhist monks formed a militia for its protection, establishing a pattern that was revived in later periods of Korean history.

B. *Paekche (18 B.C.E.–660 C.E.):* In the southwest portion of Korea, the kingdom of Paekche arose shortly after Koguryŏ. The Paekche king granted official recognition to Buddhism in 384, following the arrival of an Indian monk who had traveled to Paekche via China. The first temple was built the following year. In the sixth century, the Paekche monk Kyŏmik traveled to India to pursue Vinaya studies. He returned to Paekche in 526, accompanied by the Indian monk Paedalta (Vedatta). Together they established a productive translation institute in the capital, Wiryesong (near Seoul). As a result of their work, Kyŏmik is regarded as the father of Vinaya studies in Korea. Paekche was especially active in exporting Buddhism and other aspects of Chinese culture and technology to Japan. One of the most prominent nuns of this period, Pŏpmyŏng, was a native of Paekche who traveled to Japan in 655 and achieved fame for her ability to cure illness by chanting the *Vimalakīrti-nirdeśa Sūtra.* Her regional Korean accent is said to be responsible for the way the Japanese chant Chinese Sūtra passages to this day.

C. *Silla (57 B.C.E.–668 C.E.):* Situated in the mountainous hinterlands of southeast Korea, Silla was the most isolated of the three kingdoms and thus the last to recognize Buddhism officially. The missionary monk Ado (b. 357?) is said to have dazzled the Silla court with his miraculous powers. Other sources credit a monk from Koguryŏ with introducing Buddhism to the Silla kingdom in the fifth century. Buddhism did not become the state religion until the sixth century, however, largely because the government was less centralized than in the other two kingdoms and the aristocracy was able to put up more resistance to what it viewed as a political tool for strengthening royal power. Then in 527 the Buddhist devotee Ich'adon conspired with his uncle the king to remove aristocratic opposition to the religion by becoming a martyr to the cause. The solar eclipse that followed his execution convinced the people of the power of the Dharma. Within 25 years after Ich'adon's death, scores of Silla aristocrats had become Buddhist converts. Scholars have pointed out, however, that the Silla aristocracy had political motives for embracing the religion as a way of fostering the diplomatic ties it was seeking with China.

9.3 THE UNIFIED SILLA DYNASTY (668–918)

In the seventh century, the Silla kings succeeded in conquering their neighbors by playing them off against the Chinese. The unification of the peninsula paved the way for an outstanding period for Korean culture, in which syncretic tendencies, paralleling the political unification of the country, were dominant. Elements from Confucianism, Buddhism, Taoism, and native shamanism were merged in a common religious ideology, with Buddhism playing primarily a cultic role. The opportunity to make merit with the monastic Sangha, and the ability of the Sangha to intercede with Buddhas and bodhisattvas, were seen as guaranteeing the stability and security of the nation.

An instance of this syncretic pattern appears in the *hwarang* ("flower squires"), a select corps of aristocratic youth who were sent to an exclusive military academy as a means of providing the nation with a civilized elite. In the academy they were taught the six traditional Chinese arts (etiquette, music, archery, riding, writing, arithmetic) and cultivated a sumptuous personal aesthetic. Although the moral code they adhered to was primarily Confucian—with a nod to Buddhist precepts in that they were to kill only "discriminately"—they took the bodhisattva Maitreya (Mirŭk-bosal) as their patron deity.

Maitreya was popular on other levels of society as well. In contrast to the situation in China, his cult was never superseded by that of Amitābha. In fact, one of the distinctive features of the Korean Pure Land sect has been its recognition of Maitreya and Amitābha as equals. During the Silla period, the Maitreya cult involved two modes of movement, serving two functions in the society. In the "descent" mode, kings and would-be kings portrayed themselves as incarnations of Maitreya in order to justify their claims to power. In the "ascent" mode, other members of society sought to attain Maitreya's abode in the Tuṣita heaven after death. Other members of the Buddhist pantheon who became popular included Bhaiṣajyaguru (Yaksa-yorae), Amitābha (Amita-bul), Avalokiteśvara (Kwanse'ŭm-bosal), and Kṣitigarbha (Chijang-bosal). The historical Buddha, Śākyamuni (Sŏkkamuni), was also accorded the highest reverence, as were his purported relics, such as skull fragments, teeth, and bits of clothing. Temples were built specifically to house these relics, as well as to channel their powers to individual devotees and to the country as a whole.

The Buddhist pantheon inspired monumental works of art. The cave temple at Sokkuram is probably the most impressive example of the dynasty's devotion to the religion. Begun in 751, it was inspired by the cave temples of China, yet reflects a Korean aesthetic. The main Buddha-figure, a seated Śākyamuni Buddha nearly 10 feet tall, is surrounded by statues of various bodhisattvas and disciples. Many wooden temples were built but have not survived the rigors of time.

On the doctrinal level, early interest focused on the *Avataṃsaka* and *Lotus Sūtra*. Ironically, it was during this period of unification that Korean Buddhism split into five doctrinal schools (under the influence of trends in China): Vinaya (Kyeyul chŏng), Nirvāṇa (Yŏlban chŏng), Dharma Characteristic (Pŏpsŏng chŏng/Haedong), Hua-yen (Wonyung chŏng/Hwaŏm), and "Old" (pre-Hsüan-tsang) Yogācārin (Pŏpsang chŏng). Ch'an (Sŏn) and Pure Land (Chŏng-t'o) also came to Korea during this time, as did T'ien t'ai (Ch'ŏnt'ae), although this last school did not become well established until the following dynasty. Chen-yen (Sinan) became popular with the royal family, but the fall of the dynasty seems to have brought about the end of the school as well.

9.3.1 Hwaŏm (Hua-yen)

Of the doctrinal schools, Hwaŏm became the most important. Its Korean systematizer, Ŭisang (625–702), studied in China as a disciple of the second Hua-yen Patriarch, Chih-yen (602–68). Ŭisang not only introduced Hwaŏm to Korea, founding the school's Korean headquarters at Pusok Temple, but also continued to shape its doctrine in China through his correspondence with Fa-tsang (see Section 8.5.2).

Another Korean monk who influenced Hua-yen/Hwaŏm doctrine both in China and Korea was Ŭisang's friend and fellow student, Wŏnhyo Daesa (617–86). Koreans generally regard Wŏnhyo as one of their great philosophers, and his career is remarkable for the way in which his life mirrored his thought. His main agenda as a scholar was to unite all the diverse Buddhist schools. He delineated two main approaches to Awakening: the analytic approach, in which one tried to develop the full range of pāramīs, and the synthetic approach, in which one tried to return to the One Mind. He then worked out a scholarly method that revealed how the two approaches applied to all issues in Buddhist thought and yet ultimately could be syncretized by demonstrating how each contained the other in a totally unhindered way. After he had written 240 volumes applying his method to major Mahāyāna texts, his principle of unhindered thought led to a life of unhindered action. Fathering a son with a widowed princess, he abandoned his robes and began wandering, teaching that meritorious and demeritorious action were one and the same for the truly wise person. He used song, music, and dance to spread Pure Land teachings among the common people, and made a career of bringing the Dharma into brothels and taverns.

9.3.2 Sŏn (Ch'an)

Pŏmnang (fl. 632–46), a Korean disciple of Fourth Ch'an Patriarch Tao-hsin (580–651), is credited with bringing Ch'an to his homeland, although his lineage soon died out. Other Ch'an lineages arrived later, becoming organized into the *kusan* (Nine Mountains) system by the early tenth century. Almost all were founded by disciples trained in the tradition of Ma-tsu Tao-i (see Section 8.5.5). In emulating their master's idiosyncrasies, these disciples soon found themselves at odds with the five doctrinal schools. Frustrated by the obstacles the schools placed in their way, some of them began mounting direct attacks on their opponents. Thus as the Unified Silla dynasty drew to a close, Korean Buddhism found itself radically split between textual study and practice, the widespread perception being that the two approaches were irreconcilable.

9.4 THE KORYŎ DYNASTY (918–1392)

Under the Koryŏ dynasty, Buddhism continued in its cultic role as the state religion, reaching a high point in its Korean history. The founding king of the dynasty, Wang Kon (T'aejo, r. 918–43), regarded the Dharma as the foundation for his rule and instituted an examination system for Buddhist monks, modeled on the Confucian civil service exams, that provided avenues for monks to become advisers to the court.

Perhaps the main reason for government patronage of Buddhism was an unstable military situation that plagued the dynasty and fueled the perceived need for supernatural assistance. The most striking monument to this perceived need is the Korean Tripiṭaka. Around the turn of the eleventh century, Korea was harassed by the Khitans, an invading tribe from Manchuria. Thus, by royal decree, a complete canon of all available Chinese and Korean Buddhist texts was compiled and carved in wooden printing blocks in hopes of securing Śākyamuni's protection for the country. The project—utilizing more than eighty thousand blocks—took two decades to complete, but had little effect on the ongoing warfare. The Khitan menace did not end until 1218, when the tribe was stamped out by the Mongols, who posed an even bigger threat to the peninsula and actually put the Tripiṭaka blocks to the torch. In 1236, a royal decree ordered that another set of blocks be carved. Again, the more than eighty thousand blocks completed in 1251 did not immediately drive away the Mongols, although the country suffered less than many others from Mongol depredations. Eventually Mongol power in Korea began to wane in the 1350s, and ended altogether in 1381 with the downfall of the Yüan dynasty in China. This second set of blocks has survived to the present, and in the early twentieth century formed the basis for the massive Japanese Taishō edition of the Chinese Canon.

Benefiting from strong political patronage from the Koryŏs, monasteries grew in size, wealth, and influence. Many became major landholders, with large numbers of serfs. Some even embarked on commercial ventures such as alcohol, noodle, and tea production, and monks became embroiled in court politics. Sŏn monks in particular were renowned for their mastery of geomancy, which kept them involved in building projects and ceremonies and pulled them away from their meditation practice. As had happened in many other countries, worldly success began to corrupt the Korean Sangha. This sparked a backlash from both inside and outside the Buddhist community. Confucians mounted their usual attacks on the religion as a whole, whereas Buddhist government officials accused individual monks of ordaining not for spiritual reasons but merely to avoid military service and to exploit the lucrative potential of monastic life. In the tenth century, the government instituted a series of restrictions to limit the participation of monks in secular affairs; in the twelfth century, it ordered that all monks breaking their precepts be forcibly disrobed.

In the midst of the political and ecclesiastical turmoil of the period, three Korean monks—Ŭich'ŏn, Chinul, and T'aego—applied working models from China to raise the standards of the religion and to heal the split between doctrine and practice that had begun under the previous dynasty. Their efforts, which transformed the original divisions of five teachings and nine mountains (major Sŏn temples) into five teachings and two sects, have shaped Korean Buddhism ever since.

9.4.1 Ŭich'ŏn

Ŭich'ŏn (1055–1101) began his life as a royal prince. At the age of 11 he entered a Hwaŏm monastery; in 1085 he went to China to collect texts and further his studies. There he studied widely with noted masters from various schools, but was especially drawn to T'ien-t'ai. He vowed to the memory of the Chinese master Chih-i (see Section 8.5.1) that he would expound the school's doctrine in his homeland, viewing it as the ideal means to synthesize competing traditions by avoiding the pitfalls inherent both in study without practice (represented by the five orthodox schools) and practice without study (represented by Sŏn). In particular, Ŭich'ŏn criticized contemporary Sŏn practitioners for abandoning what he saw as their school's original reliance on study as a basis for meditation.

Enjoying the advantages of royal patronage, Ŭich'ŏn's order soon flourished, attracting members from all quarters of the Buddhist community. His early death, however, put a halt to his attempted unification of Korean Buddhism. Instead of bringing Buddhists together, Ŭich'ŏn succeeded simply in adding one more school to the already crowded field. Nonetheless, the example of his attempts provided important lessons for the more successful reformer, Chinul, one century later.

9.4.2 Chinul

Chinul (1158–1210; posthumously named Pojo) was largely responsible for molding Sŏn into its present form. As a result of his efforts, almost all of Korean Buddhism is now in a sense Sŏn.

Severe childhood illness provided the occasion for Chinul's entry into the monkhood. When all attempts at healing failed, his father promised his son to the Sangha if the Buddha would provide a cure. The cure came, and so Chinul received tonsure at the tender age of 7, followed by the novice precepts at age 15. Bound to no permanent teacher, he began practicing meditation from an early age based on his own reading of texts. This combination of scholarship and practice, rare in his day, was to provide the pattern for his life and teachings.

In 1182, the young Chinul traveled to the capital to sit for the Sŏn examinations. Although he passed them easily, he was disgusted with the worldly climate surrounding them, and so made a pact with a handful of fellow examinees to retreat into the mountains and start a reform-minded religious society, the Samādhi and Prajñā Community, for both lay people and monastics. This was to be the first such society in Korea, although it followed a pattern popular in China since the fifth century (see Section 8.5.3). Delays in realizing his plans for the community, however, set him on an itinerant life. In the course of his wanderings he settled in the extreme southwest, where he experienced the first of his three major meditative insights. Each insight came as a result of reading a text, underscoring his conviction that doctrinal knowledge and meditative experience were meant to go hand in hand. His first insight came from a passage in the *Platform Sūtra* (see Section 8.5.5) that identified the mind with the self-nature of suchness. The insight this gave him into his own mind convinced him of the truth of the *Platform Sūtra*'s teaching on the unity of samādhi and prajñā, and of Tsung-mi's teachings on sudden Awakening and gradual cultivation (see Section 8.5.2). His second insight came while reading a commentary on the *Avataṃsaka Sūtra* that identified the original mind with the wisdom of universal brightness that awoke suddenly and completely to the dharmadhātu, or the true nature of reality. This insight underscored for him the essential unity of Hwaŏm doctrine and Sŏn practice.

Soon after this second insight, Chinul's Samādhi and Prajñā Community finally became a reality in 1188. By 1197 the community had become well known throughout Korea, attracting large numbers of followers from all walks of life. To accommodate the growing numbers, the group chose Sŏnggwang Mountain as the site for an enlarged temple. Chinul's third and definitive insight came during a short retreat he took en route to the new center. Although the political situation in Korea had curtailed contacts with China, Chinul had somehow gained access to the *Record* of Ta-hui Tsung-kao (see Section 8.6), whose distinction between live and dead utterances sparked Chinul's final experience of Awakening. This final Awakening, however, did not erase Chinul's respect for the texts that had inspired his earlier insights. For him, understanding the meaning of words as dead utterances remained a necessary precursor to approaching them as live utterances so as to understand the process of verbalizing and then reach the radiance of the mind that lay beyond meanings and words (see also the discussions of language and perception in Sections 1.4.3 and 2.3.1). As a result, Chinul continued to use all three texts that had inspired his Awakenings as the basis for his instructions to his students. His combination of *Platform Sūtra* and Hwaŏm doctrine with k'ung-an practice set the pattern for the Chogye Order he helped spawn.

The name of the order came from the royal decree, promulgated after Chinul arrived at his new center, that renamed the mountain Chogye, after Hui-neng's mountain home in southern China. The temple on Chogye/Sŏnggwang continued to function as Sŏn headquarters for more than three hundred years; the community continues to thrive today. When Chinul died in 1210 he was succeeded by his favored disciple, Chin'gak Hyesim (1178–1234), who consolidated his master's efforts, attracted students from all the Sŏn schools and the scholastic sects, and assured the acceptance of k'ung-an meditation as the principal Sŏn practice.

9.4.3 T'aego

A native of Kwangju in southern Korea, T'aego Pou (1301–82), reconciled Chinul's Chogye sect with the remaining Sŏn practitioners of the Nine Mountains system on the basis of the personal Lin-chi (in Korean, Imje) transmission he brought back from China. Although Chinul provided the philosophical basis for the Chogye Order, some Korean monks today regard T'aego as the order's true founder by virtue of his direct link to Chinese Ch'an.

T'aego was ordained at the age of 13 and experienced a first glimmering of Awakening in his twenties. At the age of 37 he realized great Awakening after meditating on the k'ung-an, "Does a dog have Buddha-nature?—NO!" Three years later he began a vastly successful teaching career. During a visit to China (1346–48), he studied with great Chinese masters both north and south. Of these, Shih-wu, Eighteenth Patriarch in the Lin-chi lineage, certified T'aego's Awakening and convinced him to return home to spread the Dharma.

Back in Korea, T'aego lived a quiet life on Mount Sosol. The surrounding environment was anything but quiet, though, as the Yüan dynasty was coming to an end in China. For the Koryŏ king, Kongmin (r. 1351–74), this presented a golden opportunity to reassert Korean independence from the Mongols and to consolidate his power within his realm. In the very year that he assumed the throne, he called T'aego to the capital. Whatever the king's motives for the summons—a desire for Buddhist wisdom or to tap into T'aego's popularity—T'aego took advantage of his new position both to lecture the court on the moral imperatives of power and to petition the king's help in unifying the fragmented Sŏn establishment. Impressed with T'aego's petition, the king appointed T'aego to the position of royal teacher in 1356 for the express purpose of carrying out the proposed unification. T'aego based his efforts for a unified Sŏn both on personal transmission through k'ung-an practice and on the monastic ordinances then current in China.

In typical Ch'an-Sŏn fashion, T'aego balanced his concern for proper form and discipline with iconoclastic rhetoric. The record of one of his lectures to the royal court depicts him as reverently offering incense to the Buddha and then taking the abbot's high seat to proclaim that all the scriptures and the Three Vehicles are just "piss left behind by an old barbarian." After serving as royal teacher off and on for 10 years, T'aego eventually sought refuge in monastic retirement. At death he was granted the title of Sŏn Master of Perfect Realization. Several Sŏn lineages claim him as a common ancestor.

9.5 THE YI/CHOSŎN DYNASTY (1392–1910)

The Yi dynasty, which bestowed the name Chosŏn (Land of Morning Calm) on the country, replaced Buddhism with Confucianism as the state cult. Buddhist monks were forced into seclusion in the mountains, leaving the political field to scholar-officials. The transition was gradual, however. The founder of the Yi dynasty, a former general under the Koryŏ kings, actually incorporated Buddhist elements in his new order. However, internal and external political factors favored the neo-Confucians. On the internal level, the new regime needed to undermine any lingering power possessed by those still loyal to the former dynasty. On the external level, it needed the support of China's neo-Confucian Ming dynasty in order to maintain power.

However, not until the reign of the third king of the dynasty did the government take active repressive measures against the Buddhists. Land and servants were confiscated, temples closed, and Buddha-images melted down to make weapons of war. Members of the social elite were not allowed to ordain, and existing monks were pressured to disrobe.

Conditions improved somewhat under later kings. The fourth king, Sejong (r. 1419–50), advocated a phonetic Korean script, Han'gŭl, which contributed greatly to the popularization of Buddhism in that it enabled Koreans to read Buddhist literature without having to learn Chinese or Sanskrit. King Sejong also consolidated the Korean Sangha into two schools: the Sŏn school, which included not only Sŏn but also Ch'ŏnt'ae; and the Doctrinal (Kyo) School, which included Hwaŏm and three other schools.

During this period Korea was plagued by invading forces, both Japanese and Manchu. Buddhist monks, following a tradition established during the Koguryŏ kingdom, took on a military role. The Sŏn master Sŏsan Hyujŏng (1520–1604), for example, led five thousand of his comrades against the Japanese. Although the Koreans were successful in driving the Japanese from their territory, the monks' involvement in the war effort incited the Japanese to burn many major monasteries to the ground.

Despite its waning influence in the court, Buddhism maintained its support among the masses. As a result, the elite linked Buddhism and shamanism as traditions to be equally avoided. In his satirical tale "The Story of a Yangban," Pak Chi-won (1737–1805) pokes fun at the attitude of a proper Confucian-trained court official: "When ill, do not call a shaman; when sacrificing, do not invite monks."

In the nineteenth century, growing Christian influence in the country sparked a small Buddhist backlash. Ch'oe Che-u (1821–64; also known as Ch'oe Sūn) founded the Eastern Learning (Tonghak) movement in response to the Western Learning (Sŏhak) movement associated with Catholicism. Also known as the Religion of the Heavenly Way (Ch'ŏndogyo), his movement incorporated meditation practices—somewhat influenced by Sŏn—with Confucian, Taoist, and native shamanic doctrines. Another reaction to Western influences was Won Buddhism, founded in 1916, which added Christian doctrines to the traditional Korean eclectic mix.

Meanwhile, beginning in the late nineteenth century, traditional Sŏn was experiencing a revival, largely through the efforts of Kyŏng Ho (1849–1907) and his student, Mang Gŏng (1872–1946). Mang Gŏng in particular was notable for his role in teaching Sŏn not only to monks but also to nuns and lay people. Of his 25 Dharma heirs, 4 were nuns. One of them, Manseŏng (1897–1975), established what is now the most highly reputed nunnery in the country, T'aeseŏng-am, on the outskirts of Pusan.

9.6 JAPANESE RULE (1910–1945) AND ITS AFTERMATH

In the late nineteenth century, Japan began actively modernizing along Western lines and mounted a program of military expansion that led (among other conquests) to the annexation of Korea in 1910. At home, the Japanese government had followed a calculated policy of using Buddhism to mold public opinion, and it followed a similar policy in Korea. At first, Korean Buddhists were pleased by the Japanese support for their religion. However, they felt betrayed upon learning of Japanese plans to subjugate the Korean Sangha to the Japanese Sōtō Zen sect. As a result, monks became increasingly involved in efforts to oppose colonial power.

The Japanese countered by pressuring the Korean Sangha to abandon its vows of celibacy. Ecclesiastical positions were granted only to married monks. Celibate monks gradually became a minority, until in 1926 the colonial government required Korean abbots to remove all rules against marriage among the clergy. The result was a marked change in the character of Sangha life, as the mundane pressures of supporting a family placed new burdens on the monks. The communal conditions that had allowed monasteries to accumulate goods and property began to break down. Most important from the Japanese point of view, family responsibilities gave the monks less time for political activity.

The one positive result of the Japanese occupation was that the threat of total Japanese domination moved the Sŏn and Doctrinal schools to patch up their differences. In 1935, after seven years of negotiations, the two schools formally merged into the Chogye Order, finally realizing the centuries-old dream of a united Korean Sangha. The union, however, was short-lived. After independence, the order was badly split between a small rural minority who had managed to preserve their celibacy throughout the Japanese occupation and the majority who had abandoned their celibate vows. The celibate monks fought to regain control of the monasteries that had gone over to the married priests, and in 1954, after the end of the Korean War, they finally won government support for their cause. Married priests were expelled from the order and formed their own separate T'aego Order. All major monasteries are now in Chogye hands, but tensions between the two groups remain strong to this day (Strong *EB*, sec. 8.8.3).

9.7 BUDDHISM IN MODERN KOREA

The success of South Korea's economic policy is changing the country so drastically that it is difficult to point out any clear trends in contemporary Buddhism, aside from two facts: an increasing proportion of the country is reported to be Buddhist, and Korean nuns now play a more prominent role in Sangha affairs than before. In addition to the Chogye and T'aego Orders, there are 16 "homegrown" sects, including Won. The Chogye Order is now dominant, whereas the T'aego Order is fast dying out. Mirroring the split between the Chogye and T'aego monks, Korean nuns now have two independent orders. The larger one, formed in 1985, is affiliated with the Chogye Order; the smaller one, founded in 1972 and heavily involved in social work, is affiliated with the T'aego Order. As for North Korea, lack of information about the society in general makes it difficult to assess the position of Buddhism there, but it is unlikely that Buddhists are free to practice.

Ordination in South Korea is controlled by government regulations. Educational standards for both monks and nuns are becoming more stringent, with a high school diploma now a minimum requirement. Once a year, candidates from various masters are convened for joint ceremonies lasting several days. In 1982, the practice of dual ordination for nuns (see Section 3.4.1) was revived by the Chogye Order after a one-hundred-year lapse. Once ordained, monastics spend three to five years studying Chinese language and Buddhist Sūtras. More and more Sangha members are also pursuing higher degrees beyond the temple, even going abroad for study.

A movement has begun to attract young people to Buddhism at the lay level. This includes a network of Sunday schools for children based on the Christian model. Massive efforts are under way to translate Sūtras and related texts into Han'gŭl, making them more accessible to the average reader, and the Korean Tripiṭaka is being put in a computer format. Monks and nuns also devote themselves to social services. Perhaps because the nuns have traditionally played a more prominent role in offering pastoral help to the laity, they are now in the forefront of finding new ways to serve the fast-changing society: counseling prisoners, running homes for the aged, hosting radio shows, offering healing through meditation, and providing instruction in such arts as painting, flower arranging, and music as forms of spiritual training.

Korean Buddhists are actively proselytizing not only at home but also abroad. Most prominent in this regard has been the Chogye monk Seung Sahn (b. 1927), famous for his teaching of "don't-know mind." His Kwan Um School, founded in 1983, now claims more than 50 affiliated groups throughout Europe and the Americas.

Not all is rosy, however. The wealth and power won by the Chogye Order have led to charges of corruption coming from within the order itself. Particularly serious have been charges of collusion with the government. In the late 1970s, as a reaction to the Christian churches' support for political dissidents, the government began promoting Buddhism as an expression of Korean identity, and the order established a Monks' Militia for National Defense. Accusations that the upper echelons of the order have funneled Sangha funds to sympathetic politicians have given rise to concern that the pattern of the Koryŏ dynasty will be repeated, whereby government patronage breeds monastic corruption.

9.8 LIFE IN A SŎN MONASTERY

Despite the rapid secularization of Korean society, the Korean Sangha is probably the strongest monastic institution in east Asia. Life in the traditional Sŏn monasteries and nunneries continues largely unchanged from the pattern it has followed for centuries, providing an accurate picture of conditions in the Sung monasteries on which they were modeled. As a result, these institutions offer an important corrective to many of the stereotypes about Ch'an/ Zen/Sŏn that fill the popular press. Reading the teachings of the ancient Ch'an masters, one would assume that they avoided books entirely and lived totally spontaneous, iconoclastic lives. Upon visiting a Sŏn monastery, one discovers, however, that the monks devote their early years to a thorough study of the classical texts, and that throughout their monastic careers they adhere to a strict code of discipline and etiquette. As we noted in Section 8.5.5, most extant Ch'an literature was composed during a period when life in Ch'an monasteries had become extremely formalized. In Korean monasteries we can see living examples of how Ch'an life and literature were originally designed to interact, each providing a corrective for the shortcomings of the other.

Four large "forest" monasteries exist in Korea today. Located on hillsides sheltered by mountains in remote areas of the country, their location reflects not only the principles of Chinese geomancy—which maintains that mountains provide protection from baleful influences—but also the geographical isolation imposed on Buddhist institutions under the Yi dynasty. In theory, each monastery preserves the four strands of tradition that have come to define Korean Buddhism—Sŏn, Hwaŏm study, Vinaya, and Pure Land—although the balance between these strands differs from monastery to monastery. In some, seminaries are maintained, offering the traditional curriculum established during the Yi dynasty, whereas others place more emphasis on meditation. All preserve traces of Hwaŏm doctrine in their formal organization. Sinuous paths winding from shrine to shrine among the buildings replicate the Hwaŏm dharmadhātu maṇḍala, a diagram that outlines the unimpeded interpenetration of phenomena (see Section 8.5.2). The monastic population is divided into two groups: the scrutinizers of principle, or meditators and scholars, and the scrutinizers of phenomena, or the support corps. The interaction between these two is an object lesson in Hwaŏm doctrine, forming a dharmadhātu maṇḍala in the four dimensions of space and time.

Each monastery is divided into several compounds, each of which is a monastery in miniature. One compound is also set aside for nuns who wish to study with the resident Sŏn master. Although they come together for the daily ceremonies of the monastery, contact between the monks and nuns is strictly curtailed. Within their compound the nuns lead a life similar to that of the monks, which is outlined in the following:

Korean folk wisdom traditionally recognizes five possible reasons for taking on the life of a monk: a sense of vocation, the fulfillment of a vow (as in the case of Chinul), family pressure, failure in love, or laziness. The fulfillment of a vow does not appear to play a role at present, and only the most devout Buddhist families would consider the life of a monk a desirable vocation for one of their sons, but the other incentives are still in force. Ironically, the sense of vocation felt by young men seeking ordination today often stems from the rampant Westernization of the country, as university students become disillusioned with the Western approach to philosophy that dominates the modern educational system and view ordination as a way to reconnect with Korea's ancient roots. The call to ordain can also come from personal experience in modern warfare, as happened in the late 1970s, when many Vietnam War veterans became monks. Young men who come to the monkhood with a sense of vocation tend to be more idealistic than their brethren, but practical experience shows that initial motivation does not necessarily determine how successful a monk's career will be.

That career goes through several stages, beginning invariably in the support corps of the monastery. The candidate spends the first six months as a postulant, working in the kitchen, the latrines, and the monastery's fields. Not only does this provide the manual labor needed to keep the monastery self-sufficient, but it also tests the stamina and commitment of the newly arrived devotees. The postulants are also expected to study basic chants and the Vinaya. As a result, their days—from the wake-up call at 3:00 A.M. to lights-out at 9:00 P.M.—are full, with little time for rest. If they last the six months, they are invited to ordain as novices and they receive the Ten Precepts (see Section 3.4.1), although here the vow to abstain from eating in the afternoon is changed to a vow to abstain from keeping domestic animals. At the end of the ordination ceremony, the novice's change in status is marked by his taking a wick, placing it inside his forearm, lighting it, and letting it burn down to the skin, as a symbol of nonattachment to the body. When the wound forms a scab, some novices have been known to pick at it to enlarge the scar, as a badge of their bravado.

Novitiate ordination carries a tacit agreement to contribute another three years of service to the monastery, usually as an attendant to the senior monk who sponsored one's ordination. Formal studies begin, focusing on chants, ritual performances, and Vinaya. Learning also proceeds on a more informal basis through interaction with senior monks. This is the period during which the young monk's sense of family identity switches away from his biological family and becomes attached to the brotherhood of his institution. After three years, the novice is eligible to ordain as a bhikṣu. This involves a ceremony during which he vows to observe the 250 precepts of the Mahīśāsaka Vinaya (see Section 3.2.4). In practice, no one expects the monks to observe the precepts related to the mendicant life—such as the prohibitions against eating after noon, eating stored-up food, handling money, and digging in the soil—but all monks are required to observe the four parājika rules strictly (see Section 3.4.1).

Bhikṣu ordination marks the point when the ordinand has committed himself to the monkhood for life. Although disrobing is possible, it is considered a great disgrace, unlike in Thailand and Burma (see Section 7.5.1). The other primary change in the life of the new ordinand is that he now has the right to travel and undertake studies at other monasteries, changing from a scrutinizer of phenomena to a scrutinizer of principle, as he has now paid his dues to the home institution. Most monks go to seminary, where they undertake a course of study covering Chinese language as well as basic texts in Sŏn and Hwaŏm doctrine. Those who take the complete course, which lasts 12 years, are eligible to become teachers themselves, either in a seminary or in programs of outreach to the laity. Other monks, after studying the *Record* of Ta-hui Tsung-kao (see Sections 8.6, 9.4.2), begin training in meditation.

Training begins in a meditation hall, which occupies its own separate compound in the large monasteries, aloof from the compounds of the support corps. In fact, most meditating monks stay away from their home monasteries to escape the pressure to return to the support corps. As a result, the contingent of meditators living at a monastery at any one time are there as privileged guests, with few assigned jobs. Despite their heavy schedules of practice, meditators as a group are remarkably independent, beholden to nothing aside from their own sense of devotion to the practice.

For six months out of the year, during the periods of "slackened rule"—roughly August to November, and February to May—the meditators are free to come and go and to schedule their individual practice as they see fit. Intensive retreats, called periods of "binding rule," are held during the summer and winter months. During these retreats the meditators are expected to stay put. Sessions are typically three to four hours long—beginning at 3 A.M., 8 A.M., 1 P.M., and 6 P.M.—subdivided into fifty-minute periods of seated meditation alternating with ten minutes of walking meditation. Lying down is prohibited except during breaks before breakfast and in the evening. Work assignments are minimal so that the meditators may devote their full energies to meditation. The most arduous period of training is the week of "ferocious effort" immediately prior to the celebration of the Buddha's Awakening (the eighth day of the twelfth lunar month, which usually falls in January). The entire period is one extended meditation session. No one sleeps; breaks are taken only for meals. In this way the participants reenact the Buddha's all-out practice on the night of his Awakening.

Although meditators will often choose to enter retreat at a particular monastery because of the reputation of its Sŏn master, few have any close contact with him. The meditator is free to choose his own k'ung-an and to find his own techniques for focusing on the hua-t'ou (crucial phrase—see Section 8.6) so as to maintain the mind in the preverbal state called the "great doubt," in which Awakening can be gained and then matured. The master will give a formal lecture once every two weeks and will conduct required private interviews once or twice during the retreat, but that is usually the extent of his interaction with the itinerant group that has taken up residence in the meditation hall. A meditator may schedule an interview with the Sŏn master at any time, but young monks are usually too timid to do so, whereas older monks tend to feel that the master has nothing to teach them that they have not already heard. The fact that Korean meditators are encouraged to stick to one k'ung-an for life may be a factor here. As a result, a master may spend his career teaching all the active meditators in the country without leaving behind a single personal disciple.

Periodically, the strict division between meditators and support corps is put aside, in keeping with the principle of unimpeded interaction. All able-bodied monks are called out to help with planting and harvesting in the monastery's fields, to fight forest fires, or to help with labor-intensive jobs in the kitchen, such as pickling vegetables or making Chinese dumplings. The lunar New Year, shortly after the period of ferocious effort, brings a three-day respite in the schedule, during which all the monks feast together, sing songs, and play games. At the end of these periods, the division of labor resumes.

If, after several years, a monk finds that he is suited to the meditative life, he will abandon the meditation-hall circuit and retreat to a forest hermitage to develop his meditation in isolation, returning to the large monasteries when he feels the need for group support to reinvigorate his practice. If his understanding develops sufficiently, he may eventually return to his home monastery, where he may be elected to one of the subsidiary positions of authority in the meditation compound, or even to the position of Sŏn master when the office falls vacant.

By far the vast majority of Korean monks, however, do not meditate. Either they never attempt the meditative life to begin with, or find that it does not suit them when they do. Thus they remain in or return to the support corps of their home monastery, filling positions in the kitchen, the field, or the office, perhaps even being elected to the position of abbot, going into retirement when they grow too old to work. In this respect they carry out a tradition of specialization within the Sangha that goes back not only to Sung China, but to the earliest centuries of Indian Buddhism; a tradition whereby a minority concentrated on gaining Awakening in this lifetime, while others facilitated that effort in hopes of acquiring merit for future lives.

As with all traditional institutions, the great Korean monasteries have found their very existence challenged by changes in modern society. One major disruption has been land reform, which has severely reduced the land holdings that used to provide their primary source of income. As a result, the monasteries have had to organize lay support groups in the major cities to ensure their financial survival. This outreach to the laity has entailed new responsibilities for the senior monks, as they must make periodic teaching visits to groups scattered throughout the country and provide lay retreat sessions on their monastic campuses. Another change has been wrought by the new tendency among the urban population to regard the monasteries as tourist spots. In some cases, the impact of tourism has proven so disruptive that monasteries have been forced to abandon their campuses to the tourists and to build unassuming retreats for monks and nuns even farther away in the mountains. Because the monastic alternative is still attracting candidates, however, solutions will probably be found to these problems, so that Korea will continue to provide, perhaps in altered form, environments conducive to a life of Buddhist practice.

VIETNAM

9.9 TWO STREAMS OF BUDDHISM CONVERGE

Vietnam as a political and cultural entity is largely a product of the modern era. For centuries the country now known by that name was divided politically and culturally into two parts, north and south. As we have already noted (see Section 7.3), southern Vietnam belonged to the area of "Further India" until the fifteenth century, and so received its Buddhism from Indian sources. Northern Vietnam has belonged to the Chinese cultural sphere—and at times was actually part of the Chinese empire—since the third century B.C.E. Although it, too, originally received its Buddhism via Indian traders and actually helped spread the religion to China in the third century C.E., the tide began to turn in the sixth century. Under the T'ang dynasty, when northern Vietnam was a part of the empire, Chinese Buddhism came to dominate the country as Chinese governors used it as a tool for civilizing the "barbarian" natives. When the Dinh dynasty (969–81) gained independence, Buddhism was proclaimed the national religion, a position it held through the Lê dynasty (1010–1225) and well into the Trân dynasty (1225–1400).

In the fifteenth century, the north annexed the Indianized Champa kingdom, based in central Vietnam, beginning a process whereby the sinicized culture of the north came to dominate the Indianized culture of the south. This process, completed in the eighteenth century, was reflected in Vietnamese

Buddhism, which—aside from a few Theravādin enclaves along the Cambodian border—came almost entirely under Chinese influence. A few remnants of the dual sources of Vietnamese Buddhism still survive, however. One of the tangible remnants is the continued practice of including Theravāda images of Śākyamuni on the same altar with Mahāyāna bodhisattvas, next to an altar devoted to Ch'an (in Vietnamese, Thiền) patriarchs. More important is the intangible remnant: a strong spirit of toleration among the various Buddhist schools, based on the principle "the same destination but different directions," with each individual free to combine elements from the various traditions as he/she sees fit.

Still, in most important respects, the development of Vietnamese Buddhism followed trends in China, such as the Sung tendency to conflate Buddhist doctrines with Confucianism and Taoism, and the Ming tendency to combine Ch'an with Pure Land practices. On the political level, the fortunes of Buddhism in the Vietnamese court followed the same trajectory as in China (as well as Korea and Japan). Confucianism came to dominate the court during the Later Lê dynasty (1428–1788), with Buddhism becoming the faith of the masses.

One important difference between Chinese and Vietnamese Buddhism is that the Chinese doctrinal schools never took root in Vietnam. Thus Thiên and Pure Land had the field to themselves. Another important difference is the close connection between Thiền and the royal court, so close that one Vietnamese king, Trân-Nhân-Tôn (1258–1308), actually became a Thiền patriarch and founded his own school. Thus Thiền, though originally a Chinese import, became associated with Vietnamese nationalism.

9.10 BUDDHISM IN POPULAR CULTURE

During the Trân dynasty, the Vietnamese evolved their own Southern Script (Chū'-Nm), a modification of Chinese characters that made possible a popular literature aimed at an audience who lacked the time to learn the Chinese system. In this literature we can see how Buddhist values, together with those of Confucianism and Taoism, infiltrated the popular consciousness. A prime example is *The Tale of Kiê'u* by Nguyên Dū' (1765–1820). Nguyên was a scholar-official born into times of political upheaval when a popular uprising toppled the reigning Later Lê dynasty. In the subsequent political struggles, the southern-based Nguyên dynasty (1802–1945) came to power. As a northerner, Nguyên was relegated to minor posts, but this gave him time to record a story, a work of more than three thousand verses, that has long since been regarded as a national literary treasure.

The essential theme of the story is romantic love, although the Confucian concept of filial duty combines with the Buddhist doctrine of karma to provide the impetus for much of the plot. Briefly, the story revolves around the beautiful and talented heroine, Kiê'u, who is forced to part with her true love, young scholar Kim. To save her family from ruin (thus answering the call of Confucian filial piety), she is driven into a life of prostitution. After years of suffering, she finds refuge in a Buddhist convent, where Kim accidentally discovers her. In the intervening years Kim has married Kiê'u's sister, Van, as Kiê'u herself had arranged before her departure from the family. He has also risen in wealth and official rank. Despite his fulfillment of the Confucian priorities in life, something is missing in his success; he has never forgotten his true love.

At first Kiê'u refuses to give up her secluded life, feeling that her past experiences have made her unworthy. Totally devoid of bitterness, she invokes the Buddhist notion of karma and her own past misdeeds to explain her terrible sufferings. Kim responds by appealing to those same Buddhist values, for karma also brought the lovers back together. When Kiê'u depicts herself as a fallen flower, Kim invokes the Buddhist image of the luminous mirror-mind from which worldly dust can be removed. Kiê'u finally relents.

The couple does indeed live happily ever after, although Kiê'u asks that their marriage be platonic. The poem ends on a Taoist note, advising an acceptance of the Tao, balanced by a recognition of inner goodness (pristine Buddha-nature) that makes human beings responsible for their actions. The shifting fortunes of all the characters in the work illustrate the Buddhist notion of impermanence as the fundamental characteristic of human existence. From this insight follows the lesson that spiritual practice—ironically symbolized by the pure love that pulls Kiê'u out of the convent—is far more valuable than fleeting sensual gratification.

9.11 THE MODERN PERIOD

Through most of the Nguyên dynasty, Buddhism's fortunes were on the wane, first because of the Confucian ideology that dominated the court, then because of the activities of the Catholic missionaries who, under French rule, were able to convert large numbers of Vietnamese, especially in the south. The end of World War II in 1945 eventually gave Vietnam an opportunity for self-rule, although the country quickly fell into a protracted civil war between a Communist north and an anti-Communist south.

The war grew to devastating proportions. The most graphic symbols of Buddhist reaction to the war were the monastics who practiced self-immolation as a way of calling world attention to their double plight: the suffering caused both by the war and by the pro-Catholic south Vietnamese government's persecution of Buddhists (Strong *EB*, sec. 8.8.4). Many of the monastics who gave their lives in this way were Theravādin, but the historical precedent for their actions came from China (see Section 8.7.1), where self-immolation had once been a devotional practice. In the context of the Vietnam War, however, its impact was primarily political. Pictures of burning monastics provoked the United Nations into investigating the Vietnamese government's history of religious persecution and played a contributing role in the downfall of the Diem regime.

Easily the most eloquent Vietnamese Buddhist spokesman during this period was the Thiên monk Thich Nhat Hanh (b. 1926), who in 1964 founded the School of Youth for Social Service and the Tiep Hien Order (Order of Interbeing), dedicated to the cause of peace and social rehabilitation. Seeing the destructiveness that can come from ideological fanaticism, the order adopted as its first precept the principle "Do not be idolatrous about or bound to any doctrine, theory, or ideology, even Buddhist ones. All systems of thought are guiding means; they are not absolute truth." Working together with other monks and nuns—in particular the nun Chân Khong (Cao Ngoc Khong; b. 1938)—Nhat Hanh organized such projects as rebuilding bombed villages, starting farmers' cooperatives, and establishing clinics. However, his efforts were not always welcomed by the government. After making a trip to the United States to plead for peace, he was declared persona non grata by both the northern and southern regimes. In exile he continued his antiwar activities; after the Communist victory, he helped in efforts to rescue the massive exodus of boat people fleeing Vietnam between 1976 and 1978; recently he has begun holding meditation retreats worldwide for Vietnamese refugees and American Vietnam War veterans as a way of healing the wounds left by the war.

Thich Nhat Hanh still lives in exile in a monastic community called Plum Village in France. A prolific scholar, writer, and poet, he has produced numerous volumes on the theme of "engaged Buddhism," the blending of meditation with social service. For Nhat Hanh, these activities are two sides of a single coin: the breaking down of barriers between mind and object, inner and outer, self and other. Central to his teaching is the notion of "being peace." For a person to help the cause of peace, he/she must embody inner peace in every act of body, speech, and mind. To gain this inner peace, it is necessary to practice mindfulness, which Nhat Hanh defines as the ability to appreciate the miracle of each present moment as it happens, to accept and embrace even negative things so as to discover their positives uses. In this way, suffering is not to be escaped from, but to be transformed. Rather than trying to leave saṃsāra, one breaks down one's defensive barriers so as to enter into the principle of the interrelatedness of all things. With this insight, one can take the wisdom and compassion used in pacifying one's own greed, anger, and delusion, and use them to pacify the forces of greed, anger, and delusion in the world at large. Nhat Hanh thus takes Fa-tsang's view of Buddhist practice (see Section 8.5.2) and gives it a political slant.

Within Vietnam, despite the antireligious ideology of the Communist state, 80 percent of the population are currently estimated to be Buddhist. A state-sponsored Vietnam Buddhist Church was established in 1975, but many dissidents have resisted government control. Prominent among the resistance organizations is the Unified Buddhist Church of Vietnam (UBCV), a union of Theravāda and Mahāyāna groups. Officially banned in 1981, the UBCV has nonetheless marshaled the support of Vietnamese overseas to pressure the government into reinstating it. Its concerns include the release of imprisoned activists and the return of Sangha properties confiscated by the state. Although the situation for Buddhism is still uncertain, the dissidents take comfort in Buddhism's having outlived many other regimes in its past, and so feel that time is on their side.

10

Buddhism in Japan

10.1 THE CULT OF CHARISMA

Prior to the importation of Buddhism from Korea and China, Japan had no speculative tradition of its own. However, it had developed a unique approach to the role of religion in political and cultural life that shaped the way it adopted and adapted Buddhism. Pre-Buddhist Japanese religion centered on the worship of *kami:* beings (spirits, people, animals), objects, and places possessing charismatic power. This charisma was perceived to have not only a religious dimension, but also political and aesthetic dimensions as well. The long-term historical impact of this perception has been to blur the line between religious and political life on the one hand, and between religious and aesthetic sensitivity on the other. The interpenetration of these three dimensions can be regarded as the distinctive feature of Japan's participation in the Buddhist religion.

Kami worship interpenetrated political life in that the basic unit of political organization—the *uji* (tribe or clan)—was defined by all members of the clan, whether related or not, owing ultimate allegiance to the same kami. The political leader of the clan was also the clan's chief priest and sometimes its shaman, conducting rituals with the aim of appeasing the clan's kami and augmenting his/her own charisma (Japan from early on had a tradition of strong female rulers). There were even cases in which the leader became so charismatic as to be identified with the kami itself. A true leader was supposed to be particularly sensitive to the kami's wishes and to rule the clan accordingly.

Thus ritual and political administration were viewed as two facets of a single process. Because the kami were numerous and essentially amoral, with no established order among them, this system was inherently unstable and fractious. One of the principal problems in unifying Japan as a country thus lay in establishing a fixed narrative cycle to explain the hierarchy among the kami so that the various clans could be brought into a hierarchical relationship as well. The truth of these narratives was tested in the battlefield, and a shift in the balance of power would be reflected in a retelling of the relevant narrative.

In the sixth century, as Japan became exposed to the religions of Korea and China, the imperial uji began to look to Buddhism and Confucianism to shore up its ideological credentials. This seems to have been due both to the success the Sui dynasty had in using these two religions to unify China, and to the claims made by both religions that they were based on universal principles rather than uncertain narratives. At any rate, Buddhism functioned primarily as a state religion for its first six centuries in Japan, and—until the rise of the Tokugawa shogunate in the seventeenth century—it predominated over Confucianism in the syncretic state ideology. Buddha-images were worshiped as the highest kami, monks served largely as ritual experts for the court, and—because of their close political connections—monasteries soon rivaled the court in their reputation for financial, political, and sexual intrigue. Unlike the rulers of Southeast Asia and Tibet, however, the imperial clan took little interest in enforcing the Vinaya among the monks it sponsored, and thus a tradition of lax monastic discipline developed in Japan that eventually led Japanese society to accept the practice of monks' taking wives.

One problem to which the ruling establishment did become very sensitive, however, was that by the time Buddhism reached Japan it had split into several sects—in some cases worshiping different Buddhas—and thus could function as a force for disunity as well as unity. The court tended to favor syncretic, all-inclusive forms of Buddhism, especially those that had room for kami worship—which, to distinguish it from Buddhism, was given now the name Shintō. However, the corruption in state Buddhism, as well as its indifference to the religious needs of the general populace, led to the development of more independent popular Buddhist and folk-Buddhist sects that gathered around charismatic individuals. Some of these sects, such as Sōtō Zen, retired from the political scene entirely by going into the wilderness, whereas others, such as Nichiren-sho-shū, were more confrontational. The possibility that these breakaway sects could function as rebellious uji and thus threaten political stability explains the vehemence with which the establishment has from time to time suppressed such movements. Again, this pattern of breakaway sects in opposition to established sects has been a recurrent theme in the history of Japanese Buddhism up to the present, especially during times of social turmoil. One of the great ironies of the history of Buddhism in Japan is that although the Japanese originally imported Buddhism as a means of fostering national unity, what they made of it proved so divisive that the political establishment eventually saw the need to suppress it.

On the aesthetic side, early Japanese poetry addressed to the kami of natural objects fostered the idea that religious sensitivity and aesthetic sensitivity to the beauties of nature were two sides of a single faculty. Because the leader of an uji was expected to be especially sensitive to the charisma of the kami, he/she was expected to have a highly developed aesthetic sense as well. Artistic sensitivities, and the disciplines that fostered them, were thus regarded as credentials for leadership, which explains the eagerness with which warriors and others in high positions of power have tried to establish their reputations as sensitive aesthetes in order to validate their rule. As the various forms of Buddhism came to Japan, the aristocracy was especially attuned to the style of each form, and took it for granted that one could intuit the essential message of the teaching by intuiting its style, much as one could intuit the character of another person through the aesthetic appreciation of an object that the person had made. Thus each school of Buddhism became associated with a particular style: Shingon was sumptuous, Tendai and Zen were spare and vigorous. These styles had a strong influence on Japanese arts and crafts. Particular skills, such as the tea ceremony and the training of warriors, adopted the Zen style and were pursued as "ways," *(dō* or *tō,* from Chinese *tao),* similar to the ways of Buddhism (Butsudō) and Shintō.

The cult of charisma came to surround these aesthetic disciplines so strongly that the belief arose that the discipline of the craft or skill enabled one to develop one's spirit to the same pitch of sensitivity that one could achieve through overt religious training. At its best, this fusion of aesthetic and religious faculties fostered the realization that all one's activities reflected the depths of one's mind, and that one should give oneself with total sincerity to one's present activities, however minor, for the sake of one's spiritual development. At its worst, this attitude trivialized religious life into sentimentality and the pursuit of ever-heightened sophistication in sensual beauty. In either event, this fusion of aesthetic and religious faculties was one of the Japanese nation's primary contributions to the Buddhist tradition.

10.2 THE IMPORTATION OF KOREAN BUDDHISM

Buddhism was probably first brought to Japan by Korean immigrants who settled in the Asuka-Nara area of central Japan. The first recorded contact on the royal level, however, was in 552, when King Syŏng-myŏng of Paekche sent Buddhist statues and Sūtras to the Japanese imperial court, motivated in part by hopes of forging an alliance with the Japanese against his Silla rivals. The Korean case for Buddhism was that the Triple Gem functioned as a very high level of universal kami. If worshiped, it would safeguard the nation. Thus, from the very beginning the Japanese regarded Buddhism as a political force, centered in Buddha-images, and soon embroiled it in political controversies. The ambitious Soga clan, descended from Korean immigrants, championed the Buddhist cause and obtained the right to build a temple to house a Buddha-image, at the same time arranging to have the first Japanese monks and nuns ordained. When a plague then broke out, anti-Soga forces claimed that the worship of foreign kami had angered native kami. To appease the native kami, they drowned the image in a canal and forced Buddhist nuns to disrobe. When this had no apparent effect on the plague, the image was fished out of the water and Buddhists were allowed to resume their practice.

The Sogas eventually came to dominate the imperial court, thus assuring Buddhism's adoption as a state religion. The individual most instrumental in this adoption was Prince Shōtoku (573–622), who was later regarded as the founder of Japanese Buddhism (Strong *EB*, sec. 8.1.2). As regent for Empress Suiko (r. 592–628), in 604 he formulated Japan's first constitution, a statement of governing principles covering the areas of ethics, religion, and the psychology of leadership. The constitution combined elements from Buddhism, Confucianism, and kami worship, foreshadowing the way in which these three traditions were to function together as the national ideology for the following millennium. Shōtoku advocated the Triple Gem as the highest refuge for all beings; only by taking refuge in it could morally crooked people be motivated to become straight. Straightness, however, was a function of the Confucian principle of li (propriety), according to which one was to adhere closely to the duties implicit in one's social position. Finally, the citizenry were called on to continue worshiping the kami so as to keep the male and female forces of the cosmos in balance and to ensure the proper course of the seasons.

To implement the Buddhist side of his policy, Prince Shōtoku imported Korean artisans to build temples—including the Hōryū-ji, the oldest surviving temple complex in the nation, with what are now among the oldest wooden buildings in the world—as well as Korean monks and nuns to staff them. Three Japanese nuns—Zenshin, Zensō, and Eizen—were sent to Paekche in 587 to study the Vinaya. On their return in 590, they established an ordination center for nuns. Prince Shōtoku himself studied under Hye-cha, a monk from Koguryŏ, and is credited with writing commentaries on a number of Mahāyāna Sūtras.

In bringing Buddhism to Japan, the Koreans also brought elements of Chinese culture, such as the Chinese writing system, which the Japanese adopted for their own language. Because Buddhist Sūtras were all written in Chinese, it became plain to the Japanese that they might do better to establish direct contact with China, rather than go through Korean intermediaries. Thus Prince Shōtoku initiated diplomatic relations with the Sui court in 607 and sent talented young monks and scholars there to study. Although his untimely death aborted many of his policies, these contacts with China shaped the political and cultural future of Japan as a whole. On the one hand, the contacts provided the catalyst for the emergence of a pro-Chinese, anti-Soga clan, the Fujiwaras, who were to dominate the court up through the Heian period. On the other hand, they set the stage for the wholesale importation of Chinese Buddhism and other features of Chinese culture, which provided the Japanese with models for what civilization should be. Thus, Chinese Buddhism came to supplant the Korean models that Shōtoku himself had followed.

10.3 THE IMPORTATION OF CHINESE BUDDHISM

Under Emperor Temmu (r. 672–86), a Chinese form of government was instituted, including laws for the support and control of religion. As a result, Buddhist temples came under the jurisdiction of the Department of Kami Affairs, and tight control was exerted over who could obtain ordination and where. This was to ensure that Buddhism would not develop into a force inimical to the state interests.

Meanwhile, a number of Chinese Buddhist schools had been imported to Japan, with little or no modification. In 625, a Korean monk who had studied in China introduced the study of Mādhyamika (Three Treatise; in Japanese, Sanron) and the *Satyasiddhi* (Jōjitsu) treatise (see Section 8.4.2). In 658, two Japanese monks who had studied under Hsüan-tsang (see Section 8.5) introduced the study of Vasubandhu's *Abhidharmakośa* (Kusha). Another Japanese monk went to China in 653, studied the Fa-hsiang (Hossō) teaching under Hsüan-tsang for more than ten years, and then introduced it to Japan. Other Koreans as well as Japanese returned from China and reinforced the initial transmissions. Kusha, Jojitsu, and Sanron were never more than curriculum subjects, but Hossō became a wealthy, politically influential sect and has maintained an institutional existence to the present day.

In 710 the imperial court was moved to Heijō-kyō (Capital of the Peaceful Citadel) at present-day Nara, where a city based on the design of the Chinese capital at Ch'ang-an had been laid out. The Hua-yen (Kegon) school was introduced from China by several teachers—Korean, Chinese, and Indian—and rapidly acquired great influence (see Section 8.5.2). The Hua-yen worldview was adapted to political ideology by equating Vairocana, the Cosmic Sun Buddha, with the emperor, whose uji claimed to be descendants of the sun. The fourth Dharma-realm, that of the unimpeded interpenetration of phenomena, was made the model for Japanese society, in hopes that the various ujis would interact harmoniously. Kegon, like Hossō, has continued as a sect up to the present.

Throughout the Nara period, the number of Buddhist temples continued to proliferate. In 741, every province was ordered to construct a temple and pagoda with at least 20 monks and 10 nuns. In 752, Tōdai-ji (Great Eastern Temple), the largest wooden structure in the world today, was designated the head temple in Nara. Two years later, the Chinese Vinaya master Ganjin established an ordination center there. In keeping with the laws passed under Emperor Temmu, the government permitted ordinations only at approved centers, which were intentionally kept limited to a few. Although the purpose of this restriction was to keep tight rein on the Sangha, in practice it led to strongly organized sects, with branch temples in the provinces dependent on the head temple to provide properly ordained monastics, whereas the head temple was dependent on the local temples for income.

Nara Buddhism was primarily a state cult, with little impact on the general populace, but Buddhist ideas and practices at this time did begin to penetrate Japanese folk religion in three forms. The first was the Nature Wisdom school (Jinenchishū), whose members—some of them Buddhist monks—sought Buddhist-like Awakening in the mountains and forests using non-Buddhist, "natural" ascetic practices. The second form included *ubasoku* (from the Sanskrit *upāsaka*), the "private monks" or "unordained monks," charismatic religious leaders who combined Buddhist teachings with native Japanese shamanic practices, such as healing and divination. In this form we can see the predecessors of the new religions of the nineteenth and twentieth centuries. The third form, which was also to have long-term impact, was the integration of Buddhist and Shintō beliefs (Strong *EB*, sec. 8.2.2). Certain kami were alleged to have encouraged the construction of Buddhist temples, in return for which they were declared to be bodhisattvas, so that shrines to them could be constructed in the temple compounds. This arrangement, which began as ad hoc inter-kami politics in the eighth century, was later given a theoretical justification in the ninth century, when both the Tendai and Shingon sects explained that the Shintō kami were actually *nirmāṇakāya* (emanation bodies) of the great Cosmic Buddhas (see Section 5.5.1).

During this period, Buddhism's main impact on lay life, at least in aristocratic circles, was felt in its advocacy of nonviolence. Hunting for sport was abandoned, and cooks began to develop a Japanese vegetarian cuisine. The artisans imported from China to work on temple construction also influenced Japanese arts and crafts not only in temples but also in the court and in private homes.

Close relations between state Buddhism and the court eventually led to the thorough corruption of the former. The *inke* system, whereby wealthy clans could receive income from land they had donated to monasteries, meant that monasteries became closely tied to the interests of their sponsors. The *insei* system, whereby an emperor could abdicate the throne, ordain as a monk, and yet continue to rule from behind the scenes, brought political intrigue directly into the monasteries. The government decrees ordering a certain number of men ordained as monks every year ensured that the monasteries would remain fully staffed, but also brought into the orders men with no real religious vocation. Eventually, a monk by the name of Dōkyō, having worked his way up the political hierarchy as the paramour of the Empress Kōken (r. 749–58), was accused of trying to usurp the throne. Although banished after the empress's death, he was apparently not the last monk to get overly involved in political affairs, for in 794 the capital was removed to a remote place to isolate the government from the political machinations of the Nara monasteries. Ten years later it was again moved, to Kyōto, thus beginning a new era in Japanese history.

10.4 THE HEIAN PERIOD (804–1185)

In 788, a young monk named Saichō (Dengyō Daishi, 767–822) left the corruption of the Nara monasteries and established a new monastery on Mount Hiei, northeast of Kyōto, with the intention of creating a community that would adhere strictly to the Vinaya. When the new capital was established in the city in 804, Saichō won the patronage of the emperor, who sent him to study in China. During his year there, he studied primarily T'ien-t'ai but also other schools: Ch'an, Vinaya, and Chen-yen. On his return, he combined these with Shintō elements into a single system, Tendai, which was thus broader in scope than its Chinese namesake. This system was the first of two distinctly Japanese attempts to amalgamate various Buddhist teachings into comprehensive One Vehicle schools. Saichō kept his monks in seclusion on Mount Hiei while they underwent a 12-year period to cultivate the three requirements of "the true Path of the complete teaching": discipline, meditation, and study. Some of his graduates stayed on the mountain, whereas others left to serve the state as scribes, engineers, and teachers. Saichō campaigned to get an ordination center, one using purely Mahāyāna vows, established on Mount Hiei; due to the opposition of the Nara clerics, however, the center was authorized in 827, five years after his death (Strong *EB*, sec. 8.4).

Mount Hiei went on to become the major monastic center in Japan and remained so until its destruction at the end of the sixteenth century. In its heyday, it housed thirty thousand monks and contained more than three thousand buildings. Its success as an institution, however, meant that it began to take on a life of its own, ultimately betraying the vision of its founder. New elements were added to the scholastic synthesis, to the point where the unifying thread of the doctrine became more and more difficult to discern. Imperial support focused the practice of inke and insei on Mount Hiei, engendering the kind of corruption that Saichō had left Nara to avoid. The vast amount of wealth donated to the temple required that some of the monks be armed to protect it from thieves. These armed monks formed factions that then became involved in disputes over succession to the position of abbot. Toward the end of the Heian period, bands of these *akuso* ("vicious monks") conducted demonstrations in the streets of Kyōto to press their claims on the government.

Perhaps the most radical—and negative—contribution of the Tendai school to Japanese Buddhism was its misogyny. Women were banned from Mount Hiei so as to prevent the sexual liaisons that had characterized the Nara monasteries. Although this policy may have had its desired effect in the beginning, in the long run it succeeded primarily in stigmatizing women, giving the impression that they were at fault for the original problem and were somehow spiritually defiling and inferior. As for the desired goal of fostering celibacy among the monks, the policy was ultimately a failure. Trapped on the mountain by their 12-year vows, many of the monks began having sexual liaisons among themselves, which led to further complications in the monastery's political life. Writers have frequently commented on the fact that all the major monastic reformers of the following period—Eisai, Dōgen,

Hōnen, Shinran, and Nichiren—spent their early monastic careers at Mount Hiei and were largely motivated in their efforts at reform by the corruption they witnessed there; it is equally noteworthy that many of them explicitly repudiated the Tendai view of women by asserting that women were spiritually equal to men.

Shingon was the other new "One Vehicle" Buddhist school, and the only Tantric sect to survive in east Asia. Shingon (in Chinese, Chen-yen) was brought to Japan by Kūkai (Kōbō Daishi; 774–835), a remarkably erudite and talented man. In addition to founding the Shingon sect, he devised a syllabary that greatly simplified the reading and writing of Japanese. He also opened the first school in Kyōto for the poor. Like Saichō, he had gone to China in 804, hoping to find order among the plethora of Buddhist schools. Unlike Saichō, he found the highest expression of the Buddha's teachings not in the *Lotus Sūtra,* but in Yoga Tantra. For him, Tantra was the direct teaching of the Dharmakāya, whereas the non-Tantric Sūtras were simply the word of the nirmāṇakāya, Śākyamuni. On returning from China, he founded the great monastic center at Mount Kōya—which, like Mount Hiei, remained closed to women until very recently. He later founded a second center, the Tōji, in the capital, once he began developing a following in the imperial court. Writing voluminously on Buddhist theory and practice, he drew up a map of the spiritual Path consisting of ten stages of increasingly profound insight into the nature of one's own body and mind. The first stage was the "goat level" of totally undeveloped realization, whereas the remaining nine corresponded to various Confucian, Brahmanical, and Buddhist schools. The tenth and uppermost realization, perfecting those below it, was the realization of the "glorious mind, most secret and sacred," to be found only through the Tantric practice taught in Shingon.

Like Chen-yen, Shingon was based on Tantras of the Yoga class (see Section 6.3.2)—those that taught deva-yoga, the practice of imitating the body, speech, and mind of the Buddha Mahāvairocana (The Great Sun), so as to assume the identity of that great being. However, Kūkai worked out the theoretical side of Yoga Tantra in much more detail than had his Chinese predecessors. Adopting a Hua-yen theory (see Section 8.5.2), he viewed Mahāvairocana as the entire cosmos itself, in both its physical and mental aspects. Developing this theory, he taught that Mahāvairocana was, on an impersonal level, all six great elements: earth, water, fire, wind, space, and consciousness. On a personal level, he was expressed in terms of body, speech, mind, and action. Mahāvairocana's speech, for example, consisted of mantras coupled with all the colors, forms, and sounds of the cosmos, as symbolically interpreted by the Tantric initiate.

Kūkai taught that each living being is a microcosm of the Dharmakāya, and although the various aspects of Mahāvairocana are all in perfect union and harmony on the macrocosmic level, they are not in harmony in the microcosm of the individual. The purpose of practice is to bring the microcosm into harmony with the macrocosm and to realize the essential identity between the two. The first step is to observe the Vinaya precepts, so as to bring one's actions into harmony with macrocosmic action. The next is to bring body and speech into harmony through the use of the mudrās and mantras taught by Mahāvairocana. Then, by absorbing one's mind in these physical manifestations along with visualization of chaste but colorful maṇḍalas, total harmony can be attained as one realizes that Mahāvairocana's Body of Principle—that is, all that is to be realized—is identical with the Body of Wisdom that attains the realization.

Kūkai's interpretation of Buddhist cosmology resonated well with native Japanese beliefs, which helps account for its quick acceptance by the imperial court. The solar imagery and pantheism in his portrait of Mahāvairocana corresponded with the ancient imperial sun cult, and his emphasis on form, color, and sound as means of expressing religious truths—especially in the sumptuous and sonorous rituals he devised for the court—satisfied the traditional Japanese sense that art and religion are essentially one. During Kūkai's lifetime, Shingon eclipsed Tendai in popularity, although its popularity declined somewhat after his death—partly because Tendai began appropriating Tantric teachings as well, partly because Shingon produced no new leaders of Kūkai's caliber. Nevertheless, the school remained a major religious and political force until the civil wars of the fifteenth century and continues to be moderately popular even to this day.

Although both Tendai and Shingon ministered primarily to the ritual needs of the court, they also began to participate in the spread of popular Buddhism. The Heian period witnessed the emergence of *shugenja,* mountain ascetics who combined Buddhism and shamanic practices, like the ubasoku of the Nara period, and who affiliated themselves, albeit loosely, with the two new sects. Tendai also played an important role in the rise of Japanese Pure Land Buddhism. The *Nembutsu* (nien-fo), or repetition of the name of the Buddha Amitābha (in Japanese, Amida), had very early formed a part of the Tendai synthesis, where it functioned primarily in rituals for the dead and as a means of gaining merit devoted to the attainment of nirvāṇa. Tenth-century Kyōto, however, suffered a string of natural disasters that led to the belief that the Mappō—the age of Degenerate Dharma, when people would be unable to practice under their own power—was near at hand. This inspired a number of Tendai monks to divorce the Nembutsu from its context in the Tendai synthesis and to recommend that it be made the sole focus of practice for the sake of attaining Amida's Pure Land (Jōdo). One of these monks, Kūya (903–72), danced in the streets singing simple hymns about Amida and organized self-help projects among the common people. Another, Genshin (942–1017), wrote an influential treatise, *The Compendium of Rebirth,* advocating the Nembutsu, not because he considered other paths wrong but because it was open to all: saint and sinner, monk and lay person, man and woman, emperor and peasant. Genshin was followed by Ryōnin (1072–1132), who, like Kūya, spread the practice of Nembutsu in song, attracting followers in court and countryside. Not until the Heian period had ended, however, did Pure Land become a separate sect.

A major source for understanding the day-to-day religious life of the Heian period is the popular literature that began developing at this time. Its early masterpieces—such as *The Tale of Genji,* by Lady Murasaki Shikibu

(978–circa 1025)—reveal how Buddhism functioned in the life and worldview of Japanese society in general (see also Strong *EB*, secs. 8.8.1, 8.5.2). According to Murasaki, temples served as locations for secret trysts, as retreats for young widows caught in the chess of marital politics, and as harbors of seclusion in which retired emperors could pursue their literary and artistic interests undisturbed. Religious pilgrimages allowed members of the court to escape the confines of court life, while at the same time exploring the mysterious world of the common folk.

The worldview portrayed in the book combines views of karma and spirit agency similar to what we noticed in Thai popular Buddhism (see Section 7.5.1). Calamities—from earthquakes to marital spats—are blamed on the influence of angry spirits, called *goryo.* To appease these spirits, festivals are held, partly to entertain them with shows of wrestling, dancing, music, archery, and horse racing; partly to exorcise them with Buddhist and Shintō rituals. Karma plays an integral role in Murasaki's plots, in that good and bad fortune are traced back to the characters' own actions, either in present or past lives, but it is viewed less as a means of shaping the future than as a force for being punished or rewarded by the past. This view gives a non-Buddhist, fatalistic coloring to the doctrine. Romantic entanglements, for instance, are predestined and thus unavoidable. The ancient Chinese view of the sins of the parents being inflicted on their children also plays a role: A bastard son is cursed by his parents' adultery. Ultimately, fatalism—perhaps influenced by the Mappō movement—proves more pervasive than a truly Buddhist view of karma. The characters are essentially helpless "bits of driftwood in a floating world"—an image that was to have a lasting influence on subsequent Japanese literature.

10.5 THE KAMAKURA PERIOD (1185–1333)

Toward the end of the twelfth century, courtiers and provincial warriors became involved in a series of battles that led to a decisive victory for the warriors in 1185. This ushered in a new era for Japan, politically, socially, and culturally. Political power was now in the hands of the Bakufu ("tent government"), or shogunate, which moved the seat of government to Kamakura. While the warriors ruled, the emperor and his court remained in Kyōto, where they were allowed to "reign" in a ritual sense, deprived of any real power. Emperors sporadically attempted to regain control of the government, but feudal military rulers remained in power until the mid-nineteenth century.

The Bakufu greatly simplified the legal code for the country and, in doing so, gave religious institutions much greater freedom to operate. This resulted in the growth of a number of new Buddhist sects, many of them advocating a single practice rather than the amalgam of practices taught by Shingon and Tendai, and focusing their efforts on serving the populace as a whole, rather than just the court.

10.5.1 Zen

Overcoming strong opposition from Mount Hiei, Myōan Eisai (1141–1215) established the first Zen (in Chinese, Ch'an) temple in Kyōto in 1202, after having received the seal of transmission from a Lin-chi master in China in 1191. Eisai himself, however, was essentially a Tendai man. Of his extant writings, only one piece deals with Zen—recommending it as a tool for unifying the nation—whereas his remaining writings focus on restoring Tendai to its earlier stature. Dissatisfaction with the eclecticism of Eisai's Zen led a number of monks in the following generation to travel to China on their own to receive transmission of a less adulterated teaching to bring back to Japan.

The first to do so was Dōgen Kigen (1200–53). Born into an aristocratic family but then orphaned at age 7, Dōgen was ordained a monk at age 14 at Mount Hiei. An extremely precocious child, he quickly mastered Tendai doctrine and became puzzled by what he viewed as its central inconsistency, one common to all Dharmakāya thought: If all human beings already have Dharma-nature, why is there any need to practice so as to gain Awakening? Leaving the monastery, he traveled from master to master to gain an answer to his question, but found none to satisfy him. In 1223 he left for China, where he eventually began intensive practice under the Ch'an master Ju-ching (1163–1228) and had an Awakening experience that he called "the dropping away of body and mind." In 1227 he returned to Japan to spread his vision of the true Buddhist teaching to counteract what he viewed as the gross misunderstandings of Buddhism rampant there. Although he first settled near Kyōto, ecclesiastical politics forced him to retreat to the mountains far to the northeast of the city, where he founded Eihei-ji, which after his death became the principal temple of the Sōtō (in Chinese, T'sao-tung) Zen sect.

Dōgen's major life work was a collection of talks and essays entitled *Shōbōgenzō*, or the *Treasury of the True Dharma-eye.* This was the first philosophical work to be written in Japanese and is today widely regarded as one of the most difficult and profound. Dōgen's presentation is subtle and complex, often pushing language to the breaking point, and in fact his extreme manipulation of language lies at the essence of his message. The *Shōbōgenzō* is primarily an answer to the question that took him to China, although his answer indicates that he had originally formulated the question in the wrong terms. Instead of treating Awakening as a static state that lies at the end of practice, he rephrases the question so as to deal with the relationship of cultivation to authentication. According to him, the authentication of Dharma-nature is to be found in the very process of cultivating Zen, and is in no way distinct from it. Zen, he says, is essentially "dethinking thinking." With what means is dethinking to be thought? "Beyond thinking" (*Shōbōgenzō:* "Zazengi"). Beyond thinking is the Dharma-nature that lies at the heart of dethinking thinking.

This can be explained by what Dōgen calls *genjō kōan,* or the practice of regarding the immediate present as one's object of meditation, taking apart all one's most subtle thoughts and attitudes about what is happening in the here and now in order to exhaust the limits of thinking. When one sits in meditation, for instance, Dōgen recommends that one be involved in *shikantaza* ("just sitting"). His analysis of what this entails, though, reveals that there are many complex levels of thought that have to be dethought, many subtle presuppositions that have to be dismantled, for a sitting to be "just sitting." He gives an example of how thought might dethink in this case: "Do we sit in the sitting or in our body and mind? Or do we sit dropping off sitting in the seated body and mind, or is sitting still something else? We must investigate these and other countless details in Zen-sitting. . . . There is sitting of the mind, which is different from sitting of the body. There is sitting of the body, which is different from sitting of the mind. There is sitting of dropping off the body and mind, which is different from sitting of dropping off the body and mind. . . . You must thoroughly investigate perception, intention, and consciousness" (*Shōbōgenzō:* "Zanmai Ōzanmai"). This passage provides an example of why the language of the *Shōbōgenzō* is so difficult, for much of the work is essentially an example of dethinking thinking in action.

In other parts of the *Shōbōgenzō*, Dōgen demonstrates how dethinking thinking can be applied to classical kōans (in Chinese, k'ung-an) as well, but he makes clear that the purpose of asking these questions from all possible sides is not to come to any conclusive answers, but to become more and more familiar with the dynamic of "beyond thinking" that enables one to do the questioning of dethinking thinking here and now in the first place. Thus, full familiarity with or authentication of Dharma-nature—the dropping away of body and mind—is to be found in the process of cultivation itself, and is not its end result.

True to his penchant for dethinking thinking, Dōgen demolished both sides of the question as to whether transmission outside of the texts was related to transmission in the texts. Still, especially in his later writings, he often quoted not only from the Mahāyāna Sūtras, but also from Hīnayāna works. As did his teacher, he insisted that he was transmitting not a Zen or Ch'an school, but simply the true Dharma-eye, the true Buddha Way. It is even possible to see strong parallels between his thought and that of early Buddhism: Dethinking thinking corresponds to the use of right view to go beyond views, and his teaching that authentication is to be found in the process of cultivation parallels the teaching that the realization of the Third Noble Truth is part of the same process as the development of the Fourth (see Section 2.3.1).

Nevertheless, soon after his death, Dōgen became regarded as the founder of the Sōtō school of Zen. The Fourth Sōtō Patriarch, Keizan Jōkin (1268–1325), simplified the doctrine and practice of the school, dropping Dōgen's complex approach to kōan study in favor of a more quietistic, silent illumination. At the same time, he added Shingon and kami ritual elements to make the sect more popular with the peasant classes and rural aristocracy. His program was so successful that Sōtō became known as "farmer's Zen." Although the school became one of the largest in Japan, it never gained popularity among the aristocratic elite, probably because it followed Dōgen's stern warnings not to combine Buddhist teachings with neo-Confucianism or to seek political influence. Dōgen's thought was virtually forgotten, even in his own school, from the fifteenth to the eighteenth century. Only in the past century have scholars resuscitated his writings and made them available to the Japanese intellectual mainstream.

Soon after Dōgen returned from China, he was followed by a number of Chinese and Japanese masters who brought Rinzai Zen (in Chinese, Lin-chi Ch'an) to Japan. Most of the Chinese masters were refugees from the Mongol invasions of China or—in following generations—members of Lin-chi lineages that were out of favor with the new Yüan dynasty. Unlike Dōgen, many of these teachers followed the Sung Ch'an tendency of combining their teachings with neo-Confucian social and political doctrines, and so were willing to act as scribes and teachers of Chinese culture for their aristocratic supporters. This helped make Rinzai popular with the ruling classes. Rinzai was quickly accepted by both the shogunate and the imperial court, which helped the sect withstand the political pressures exerted by the more established schools. The only Rinzai school established in the thirteenth century that is still extant today is the Ō-Tō-Kan school, founded by Nampo Jōmyō (1235–1309), who emphasized classical kōan study and resisted the temptation to combine Rinzai teachings with those of other Buddhist or Confucian schools. His follower Shūhō Myōchō organized the first systematic program of kōan study in Japan and founded the Daitoku-ji temple in Kyōto, which is today the head temple of the Rinzai sect, justifiably famous for the quiet sophistication of its buildings and gardens.

One noteworthy feature of Rinzai Zen during this period was its appeal to the relatively uneducated warriors of the Kamakura shogunate. It provided them with an avenue to Chinese culture, bypassing the court-dominated Tendai and Shingon sects. At the same time, its style—direct, one-on-one, forcing the student to be quick on his feet—appealed to their warrior spirit. This lay the seeds for one of the great ironies of Japanese Buddhism, a long-term development whereby Rinzai was incorporated into the *bushidō* (Way of the Warrior) in the seventeenth century (see Section 10.7), and later used to justify Japan's militaristic policy in the nineteenth and twentieth centuries (see Section 10.8).

10.5.2 Pure Land

Belief in the imminence of the Mappō—the age of Degenerate Dharma—continued to gain widespread credence into the Kamakura period, leading to the formation of three major popular sects that have continued up to the present time. The history of these sects is especially interesting in that it provides us with the earliest detailed records of the way in which Japanese folk religious groups formed around charismatic leaders, were distorted by their early following, and suffered at the hands of the authorities.

The first of these sects was the Jōdo-shū (Pure Land sect), founded by the Tendai monk Hōnen (1133–1212). Strongly influenced by the views of Chinese Pure Land Master Shan-tao (see Section 8.5.3), Hōnen wrote a long work systematizing Pure Land doctrines under the title *The Treatise on the Selection of the Nembutsu of the Original Vow* (1197). A charismatic leader, he practiced what he preached—chanting the Nembutsu up to seventy thousand times a day—and drew disciples from all levels of society, including aristocrats and samurai. Of these the most important was the Fujiwara regent Kujo Kanezane (1148–1207), whose enthusiastic support greatly advanced the position of the school. Hōnen might have followed the example set by Kūya and Genshin (see Section 10.4), who remained in the Tendai fold, had it not been for his getting into trouble with the conservative Tendai establishment on two counts: He was extremely popular, and his enthusiastic claims for the all-encompassing powers of the Nembutsu could be interpreted as granting license to sin, as all wrongdoing could supposedly be cleansed by chanting. Hōnen himself adhered closely to what he regarded as the spirit of the Vinaya, but his insistence that the practice of Nembutsu was sufficient for salvation, with no need for meditation or merit making, led many of his followers to interpret his doctrine as a release from moral strictures.

Hōnen's political connections protected him for a while, and even the reigning emperor took on the role of mediator between the contending factions. However, in 1207, when four of Hōnen's followers were executed for alleged indiscretions with ladies of the court, he was stripped of his monastic title and ordered into exile, together with a handful of his closest disciples. The order was rescinded in 1211, but he died soon thereafter. Fifteen years after his death, in 1227, his *Treatise on the Selection of the Nembutsu of the Original Vow* was burned in public on the grounds that it was a threat to the Dharma.

Shinran (1173-1262), the inspiration for the Jōdo-shin-shū (True Pure Land sect), was one of the disciples ordered into exile with Hōnen. Although he had no intention of founding a separate school, dramatic visions inspired him to make two important changes in the tradition—one institutional, the other doctrinal—that led his followers to form a separate sect. The first vision came while Shinran was still a Tendai monk. After twenty years on Mount Hiei, grappling with the constraints of celibacy, he experienced a revelation, in which the Bodhisattva Kuan-yin (in Japanese, Kannon) appeared to him in a dream and promised to come to him in the form of a young woman whom he should marry. Shinran did as he was told and for the remainder of his life assumed the status of "neither monk nor layman," which accurately describes the married clergy of the sect that took him as its inspiration. These clerics continued to live in temples and perform religious services, but also led a family life and expected the eldest son to take over the temple from his father.

Shinran's place of exile was the northern province of Echigo, where he propagated the Nembutsu among the common people. Because Hōnen died soon after both of them were pardoned, Shinran did not return to Kyōto, but traveled through the towns and villages of east Japan, spreading the teaching and founding *dojo nembutsu* (Nembutsu temples). During this period he had his second major revelation—that the saving grace of Amida required only one Nembutsu. This provided Shinran's answer to a question that had divided members of the Pure Land school for decades: How many times was it necessary to repeat the name of Amida in order to be assured a place in his paradise? (See Strong *EB*, sec. 8.3.2.) The *Sukhāvatī-vyūha Sūtra* (see Section 5.5.4), which had formed the basis for the Pure Land school, stated that one need repeat Amida's name only 10 times to qualify for the benefit of his saving vow, whereas Shan-tao had recommended repeating the Nembutsu as many times as possible, as a mantra, throughout the waking day. Shinran's position—formulated in his work *Teaching, Practice, Faith, and Attainment* (1224)—was that the original question had been misconceived. The Nembutsu was not to be viewed as a means of earning one's way to the Pure Land, for such a view implied a lack of total faith in the saving power of Amida's grace and deceived one into believing that one's own efforts could actually effect salvation. Rather, one Nembutsu was enough to acknowledge and accept Amida's grace; the remaining repetitions were simply to express gratitude. Human effort was in no way sufficient to achieve salvation. Even one's ability to accept Amida's grace had nothing to do with one's own merit, but was a result of Amida's grace as well. Whereas Hōnen had stripped meditation and merit making away from the teaching, leaving only faith and the Nembutsu, Shinran stripped it down still further, leaving only faith in *tariki* (other-power), with no trace of *jiriki* (self-power) at all. By doing so, he took the abstract Yogācārin teaching that Awakening is possible only because of the seeds of the Buddha-nature implanted in the consciousness, and gave it a personal cast.

Shinran's frequent references to himself as having sinned in taking on a wife must be viewed in the context of his radical emphasis on faith. Evil individuals who recognize their evil nature, he said, are more likely to be born into the Pure Land than good individuals, for the good are deluded by the pride they take in their virtue, and thus are blocked from accepting the gift of grace.

Shinran's doctrine, similar to Hōnen's, opened itself to all sorts of abuses and misinterpretations. His own son, Zenran, preached such an inflammatory version of the teaching as to make it an outright invitation to sin. Shinran eventually had to sever all relations with him. Dojo leaders became autocratic, treating the sect's funds as their own, and government officials intervened in 1235. Shinran returned to Kyōto in that year and lived quietly until his death at the age of ninety. Only after his death did his followers organize themselves into a sect.

10.5.3 Nichiren (Strong *EB*, sec. 8.9)

Nichiren-sho-shū, the third Mappō sect formed during the Kamakura period, was the first major sect of Japanese Buddhism with no foreign antecedents. It was also the first to be named after its founder. The son of a fisherman, Nichiren (1222–82) was ordained at the age of 15 and given the name Rencho (Eternal Lotus). As he grew older, he became greatly concerned with the calamities befalling the nation and the imperial family, convinced that they had a religious cause. Thus he resolved to study all of the Buddhist teachings then available so as to find the solution to this problem and to save the nation from what he saw as sure disaster.

After pursuing many paths, his studies eventually took him to Mount Hiei, where he was drawn by the nationalistic elements in Saichō's teachings. He came to the conclusion that Saichō had been right in basing his teachings on the *Lotus Sūtra,* but wrong in adding to it teachings from other Sūtras and schools. Only the *Lotus Sūtra,* Nichiren felt, contained the unadulterated True Dharma. All other Buddhist sects were wrong—and not only wrong, but actually evil in that they obscured and distorted the truth, advocating the worship of false Buddhas. The chief culprit in this regard was the Pure Land movement. Instead of viewing this movement as a possible solution to the Mappō, Nichiren viewed it as the Mappō's primary cause. The calamities befalling the nation and the imperial family could be traced to the emperor's having allowed false Dharma to be propagated in the country. The only solution was to punish the evil individuals who were responsible for the situation, and to bring the entire nation to the worship of the truth as contained in the *Lotus Sūtra.* As a result of this realization, Rencho took on the name Nichiren (SunLotus), thus combining the symbols of the two concerns foremost in his mind—the *Lotus Sūtra* and the Japanese nation—with the intention of showing that hope for salvation lay in their union.

Nichiren presented his doctrines as complex meditations on the *Lotus Sūtra*'s teaching of the original Buddha-nature and on the Tantric doctrine of the dhāriṇī that contains in one phrase the truth of all true Dharma statements. However, the practice he recommended was simplicity itself: the repetition of the *daimoku* (mantra) "Namu Myōhō Renge Kyō"—Homage to the Scripture of the Lotus of the Perfect Truth—while at the same time placing faith in the conviction that the Eternal Buddha Śākyamuni, the truth of the Sūtra, and all beings were ultimately one, fully encompassed by the daimoku. Later he worked out a maṇḍala representing his beliefs, called the *gohonzon,* at which one was to stare while repeating one's declaration of homage.

Nichiren's life followed the pattern of a Shintō shaman more than that of a Buddhist leader. He attracted a following largely through his courage and the incandescent intensity of his personality, which at times resembled that of a medium possessed. His life was reportedly marked by omens and portents, and he was hailed as a great diviner when the Mongol invasion that he had predicted in 1260 and 1268 was actually attempted in 1274. His utopian vision predicted that Japan, by following his teaching alone, would become a Buddha-land on Earth, from which the revived and purified Dharma would spread to the rest of the world. Later in life, he became convinced that he was an incarnation of the Bodhisattva Viśiṣṭacāritra (Superb Conduct), the leader of the bodhisattva hosts whom Śākyamuni had summoned out of the earth with the command to worship and protect the *Lotus Sūtra.* All who followed him were identified with the bodhisattva hosts. Of all the medieval Japanese Buddhist sects, Nichiren-sho-shū conceived a Buddha closest to the traditional kami, and followed a leader closest to the traditional prophet/leader of an uji. Nichiren's following, in terms of its intolerance of others and its sense of its own special identity and mission, embodied the traditional uji's tribal side. The school's only Buddhist competition in terms of these traits comes from the new religions in the twentieth century. It is no accident that the largest of the new religions are offshoots of this sect.

As might be expected, Nichiren ran afoul of the authorities for his inflammatory accusations. He was twice exiled and once narrowly escaped execution. Each suffering was in his eyes a glorious martyrdom. He died in poverty and relative obscurity, but his sect continues to thrive.

10.6 DECLINE AND FALL (1336–1603)

After an abortive three-year period of imperial rule, a new shogunate established its capital in Kyōto in 1336, ushering in a new period in Japanese history that, in retrospect, seemed to confirm earlier predictions that the Mappō, or Dharma-ending age, was at hand. The new period began auspiciously enough, with the first shogun establishing a temple "for the peace of the nation" in every province. Before the period ended, however, the country had been plunged into a devastating series of civil wars. All Buddhist sects aside from Sōtō and Rinzai had formed armed societies to protect their interests, only to be slaughtered by the hundreds of thousands, which destroyed Buddhism's credibility as an instrument for national unity.

The first shogun's religious adviser, Musō Soseki (1275–1351), was a Rinzai monk who had also received training in the Tantric traditions. After spending his youth in seclusion, he became one of the most politically active monks in Rinzai history, numbering not only shoguns but also emperors among his pupils. He thus cemented the bond that had been developing between Rinzai and the ruling classes, making it the new de facto state religion. Although he himself was a serious meditator, the school he founded quickly became immersed in the political and cultural life of the capital. Zen monasteries mounted trade expeditions to China to help shore up the financial base of the new government; monks served as diplomats, accountants, and teachers of Chinese arts and culture, neo-Confucianism in particular. This left little time for meditation. With few exceptions, the Zen of the Muromachi period is remembered more for its contributions to the arts than for its dedication to actual practice.

This period ultimately came to be regarded as a dark age in Zen practice, with textbooks offering the "right" answers to kōans readily available, and certificates of *satori* (Awakening) to be had for a price. Classical kōan cases were used not for meditation training but as literary and educational devices, and the monks became renowned for their skill in the arts of poetry, flower arrangement, garden design, painting, calligraphy, and the cult of *chadō* (tea). In doing so, they developed a fastidious style, blending the sophistication of Chinese and Kyōto court culture with the austerity and attention to subtle detail that they saw as distinctively Zen. As education and opportunities for social mobility became more widely available during this period, this style proved immensely popular not only among the ruling classes, but also among the newly enfranchised, who adopted a self-consciously rustic version of the Zen style as a badge of their newfound status and cultural sophistication. It was thus that Zen began to percolate throughout Japanese culture, less as a philosophy or path of practice than as an attitude: the belief that anything, if done in the proper style with the proper frame of mind, could count as Zen.

This style was best expressed in the *nō* drama, particularly in the plays of Zeami Motokiyo (1363–1443), which developed at this time. The structure of nō drama in general is based on a generic Mahāyāna teaching that claims that beings suffer if they view saṃsāra as separate from nirvāṇa, but can gain tranquility if they can break through dualities to realize the nirvāṇa in saṃsāra here and now. Zeami's plays drew on incidents that conveyed Buddhist themes, including the teachings of Tendai, Shingon, and Pure Land, while the aristocratic Zen style provided the stark stage settings and the overriding aesthetic. In his theoretical writings on nō, Zeami maintained that the training of the nō actor was analogous to that of a Zen monk. Each performance of a play was part of the ongoing training, in which the actor, while acting, was to attain a particular state of mind as a result of the performance. In Zeami's phrase, the performance is the seed, and the mind is the flower. Thus the actor was to direct his efforts at his own state of mind, rather than at pleasing the audience. If the audience was sufficiently sensitive, of course, it would be able to intuit the actor's success at internal transformation, but even if it couldn't, the true measure of the actor's performance would be something that he could gauge from within. Later writers, such as Komparu Zenchiku (1405–68), made the Zen-nō connection even more obvious as they fashioned their dramas around explicit Zen themes.

As had happened in the Nara and Heian periods, the close relationship between monasteries and the ruling elite led to the corruption of the monks. This is attested to in the life and writings of the Rinzai monk Ikkyū Sōjun (1394–1481). The illegitimate son of an emperor, Ikkyū was forced into a Rinzai monastery at the age of five to escape the political intrigues of the court, only to encounter the political and sexual intrigues of monks close to the court and the shogunate. Trained in a Kyōto temple to be an accomplished poet, he eventually left the capital to undergo spartan kōan training in a provincial center, where he claimed to have gained Awakening. His uncompromising temperament, though, led him to rebel against the hypocrisy he saw around him, both in the capital and in the provinces. He began using his poetic skills to mount scathing attacks on the "leprous and perverted" Zen establishment. He also flagrantly broke monastic rules as a form of protest, eating meat, drinking alcohol, and even fathering a child.

Styling himself a "crazy cloud," Ikkyū frequented the company of honestly dishonest commoners and was not averse to taking ruffians and streetwalkers as disciples. Nevertheless, he insisted on rigorous standards of meditation practice. His distinctive contribution to Zen thought was his doctrine of "the red thread of passion," in which lust became the testing ground for the doctrine of the nonduality of the realm of Awakening and the realm of desire. In his old age Ikkyū wrote explicitly erotic poetry to compare his mistress, Lady Mori—a blind street singer, some forty years his junior—to the Buddha. Later generations of Zen practitioners revered him, but he left no Dharma heir.

During the fifteenth century, the sophisticated Muromachi aesthetic had been reduced to a thin veneer over a society that was essentially falling apart. Bloody power struggles rent the shogunate; famines and epidemics led to peasant uprisings. The ruinous Ōnin War (1467–78) effectively brought an end to central control, and provincial warlords began asserting their independence. Merchants and artisans in the cities and towns formed guilds that centered on Buddhist temples and Shintō shrines in order to defend their interests. Rennyo (1415–99), the Eighth Patriarch of the Jōdo-shin-shū sect, organized his followers into a feudal state that was protected by peasant armies; the other Pure Land sects and the Nichiren sect soon followed suit, staging peasant revolts to assert their interests.

In the sixteenth century, a string of warlords tried to reunify the country, only to find their path blocked by the armed Buddhist groups. Oda Nobunaga (1534–82) was especially ruthless in his suppression of Buddhist institutions. He burned the monastery at Mount Hiei to the ground, putting its monks to the sword. He also attacked the Shingon stronghold on Mount Kōya and suppressed the Nichiren and Pure Land armies. In one province alone (Echizen) he slaughtered thirty to forty thousand followers of the Jōdo-shin-shū Ikkō (Single-Minded) sect. Rinzai Zen, like Sōtō, was able to escape his ire largely because it remained unarmed and also because it had begun to decentralize, spreading out to the country after many of its main monasteries in Kyōto had been destroyed during the Ōnin War. Nobunaga's successor, Toyotomi Hideyoshi (1536–98), was somewhat less savage in his policies, disarming rather than killing the peasantry, although he too attacked rebellious monastic communities, such as the Shingon center in Negoro, and conducted sword hunts in monasteries throughout the land. National unification finally came under Tokugawa Ieyasu (1542–1616), who moved the capital to Edo, modern-day Tokyo, and opened a new era in Japanese history.

10.7 CONFUCIANISM IN CONTROL (1603–1868)

The Tokugawa shogunate was more than just another feudal regime. It was a military dictatorship with an all-embracing ideology aimed at the total restructuring and control of Japanese society. The ideology was founded on Confucian ideals. The role of the government was to be based not on transcendent principles, but on the order of heaven, which was immanent in the natural norms implicit in human, social, and political order. Society was to be divided into rigidly defined classes, and the duty of each citizen was to fulfill the obligations of his/her class. Religions were allowed to function to the extent of supporting this order, but were not to pass judgment on the government or disturb social peace and unity in any way.

The rise of Confucianism under the Tokugawas can be explained both by what was perceived as the Buddhist-inspired disunity of the previous century, and by the success that the Ming dynasty had in using neo-Confucianism to unite China. Neo-Confucian scholars in Japan managed to separate themselves from the Zen monks who had been their teachers and to devise an anti-Buddhist, pro-Shintō version of their philosophy to serve the new government's needs.

On the surface, Tokugawa policy seemed to support Buddhism. For example, all families were required to register as members of a Buddhist temple of any sect. An edict was published denouncing the activities of Christian missionaries and noting that Japan was essentially a Buddhist and Shintō nation. In actuality, the registration of families was a means of keeping tabs on the population and preventing proselytizing by any religious group. No one was allowed to change religious affiliation without the entire household changing. Clerics became not only census takers but also government informers. Although the state used Buddhist institutions as an arm of its policy, it provided them with no financial support.

In the midst of this bleak situation, a number of individual Buddhists shined. In 1654, Yin-yüan Lung-ch'i (Ingen Ryūki; 1592–1673) came to Japan and founded a new Zen sect, the Ōbaku sect, which combined Rinzai and Pure Land teachings. This helped revivify the almost dormant state of Japanese Sōtō and Rinzai. In the provinces, Bankei Yōtaku (1622–93) taught that Rinzai practice consisted simply of letting things be while one dwelled in the innate "knowingness" of the mind, which Bankei equated with the Unborn Buddha-mind. This made Zen more widely accessible to the general populace. Rinzai's new social status, tied more closely to commoners, was reflected in the fact that the Zen style of this period was totally dominated by its more rustic version, in which spiritual significance was sought in the most ordinary, mundane details, rather than in fastidious sophistication. The best exemplar of this style is the poet Matsuo Bashō ("Banana Tree"; 1644–94), the foremost practitioner of the art of haiku poetry. Assuming in the fourth decade of his life the persona of a wandering Zen monk, he wrote travel essays recording aesthetic experiences analogous to satori, composing short, impromptu verses in an attempt to capture the transcendent in a single cluster of images. His aesthetic emphasized the values of lightness, contented solitude, and an appreciation of the commonplace. For example, late in his life he composed the following reflection on no-self: "On this road / With no traveler / Autumn night falls."

The most influential Zen practitioner of this period was Hakuin Ekaku (1686–1769). An extremely high-strung, sensitive child, Hakuin entered the monkhood at an early age and vigorously pursued kōan study under numerous masters (Strong *EB*, sec. 8.6). Controversy has ensued over whether any of his masters certified his satori, but the broad nature of his training enabled him to devise a comprehensive system of kōan study, drawing on many traditions, that has served ever since as the universal Rinzai curriculum.

Hakuin's own dramatic experiences as a meditator led him to agree with Tsung-mi (see Section 8.5.2) that satori was a sudden event that then had to be cultivated through further practice. He classified the kōans of the classical tradition into five grades, based on—interestingly enough—the system of five ranks formulated in the Chinese T'sao-tung school. These were supposed to take the meditator to total Awakening through five stages of realization of the interpenetration of principle and phenomena: the Apparent within the Real, the Real within the Apparent, Coming from within the Real, Arrival at Mutual Interpenetration, and Unity Attained. The purpose of the first-stage kōans was to gain *kenshō* (insight into one's own true nature). This was the sudden Awakening that was then to be cultivated through further study. Although Hakuin drew almost entirely on classical kōans for his instruction, he devised a first-stage kōan that has since become one of the best known in the Zen repertoire: "What is the sound of one hand?"

Hakuin taught his lay followers various syncretic teachings—including some Pure Land practices—but he was strong in his insistence that Zen monks should devote themselves totally to kōan study, leaving no time for art, literature, or other secular pursuits. True kōan study, he said, had to be based on a strong moral foundation and required three basic attitudes: great belief in the kōan, great questioning of one's assumptions, and great aspiration and perseverance. He was strongly critical of the "silent illumination" approach, by which he was probably referring to the teachings of Bankei and what had become of Sōtō Zen. His analysis of the psychological dynamics of the practice, along with his map of the practice itself, is now the established norm in the Rinzai tradition. All present-day Rinzai masters take him as a model and trace their lineage to him.

One other important development in the Tokugawa period that was to have a long-term effect on Japanese Buddhism was the work of the nationalistic scholar Yamaga Sokō (1622–85) in formulating the ideals of bushido, the Way of the Warrior. This was a code of military virtues, drawn from various strands of Japanese tradition, intended to justify the continued existence of a largely idle samurai class. In essence, bushidō was a Confucian code, in that the warrior's duty was to be as effective as possible in going to battle for his ruler. Although it had no relation to Buddhist ethics, it picked up what the Japanese perceived as the Zen style: a quick and total awareness of the present, so free from distracting thoughts and dualisms that the swordsman attained a state of *mushin* (no-mind), at one with his sword. Japanese writings on Rinzai Zen that appeared in the West in the early twentieth century asserted a deep connection between Rinzai and bushidō, but the warrior code itself never gained popular currency or connection with Zen institutions in Japan itself until the end of the nineteenth century.

At the beginning of the nineteenth century, pressures from inside and outside Japan made the tight Tokugawa control over the society more and more untenable. Millennial cults appeared, and pro-Shintō forces asserted their independence from the Confucian ideologues who had previously supported them. In 1868 they restored the imperial system by bringing the Meiji emperor to power.

10.8 STATE SHINTŌ IN CONTROL (1868–1945)

The Shintō forces behind the Meiji restoration were initially hostile to Buddhism, viewing it as a decadent foreign influence that had polluted the original purity of Japanese culture and prevented the modernization of the Japanese state. After passing a law separating Buddhism and Shintō, the new government pursued an active policy of persecuting Buddhists, denouncing their traditions, expropriating temple lands, and converting Buddhist temples into Shintō shrines. A decree went out that Buddhist monks of all sects should be allowed to marry; at the same time, the monks were pressed into service to teach the new state religion—State Shintō—throughout the countryside. Only the intervention of a foreign businessman saved Prince Shōtoku's Hōryū-ji (see Section 10.2) from being turned into kindling wood for a public bath. The anti-Buddhist fervor peaked in 1871, after which it became clear that the policy of outright suppression was proving counterproductive. Some of the policies were dismantled—monks no longer had to propagate Shintō—but the decree allowing marriage stuck. At present, there are very few celibate monks in Japan except for young men in training, although the nuns' orders have maintained their celibate vows.

Toward the end of the nineteenth century, the state mounted an expansionist, militaristic policy that was to lead Japan into a long string of wars: the Sino-Japanese War (1894–95), the Russo-Japanese War (1904–1905), the annexation of Korea (1910), World War I, and the invasion of Manchuria followed by World War II. This new national mission provided the context in which a new generation of Buddhist scholars—mostly educated in the institutions of Western learning established by the Meiji government—began a concerted effort to reclaim Buddhism's place in Japanese culture. To do so, however, they had to redefine the Buddhist tradition in such a way that would make it respectable, not only to Japanese nationalists, but also to the younger generation educated in Western rationalism and science. In a way, the Japanese redefinition of Buddhism in the light of Western thought was simply one instance of a trend sweeping throughout Asian Buddhism, but its imperialistic overtones gave it a tenor quite unlike anything else that was happening in Asian Buddhism at the time.

Borrowing principles from the European Enlightenment (see Section 12.2), the proponents of *shin bukkyō* (New Buddhism) distinguished the monastic institutional form of Buddhism from its original and pure principles. Contemporary Japanese Buddhist institutions, they conceded, were decadent and corrupt, but the original principles of the religion were consonant with modern ideals—humanistic, cosmopolitan, and socially responsible—that would aid the nation in its efforts toward modernization. At the same time, borrowing a page from the social Darwinists, they insisted that the turmoil of Japanese history, including the recent Shintō suppression of Buddhism, had ensured that only the fittest and most developed expressions of Buddhism had survived on Japanese soil. The obvious contradictions in these two positions they reconciled by appealing to a Japanese version of the racism rampant in the West at the time. The Japanese, they insisted, had a unique talent for combining refined aesthetic/religious sensitivity with ruthless courage, and thus had managed to remain true to the inner essence of Buddhism while simultaneously taking it to a heightened pitch.

Zen priests, such as Kōsen Sōon (1816–92) and his student Shaku Sōen (1859–1919), insisted that Rinzai Zen in particular, when stripped of its institutional forms, embodied the essence of Buddhism with a purity matched nowhere else. This essence consisted of a direct experience attained through a radically empirical and scientific inquiry into the true nature of things. In fact, the total stripping away of all conventionalities was in and of itself Zen. Thus the New Rinzai took the more iconoclastic side of Zen and made it represent the whole tradition, while dismissing as historical baggage the institutional forms that had balanced that iconoclasm and formed its reason for being. To answer Western charges of the effeminacy of Oriental culture, these priests also insisted on Zen's ties with the bushidō code of manly self-sacrifice, discipline, and single-minded fearlessness. Thus their vision of Zen was the ultimate expression both of the spirit of Buddhism and of the unique strengths of the Japanese race. As a political creed, New Rinzai answered Japan's need for a national ethos, immune to Western criticisms, that would support the national war effort and justify the disregard of conventional morality in its political designs on its spiritually "effete" neighbors. As the movement developed, its advocates began to view themselves as guardians of the primary essence of all world spirituality, and Japan as the vanguard of the spiritual regeneration of the human race. It is no accident that the primary exponent of Zen to the West in the twentieth century, D. T. Suzuki (1870–1966), was a student of this movement.

The books and courses offered by the New Buddhists were so successful that government ideologues began to reassess Buddhism's role in Japanese history. As a result, they came to glorify the Rinzai contribution to the Way of the Warrior and the Muromachi aesthetic as signs of Japan's innate racial and cultural superiority. Rinzai monks were called on to teach the Zen aesthetic to members of the society as a way of fostering national pride, and to teach meditation as a way of instilling the single-minded "no-mindedness" of the Way of the Warrior—not only to soldiers, but to all whose total commitment would be needed to support the war effort. Monks from all Buddhist schools were also called on to justify militarism as a spiritual duty by teaching that the "bodies and hearts broken by war" were a noble sacrifice to a greater cause. The monks, aside from a handful of pacifists, did not refuse.

Until its collapse during World War II, the militaristic policy was a stunning success. Nevertheless, it created severe dislocations in Japanese society, which, as always, led to new religious movements centered on charismatic leaders. The number of quasi-religious groups skyrocketed from 98 in 1924 to more than 1,000 in 1935. To escape government harassment, many of them affiliated themselves with official Buddhist organizations. Prominent among these new groups were Sōka Gakkai and Risshō Kōsei-kai, both associated with the Nichiren sect. After World War II, these and similar movements were to overshadow the traditional organizations that had offered them shelter before and during the war.

10.9 THE RISE OF MODERN URBAN FOLK BUDDHISM

Japan's defeat in World War II, together with the subsequent American occupation and rapid postwar industrialization, brought about radical changes in the nation's religious life. Defeat meant that religious institutions that had collaborated with the government's war effort were discredited in the public eye. Occupation meant that American notions of religious freedom, democracy, and the separation of church and state became the law of the land. Industrialization and urbanization meant that the family and village social structure began to break down. These factors combined to hurt the cause of traditional Buddhism and to spark a phenomenal growth in the new religions, some of which incorporated Buddhist elements.

In 1945, the occupation force dissolved the official structure of State Shintō; in 1946, the emperor publicly denied his divinity; in 1947, the traditional system of interlocking households was dismantled, so that individuals were no longer bound by their family religion. A policy of land distribution was enacted to help create the stable middle class that a secure democracy would require, but this involved confiscating much of the land that had provided the income for Buddhist temples. The combined effect of these directives was to create, for the first time in Japanese history, a totally secular government; to give individuals total religious freedom; and to force many Buddhist priests into taking on lay occupations so as to support their families, thus limiting their time and ability to meet the new religious needs of the laity.

The government pursued its new secular role with the same single-minded determination with which it had pursued its earlier religious and militaristic goals. As was traditional in Japanese society, it functioned essentially as a federation of ujis, although now the ujis were industrial conglomerates. The lesson of the war was that pure spirit alone could not overcome technological superiority, so the government's efforts were now aimed at technological and economic progress. Much of Japan's postwar economic success can be traced to the same combination of Zen single-mindedness and Confucian devotion to one's social duty that had marked the Way of the Warrior. Zen monks were again called upon to teach meditation, this time to corporate workers and executives so that they would be able to devote themselves totally to their sales and production goals. Traditional manuals on military strategy were studied as guides to capturing domestic and foreign markets.

This single-minded focus on economic success has created one of the most secular societies on Earth. Polls indicate that large numbers of Japanese do not view themselves as belonging to any particular religion. Interest in traditional Buddhism is largely confined to two widely disparate groups: (1) the rural agricultural classes, who look to Buddhist institutions for the same services they have performed for centuries; and (2) the urban intelligentsia, who look to Buddhist thought as a model for creating distinctively Japanese forms of such Western enterprises as critical philosophy and psychotherapy.

For the remainder of society, however, traditional Buddhism has lost much of its appeal, except as a relic of Japan's cultural past. "Funeral Buddhism" is the name that many people use to refer to the traditional sects, in light of the ritual role to which many of the priests have been reduced. The Japanese point to their continued appreciation of art and the beauties of nature as a sign that their religious sensitivities have not atrophied, but this simply means that they are still sensitive to the old notion of kami. Because the ujis currently in power, unlike the ujis of the past, are devoted to no kami at all, many Japanese have turned to the new religions of charismatic leaders to provide them with the traditional connection between their religious and social/political life; that is, to ujis that have reestablished the kami connection.

The postwar growth of the new religions came in two waves: first, during the rapid industrialization following the Korean War, and then during the dislocations of the 1980s, when the conglomerates that had once promised their workers lifetime job security began to abandon the home labor force in search of cheaper labor abroad. The first wave involved what were termed *shinkō shūkyō* (the new religions); the second, *shinkō shinkō shūkyō* (the new new religions). Both waves consisted of widely disparate groups, some claiming connections with Buddhism, others not, but what they have in common is a modern urban version of a pattern typical of traditional Japanese folk religions: utopian, sometimes apocalyptic, visions; direct connection with divinities or divine agents; healing—now expanded to include not only physical healing but also psychological healing and subsequent social and economic success; and a concern for physical and mental purification. Where these new religions differ from older Japanese folk religions is in their use of modern organizational skills and the mass media to win and maintain their followings. They are essentially ujis, but the pattern for a successful uji is now no longer the tribe, but the modern industrial corporation. The new religions have this pattern down pat.

The most successful of the new religions is Sōka Gakkai, or the Society of Creation of Values, founded in 1938 by Tsunesabarō Makiguchi, who combined classical Nichiren doctrine and practice with his own secular views on value creation. The sect recommends the traditional Nichiren practice of chanting the daimoku *Namu Myōhō Renge Kyo,* although the purpose of the chant is to attain this-worldly goals: job promotion, financial success, family harmony, and the alleviation of physical and psychological ills. The sect is known for its aggressive proselytizing, not only in Japan but also throughout Asia and the West, employing such tactics as "smash and flatten," whereby any resistance on the part of the prospective convert is worn down by physical and psychological threats and violence. Each follower is duty-bound to convert his or her family and friends. The aims of the sect include political control of Japan—its political party, Kōmeitō, has a block of seats in the Japanese Diet—and conversion of the entire world to its fold. It is extremely intolerant of other religions; its followers are chiefly among the socially disadvantaged. Formally a lay wing of the traditional Nichiren sect for its first fifty years, it was excommunicated in 1991, although this has had little effect on its programs.

Of the new new religions, the most notorious has been Aumshinrikyō, which gained international notoriety after an urban guerrilla attack on the Tokyo subway in 1995. The most successful of these groups, however, has been Kōkufu-no-Kagaku, or the Institute for Research in Human Happiness. This group was founded in 1986 by Ryuho Okawa, a self-proclaimed incarnation of a "core spirit" named El Cantare, whose previous incarnations include the Buddha and Hermes, the Greek god of the sun. Ryuho's teachings, as presented in the book *Laws of the Sun,* combine the apocalyptic forecasts of Nostradamus (the sect has produced a popular movie on this theme) with the laws of the Buddha for a new age—self-reflection and conservative living in line with the Noble Eightfold Path. In ancient Japan, Ryuho's solar pretensions would have been sufficient grounds for execution, but in modern Japan they simply pass as a sentimental connection with the kami that inspired Japan's past imperial glories.

10.10 A RELIGIOUS LIFE IN A SECULAR WORLD

Risshō Kōsei-kai, the second largest of the new religions and probably the most Buddhist in orientation, offers an interesting case study in the inner dynamics of these organizations, in terms of institutional development, worldview, and religious life. The name of the organization is an acronym. *Risshō* stands for "establishing the true law [of the *Lotus Sūtra*] in the world"; *kō* for "mutual exchange of thought among people of faith"; and *sei* for "the perfection of the personality and attainment of Buddhahood." The organization was founded in 1938 by a man, Niwano Nikkyō (b. 1906), and a woman, Nagamuna Myōkō (1889–1957), who were members of Tokyo's small merchant class. Its early days were similar to those of many other folk religions. Niwano and Nagamuna specialized in faith healing, a popular activity in the days when medical care for Japan's urban poor was uncertain at best. They taught that serious and mysterious diseases were the result of bad karma inherited from one's ancestors. Using their combined talents to diagnose the precise causes of a particular disease—Nagamuna heard inner voices that identified themselves as Buddhist guardian deities and other kami, Niwano practiced name divination—they advised the patient or the immediate family to chant the *Lotus Sūtra,* dedicating the merit to the ancestor responsible for the disease. With his/her stock of merit thus improved, the ancestor would then be in a position to bless the patient and so effect a cure. To maintain health, however, the patient also had to undergo a change of heart, for one's laxity in having ignored the needs of one's ancestors in the first place was symptomatic of a deeper attitudinal problem. If this problem went unchecked, one would be subject to further disease. Thus the patient was told to attend counseling sessions, in which he/she was trained to use the teachings of the *Lotus Sūtra* to bring about a change of heart and a happier life within the entire family circle. These counseling sessions—called *hōza* (Dharma-sittings)—seem to account for the strong sense of group identity that kept the movement intact during the difficult years of World War II.

During the occupation years, Kōsei-kai—as it calls itself for short—became the fastest growing of the new religions. After the occupation it was overtaken by Sōka Gakkai, but its growth rate has continued to be dramatic. At the end of the war it claimed 1,000 households. By 1960, it claimed 399,000; in 1980, 1,640,000. At present it claims 6 million individual members worldwide. The turning point for the organization came in the late 1950s and early 1960s. Prior to Nagamuna's death in 1957, the leaders of the group undertook fasts and cold-water austerities to develop shamanic powers similar to hers. The contrary messages that these various shamans received, however, threatened to split the group on at least one occasion. After 1957, Niwano decided that the group had entered a new period in its history that would no longer depend on shamanism. The sole source of authority from then on would be the Eternal Buddha revealed in the *Lotus Sūtra.* At about this time, the concerns of the membership began to shift, in response to Japan's increasing affluence. More and more of the members, in addition to seeking relief from specific worldly problems, began seeking a more meaningful life in general. As a result, the organization began to place less emphasis on physical healing, and more on the "sei" part of its name: the perfection of the personality. In this, it followed a pattern common to all the new religions that have survived their first generation.

The Kōsei-kai approach to personal perfection is best revealed in Niwano's writings on the subject. According to him, the personality is composed of two parts: the observed self and the seeing self. The observed self is the ordinary sense of separate identity that, if left to its own resources, would simply act out its selfish instincts. However, each person also has a seeing self, composed of introspection and conscience, which can contemplate the actions of the observed self and redirect the personality to higher ends. This seeing self is identical with the Buddha-nature present in all beings. It can be actualized only through one's relationships in society, due to the dual dynamic taught by the Buddhist doctrine of the interdependence of all things. To begin with, one activates the seeing self through appreciation of one's debts to others by fostering a sense of gratitude for those who have given one life: the Eternal Buddha; one's ancestors, distant and immediate; and the kami. One should also feel gratitude for one's teachers and superiors in general. To express gratitude, one should develop sincerity, which means a willingness to fulfill one's duties, learning the lessons that one's superiors have to teach and thus growing as a person. Of course, the lessons of the Eternal Buddha are the most important to learn. These come in two forms: (1) the verbal instructions given in the *Lotus Sūtra,* and (2) the trials and tribulations of everyday life, which—according to the *Lotus Sūtra*—are to be regarded as expedient lessons given by the Eternal Buddha to help one grow in the direction of Awakening.

By mastering these lessons, one enters the second half of the dynamic of perfecting the personality. In light of the interdependence of all things, one realizes one's own ability to change the world through a change of one's attitude. A common Japanese saying states that other people are a mirror of oneself, and Kōsei-kai, similar to other new religions, takes this saying literally. Problems at home, at work, or in school are regarded as signs that one's attitude is problematic and needs changing. The smooth functioning of society is a sign of one's own self-perfection. This explains why one's own perfection cannot be regarded as separate from the perfection of society. Although this viewpoint places heavy responsibility on each person, it is also empowering, as it implies that within each person is the potential for perfection both within and without. According to Niwano, only when one keeps the ideal of perfection alive in one's thoughts and actions is it possible to head in the direction of the true Mahāyāna teaching: the cultivation of the higher self and the creation of a Pure Land on Earth.

These themes find expression in the three primary activities of the Kōsei-kai religious life: hōza, family ancestor rites, and proselytization of new members. Hōza sessions typically number 12 or so participants, including one trained leader. Some members attend them daily, others at less frequent intervals. Each participant is encouraged to speak frankly of particular problems in his/her personal life, to repent the attitudinal error that brought on the problem, and then to seek advice from the other members as to how to bring about a change of heart. Although the *Lotus Sūtra* is recognized as the ultimate source for wise advice, all manner of practical advice from other sources is also admissible at these sessions. Niwano's writings, for instance, contain anecdotes from the lives of Zen masters, quotations from Chekhov, Confucian maxims, and lessons from business management to demonstrate how to improve one's attitude at work in such a way that will engender personal growth, increase productivity, and advance one's position, all at the same time. Similarly, he advises managers on how to improve productivity from workers while at the same time exhibiting greater responsibility for the environment. Hōza leaders are trained to be similarly resourceful in providing advice pertaining to family life, neighborhood relations, and other aspects of daily life. The basic dynamic of hōza sessions is thus twofold: calling forth repentance for following the selfish instincts of the observed self, and gaining confidence in the power of the seeing self to correct one's problems and work toward one's highest ideals.

The basic premise is that secular activity, when approached with the proper attitude, provides the ideal arena for a fulfilling religious life of self-cultivation.

Ancestor rites, as we have seen, function to improve one's ongoing relationship with one's ancestors, living and dead. They also function to improve family ties among the living, based on the principle that "the family that recites together remains together." The act of chanting offers an opportunity for change of heart, as one reflects on debts owed to one's forebears; the daily repetition of the chant demonstrates one's sincere appreciation for the gift of life. The ancestors, in turn, are expected to bless one's current affairs and may even find ways of offering valuable lessons or timely warnings through dreams. Thus the active interdependence of all things includes the dead as well as the living.

Proselytizing is an opportunity to show gratitude to the Eternal Buddha and to the organization for the benefits that one has received through membership. It is also an opportunity to do good for the world by making the Buddha's message more widely available. In addition, it acts as a test of one's purity of heart, as success or failure in winning converts is believed to be a measure of the sincerity of one's motives. Kōsei-kai's methods of proselytization are fairly nonconfrontational. In fact, cooperation with other groups, both religious and secular, has been a major theme in the organization's work. In 1970, Kōsei-kai convened the first World Conference on Religion and Peace and has since continued to take a leading role in the activities of the conference, which now meets on a regular basis and includes members from sixty nations. At approximately the same time, Kōsei-kai helped to form the Brighter Society Movement, a public-spirited consortium of government and private organizations working together for the general improvement of the quality of life in Japan. Kōsei-kai members are also active in relief work. Each member of the organization is asked to fast for three days a month and to donate the resulting savings for overseas aid. The organization hopes that people exposed to the pure hearts of Kōsei-kai members involved in these good works will be attracted to the faith, thus hastening the day of the Pure Land on Earth.

Interestingly enough, the one area in which Kōsei-kai's efforts at external cooperation have been least successful is with other new religions. Niwano made an effort to forge an alliance with other groups whose teachings center on the *Lotus Sūtra,* but the effort came to nothing, as each group feared domination by the others. In the 1970s, Kōsei-kai and other new religions banded with the Liberal Democrat and Democratic Socialist parties to turn the tide against Kōmeitō, the Sōka Gakkai party—a paradoxical case of religions uniting with political parties to protect the separation of politics and religion—but the concerns of this union have not spread to other areas. This tendency to unite only around ad hoc issues is typical of the uji pattern that these new religions follow; it suggests that they will maintain their separate identities as long as no major crises face Japan.

Scholarly discussions of the new religions tend to focus on two themes: what do the religions represent, and what do they augur for the future? The second question is impossible to answer with any certainty, but an answer can be found for the first. The development of almost all of these movements falls into the two phases that we have noted in the history of Risshō Kōsei-kai. Niwano, using terminology from the *Lotus Sūtra,* refers to the phases as the period of expedient truth, in which charismatic leaders provided a personal, ad hoc kami connection to deal with immediate crises; and the period of absolute truth, in which the larger issues of the perfection of the personality can be more systematically addressed once the crises have passed. The first phase represents a revival of the traditional uji in a form least integrated with the rest of society. The second phase represents a combination of the uji ideal of devotion to the clan and the clan's deity, with congruent elements from neo-Confucianism. Although some of the new religions use Buddhist terminology to describe their teachings during this phase, the basic pattern of religious life is Confucian. There is no role for the monastic Sangha, and solitary meditation is not encouraged except as a means of strengthening the mind in pursuit of this-worldly ends. Lay people take full responsibility for their ritual obligations to their ancestors, secular life is the ideal arena for religious practice, and one's perfection as an individual is to be found by sincerely fulfilling one's social duties so as to bring about the perfection of society as a whole. By adopting this neo-Confucian pattern, these new ujis have integrated more or less peacefully with the rest of society and have taken on the status of established religions. Thus, even when they are nominally Buddhist, they represent—in both phases of their development—the ascendancy of pre-Buddhist and non-Buddhist elements in Japanese religious life.

There will inevitably be more periods of crisis in the future of Japan, and further new religious leaders can be expected to formulate creative solutions in response. Whether they will continue the current trend or bring about a return to more traditional forms of Buddhism, only time will tell.

11

Buddhism in the Tibetan Cultural Area

11.1 A TANTRIC ORTHODOXY

The Tibetan cultural area covers the lands in which the Tibetan form of the Buddhist Unexcelled Yoga traditions became established as the dominant religion. This includes not only Tibet, but also the Himalayan valleys immediately bordering Tibet—such as Ladakh, Spiti, Bhutan, Sikkim, and Mustang in northwestern Nepal—as well as areas further afield that the Tibetans converted to their form of Buddhism, such as Mongolia, the Buryats in Siberia, and the Kalmyks in the steppes north of the Caspian Sea. All of these lands had strong shamanic traditions prior to their adoption of Buddhism, traditions that played a major role not only in determining which form of Buddhism was to become dominant in this area but also in reshaping Buddhist practice as it became established.

The question of the relationship between Buddhism and the preexisting shamanic practices provided a recurring point of disagreement and creative compromise throughout the history of Buddhism in these lands. On the popular level, the issues were similar to those surrounding Theravāda syncretism in Southeast Asia: how the beliefs and rituals dealing with the spirit world were to be rationalized in terms of the Buddhist doctrine of karma. The primary difference here was that the dominant orthodoxy—Tantra, with its mantras, rituals, visualizations, and assumption of divine identities—acted as a primary source of techniques for the shaman's arsenal. On the level of meditation practice, the tension between shamanism and Buddhism revolved around the question of how the states attained in Buddhist mind development corresponded to the altered states of consciousness attained by shamanic adepts. As we noted in Chapter 1, the Buddha's Awakening contained shamanic elements but also something more: a strongly ethical orientation and a phenomenological analysis of the causal process by which the mind gives rise to suffering. The question for the Tibetans as they gained exposure to Buddhism was quite simply how essential this "something more" was to the attainment of the Buddhist goal.

Related to this question was the social issue of how Buddhist Tantrism, a movement that glorified the personal powers derived from systematic transgression, could provide the dominant ideology for a society without undercutting ethical norms. For the Tibetan shamans who sought and paid for initiations into Buddhist Tantra from Indian adepts, this was hardly an issue. But for the Tibetan kings who actively sponsored the importation of Buddhism into their country—and later for the ecclesiastical leaders who took over the central government—the creation of ethical restraints on the more antisocial tendencies inherent in Tantra was a primary concern.

One final point that needs addressing before we begin our coverage of the history of Tibetan Buddhism concerns the way the practice of Tantra has affected how the Tibetans themselves view that history. In performing a Tantric ritual, one is dealing with strong and potentially dangerous forces. One must have unshakable confidence in the techniques learned from one's teachers, and this means that one must believe these techniques have been handed down, unchanged, from a supremely reliable source. Because none of the rituals can claim to originate with Śākyamuni, they are generally attributed to Cosmic Buddhas whose mode of being supersedes all questions of historical proof. If changes are introduced into the tradition, they must be justified either by rewriting history or by claiming special forms of transmission that circumvent normal means. This has led to a cultural pattern whereby history is valued not for its accuracy but for its usefulness in helping to empower the ritual participant. When asked by westerners what "really" happened at a particular point in history, Tibetans have been known to respond that the question is irrelevant. What matters to them is the interpretation that can support the ritual.

At the same time, the Tantric practice of deva-yoga (see Section 6.1), combined with the Yogācāra doctrine of the Dharmakāya underlying all minds, tends to blur the whole issue of personal identity. This has led to the creation of histories in which important individuals are emanations of great deities, bodhisattvas, and Cosmic Buddhas acting out an epic drama for the protection and prosperity of the Tibetan nation and its form of Buddhism—the more dramatic the epic, the better. Although both of these tendencies serve to obstruct the modern historian's quest for accuracy, they are important historical facts in and of themselves, and must be kept in mind when trying to understand how Tibetan Buddhism has developed over the centuries.

11.2 THE CONVERSION OF TIBET

What little is known of pre-Buddhist Tibetan religion indicates that it dealt with what were later called the four ways of gods and men: divination, exorcism, magical coercion, and the guidance of the human spirit after death. A cult centering on the divinity of the king involved elaborate sacrifices for the maintenance of the king's power while he was alive, and for the provision of his eternal happiness in the heavenly world after death. Ritual experts were hired for both sorts of occasions, and some seem to have acted as the king's advisers in the day-to-day running of the kingdom. Scholars have suggested that this pattern, which focused political and sacred power on a single figure, set the stage for the later period in Tibetan history when monasteries assumed the role of noble families and their abbots the role of kings, but as we shall see, there were also economic reasons for this later development.

Considering Tibet's proximity to India, Buddhism reached it remarkably late. The Tibetans themselves recorded that Buddhism was introduced twice into their country, first in the seventh to ninth centuries, and then again beginning at the end of the tenth, with a dark period of anti-Buddhist persecution in between. We must qualify this scenario, however, by noting that it covers only the periods in which the rulers of Tibet took an active interest in the propagation of Buddhism, and that the persecution was more antimonastic than anti-Buddhist. From the seventh century to the Muslim conquest of India at the beginning of the thirteenth century, a fairly constant stream of individual Tibetans filtered down through the Himalayan passes to acquire initiations and instructions from the Buddhist Tantric adepts in northeastern India and Kashmir. Their interest in Tantric powers, as opposed to Buddhist philosophy, played a major role in shaping Tibetan Buddhism.

11.2.1 The First Propagation

The first king credited with bringing Buddhism to Tibet was Song-tsen Gampo (full transliterated form: Srong-brtsan sgam-po; d. circa 650). King Song-tsen inherited a united Tibetan kingdom from his father and started Tibet on a campaign of imperial conquest that made it the dominant power in central Asia, with control over the Silk Road, until the middle of the ninth century (see Section 8.1.3). He had two Buddhist wives, a princess from China and one from Nepal. To please them, he built Tibet's first Buddhist temple, the Jo-khang in Lhasa (Strong *EB*, sec. 7.1). Later Tibetan historians identified King Song-tsen as an emanation of Avalokiteśvara, and his Chinese wife as an emanation of Tārā (see Section 5.4.4). After his reign, Lhasa began to attract Buddhist monks whose homelands had been decimated by the Tibetan conquests, but these monks, along with the handful of Tibetan monks they had managed to ordain, were later forced to leave Tibet when they were blamed for a smallpox epidemic in the capital. Nevertheless, they left behind a legacy of texts that served to convert Tibet's first truly Buddhist monarch, Trhisong Detsen (Khri-srong lde-brtsan; r. 755–circa 797).

Tibet's imperial power reached its peak during Trhisong Detsen's reign, as China was in the throes of the An Lu-shan rebellion (see Section 8.5). Tibetan armies occupied the Chinese capital at Ch'ang-an in 763, and captured Tun-huang, the great Buddhist translation center on the Silk Road, in 787, after which scholars there turned to translating Chinese Buddhist texts into Tibetan for their new overlords. Trhisong Detsen took advantage of this situation to send emissaries to India, China, and central Asia to obtain Buddhist texts; to invite Buddhist scholars to the Tibetan court; and to submit lists of questions concerning Buddhist doctrine to any renowned scholars who were unable to make the trip. One such list has been found in the caves of Tun-huang. It is a remarkable document revealing that Yogācāra was the primary school of Buddhist thought entering Tibet during this period, and that the king had a sophisticated grasp of its teachings and controversial points. Later Tibetans regard him, with good reason, as an emanation of Mañjuśrī (see Section 5.4.2).

Two other significant events in the history of Tibetan Buddhism occurred during King Trhisong's reign. The first was the building of the monastery at Sam-ye (bSam-yas), southeast of Lhasa, a process that took a total of 12 years, from 763 to 775 (Strong *EB*, sec. 7.1). The great Indian scholar Śāntarakṣita was invited from Nalanda to preside over the founding of what was to become Tibet's first native monastery, but a series of natural disasters, which the anti-Buddhist faction at court attributed to his presence in the country, forced him to return to India. Before leaving, however, he counseled the king to invite to Tibet an Indian Tantric adept, Padmasambhava, who would tame the local gods and demons, making them more amenable to the establishment of Buddhism on Tibetan soil. The king followed his advice, and Padmasambhava accepted the invitation. Tibetan traditions report that Padmasambhava was a fabulous wonder-worker, subduing a vast number of demonic forces and forcing pledges from them to protect Tibetan Buddhism.

Construction was then resumed on the monastery at Sam-ye. Śāntarakṣita was invited to its consecration, and the king swore in an edict, still extant, that Tibet would dedicate itself in perpetuity to the support of the Triple Gem. At the same time, seven hand-picked members of the Tibet nobility, called the Seven Elect, were ordained to form the first native Tibetan Sangha. The Mūlasarvāstivādin Vinaya was chosen as the guide for monastic discipline. This is one of the few Hīnayāna texts to be translated into Tibetan and has formed the disciplinary code for all Tibetan monastic orders ever since. It is important to note, however, that the monastic form introduced into Tibet had little in common with the original Buddhist pattern of small, loosely organized communities of alms-goers. Rather, life at Sam-ye was patterned on that of the great Buddhist universities in India: large, organized communities dependent on landed grants for their continued existence. This was one of the factors that eventually led Tibetan monasticism to become thoroughly politicized.

Historical records have little more to say about Padmasambhava after the consecration of the monastery at Sam-ye, but Tibetan legends credit him with spending decades in Tibet, subduing gods and demons throughout the land.

Tibetans regard him as a second Buddha, eclipsing Śākyamuni in importance for their country. In later centuries the Nyingma order claimed him as their founder and as the conduit—from the great Cosmic Buddha Samantabhadra (see Section 5.4.4)—of their central meditation tradition, Dzogchen (rDzogs-ch'en, The Great Perfection).

Whatever the truth of these legends, Padmasambhava had little influence over the policies adopted at Sam-ye. The king appointed a council, composed of the chief monks, to oversee the translation of Buddhist works into Tibetan and, in particular, to prevent the translation of Tantras. The large number of Tantric works that did make their way into Tibetan during this period were thus the result of independent efforts, and not of royal sponsorship.

The second major event occurring during Trhisong Detsen's reign was the Great Debate on the issue of sudden versus gradual Awakening, held at Sam-ye from approximately 790 to 792 (Strong *EB*, sec. 7.3). Historical sources covering this event are contradictory, with some even suggesting that no direct debate was held, but rather that different scholars from India and China were invited to present their positions separately to the king. One of the few sources dating from the time of the debate—the report of Hwa-shang Mo-ho-yan, the major Chinese participant and a student of the Northern School of Ch'an—claims that the Chinese defense of sudden Awakening won the king's favor. Later Tibetan sources, however, all maintain that the Chinese lost the debate and that the king banned any further Chinese missionary activity in the country. There is strong evidence that this ban was never enacted, but the accepted version of the event had an important effect on later Tibetan thought and is in fact a major source for our understanding of the issues alive in the period during which this version crystallized, the thirteenth and fourteenth centuries. Therefore we will discuss it in connection with that period in Section 11.3.1.

Two of Trhisong Detsen's successors, his son and grandson, continued his enthusiastic support of Buddhism. The grandson, Ralpachen (Ral-pa-can; r. 823–40), even appointed a Buddhist monk as his chief minister. However, this appointment, along with the growing power of the Buddhist monasteries in general, appears to have been unpopular with members of his court, for in 840 both the king and his chief minister were assassinated. Ralpachen's brother, Lang Dar-ma (gLang Dar-ma), ascended to the throne and proceeded to crack down on the monasteries. He is depicted in the traditional histories as an anti-Buddhist fanatic, although Tun-huang records portray him as opposed not to the religion per se, but simply to the inordinate power that the monasteries had begun to acquire based on their land grants. He in turn was assassinated by a Buddhist monk—the assassination was later justified on the grounds that it was an act of "kindness" to prevent the king from creating further bad karma—and the ensuing political chaos brought about the end of the Tibetan empire and any semblance of centralized control in Tibet. The monasteries were depopulated, and thus the period of the First Propagation ended.

Although the political order in the following period was too fragmented to provide any support to Buddhism, individual Tibetans continued to pursue

Buddhist Tantric practices, and a number of them made the trip to India for further initiations and texts. One of the most famous practitioners of this time was Ma-cig (Ma-gcig, The One Mother; 1055–1145), a nun who was forced to renounce her vows after having intercourse with the man who later became her husband. After his death, she began to suffer a variety of ailments resulting from breaking her vows and engaging in indiscriminate Tantric practice with improperly initiated adepts. Eventually she met up with an adept who had studied in Nalanda and who was able to diagnose the cause of her trouble. After arranging for her to undergo an elaborate ceremony of atonement, he became her new principal partner, and from that point onward she met with nothing but success. Eventually her fame eclipsed his; Tibetans continue to worship her as an emanation of Tārā to this day.

Without royal patronage to encourage doctrinal orthodoxy and monastic discipline, Buddhist practice in Tibet mixed freely with shamanic customs. In the latter part of the tenth century, as various minor Tibetan kingdoms began to attain a measure of stability, the new kings came to regard this situation with concern, viewing Tantrism as detrimental to the moral fiber of their societies. Their concern is what led to the Second Propagation of the Dharma.

11.2.2 The Second Propagation

The Second Propagation began in the newly stabilized kingdoms to the south of Mount Kailāsa (Strong *EB*, sec. 7.5.1), in the extreme southwest of Tibet, as the central area around Lhasa was still in disarray. The prime mover in this Buddhist renaissance was the king of Purang, Yeshe-od (Ye-shes-'od), who abdicated his throne in favor of his son and took ordination in order to devote himself fully to the Buddhist revival. He wrote an ordinance denouncing sexual yoga and animal sacrifice as practiced in Unexcelled Yoga. Sending a group of followers to Kashmir to collect reliable texts, he set forth the principle that only those practices that were clearly derived from Indian Buddhist texts should be accepted as true Dharma. This principle formed the guiding standard behind the entire Second Propagation.

After Yeshe-od's death, his grandson, O-de ('Od-Ide), invited the great Indian scholar Atīśa (982–1054) from the university at Vikramasila, near Nalanda, to help spread the Dharma in Tibet. This was perhaps the most influential single event in the conversion of Tibet to the Buddhist religion. Scholars have often noted the symbolism of the founding of the monastery at Sam-ye, with Śāntarakṣita representing the monastic/university strain of Buddhism, and Padmasambhava the Tantric strain. Atīśa serves as a symbol of the Indian tradition that became the orthodoxy in Tibet, in that he combined both strains in one person. On the one hand, he advanced the Prāsangika interpretation of Mādhyamika philosophy (see Section 4.2), which was to become the dominant school of Tibetan academic thought. Together with his Tibetan disciple Dromtön ('Brom-ston; 1003–65), he founded the first of the great Tibetan monastic orders, the Kadam (bK' gdams, Bound to [the Buddha's] Command), which became renowned for its high standard of scholarship and strict adherence to the Vinaya (Strong *EB*, sec. 7.4). On the other hand, he himself had studied under the famous Indian Tantric adept Nāropa (see Section 6.3.4), and is remembered as the conduit of a great number of Tantric initiation lineages in the monastic version of Unexcelled Yoga (see Section 6.3.5). He was also responsible for the importation of the cult of Tārā, which was to become Tibet's most widespread bodhisattva cult.

The dual nature of Atīśa's thought is best illustrated by his analysis of the Buddhist Path into three stages: renouncing of the world of saṃsāra, arousing the thought of Awakening, and attaining a correct view of emptiness. Viewed from an academic standpoint, this is a fairly standard interpretation of Mahāyāna thought. At the same time, however, it also follows the process of generation in deva-yoga. The renunciation of the world corresponds to the adept's renunciation of the everyday level of experience to enter into the maṇḍala he/she is visualizing. The arousing of the bodhicitta corresponds to the adoption of the deity's mind-set, and the correct view of emptiness corresponds to the recollection of purity, in which the adept stops to reflect that all levels of reality—everyday and visualized—are equally empty of any self-nature, so as to prevent the mind from placing any thought constructs on the ritual experience before proceeding with the remainder of the ritual. It is important to remember that this pattern of dual meanings applies not only to Atīśa's thought, but also to Tibetan Buddhist thought in general.

The story of Atīśa's invitation is interesting for the light it casts on the economics of institutional Buddhism both in India and in Tibet at this time. To induce Atīśa to come to Tibet, King O-de had to pledge a large sum of gold to the university at Vikramasila for what was essentially a three-year contract. When the three years were up, Atīśa's return to India was blocked by political unrest in the Himalayas. Thus he agreed to stay on, provided that additional payments be sent back to the university. All of this suggests that the Indian universities' day-to-day operating expenses and the vagaries of royal support had forced them to depart from the traditional Buddhist willingness to offer teachings for free. This, together with the practice among lay Indian Tantric adepts of charging for their initiations, established the custom among Tibetans that it was legitimate to charge for the teaching, a custom that continues today.

The Second Propagation continued until the demise of Buddhism in northern India and Kashmir, and was largely a story of how the new Kadam movement interacted with other Tantric lineages being brought from India during this period and with the earlier Buddhist traditions derived from the First Propagation. Many Tibetans continued traveling to India to collect texts and initiations throughout this period, but two in particular stand out: Drok-mi ('Brog-mi, Nomad) and Marpa. Drok-mi (992–1074) collected a large number of initiations while in India, principally from the lineage of the Tantric adept Virūpa. After his return to Tibet, another Indian, Gayadhara, sought him out and gave him exclusive Tibetan rights over his lineage as well. One of Drok-mi's disciples, Kon-chog Gyalpo (Dkon-mchog Rgyal-po), established a monastery in Sakya (Sa-skya); his son, adopting the discipline of the Kadams, became the first hierarch of the Sakya order, which was to become the dominant political power in Tibet in the thirteenth and fourteenth centuries.

As for Marpa (1012–96), he originally began studying with Drok-mi but objected to Drok-mi's high initiation fees and so went to India to acquire Tantric initiations on his own. He studied primarily with Nāropa, who taught him the *Cakrasaṃvara Tantra*. On his return to Tibet, Marpa married and set himself up as a householder, revealing his mastery of the Tantras only to a chosen few. His main student was Milarepa (Mi-la ras-pa, Cotton-clad Mila; 1040–1123), who was to become one of the most beloved figures in Tibetan history. Mila, as a youth, had learned magic in order to take revenge on a wicked uncle who had dispossessed and maltreated Mila's widowed mother. Seized with remorse after destroying his uncle, he sought first to expiate his bad karma and then to attain liberation. At age 38 he became Marpa's disciple. For six years the master subjected him to harsh ordeals (Strong *EB*, sec. 7.9) before finally granting him the initiation he sought. Milarepa spent the remainder of his life meditating in the caves and wandering on the slopes of the high Himalayas. After a long period of solitude, he gradually attracted a following, converted many disciples, and worked wonders for people's benefit. A fictionalized "autobiography" of Milarepa, composed in the fifteenth century, is one of the great classics of Tibetan literature.

Mila's primary student was Gampopa (Sgam-po-pa; 1079–1153), a monk of the Kadam lineage. Mila taught Gampopa a version of the Mahāmudrā meditation, called Sūtra Mahāmudrā, that would not violate the latter's vows of celibacy. In the original Unexcelled Yoga teachings, Mahāmudrā was the state of innate blank joy that the adept would attain at the climax of the sexual union. Sūtra Mahāmudrā was a technique by which a celibate meditator could attain the same state through a union of the male and female "energy channels" in the body. This method was originally denounced outside of Gampopa's following, but eventually became one of the dominant meditation methods in Tibet. However, an entire book could be written on the various permutations it underwent as it was passed down from master to master and school to school, combining with Dzogchen and other methods. (See Strong *EB*, sec. 7.6, for a version that closely parallels early Buddhist dhyāna practices.)

Gampopa's combination of Kadam monastic discipline and Mahāmudrā meditation formed the basis for a new school, the Kagyü (bKa' brgyud, the Followers or the Transmitted Command). His disciples split into five subschools, chief of which was the Karma school. Although monks of both the Kagyü and Sakya schools were expected to follow the Mūlasarvāstivādin Vinaya, because their lineages were ultimately derived from laymen, they were somewhat more lax in their discipline than the Kadams.

Various other small schools and monastic orders formed as the Kadams combined with other Tantric lineages newly arrived from India, but none of them gained prominence. Quite a few of the older Tantric lineages, however, refused to have anything to do with the new reform movement. These older lineages were composed largely of lay practitioners whose traditions contained not only authentic Buddhist texts but also apocryphal texts, doctrines, and practices—such as Tantric rituals centered on native Tibetan deities—for which no Indian texts could be cited as precedents. The question of how to meet the challenge of the reform movement's new standards and at the same time hold on to their old traditions brought these lineages together into two broad camps that eventually developed into two loosely organized lineages of their own. One was the Bon lineage, which declared itself a separate religion, maintaining that the Śākyamuni of the reform movement was an impostor Buddha, and that they held the lineage of the true Buddha, named Shenrab (gShen-rab, Best of Holy Beings), a native of a land to the west of Tibet called Ta-zig (present-day Tadjikistan?). Thus they had no need to justify their traditions as coming from India and were able to develop a tradition that is an unabashed amalgam of Buddhist teachings—generally following the Yogācārins—and older shamanic beliefs, including a myth of the universe being created from light (Strong *EB*, sec. 7.2).

The other camp, which accepted that they and the reformers worshiped the same Buddha, called themselves the Nyingma (rNying-ma, Ancient) school. This school maintained that its allegedly apocryphal texts were actually authentic in that they had been hidden by Padmasambhava and later discovered by spiritual adepts. Thus the Nyingmas reopened the old controversy that had split the Sthaviras and Mahāsanghikas (see Section 3.2.1) over what constitutes an authentic transmission. In the long run, the Nyingmas won the battle in Tibet, for the tradition of *termas* (gter-ma)—hidden treasure texts reputedly placed underground, underwater, in the sky, or in "mind" (conceived as the Dharmakāya)—spread to other schools as well. In the eyes of some, termas discovered by *tertons* (gter-ston), or treasure-finders, were a more profound transmission than texts with an established historical pedigree. At any rate, termas provided the mechanism whereby new teachings could be accepted as authentic in a culture obsessed with lineages and precedents.

The primary Nyingma terma of this period was the *Mani Kabum* (Maṇi bka' 'bum), which set forth the eclectic proposition that all interpretations of the Buddhist path were equally correct, and that all altered states of consciousness realized at the ends of these paths were equivalent. It also set forth a system—which was to influence all subsequent Nyingma thought—whereby the Unexcelled Yoga level of Tantra was divided into three sublevels, with the Nyingma/Bon form of meditation, Dzogchen, forming the highest of the three.

Dzogchen, unlike more standard methods of Buddhist meditation, asserted that Awakening wasn't "brought about" at all. Awareness in and of itself, the Nyingmas claimed, was already innately pure and nondual, and all that needed to be done in order to realize its innate purity and nonduality was to let thought processes come to a stop. The approach they prescribed was thus one of spontaneity and nonstriving, effortless abiding with the "Primordial Basis." They offered no analytical path for how to accomplish this, however, for they said that any analysis would simply add to the mind's thought processes.

The obvious parallels between the Dzogchen and Ch'an doctrines of spontaneity have caused some scholars to assume that Ch'an was the source for the

Dzogchen tradition, but early Dzogchen documents from the tenth and eleventh centuries were careful to point out the very real differences between their school and Ch'an, which was also practiced in Tibet at that time. For their part, the Ch'an adepts had derived their doctrine of spontaneity from the Taoists, and it may be that the doctrine of spontaneous nonstriving had its roots ultimately in shamanic traditions common to Tibet, China, and central Asia. Thus the relation between Dzogchen and Ch'an may have been one of common ancestry rather than direct influence.

Thus, by the end of the Second Propagation, there were four major schools of Buddhism in Tibet—Kadam, Sakya, Kagyü, and Nyingma—with a fifth offshoot school, Bon, which maintained that it was a separate religion even though it held many doctrines in common with the Nyingma school. Kadam, Sakya, and Kagyü had well-established monastic orders for both men and women. Nyingma and Bon did not develop monastic orders until the fourteenth and fifteenth centuries, and even then their monastic impulse was never strong.

As was the case with the schools of early Buddhism, no hard-and-fast lines existed between the various Tibetan schools, largely because of the tendency for individual monks, nuns, and lay adepts to travel about, gathering up instructions and initiations from as many authorized teachers—termed lamas (bla-mas)—as possible, regardless of affiliation. The Kadams retained their reputation as the strictest in terms of celibacy, but otherwise the schools were distinguished primarily by which Tantra they followed and which Cosmic Buddha they regarded as the source of their particular lineage.

11.3 THE PERIOD OF CONSOLIDATION

During the first two centuries after the demise of Buddhism in northern India in the early thirteenth century, the Tibetans succeeded in consolidating their religion into the form it was to maintain, largely unchanged, until the early twentieth century. This involved four processes: studying the history of Buddhism so as to provide a background for textual study, gathering texts to form a standard canon, establishing doctrinal syntheses to interpret and accommodate the many schools of thought inherited from the two propagations, and forming a political system that reflected the increasing institutional power of the monastic communities.

11.3.1 Historical Issues

The first task confronting the scholars of this period was to establish a standardized canon from the mass of texts they had inherited from the two propagations of Dharma; this, in turn, required that they research the history of Buddhism, both in India and Tibet, so as to provide a framework for their textual studies. In part, their research was motivated by a genuine quest for historical truth, and the resulting histories remain among the most reliable sources for modern historical study of Buddhism's last centuries in India.

However, because the two propagations of Dharma to Tibet had resulted in two distinct camps of thought, partisan concerns occasionally eclipsed the historians' concern for factual truth. As a result, they came to focus on a handful of specific incidents that they polemicized to the point where it is virtually impossible to determine what actually transpired during the events in question. The histories written during this period, however, provide excellent source material for studying the issues that were uppermost in the historians' own minds.

One prime example of this partisan historiography was the controversy that developed over the correct record of the Great Debate held at Sam-ye in 790–92 on the issue of sudden versus gradual Awakening (see Section 11.2.2). The crux of the debate—if in fact the debate did occur—was not so much over the sudden or gradual nature of Awakening as it was over how necessary morality and analytical insight were in bringing Awakening about. This was a primary point of disagreement between the two major camps: the old schools, following their practice of Dzogchen, maintaining that simply stilling the processes of thought is enough to realize Awakening; the newer schools, following their monastic Mādhyamika teachings, maintaining that morality and analytical insight were indispensable components of the Path. Thus the two camps focused on what support they could find for their positions in King Trhisong Detsen's handling of the case. It is interesting to note how, in the course of the controversy, the battle lines were redrawn, with the Kagyü school and its practice of Sūtra Mahāmudrā finding itself aligned with the Nyingmas. This realignment was to last up through modern times.

The controversy began with Kunga Gyalts'en (Kund-dga' rGyal-mtshan; 1182–1251), leader of the Sakyan school, who is one of the few figures in Tibetan history to be remembered primarily by his Sanskrit name, Sakya Paṇḍita. Sakya Paṇḍita depicted the Chinese side of the Great Debate as being identical with the Sūtra Mahāmudrā and "Chinese" Dzogchen methods of meditation that were being propagated during his time. According to him, Trhisong Detsen clearly repudiated the Chinese position, forbidding that it ever be taught in Tibet again. This, he said, was proof that Sūtra Mahāmudrā and Chinese Dzogchen were invalid as well.

To counter Sakya Paṇḍita's attack, the Nyingmas produced their own interpretation of Trhisong Detsen's reign, in which the king's daughter, Yeshe Tsogyel (Ye-shes mTsho-rgyal), became Padmasambhava's primary consort, and the king himself became a trained Dzogchen adept. In addition, the twelfth-century Nyingma historian Nyang Nyi-ma 'od-zer provided an alternative version of the outcome of the debate, in which Trhisong Detsen decreed that the gradual and sudden approaches to Awakening were essentially the same, the gradual mode being generally preferable simply because it was better suited for people of ordinary talents, whereas the sudden method was better for those with extraordinary talents. Thus, according to this account, both sides emerged victorious from the debate.

Butön (Bu-ston; 1290–1364), a monk belonging to an independent branch of the Kadams, later reasserted Sakya Paṇḍita's position in his definitive history of Buddhism (Strong *EB*, sec. 7.3), and this was to become the position accepted by Tibetan officialdom. Hwa-shang, the Chinese representative at the debate, came to be depicted as a buffoon in the dances staged by the state to celebrate the Tibetan New Year, although this development was as much due to Tibetan nationalism as it was to historical beliefs. Nevertheless, the Nyingmas continued to uphold their version of the debate, and the matter was left at an impasse.

11.3.2 Texts

Scholars worked throughout the thirteenth century to gather, standardize, and collate the various texts that had been brought over from India and translated into Tibetan during the previous centuries. The connection between this process and that of historical research is demonstrated by the collation's having been completed in the beginning of the fourteenth century by Butön, the author of the definitive history of Buddhism mentioned previously. Butön's canon consisted of two parts: the Kanjur (bKa'-'gyur), which contained the word of Śākyamuni and other Buddhas; and the Tenjur (bsTan'gyur), which consisted of later treatises not only on Buddhist doctrine, but also on other subjects—such as medicine, astrology, and grammar—that had been taught in the great Buddhist universities during the period when Tibetans were gathering texts there. The Kanjur fell into four parts: the *Mūlasarvāstivādin Vinaya,* the *Perfection of Wisdom Sūtras,* other Sūtras, and Tantras. Very few Hīnayāna Sūtras made their way into the collection. The first printed Kanjur was completed in Peking in 1411, and the first complete printings of the canon in Tibet were carried out at Narthang in 1742, utilizing 108 volumes for the Kanjur and 225 for the Tenjur.

Butön did not include Nyingma Tantras in his compilation of the canon, so in the fifteenth century a Nyingma scholar, Ratna Lingpa (Ratna gLing-pa; 1403–78), collected the Nyingma texts then available in a work called the *Nyingma Gyudbum* (rNying ma rgyud 'bum), or *One Hundred Thousand Nyingma Tantras.*

11.3.3 Doctrinal Systems

The compilation of a standardized canon was only the first step toward resolving the most bewildering problem facing Tibetan Buddhists during this period—that of finding order in the welter of conflicting doctrines and practices contained in the legacy of Sūtras, Tantras, and treatises they had inherited from the past. Many monks of high intellectual caliber tackled the problem, but only two provided syntheses that were to prove enduring, forming the two basic approaches to doctrine and practice that have continued to characterize Tibetan Buddhism up through the present.

The first of the two syntheses was provided by the great Nyingma scholar Longch'en Rabjam (Klong-ch'en rab-'byams; 1308–63), who produced a series of texts called the Seven Treasuries, formulating the Nyingma path of practice in such a way as to make Dzogchen respectable in terms of Indian Buddhist doctrines. Longch'en Rabjam was less interested in systematizing

Buddhist doctrine as a whole than in systematizing Dzogchen theory and practice. He held to the Nyingma position that all Buddhist teachings, no matter how contradictory they might seem on the surface, were equally valid as alternative approaches to the truth—as different teachings were suitable for different temperaments—but that they all were ultimately inadequate as descriptions of the realizations to be gained through the practice of Dzogchen. However, by his time a variety of Dzogchen traditions had developed, and he felt called upon to impose some order on them.

He ultimately delineated three valid Dzogchen traditions, two lower ones tracing their lineage from a Chinese monk in Kashmir, and a higher one purportedly founded by Samantabhadra (see Section 5.4.4) and brought from India to Tibet by Vimalamitra. The higher one taught two approaches to Awakening—both equally effective, but the second the more spectacular of the two. The first, a sudden method, was *trekchö* (khregs chod, cutting through rigidity), in which one simply broke through to the innate purity and simplicity of awareness and then stabilized one's ability to remain in touch with that purity. The second, a more gradual method, was *tögal* (thod gral, passing over the crest), in which yogic techniques were used to stabilize the attainment of light acquired in the earlier stages to the point where one attained the rainbow-body, whereby one's physical body would dissolve into light after death.

These practices are obviously shamanic in origin, related to the Bon myth of the creation of the world from light. Longch'en, however, rationalized them with Buddhist doctrine by identifying the pure awareness realized in trekchö with the Dharmakāya, and the rainbow-body attained in tögal with the sambhogakāya. However, he was careful to point out that the Dharmakāya was not identical to the store-consciousness (see Section 4.3), for unlike the store-consciousness it has been pure and nondual all along. Thus a recurrent question in later Dzogchen teachings has been how to distinguish the two in practice.

Longch'en Rabjam's systemization of Dzogchen has remained definitive up to the present, but it solved few problems for those thinkers who respected the inconsistencies they found among the various schools of Buddhist thought. At the same time, his life—he reportedly sired a number of illegitimate children—did not provide a satisfying model for those who respected the Buddhist teachings on morality. Only later in the fourteenth century did Tsongkhapa (Tsong kha-pa; 1357-1419), a native of northeast Tibet, formulate a system accommodating both of these concerns that was to win widespread approval.

Tsongkhapa had become a novice in boyhood and received Tantric initiations before going to central Tibet. There he studied the exoteric Mahāyāna treatises for years and visited all the notable centers of learning, regardless of their affiliation, his special interests being logic and Vinaya. Taking full ordination in the Kadam order at age 25, he began to ponder the central question of Mahāyāna philosophy: the meaning of the doctrine of emptiness. Did it completely negate the validity of conventional norms and reality—including other Buddhist doctrines—or did it leave them intact? After years of study and meditation, he was introduced to a text by Candrakīrti, the founder of the Prāsangika Mādhyamika school (see Section 4.2), and in 1398 this inspired a vision in which he saw all Buddhist teachings as being mutually reinforcing rather than contradictory. According to his vision, the doctrine of emptiness, if properly understood, did not invalidate ethical norms, logic, or the doctrine of dependent co-arising. This realization formed the basis for the remainder of his life's work.

Tsongkhapa's *Sung-bum* (gSung 'bum), or *Collected Works,* total well over two hundred titles. They cover the entire range of Buddhist philosophy and Tantric practice under the rubric of Atīśa's threefold analysis of the Buddhist Path—renunciation, bodhicitta, and right view concerning emptiness—with a special emphasis on the last category. According to Tsongkhapa, the emptiness of the exoteric Mahāyāna treatises was in no way different from or inferior to the emptiness induced by Tantric practices; one needed to have a proper understanding of emptiness, arrived at through the processes of logic and textual study, for one's Tantric practice to succeed. Logic was needed because it made clear the "object of negation," that is, precisely what was and was not negated by the doctrine of emptiness. Textual study was needed for the same reason, for as one worked through the various formulations of Buddhist doctrine produced over the centuries, one's understanding of emptiness would gradually become more subtle and precise.

Tsongkhapa rated, in ascending order, the various schools of Buddhist thought known to him as follows: Vaibhāṣka, Sautrāntika, Yogācāra, Svātantrika Mādhyamika, and Prāsangika Mādhyamika. The rating was based on the thoroughness with which the school understood the doctrine of emptiness, although Tsongkhapa viewed the higher schools as perfecting rather than negating the lower ones. Sautrāntika and Vaibhāṣka he faulted as giving too much reality to mental objects; Yogācāra he faulted as giving too much reality to mind. For him, Prāsangika Mādhyamika provided the middle way in that it did not negate too little, as did the earlier Buddhist schools, nor did it negate too much, as did some of Tsongkhapa's contemporaries, who saw emptiness as negating moral norms and other conventional truths.

To implement his proposed course of study, Tsongkhapa founded a monastic university on Mount Ganden (dGa'-Idan), near Lhasa, in 1409. Soon his students founded two additional universities, also near Lhasa, at Dre-bung ('Bras spungs) in 1416, and Sera (Se-rwa) in 1419. In their heyday, the three universities housed a total of more than twenty thousand monks. Their curriculum started with basic study in logic and then proceeded through what were termed the five great texts: six to seven years on Asanga/Maitreya's *Abhisamayālaṃkāra,* a text on the bodhisattva Path (see Section 4.3); two years on Candrakīrti's *Madhyamakāvatāra,* a commentary on Nāgārjuna's Stanzas on the Middle Way, to introduce the proper understanding of emptiness (see Section 4.2); two years on Vasubandhu's *Abhidharmakośa* (see Section 4.4); and two years on a Vinaya commentary by Guṇaprabhā. Each year throughout the course of study, time would be taken out to review the fifth great text, Dharmakīrti's major work on logic and epistemology (see Section 6.2).

The curriculum as a whole was an attempt to recreate the atmosphere of the great Indian universities. The student body in each university was divided into two debating teams, which were encouraged to be ruthless in their attack of each other's positions. The course of study would culminate in several years of review before the student would attain his *geshe* (dse-bshes, Refined Knowledge) degree and participate in a final debating contest. This contest ultimately grew into a major national event, with each year's winner becoming a national hero.

Throughout the course of study, the monks also pursued preliminary Tantric practices. Only after the completion of their studies, however, were they allowed to pursue higher Tantric practices on full-scale retreats. Tsongkhapa insisted on strict adherence to the monastic discipline throughout the course of the practice. Although he did not deny the possibility that one might be able to pursue the Tantric Path with a partner, he set out a stringent—virtually impossible—list of qualifications that both partners would have to fulfill if they did not want their practice to lead them to hell. As a result, his followers for the most part stuck to celibate Tantrism.

Tsongkhapa's program was so distinctive that it developed into a new school, the Gelug (dGe-lugs, Virtuous Ones), and became so popular that it took over the Kadam school and in effect replaced it. His program influenced studies in the other major schools as well. The curriculum he set out remained unchanged until Lhasa fell to the Chinese in the middle of the twentieth century, and is still followed in Gelug monasteries scattered throughout the world. When Tibetan Buddhism spread to Mongolia and Siberia in later centuries, the Gelug curriculum formed the heart of the movement. Although it succeeded in producing a line of brilliant scholars and academicians, it put a freeze on creativity in Tibetan monastic academic circles. In the later centuries of Tibetan Buddhism, which we will touch on in the following, the creative impulse tended to come from sources that found their inspiration in Longch'en Rabjam's more eclectic approach.

11.3.4 Politics

Tibet, in inheriting the tradition of the monastic universities from India, inherited a logistical problem as well: how to maintain these large institutions. Unlike the early Buddhist monks, the students at the Tibetan monasteries could not rely simply on the alms they might gather, for in many cases they formed enormous communities. The problem of maintaining these communities—many of which became well endowed—as stable institutions with a minimum of hardship and dissension became a major political issue on both internal and external levels.

On the internal level, the primary question was how to provide for a smooth transition in the leadership. In some of the orders, such as the Sakyas, this problem was solved by making the highest office hereditary, passing from uncle to nephew. In others, such as the Karmas and eventually the Gelugs, a more innovative approach was settled on, whereby the leader, at death, would intentionally reincarnate in such a way that he would resume leadership after his reincarnated form, a *tülku* (sprul-sku), gained maturity. The story of how this tradition developed is a fascinating study of how shamanic and Buddhist strands combined in the development of Tibetan Buddhist traditions.

The tülku tradition originated in the Karma subschool of the Kagyüs. One of Marpa's reputed magical skills had been the ability to transfer his spirit to animate the body of a person newly dead. The purpose of this skill, aside from its entertainment value, was to cheat death. If one were approaching death oneself, one could continue life in a younger body of one's choosing. Marpa had been unable to pass along this particular skill to any of his followers, but the tradition of its existence led the second hierarch of the Karma school, Karma Paksi (1204–83)—reputedly skilled at both Mahāmudrā and Dzogchen practices—to attempt to inject his spirit at death into the corpse of a boy. He failed in his attempt and ended up injecting his spirit into the womb of an expectant mother. After his rebirth, he was able to recount the details of his experience and was ultimately accepted as the next leader of the Karma school.

As this tradition became standard in the Karma school, it spread to other orders and monasteries as well, until eventually Tibet had more than three hundred recognized tülkus. The dying leader would leave signs to indicate the location of his/her next rebirth; followers would attempt to interpret the signs and find the child who matched them, and then bring up the child until it was old enough to resume authority. This method had a number of advantages in that it freed the school or monastery from having to depend on the uncertain ability of a single family to provide it with a string of suitable incumbents, at the same time arranging for talented children to be groomed for leadership from an early age. However, it also was open to serious abuses, especially in the case of wealthy or politically powerful institutions, within which differing factions might propose different children as the genuine tülku, or the regents might refuse to pass power along to the tülku when the latter reached maturity (Strong *EB*, sec. 7.8).

The tülku tradition has been explained as an application of the doctrine of rebirth, and in its early years it may have been rationalized with Buddhist doctrine in those terms. However, in the seventeenth century, the tradition began to combine with the tradition of bodhisattva emanations, and thus was explained in terms of the nirmāṇakāya theory (see Sections 4.3, 5.5.1). This proved expedient in a number of ways. Tülkus who turned out to be obvious poor choices could be removed from office on the grounds that their bodhisattva had abandoned them. If several tülkus were proposed for the same position, an arrangement could be worked out to accommodate the political interests of all the parties in the dispute. The most striking example of this was a case in Bhutan where three children were proposed by different factions as the rightful hierarch of the Drugpa ('Brug-pa) branch of the Kagyüs in charge of that country. Finally the decision was made that the previous hierarch had split his body, speech, and mind among three incarnations, and that the speech and mind incarnations should assume authority. From that point onward, this tülku developed a habit of making this three-way split.

Questions of internal politics, however, were relatively mild in comparison to those of external politics. As we have noted, monks have participated in Tibetan politics from the time of the First Propagation; their erudition made them ideal diplomats, similar to the clerics of medieval Europe, and thus they followed a precedent established by their forerunners in India and central Asia. They also followed the Indian precedent—the priest/patron relationship—whereby the patron would reward a monk's political work by granting him or his monastery full rights over a gift of land, free from taxation, thereby establishing the monastery as the governing power in a small fiefdom. By the thirteenth century, some of these fiefdoms were no longer small. Because they were the only institutions in the country transcending the clan level, they became major players on the political scene.

Ultimately, one of the orders, the Sakya school, parlayed this position to full government of Tibet by transposing the priest/patron relationship to the international level. In 1247 the ruling clans of Tibet realized that the Mongols, who by then had become the dominant power in central Asia, were planning to invade. In order to prevent this catastrophe, they sent Sakya Paṇḍita (see Section 11.3.1) to negotiate a truce with the Mongol ruler, Ködön Khan. Sakya Paṇḍita was famed not only for his scholarship but also for his practical wisdom, which he used on this occasion to play both sides to his advantage. By offering Tibet's submission to Mongol rule, he persuaded the Khan not to invade Tibet. He then talked the Khan into placing him and his descendants in the position of viceroys over the entire country.

Scholars have argued that the long intermingling of politics and religion in Tibetan history from pre-Buddhist times has inclined the Tibetans to see nothing wrong with the notion of a monk as ruler of their country, but Sakya Paṇḍita's maneuvering on this occasion was extremely unpopular with his countrymen. The Sakyans were able to use their power to their advantage in the short run, waging war on and destroying any monasteries who opposed them, but their rule was short lived, and they fell from power in 1354 as their patrons, the Mongols, also fell. Nevertheless, they set a precedent that was to prove decisive for Tibetan history. During their reign, other schools tried to follow their example by establishing priest/patron relationships of their own with the Mongols. After their reign, the Kagyü school closely affiliated with the clan who overthrew the Sakyas became thoroughly embroiled in the political scene and benefited mightily in terms of wealth and prestige. However, the Gelugs in the long run ultimately benefited most from the Sakyan precedent. The story of how this occurred takes us into a new era of Tibetan history.

11.4 THE AGE OF THE DALAI LAMAS

The Gelug monasteries, in carrying on the traditions of the Indian universities, continued the tradition of producing missionaries as well. In 1578, Tsongkhapa's third successor as head of the school, Sonam Gyatsho (bSod-nams-rgya-ntsho; 1543–88), converted the Mongol ruler, Altan Khan, to

Buddhism. This set into motion a process whereby the Mongols and other inhabitants of the central Asian steppes took on the Gelug system of monastic education and came to regard Lhasa as the cultural and religious capital of their lands. The Khan bestowed the name of Dalai Lama (Ocean [of Wisdom] Teacher) on Sonam Gyatsho, but because Gyatsho was regarded as the tülku of his two predecessors, he became known as the Third Dalai Lama, with the title of First and Second granted retroactively to them.

In a shrewd political move, the Fourth Dalai Lama was born in the family of the Mongol Khan, but not until the reign of the Fifth Dalai Lama (1617–82) did this priest/patron relationship bring political power to the Gelugs. With the help of Mongol troops, the Fifth Dalai Lama crushed his enemies in central Tibet and became ruler of the entire country. His repressive measures forced monks of other politically active sects to take refuge in outlying areas of Tibet, Sikkim, and Bhutan, but he was very generous with sects exhibiting no political ambitions. In particular, he showed a great interest in Nyingma doctrines—he was reputed to be a Dzogchen adept—and bestowed on the Nyingma order property he had seized from the Kagyüs. Styling himself an emanation of Avalokiteśvara, he built an enormous maṇḍala-palace on a hill overlooking Lhasa and named it the Potala, after the mountain in southern India reputed to be Avalokiteśvara's home. Thus he became the first figure in Tibetan history to combine the traditions of tülku and bodhisattva emanation in one person.

Nine years after the Manchus took power in China in 1644 (see Section 8.7), the Fifth Dalai Lama visited Peking and established a special priest/patron relationship with the new dynasty, thus setting the stage for the Gelugs to rule Tibet well into the twentieth century. With considerably more skill than the Sakyas—and considerably more luck, in that their patrons held power for an unusually long time—the Gelugs were able to use Chinese power to keep their political enemies under control, while using their own wits to keep the Chinese from interfering excessively in Tibet's internal affairs. This position lasted, somewhat precariously, until 1951, when the priest/patron relationship finally backfired on the entire country.

Only two of the Fifth Dalai Lama's successors, however, shared his political acumen. During the reigns of the Sixth through the Twelfth, most of the political maneuvering was done by the Gelug regents. The Sixth Dalai Lama, born to a Nyingma family, proved remarkably unsuited for monastic life; he is credited with being the author of a series of erotic poems based on his exploits in the brothels of Lhasa. For a period, his fellow lamas debated whether he was a Tantric adept of the old school or a mere lecher. They finally decided that Avalokiteśvara had abandoned him and entered another lama. Before they could act, however, the Mongols attacked Lhasa, killed the regent, and kidnapped the Dalai Lama, who died in captivity, perhaps murdered. The Seventh and Eighth Dalai Lamas preferred quiet contemplation to politics; the Ninth through the Twelfth died in childhood, perhaps of foul play (Strong *EB*, sec. 7.8).

The Thirteenth (1874–1933) survived the perils of childhood in the Potala only to become enmeshed in international politics, as the British and Chinese both invaded Lhasa during his reign. Seeing the long-term threat to his country if it did not modernize, he strengthened the civilian branch of the government service, raised a standing army, and instituted a number of other modernizing reforms that—after initial resistance—gradually became very popular. Toward the end of his life, however, he could see that his reforms were too little too late; his death was accompanied by bad omens that left the populace dispirited. The Fourteenth Dalai Lama (b. 1935), enthroned in 1950 just before the Chinese Communists invaded Tibet, was forced to flee the country in 1959 as the Chinese set about systematically destroying all vestiges of Tibetan culture. Realizing that the only hope for the survival of Tibetan Buddhism lies in the development of an international base of support, he has adopted the role of international spokesman for Buddhism as a whole, working tirelessly to provide for Tibetan refugees scattered throughout the world, and to reunite lamas, now becoming teachers to the world at large, from the various schools of Tibetan Buddhism.

This survey of the political fortunes of the Dalai Lamas over the past four centuries has bypassed the religious developments of the period largely because, as we noted previously, the Gelug educational system tended to preclude innovation, and the political responsibilities borne by the Gelugs tended to distract them from the purely religious life. Thus, most of the religious innovations of this period occurred outside of their school.

The primary religious development of this period was the growth of the Nyingma eclectic school of thought, and its permeation into the other non-Gelug orders. The Nyingma monastic order grew considerably as a result of the Fifth Dalai Lama's support in the seventeenth century, and the school produced one of its greatest thinkers and meditation masters in the following century, Jigme Lingpa ('Jigs-med gLing-pa; *circa* 1730–98). Jigme Lingpa, reportedly as a result of mind-to-mind transmission from Longch'en Rabjam (see Section 11.3.3), streamlined and ritualized the latter's guides to Dzogchen with an eye to making them more easily accessible, forming the basis for all Dzogchen practice ever since. He taught that individually interpreted self-discipline was more important than monastic discipline in the pursuit of the Path, and that the ultimate truth could not be captured or even approached by any verbal formulation.

These points formed the rallying point for the Ri-med (Ris-med, Unrestricted) movement that began sweeping through the non-Gelug orders in eastern Tibet in the middle of the nineteenth century. This movement was unrestricted in three ways: It drew on the traditions of all the monastic and Tantric lineages, regardless of affiliation; it offered to the general public initiations that had been kept as closely guarded secrets for many centuries; and it devalued the monastic disciplinary rules, in particular the rules concerning celibacy. Although the Ri-meds drew their leaders from the Sakyas, Kagyüs, Nyingmas, and even the Bons, the movement was primarily a triumph of the old Nyingma eclecticism, in that it emphasized Dzogchen as an element in all true Buddhist practice and supported the idea that all interpretations of Buddhist doctrine are equally valid, with no one version in a position of orthodoxy above any others.

Although the Ri-med movement was originally nonpolitical, it ran into trouble in the early twentieth century as the Gelugs began viewing it as a threat to the Thirteenth Dalai Lama's drive for the centralization of Tibet. The Gelug representative in eastern Tibet, Pabongkha (P'awongk'a) Rimpoche (1878–1943) did his best to thwart the movement. The Chinese intervention in the 1950s defused the conflict temporarily, but it is now resuming on the international stage. Virtually all of the Tibetan lamas now teaching on the international circuit are students either of Pabongkha Rimpoche or of the Ri-meds.

11.5 THE DYNAMICS OF TIBETAN RITUAL

Tibetan religious thought and practice revolve around Tantric ritual. Unless one is acquainted with the ritual patterns, it is impossible to understand the tradition at all. Although we have already discussed Tantric ritual in Chapter 6, the Tibetans have added their own style and interpretation to the ritual, derived largely from their shamanic background. Thus their distinctive amalgam deserves a separate discussion, which we will attempt here.

In the simplest terms, shamanism is the effort to gain knowledge or power from altered states of consciousness. The various shamanic traditions around the world differ primarily as to which altered states they regard as significant, how they try to induce them, and what uses of these states they regard as most worthwhile. We have already noted how early Buddhism was a variant of shamanism, although it combined shamanism with philosophy in a way that had never been attempted before. Tantra is also a variant of shamanism, in that it uses the altered state of mind induced through sexual or quasi-sexual yoga and a controlled form of spirit possession for the attainment of power. Modern shamanic practices in Tibet, which seem to continue a tradition predating Buddhism, are also largely concerned with spirit possession and the acquisition of power, which may help explain why the Tibetans were so drawn to Tantra during the propagation of Buddhism to their country.

As we noted previously, indigenous Tibetan religion involved four activities: divination, the ushering of the spirits of the dead to the afterlife, exorcism, and coercion. Of these, divination is the only practice where pre-Buddhist forms of spirit possession still predominate. Tibetans may resort to mediums, termed *lha-pa* (god-possessed) or *dpa' bo* (heroes), although there are milder forms of divination, such as astrology, brought over from India, that they may resort to as well. These mediums are used by people on all levels of society. In 1959, for instance, the decision for the Dalai Lama to flee the advancing Chinese troops was made by the State Oracle.

A manuscript found at Tun-huang suggests that, in pre-Buddhist times, the purpose of ushering spirits of the dead to the afterlife was primarily to make sure that they stayed put and did not return to bother the living. This practice has long since been brought into the framework of Tantric theory through the *Bardo T'ödröl*—known in the West as the *Tibetan Book of the Dead*—which is chanted for the first 49 days after a person's death to help him/her circumvent the fruits of karma and safely negotiate the hazards of the postdeath *bardo,* or intermediate state. Ideally, through this guidance, the spirit may escape the need for rebirth altogether; failing that, it can be directed to a decent rebirth. This guidance is intended primarily for those who have not mastered Tantric ritual, for the adept should have enough experience with the bardos experienced during lifetime that the death bardo should pose no problems.

There are four bardos in all: the mental space between two events, the space between two thoughts, the space between sleeping and waking (the dream bardo), and the space after death (the death bardo). In all of these spaces—which form the openings toward altered states of consciousness—is an intense experience of clear light that, if one is unfamiliar with it, can be terrifying. The Tibetans feel that if one feels terror at the light after death, one will not be able to deal skillfully with the various possibilities for rebirth. Thus the highest aim of all religious practice, in their eyes, is to familiarize oneself thoroughly with the "child light" appearing in the bardos that can be experienced during one's lifetime, so that one will skillfully let it be subsumed into the "mother light" appearing at death. In this way, one can master the rebirth process if one has inclinations toward being a tülku or a bodhisattva, or escape it entirely if not.

For most people, however, their ability to negotiate the dangers of the spirit world around them is of more immediate concern than their fate after death. These issues are covered under the topics of exorcism and coercion. Little is known about how Tibetans handled these issues before the propagation of Buddhism, although the Tun-huang manuscript previously mentioned suggests that one of the reasons the Tibetans adopted Buddhism was because it had more effective techniques for dealing with these problems. On the simplest level, the doctrine of karma provides a rationale by which one's good acts may tip the balance of power in one's favor. In this sense, Tibetan popular Buddhism is similar to what we have already seen in Thai popular Buddhism (see Section 7.5): Merit, interpreted in a ritual way, is a form of power that can override but does not necessarily abrogate the power of the spirit world. The Tibetans have devised a number of almost mechanical ways of increasing one's stock of merit. For people in general, this can include repeating Avalokiteśvara's mantra, *Oṃ maṇi-padme hūṃ;* writing mantras on flags, which are considered to repeat the mantra in one's stead each time the flag flaps in the wind; and spinning "prayer wheels" containing mantras inscribed on slips, which are thought to repeat the mantra each time the wheel is spun. Another popular form of acquiring merit is making pilgrimages to pay respect to important religious sites (Strong *EB*, sec. 7.5.1).

These merit rituals, however, are rather amateurish compared with the skills of a Tantric master. Although we noted the ritualistic nature of merit making in Thailand, the Tibetan Tantric master takes this ritualism to a professional level for which there are few parallels in other Buddhist cultures. Professional Tantrists come in a wide variety of forms—celibate monks and nuns, noncelibate lay practitioners, and solitary hermits—but here we will focus on the ritualism in a typical moderate-size monastery to provide an idea of how Tantric ritual has been domesticated into a socially accepted form for the acquisition of spiritual power and its application to a wide variety of ends. The monastery—a Kagyü provincial center influenced by the Ri-med movement and located in eastern Tibet—is no longer functioning, but its survivors have transported its practices to northern India and continue to maintain hope that they will someday be allowed to return and rebuild what they have lost.

The monastery was located in a valley surrounded by low, grassy hills. A large walled compound, it contained two main temples where group rituals were held, workshops for the creation of ritual implements, and row houses capable of housing three hundred monks. Farther up the hill was a hermitage where the monks were expected, at least once in their lives, to go on a retreat lasting for three years, three months, and three days. In permanent residence at the hermitage were 13 yogins, termed *vidyādharas,* who spent their entire lives following the example of Milarepa. If one of them died, one of the ordinary monks who showed the proper talent was assigned to replace him so as to keep the number constant.

Because families in the area were expected to donate a set number of their young sons to become monks—a so-called "monk tax"—to keep the monastery's population at a viable number, not all of the monks exhibited a religious avocation. The practical running of the monastery, however, offered plenty of activities for those who were less religiously inclined. The monastery needed craftsmen to provide a steady output of ritual implements, and security guards to protect it from bandits and thieves. Almost all the monks kept their own dairy cattle, tended gardens, and were expected to provide and prepare their own meals. Aside from maintaining celibacy, they led lives little touched by the Mūlasarvāstivādin rules they studied. Their support came from their families and from fees for their performance of rituals for the local laity. Generally free to come and go, they were subject to the rule of the abbot only if they happened to take him as their Tantric master. The temple as a whole, in addition to receiving donations from wealthy donors, sponsored trading ventures and caravans to supplement its income.

As one observer has noted, Tibetan Tantrism is a performing art, and the life of the monks was devoted to becoming skilled performers. This involved learning not only the techniques of the art, but also the proper altruistic motivation for performing it. A society believing firmly in the reality of ritual power could not wisely support its practice by anyone who did not have the proper motivation. Young monks, in addition to taking minor roles in the morning and afternoon group rituals, devoted their time to learning the basics of classic Tibetan. At the age of 20, they began their education in the colleges associated with the temple. Unlike the great Gelug universities in Lhasa, the course here took only 8 to 10 years, although it covered the same five basic texts. Here the emphasis was less on mastering the controversies that had built up around the texts over the centuries in the pursuit of the correct "object of negation" than on gaining familiarity with the basic ideas they contained. Upon completion of this course, the monk took a three-year training course in ritual techniques: mudrās, chanting, the making of offerings, the use of ritual musical instruments, ritual dancing, and the painting of maṇ-ḍalas. The painting of maṇḍalas was particularly important, for it aided the monk in the process of visualization so central to the practice of Tantric ritual.

Once this course had been completed, the monk was encouraged to begin his retreat, for only on retreat could he devote himself full-time to the mastery of the ritual, and only when he had completed the retreat could he be considered a lama. The training here would begin with an initiation—given by a lama, who in the course of the ceremony identified himself with the central deity of the ritual—authorizing the trainee to attempt the ritual. Without this authorization, a trainee who attempted the ritual would be considered a trespasser and would not be safe from having the ritual power backfire on him. Prior to the initiation, the trainee would have to take certain vows, in addition to his monastic and bodhisattva vows, which would include injunctions against speaking ill of one's lama, speaking ill of women, divulging secret doctrines to the uninitiated, being friendly with evil people, or dwelling among Hīnayānists.

Once the initiation was granted, the trainee would further prepare and purify himself for the ritual with the four common and uncommon preliminaries. The common preliminaries, so called because they were common to all Mahāyāna practitioners, were a reflection on the difficulty of attaining a human birth, on death and impermanence, on the principle of karma, and on the horrors of rebirth in saṃsāra. The uncommon preliminaries, specific only to Tantra, consisted of a series of purification rites accompanied by visualizations. The trainee visualized the field of hosts—the assembled deities and lamas of his lineage—and prostrated to them one hundred thousand times. He then visualized the primary deity of his ritual and recited the deity's one hundred-syllable mantra one hundred thousand times. He offered the maṇḍala one hundred thousand times to his lama lineage (Strong *EB*, sec. 7.5.3), and finally, through prayer and yoga, made their empowerment enter into himself one hundred thousand times. At the conclusion of each stage, he absorbed the maṇḍala into himself. This process completed, he was prepared to take on the central ritual.

Tantric deities have both a personal and an impersonal aspect, and thus the basic pattern of the central ritual consisted of an offering, to arouse the deity's heart, and an evocation, in which one used the deity's mantra to coerce the impersonal power set in motion by the deity's original vow or pledge to become a deity or to protect Buddhism. The deities who were the focus of these rituals fell into three classes, called the Three Basic Ones, which for Tibetan Buddhism superseded the Triple Gem in immediate importance. The three classes were members of one's lama lineage (including one's personal lama);

high Tantric patron deities subsumed under the five families of Buddhas (see Section 6.3.2); and ḍākinīs (see Section 6.3.4). To this list were added the "Lords," fierce patron deities of the particular monastery or school, who had their own special rituals that had to be practiced twenty hours every day by a monk especially assigned to the task in a small, dark, grotesquely decorated room. If these rituals were not carried out, the Lord would turn against the monastery.

As we mentioned previously, any socially approved form of Tantrism must be based on socially approved forms of motivation. Thus each time the central ritual was performed, it was bracketed by mantras representing the Three Sacred Things: awakening bodhicitta and contemplation of emptiness beforehand, and dedication of merit afterward. One standard list of the steps in the awakening bodhicitta stage included mantras for homage, offering, confession of sins, rejoicing in the merit of others; an entreaty that the deity reveal the Dharma; a prayer that the deity not pass away into nirvāṇa; and dedication of one's own merit. The "contemplation of emptiness" stage was a mantra referring to emptiness; while reciting it, the practitioner was supposed to reflect, if ever so briefly, on the proper meaning of the concept. In this and all the other steps in the ritual, the practitioner was to develop speed and accuracy not only in the repetition of the mantra and the performance of the mudrās, but also in the processes of visualization and contemplation that were supposed to accompany them, thus engaging his entire body, speech, and mind in the ritual world. In the case of the Three Sacred Things, these steps repeatedly made real to the practitioner the principle that compassion and wisdom should underlie his exercise of ritual power.

The ritual proper was the process of generation, which involved three steps: visualization of the deity's maṇḍala, abandonment of one's own world and identity so as to assume the deity's identity through the power of the mantra, and recollection of purity (see Section 11.2.2). The assumption of the deity's identity, or "pride," was crucial in that one could not expect to control the deity's power unless one "became" the deity. The recollection of purity—another reference to emptiness—was essential for returning to the emptiness from which the deity had sprung so that one could make contact with the source from which all things come, and thus be able to exercise power over them.

Next, the element of choice came into the ritual, for one could decide what to do with one's acquired power. A traditional text lists two basic uses for ritual power, extraordinary and ordinary. The one extraordinary use is the attainment of the Innate Union of Clear Light and Emptiness, which is accomplished through the process of perfection. Various texts explain this stage in different ways, depending on how much emphasis they place on physical yoga or the analytical insight needed for the proper apprehension of emptiness. Essentially it was a process whereby one coerced one's way into the deity's awareness of emptiness—called its knowledge body, as opposed to its mantra body assumed in the process of generation—and so immersed oneself in the emptiness of Awakening.

In the ordinary uses of ritual power, one generated the deity once again, this time in front of one, and then directed it into an object (say, a flask of water to be used for its ritual power), a person (such as a new initiate), or the sky (as when one wanted to drive away a hailstorm). These ordinary uses of power came in three levels: high, medium, and low. The high-level attainments were particular abilities that sprang spontaneously from one's karmic background; the medium attainments covered all the classic powers of Indian yoga—such as clairvoyance, the ability to read minds, and so forth—plus practices from traditional Tibetan shamanism; and the lower attainments covered the four functions of pacifying (for example, a quarrel, a disease), increasing (for example, crops), subjugating (for example, a person whose affections one wants to win, an obstreperous spirit), and destroying (for example, crops, buildings, roads). The last category includes the subcategory of liberating, that is, eliminating an enemy and arranging for his/her rebirth in a heaven or Buddha-realm.

The potential for these powers to be grossly misused was one of the reasons why compassion was so emphasized in the preliminary vows and the framework of each ritual performance. A text by Ngawang Lozang (Ngag-dbang bLo-bzang) argued that there were certain cases in which "liberation" could be viewed as a compassionate act, but the *Hevajra Tantra* (see Section 6.3.3) forbade all destructive applications of Tantric power. Tibetan folklore added its own restraints against the unwise or uncompassionate use of such power, stating that anyone who mastered and used Tantric powers without the proper motivation was doomed to a long and miserable rebirth as an angry demon. On occasion, troubles afflicting a particular village might be attributed to such a demon, which indicates that the misuse of Tantric powers was not unknown.

Because the Three Basic Ones contained such a wide range of personalities, different deities were regarded as appropriate for different ritual uses. For instance, Tārā was used primarily in rituals with a directly compassionate purpose; her fierce aspect, Kurukullā, was called on for more aggressive purposes, such as the subjugation of spirits. Thus a monk on retreat would try to master the mantras of as many deities as possible; when he left retreat, he continued to collect initiations, as he could afford, from wandering monks visiting his monastery or from lamas he sought out on his own. This was so that he could have rituals for as many purposes as possible in his personal arsenal. The remainder of his life would be devoted to finding a balance between the ordinary and extraordinary uses of his powers; that is, weighing his supporters' needs for his ritual help against the time he needed to devote to his own pursuit of Awakening.

Life in a Tibetan nunnery was organized around lines similar to those for a monastery, with the same division between ordinary nuns and those on retreat. The main monastic orders all had affiliated nunneries, although there were also independent nunneries run by highly regarded female tülkus (Strong *EB*, sec. 7.7). As is the case with their sisters in Southeast Asia, Tibetan nuns do not ordain as bhikṣuṇīs. With few exceptions, nuns tended to have less opportunity than monks to gain an academic education; they also tended to be less sought after than monks for their ritual powers. This was for two reasons: (1) Aside from rituals associated with Tārā, men in general were considered more capable masters of ritual power than women; and (2) nuns tended to have smaller incomes than monks, because they had fewer supporters seeking their services, which meant that they could not afford the fees charged for the more powerful initiations. This was a vicious circle, because those without the powerful initiations would then tend to attract less support. Thus, as is the case with nuns in Thailand, Tibetan nuns had more time than the monks to devote to private meditation and the extraordinary uses of their ritual powers. This pattern still holds in the Tibetan nunneries set up in India, although the steady influx of refugee nuns from Tibet has imposed added burdens on institutions already at a severe financial disadvantage.

11.6 A TRADITION AT THE CROSSROADS

The Chinese suppression of Tibetan Buddhism in the 1950s and 1960s was unusually cruel, insulting, and thorough. Nuns were raped, monks were tortured and killed, and almost all of the monasteries and nunneries were razed to the ground. Prayer books were used as shoe linings, mattress stuffing, and toilet paper; printing blocks for religious books were used to pave roads. As we noted in Chapter 8, after the death of Chairman Mao the Chinese began pursuing a policy of guarded religious tolerance throughout their country, and to some extent they applied this policy to their colony of Tibet as well. As a result, authorities gave permission for a few monasteries to resume functioning and for a handful of religious monuments to be rebuilt. However, in Tibet this policy of tolerance has been severely restricted because Tibetan monasteries have proven to be hotbeds of anti-Chinese nationalist sentiment. A constant stream of monks and nuns continue to risk the dangers of the Himalayan passes in order to make their way to safety in Bhutan and India rather than let themselves be subjected to the continued brutality of the Chinese garrison.

At the moment, the best hope for the survival of Tibetan Buddhism lies in the monasteries and nunneries being built in India, and among the groups of meditation students and financial supporters cultivated by refugee lamas throughout the West. Western children have begun to be recognized as tülkus, much as happened in Mongolia in the seventeenth century. It remains to be seen whether this will eventually lead to a priest/patron relationship that will return the Tibetans to power in their country—using the media and academia to shape world public opinion so that one of the major world powers will act as the patron—or to the development of a new home base for Tibetan Buddhism in the outside world.

12

Buddhism Comes West

12.1 EUROPE'S EARLY CONTACT WITH BUDDHISM

Prior to the opening of sea routes from Europe to Asia, the story of Europe's contact with Buddhism was one of historical oddities and undocumented possibilities. Among the possibilities, it is known that there was fairly extensive trade between India and the Mediterranean area in the era of the Greek city-states and the Roman Empire. This has led scholars to conjecture about whether the Platonic and Gnostic doctrines of the transmigration of souls originated in India, and also whether the references to Buddhism in the writings of Clement and Origen—two early Alexandrian fathers of the Christian church—can be taken as evidence that King Aśoka's emissaries to the Mediterranean countries actually reached their destination (see Section 3.3). There is also the question of whether the Egyptian Desert Fathers were influenced by Buddhists or other members of the Indian śramaṇa movement. Because the Desert Fathers were the direct inspiration for the first Christian monastic orders, it is possible that Christian monasticism derived indirectly from the same sources as did Buddhism, if not from Buddhism itself. Finally, there is the possibility that the Christian cult of relics was originally inspired by the Buddhist example.

Among the documented oddities, modern scholarship has revealed that in the sixteenth century the Catholic church unwittingly included the Buddha in its list of saints. The saints Barlaam and Josaphat (a corruption of the word *bodhisattva*) derive from the Buddha legend, which had become increasingly garbled as it traveled west from India through Georgia and, in the tenth or eleventh century, began spreading throughout Europe.

Beginning in the thirteenth century as a result of the Crusades, Europeans gradually began to travel overland to Asian Buddhist countries, primarily in the role of occasional ministers to the Khan or—like Marco Polo—as adventurous merchants. When Vasco de Gama discovered oceangoing routes in 1497, he opened Asia to European religious and commercial interests, the primary religious interest being to convert Asians to Christianity. The zeal for this mission led Jesuits to travel to India, Japan, and China in the sixteenth century, and Tibet in the seventeenth. These missionaries made detailed studies—sometimes quite accurate—of the religions they were trying to supplant, although their reports languished, unread, in the Vatican until the twentieth century. Early European colonizers, especially those from the Catholic countries, viewed it as their God-given duty to convert the natives to Christianity and stamp out heathenism. One result of this attitude was the campaign of atrocities the Portuguese committed against Sri Lankan Buddhists during their control of the island during the sixteenth and seventeenth centuries (see Section 7.4.1).

Merchants from the Protestant European countries, perhaps because of their own recent experience with religious intolerance from the Catholic church, tended to be more lenient toward Asian customs and religions. Many of them wrote glowing accounts of the highly civilized, rationally organized societies they encountered in Asia. These accounts had a telling effect in Europe, as they opened the European mind to the possibility that Europe was not the only truly civilized society on Earth. Cultural relativism—the view that cultural values and institutions were not absolutes, but were relative to geographical, historical, and other factors—thus came to be more widely accepted in European intellectual circles. This set the stage for the revolution that was to reshape Western culture at the same time it was to shape all serious Western encounters with Buddhism up to the present day. That revolution was the European and American Enlightenment of the eighteenth century.

12.2 THE AWAKENING MEETS THE ENLIGHTENMENT

The Enlightenment was essentially an effort made by a loosely organized confederation of intellectuals—including Voltaire, Hume, Kant, Diderot, Franklin, and Montesquieu—to liberate Western society from what they considered the intellectual and political tyranny of the past. Tyranny in the intellectual sphere, for most of them, meant the control that the Jesuits and other Catholic clerics had over Western thought, although some of them went so far as to equate this tyranny with the Christian mind-set itself. In the political sphere, they discerned tyranny chiefly in institutions and policies serving the narrow, shortsighted interests of a privileged few. To free the West intellectually, they advanced the view that only the scientific method, which to their minds meant the rational analysis of empirical data, could be the source of absolutely true knowledge. All other sources of knowledge—and religious sources in particular, many of them said—were culturally relative. Thus their intellectual manifesto was an amalgam of empiricism, cultural relativism, pluralism, and eclecticism. Their political manifesto, however, dealt more in absolutes: the belief that the "science of humanity"—the empirical study of human society through the fledgling disciplines of psychology, comparative sociology, and secular history (in which divine forces were not counted as players)—could yield abstract laws that would have the force of mandates for social reform. Among the absolutes they proposed as possessing scientific validity were liberty, equality, and the doctrine of human rights. Although they recognized a potential conflict between their political absolutes and intellectual relativism, they were hopeful that with the advance of the social sciences these conflicts could be resolved. With the passage of time, however, the conflicts became more marked and have consumed Western civilization ever since.

One of the unforeseen effects of the Enlightenment was the role that its program played in the introduction of Buddhism to the West. It provided the rationale for the collection, translation, and study of Buddhist texts, along with the excavation of Buddhist archaeological sites; it opened the minds of individual westerners to the possibility that there might be valuable personal lessons to learn from an Eastern religion; it was responsible for creating splits in Western culture that led westerners to look to Buddhism as a potential means of healing the splits; and it sanctioned the attitude that if Buddhism did not actually offer the solutions that westerners were seeking to solve their own cultural crises, they had the right to reform the religion in line with their knowledge of psychology and other social sciences so that it would, and that in doing so they would be making a positive contribution to the progress of the human race. These four strands of influence, in their various combinations, account for much of the complex interaction between westerners and Buddhism during the past two centuries. Because a strictly chronological survey of this process would be little more than a scattered jumble of facts, the following sections will present a thematic analysis instead.

12.2.1 Buddhism and the Science of Humanity

The Europeans who in the late eighteenth and early nineteenth centuries began the serious recovery of Buddhist texts and archaeological sites in Asia were motivated by two missions. The first was to learn enough about the customs of the nations coming under their power that they could design an enlightened form of colonial rule, one that would combine rational European principles with a sensitivity to local conditions. The second was to add to the body of data available to the growing science of humanity so that a more comprehensive view of the varieties of human experience could place the science on a more solid basis. Initially, in their view, Buddhism formed only a few scattered pieces of the larger puzzle of Asian culture they were trying to comprehend, and they often confused Buddhism with other traditions. Not until 1844 did the French philologist Eugene Burnouf put the pieces together to show that certain religions discovered in China, Tibet, India, Sri Lanka, and Southeast Asia were in fact branches of a single tradition that had had its home in India. Burnouf thus lay the foundation for Buddhology, the scholarly study of Buddhism, that has since spread throughout the west, including Russia, engaging scholars in the fields of philology, comparative religion, history, sociology, psychology, philosophy, and anthropology. The growth of Buddhology reached the point that in 1965 the University of Wisconsin established the first graduate program in Buddhist Studies, and other universities soon followed. Buddhology has also become fashionable in the East, with Japan and Sri Lanka currently providing some of the most prolific members of the field.

In the latter part of the twentieth century, Buddhology—like many other academic disciplines—became something of an end in itself, with little thought for its role in the society at large. However, the twin impulses that originally led to this professional activity—political and social-scientific—are still active to some extent. Buddhologists have been called upon to help Western governments with foreign-policy decisions and to train diplomats going to Asia. Buddhist teachings have also played a role in shaping the science of humanity in the form of the "caring professions." The most notable instance of this role is in the field of transpersonal psychology, which has created a paradigm of mental health that views the practice of meditation as a higher form of mental therapy, rather than as a reversion to infantile states, which was the view previously held by many professional psychologists. Although the theories of transpersonal psychology draw as much on Hinduism and Sufism as they do on Zen and Tibetan Buddhism, they have played an important role in making the practice of meditation in general intellectually respectable to professional psychotherapists. Some therapists even now recommend meditation to their patients, practice it themselves, and advertise their meditational background as part of their professional credentials. Similarly, the medical profession has adopted elementary techniques from Buddhist meditation to treat hypertension and enable patients to cope with chronic severe pain. Social workers in prisons and inner-city neighborhoods have adopted similar techniques to help their clients handle stress.

12.2.2 The Appropriation of Buddhist Ideas

The climate of tolerance and eclecticism in which the study of Buddhism developed has given rise, from the very beginning, to the question of whether Buddhist doctrines might have valid lessons for westerners. Buddhologists themselves have, from time to time, taken stances on this question; some, such as T. W. Rhys Davids, who founded the Pali Text Society in 1886, have regarded their study of Buddhism as a labor of love, whereas others have taken it on more as a labor of hate.

However, for a large part of the nineteenth and twentieth centuries, the most creative answers to the question of what Buddhism has to offer the West have come from outside the academic world. Some of these answers have been only tangentially related to actual Buddhist teaching, but they touch on almost all areas of Western intellectual and artistic life. A thorough account of this process would fill a book, so here we will simply note a few of the more striking examples.

The German philosopher Arthur Schopenhauer (1788–1860) was the first westerner to declare publicly his affinity for Buddhism, seeing in the First Noble Truth an expression of the thoroughgoing pessimism he advocated in his own philosophy. Schopenhauer in turn influenced Richard Wagner, who in the latter part of his life tackled the project of writing an opera on the life of the Buddha but was stymied by the problem of finding a leitmotiv, a dramatic and musical theme, for a character free from passion, aversion, and delusion.

Neither Schopenhauer nor Wagner were Buddhists in the sense of taking refuge in the Triple Gem, but the eclecticism they exemplified has played a prominent role in the West's appropriation of Buddhist ideas. One of the most influential examples of this trend is Carl Jung's theory of psychological archetypes in the collective unconscious of the human race. This theory he developed in the 1930s by taking the doctrine of karma and rebirth that he had encountered in Buddhist and Hindu texts and transforming it into a theory of psychic heredity from the collected karma of one's ancestors. A more modern example of the appropriation of Buddhist ideas is the role that Zen has played in the art and aesthetic theories of avant-garde composers such as John Cage, and of writers such as Allen Ginsberg, Jack Kerouac, Gary Snyder (Strong *EB*, sec. 9.3), and J. D. Salinger. Salinger's novel *The Catcher in the Rye* (1951), for instance, is structured as a kōan meditation on the question, "Where do the ducks in Central Park go in the winter?" No answer is given, of course, and the resolution of the kōan lies in the lessons in compassion that the main character has learned by the end of the book.

In many cases, the appropriation of Buddhist ideas has led to what might be called "extrapolated Buddhism," in that themes are taken out of their original framework and extrapolated to radically different contexts. A prime example of this tendency is the way Catholic contemplatives have adopted Zen teachings and techniques to aid them in the search for God. Pioneers in this process were Father Hugo Enomiya-Lassalle (1898–1990), a German Jesuit missionary to Japan, and Thomas Merton (1915–68), an American Trappist monk. Father Lassalle underwent Rinzai training, became recognized as a master in 1978, and later returned to Europe, where he led Zen retreats drawing kōans from the Bible. Awakening, he taught, was a culturally neutral experience that could be interpreted in terms of any worldview. Thus, for a Christian, it could lead one "along the line that ends in the vision of God." Another contemporary example of extrapolated Buddhism is "engaged Buddhism," which interprets Buddhist teachings on the interdependence of all things as a call to an activist approach to social and environmental reform. Because of the spread of Western values through modern education, this movement has found fervent supporters not only in the West, but also among activist groups in Asia.

12.2.3 The Crisis of Cultural Relativism

Closely related to the issue of eclecticism is that of cultural relativism. The eighteenth-century Enlightenment had advanced the argument that reason and empiricism offered the only absolute truths, whereas the truths of religion were culturally relative. Although this argument did not sway all of the West, it did create a cultural crisis in terms of how the breach between reason and religion could best be healed. Some early Buddhologists indicated their feelings on the matter by referring to the Buddha's Awakening as his "enlightenment." In the late nineteenth century, a number of writers, including Sir Edwin Arnold in his poem *The Light of Asia* (1879), explicitly advanced the case that Buddhism—with its tolerance, its rejection of blind faith, and its invitation for all to test its doctrines in the light of experience—was much better suited than Christianity to heal the breach. The spread of Western science and rationalism to the East meant that Eastern thinkers were confronted with the same problem, and many of them came to the same conclusion: Buddhism, when stripped of its cultural accretions, was the most scientific of all religions. In 1893, when Buddhist reverse missionaries came to America to participate in the first World's Parliament of Religions (Strong *EB*, sec. 9.1), this was the central theme of their message, and it remained a strong theme in the writings of Buddhist polemicists throughout the twentieth century. K. N. Jayatilleke, for instance, devoted books to the assertion that Buddhism was an early version of logical positivism, and his student, David Kalupahana, has been even more vocal in attempting to prove that early Buddhism and early Mādhyamika operated from the same presuppositions as Jamesian pragmatism. A more modern version of the same theme animates the writings of Fritjof Capra and Gary Zukav, who see parallels between the discoveries of quantum mechanics on the one hand and the insights of Mādhyamika and Zen on the other. These parallels, they claim, prove that the breach between scientific method and religious inspiration has been healed.

For many westerners in the twentieth century, however, this theme has seemed irrelevant at best, because the work of Nietzsche, Freud, and their contemporaries at the turn of the century used reason and empirical findings to raise the issue as to whether reason and empiricism themselves were psychologically and culturally relative. What human beings think they perceive and what they regard as reasonable, these thinkers argued, is shaped by their psychological and cultural background; thus any abstractions based on reason and perception must be culturally relative as well. Westerners who accepted these arguments found themselves faced with the question of how experience freed from the taint of cultural prejudices might be achieved. In the early part of the century, continental European philosophy—existentialism and phenomenology in particular—grappled with this issue; by mid-century, Gestalt psychotherapy was experimenting with methods to bring the mind back to a pure state of cognition, free from social and psychological structures. Meanwhile, Asian Buddhists who were aware of these trends had begun proselytizing in the West, presenting Buddhist meditation as an alternative route in the search for an awareness untainted by culture.

In 1905, Shaku Sōen (see Section 10.8), the New Rinzai delegate to the World's Parliament of Religions, had been invited to return to America to teach Zen. The visit resulted in three of his closest disciples' coming to America. One, Nyogen Senzaki, founded Zen groups from the 1920s to the 1950s on the West Coast. The second, Sokei-an, founded a Zen group in New York City in 1930 (the Buddhist Society of America, which became the First Zen Institute of America). The third, D. T. Suzuki (see Section 10.8), became—through his writings and personal influence—the primary interpreter of Zen to the West during his lifetime. His influence is felt to the present day. Suzuki's writings on Zen fell into two contradictory categories: one that insisted that Zen could not be properly understood or practiced outside of the Buddhist context, and one that maintained that the essence of Zen was transcultural or, as he put it, that "Zen is the ultimate fact of all philosophy—that final psychic fact that takes place when religious consciousness is heightened to extremity. Whether it comes to pass in Buddhists, in Christians, or in philosophers, it is in the last analysis incidental to Zen." The essence of Zen, in this light, lies in an aesthetic and spiritual realization of the beauty and perfection innate in each fleeting moment, no matter how ordinary that moment may seem to common perception (see Section 10.7).

This second category of Suzuki's writings was by far the more influential. His separation of Zen from Zen Buddhism gave rise to the impression that Zen might hold the answer to the search for pure, unfettered experience. From this it followed that Zen's connections with aspects of Buddhist doctrine that were more problematic to the modern, relativistic Western mind—such as the teachings on karma and rebirth, the seeming nihilism of nirvāṇa, and the role of ethics on the Path—were simply cultural baggage that could be dispensed with at will. This opened the Buddhist fold to a group of thinkers and artists who felt little or no allegiance toward the Buddhist tradition per se. At the same time, Suzuki's portrayal of meditation as the realization of the beauty to be found in the midst of the ordinary has had an overwhelming influence on how meditation has been taught in the West—an influence that has extended not only to Rinzai Zen, but also to Sōtō, Sŏn, Thiền, Dzogchen, and even Theravādin vipassanā.

In the 1960s, Thomas Kuhn's landmark book *The Structure of Scientific Revolutions* (1962) furthered the crisis of cultural relativism by advancing the thesis that even the physical sciences are not purely empirical, but are shaped by intellectual presuppositions, called paradigms, that determine how empirical data are selected and ignored. At the same time, the rise of the drug culture exposed large numbers of westerners to aspects of expanded consciousness and intensified perception that went beyond standard paradigms in psychology and logic, and that had obvious parallels with Buddhist and Hindu teachings on the nature of the mind. These were among the main factors leading to an explosion of interest in the possibility of unconditioned experience to be found within the mind, and two Asian Buddhist teachers came to America in time to direct part of the force of this explosion into the practice of Buddhist meditation.

One of these teachers was Shunryu Suzuki-roshi (not to be confused with D. T. Suzuki), a priest of the Sōtō Zen tradition who founded the San Francisco Zen Center in the early 1960s. His teachings made it clear to his students that many of the formalities of Sōtō practice were not mere cultural baggage, but had an intrinsic relationship to the attainment of what he called Big Mind. Suzuki-roshi's concept of Big Mind—as explained in his book *Zen Mind, Beginner's Mind* (1970)—referred to the innate oneness of consciousness from which all beings are born and to which all return after death. The purpose of meditation, he said, was to realize the perspective of Big Mind in all one's activities and perceptions so as to be able to maintain one's composure in the midst of change and to be open to the innate perfection of each moment as it passed. The image with which he illustrated this concept was Yosemite Falls. The drops of water leave the oneness of the river as they fall over the rock ledge, only to rejoin that oneness at the bottom of the cliff; Zen enables one to remain upright through the interval of separation and fall. Thus the freedom offered by Zen was one to be found within the world, and not by escaping it. Although Suzuki-roshi insisted that the insights of Zen were radically different from those induced by psychedelic drugs, some Americans could see in his depiction of meditation a safe, disciplined method for stabilizing mental states that they had already encountered in their exposure to psychedelic substances.

Although he stressed the necessity of the formalities of Zen practice, Suzuki-roshi declined to establish an ethical code for his students, on the rationale that ethics were relative to culture. Such a code, he said, would have to be developed gradually over time through trial and error, as Western practitioners applied the perspective of Big Mind to the affairs of their daily life. Again, even though Suzuki-roshi insisted that Americans might end up needing more rules than the Japanese, his general ethical relativism had an obvious appeal to the generation that had pushed through the revolution in American sexual mores.

The other teacher who had a large impact on the spread of Buddhism at this time, Chögyam Trungpa, took an even more radical approach to the question of ethics. Trained in the Tibetan Ri-med (Unrestricted) movement (see Section 11.4), Trungpa viewed ethical norms as part of the "bureaucracy of the ego" that meditation was intended to overthrow. As was the case with both Suzukis, he taught that the purpose of meditation was to attain intensified perception in this life, freed from the strictures of the ordinary mind, although—following his Dzogchen training—he viewed this level of perception as a realization of the light innate in all things. His proposed method of attaining this free mode of perception was a typically Tibetan emphasis on the centrality of the teacher–student relationship, expressed in the terminology of Gestalt psychotherapy. The ideal relationship was of a "raw, naked" variety, in which the teacher called into question all of the student's ego defenses and ruthlessly stripped them away so as to leave only the pure nature of the mind. Trungpa's writings—in particular, the book *Cutting Through Spiritual Materialism* (1973)—were quite popular, and his frank rejection of ethical norms notorious. In addition to founding the Naropa Institute, a center for Buddhist studies in Boulder, Colorado, he established a network of meditation groups and retreat centers throughout the United States and Canada.

The general mood of cultural relativism affected even the conservative Theravādin meditation methods that began appearing in the West in the 1970s. In 1975 a band of Americans—including Joseph Goldstein, Sharon Salzberg, and Jack Kornfield—who had studied the Mahasi Sayadaw method of vipassanā meditation in Asia (see Section 7.5), established the Insight Meditation Society in central Massachusetts. Through their work, this society has become the major lay center for the practice of vipassanā in the West. Although they have enforced the Five Precepts (see Section 3.4.4) during their retreats, not until the early 1990s did the group formally adopt a code of conduct for its teachers outside of the retreat context. Based on the Five Precepts, the code reflected their desire to make the precepts more appropriate to "this particular time in history and in this specific cultural setting." The precept against use of intoxicants, for example, was changed to forbid only the misuse of intoxicants. The precept against illicit sexuality was changed to forbid sexual exploitation, which in practical terms meant that a teacher should observe a three-month moratorium after a retreat before entering into a sexual relationship with a former student. There was some disagreement over whether the precept against killing would cover abortion and the killing of insect pests, so the group agreed to leave these particular issues unsettled for the time being.

Meanwhile, in 1977, Sumedho Bhikkhu, an American trained in the Thai forest tradition (see Section 7.5.2), had been invited to establish a Theravādin monastery in England. He managed to attract a large following, and his chief monastery, Amaravati, now has three branches in other parts of England, as well as affiliates in Switzerland, Italy, Australia, New Zealand, and America. Although the monks and nuns at these monasteries have made only slight adjustments in the precepts they follow, eclecticism and cultural relativism play a role in the Dharma they teach. The purpose of religious practice, according to Venerable Sumedho, is to realize the ultimate reality that is found by transcending one's cultural conditioning. He calls the Buddhist approach to this process the practice of being, rather than trying to become, enlightened. It involves maintaining a reflective attitude toward the way things are in the body and mind in the present, letting events arise and go to cessation on their own, and opening to the state of peaceful emptiness that contains their arising and ceasing. He notes, however, that contemplative traditions in all major religions can lead to the same state. Thus one's choice of a religious path is a matter of personal preference, as no one religion can claim to possess the only true way. What matters most is that one trust in the conventions of one's chosen tradition and devote oneself fully to a life of wisdom. In saying this, he breaks from the traditional Theravāda assertion that nirvāṇa is unlike the goals of other religions, and that the Noble Eightfold Path is the only way there.

Suzuki-roshi died in 1971, and Chögyam Trungpa in 1987. Both had appointed American Dharma heirs shortly before their deaths; both of their heirs quickly became involved in sex scandals and were eventually removed from their appointments by their organizations. Soon similar scandals in other Zen, Sŏn, and Tibetan centers, involving Asian as well as American teachers, brought home that these were not isolated instances but part of a general pattern: the unsettled questions of whether a person officially recognized as Awakened is subject to ethical norms; whether "officially recognized" Awakening is a valid institution; and whether the power of a practice group is to be invested in the teacher or in the group as a whole. The role that cultural relativism had played in bringing these groups into existence made the issue of ethical norms particularly slippery in resolving these questions. Some members of these groups maintained that such norms are part of the puritanical tradition that American Buddhists will have to abandon, whereas others pointed out the central role that ethics has played in Buddhism from its earliest days. Thus, the crisis of cultural relativism that brought many to the practice of Buddhist meditation in the first place has now become a crisis within Western Buddhism itself.

12.2.4 Calls for Reform

Like their Enlightenment forebears, Western Buddhists have combined their cultural relativism with a fairly absolutist program for institutional reform. The Enlightenment's belief that absolute truths could be found through the social sciences has long given westerners a strong sense that not only their own culture, but also the cultures of other people, should bend to the findings and hypotheses of these disciplines. As westerners began entering the Buddhist fold, this attitude led them quickly to begin calling for reforms, subjecting what they viewed as the relative truths of Buddhism to the absolute truths of their vision of comparative religion, history, psychology, and other social sciences.

This Western tendency has been present since the nineteenth century. Henry Steel Olcott and Helena Blavatsky, the American and Russian founders of the Theosophical Society, sailed to Sri Lanka in 1880 and amid much publicity became the first westerners to take refuge in the Triple Gem (see Section 7.4.1). They quickly assumed the role of Buddhist leaders, recommending such extensive reforms to remove what they viewed as superstitious elements in Sri Lankan Buddhism that most of their newfound following eventually left them. Other Western reformers took the anticlericism they had inherited from the Enlightenment and focused it on Buddhist monks. In the 1920s, Caroline A. F. Rhys Davids, president of the Pali Text Society, argued that all great religions must be life affirming; the life-negating ideas recorded in the early Buddhist texts thus were monkish inventions that could not possibly have come from the mouth of such a great religious figure as the Buddha. As a result, she said, the job of a Western Buddhologist was to ferret out the few remaining glimmerings of the original teachings and to expose all life-negating elements as later interpolations. Throughout the first half of the twentieth century, westerners who went to Asia in search of Buddhist truths—including Alexandra David-Neel, Dennis Lingwood (Sangharakshita), and Ernst Hoffman (Lama Anagarika Govinda)—lectured their Asian hosts on how monasticism had perverted the Buddha's doctrines. Although a number of westerners, beginning in 1900, went to Asia for ordination, not until the 1950s did any of them submit to long-term training under an Asian Buddhist master on Asian terms. The year 1962 marked the first time a Western Theravādin bhikṣu undertook the requisite five-year apprenticeship under a senior Asian mentor. Prior to that, all Western bhikṣus had either returned to the West soon after ordination or had established their own centers in Asia where they could study and practice the Dharma as they saw fit, thus effecting their own personal reforms in the tradition.

With the establishment of Buddhist centers in the West in the latter half of the twentieth century, the clamor for reform has become more widespread and intense. Some of the proposed reforms simply combine various Buddhist traditions, a combination now possible because, for the first time since Buddhism left India, all surviving Buddhist schools speak a common language (Strong *EB*, sec. 9.2). Whether or not this eclecticism becomes institutionalized, it is already a fact of life, with Theravādin vipassanā teachers studying Dzogchen, Zen priests studying the Pali Pāṭimokkha, Tibetan lamas quoting Zen masters in their talks, and practicing Buddhists of all schools reading books by Buddhist masters of every available tradition.

Other de facto reforms have integrated Western values into Buddhist practice. These include the increasing role played by women in the running of Buddhist organizations and the larger role played by laity in the teaching and practice of meditation. These reforms, however, are not without precedent in the Asian traditions (see Sections 6.3.4, 10.5.2, 10.10). What is unprecedented is a reform that has gone virtually unnoticed: the redefinition of the Third Refuge, the Sangha, to include all people who practice Buddhist meditation, regardless of whether they regard themselves as Buddhist or not. This concept—fostered in particular by Chögyam Trungpa and Thich Nhat Hanh (see Section 9.11), and accepted by many Western Buddhists of all schools—has expanded the notion of Sangha to cover an area wider than that of even the classical notion of pariṣad (see Section 2.4), including in the Third Refuge people who have not taken refuge themselves. It has also changed the notion of the kind of refuge one might expect from the Triple Gem—in this case, the psychological support one might receive from those who are sympathetic to one's chosen path of practice.

Whether these reforms will become distinctive, long-term features of Western Buddhism or are simply part of a passing phase is too early to tell. But a number of writers have advanced the case that the reforms should become normative—not only for Western Buddhism, but for Asian Buddhism as well. The most comprehensive and systematic argument for this case has been presented by a student of Chögyam Trungpa, Rita Gross, in her book *Buddhism After Patriarchy* (1993). Following the classical pattern of Enlightenment scholarship, Gross's absolute values are abstractions drawn from the study of history, psychology, and comparative religion. She argues that Buddhism, like all other religions, must accept that it is a system of myths with no absolute claims to scientific or historical truth. It should also abandon as inappropriate any concepts of dualistic, other-worldly freedom—such as a nirvāṇa beyond this world—and reject as irrelevant such questions as rebirth and the individual's preparation for death. Instead, it should focus on its sufficient role: mandating gender equality and providing a psychological grounding of wholeness, balance, tranquility, and deep peace so that one may (1) find the freedom within the world by developing composure amid change, (2) communicate with and provide comfort for other people, and (3) develop a sense of care and appreciation for the Earth. Any Buddhist doctrines, practices, or institutions that deemphasize this role for the sake of other goals, she argues, are holdovers from a patriarchal mind-set and so should be dropped from the tradition altogether.

Another reformer who uses social science paradigms to rethink the Buddhist Path is Jack Kornfield. In his book *A Path with Heart* (1993), he combines his background in humanistic psychology and meditation with his extensive reading in comparative religion to present a picture of the Buddhist Path that transcends the limitations that he claims are inherent in all practice lineages. He asserts that spiritual practice should center on issues of relationship and personal integration. Many would-be meditators are so wounded psychologically by modern society, however, that meditation alone cannot deal effectively with these issues in their lives. Thus they might benefit by combining humanistic psychotherapy with their meditation. This does not mean that one gets one's psychological house in order and then strikes out for nirvāṇa, he says. Rather, one should use psychotherapy step-by-step along one's way to heal the mental wounds uncovered in meditation and to integrate newfound insights into one's life. Although he warns against becoming obsessed with goals in the practice, he concludes his discussion with a personality profile of the type of maturity that spiritual practice should produce: a sense of the sacred that is both integrated and personal; an embracing of opposites; an attitude of nonidealism, kindness, immediacy, questioning, flexibility, and ordinariness; and the ability to express these qualities in the entire range of one's relationships—to one's family, one's sexuality, the community, the environment, politics, money—every being and action. Spiritual practice begins and culminates, he claims, in the simple presence of intimacy. The ultimate test of the success of one's practice should be the ability to love well, live fully, and let go.

Other reformers limit themselves more to institutional restructuring. For instance, there are attempts to revive the Tibetan and Theravādin Bhikṣuṇī Sanghas (Strong *EB*, sec. 9.2) and to design new formats for teaching and practicing meditation so that lay people may devote more time to the practice without sacrificing their families and careers. However, there is wide disagreement among reformers as to what in the Buddhist tradition is dispensable and what needs to be retained. Even the doctrine of rebirth, which is one of the few common denominators among the various Asian traditions, is controversial in Western Buddhist circles. Commentators writing on the Western Buddhist movement as a whole, when trying to define its unifying thread, are often reduced to such statements as "the essence of Buddhism is an inexpressible living force" or "the Zen that tries to define itself isn't true Zen." As long as there continues to be this inability to define or agree on what in the tradition is distinctively and essentially Buddhist, any attempted reforms will probably further fragment Western Buddhism rather than provide it with a distinctive, unified form.

12.3 THE TWO SIDES OF NORTH AMERICAN BUDDHISM

We have so far touched on one side of the Buddhist tradition in the West, what might be called Euro-Buddhism in that it has been shaped by European and Euro-American cultural norms. In North America at present, this side of the tradition includes transmissions from all the major divisions of Buddhism existing in the world today: Rinzai, Sōtō, Jōdo-shū, Jōdo-shin-shū, Nichiren, and Shingon from Japan; Ch'an and Ching-t'u (Pure Land) from China; Sŏn from Korea; Thiền from Vietnam; all four major lineages from Tibet; and a variety of meditational schools from the Theravādin countries, including the Mahasi Sayadaw and U Ba Khin methods from Burma, and the forest traditions from Thailand. Although Rinzai Zen had a virtual monopoly on Euro-Buddhism in North America prior to the 1960s, Tibetan forms have since become predominant through the missionary work fueled by the Tibetan diaspora. For all the differences among these various groups, however, they share a common universe of discourse that rarely includes the other side of North American Buddhism: Asian-American Buddhism, or that practiced by Asian immigrants and their descendants.

The largest and most organized of the various Asian-American groups are the Buddhist Churches of America, which follow the Jōdo-shin-shū tradition and draw their membership largely from the Japanese-American community. Founded prior to World War I, their umbrella organization links sixty independent churches and sponsors educational programs and publications. As their designation *churches* suggests, these groups have adopted a Protestant American style of Sunday-morning worship. Other Asian-American Buddhist groups include large Chinese Buddhist organizations on the West Coast, and more than 150 loosely organized Theravādin temples serving Southeast Asian refugees and immigrants scattered throughout the United States and Canada. Few of these groups are engaged in outreach work to the larger American community, and few have any interest in Euro-Buddhism of any variety.

The reasons for the lack of interest are many, but they center around the feeling that Euro-Buddhists have little respect for or understanding of the Buddhist tradition. The Western tendency, born of cultural relativism, to glorify a playful attitude toward the tradition (Strong *EB*, sec. 9.3) they find particularly offensive. Some Asian-American Buddhists also see Euro-Buddhists repeating what they regard as the mistakes in their own native traditions. For instance, the call to restructure meditation to fit it better into the constraints of lay life, in their eyes, is little more than an attempt to domesticate Buddhism in a thoroughgoing way (see Section 7.5.1). Finally, Asian-American Buddhists question whether a Buddhism that bends too readily to Western secular norms will have the authority or vision to offer a valid critique of the spiritual limitations of Western secular society. Euro-Buddhists, however, view Asian-American Buddhists as being too engaged with the cultural trappings of their traditions to be able to communicate meaningfully to Western spiritual and intellectual concerns. In short, each side is alienated by what it views as elements of "designer Buddhism" in the other.

Perhaps the most basic difference dividing the two sides of North American Buddhism lies in their reading of Buddhist history. Euro-Buddhists tend to focus on the bewildering variety of forms that Buddhism has assumed as it has adapted to the various countries to which it has spread in the past. This was especially true when it spread to a civilization such as China—with a well-established, sophisticated culture of its own—so it is only to be expected that Buddhism will have to adapt radically as it comes to the established cultures of the West. Asian-Americans, however, tend to focus on Buddhism's having survived in a recognizable, integral form only through repeated efforts to return to its roots, as with the forest movements in Theravādin countries (see Section 7.5.2), and the many missions from China to India in search of more accurate, authentic texts (see Sections 8.4.2, 8.5). These efforts to stay true to its roots, they say, will be especially necessary in a culture such as modern America, where the impulse to eclecticism and syncretism—to swallow things up in the melting pot—is so strong.

At present, the few meeting grounds for the two sides of North American Buddhism consist of a handful of metropolitan Buddhist councils, the small number of monasteries run for or by westerners, and occasionally an academic classroom. From a historian's point of view, however, it would seem that Buddhism's potential for survival as an integral but culturally relevant religion in America will depend on the ability of the two sides of North American Buddhism to meet and overcome their differences so as to learn from each other's vision of what is essential to their tradition and what it has to offer the modern world.

An Overview of the Buddhist Scriptures

A. The Pali Canon: The *Tipiṭaka* ("Three Baskets")

I. *Vinaya-piṭaka* ("Basket of Discipline")
   1. *Sutta-vibhanga* ("Analysis of the Text")—the rules of the Pāṭimokkha codes with explanations and commentary.
      a. *Mahāvibhanga* ("Great Analysis")—the 227 rules for monks.
      b. *Bhikkhuṇī-vibhanga* ("Nuns' Analysis")—the 310 rules for nuns.
   2. *Khandhaka* ("Groupings")
      a. *Mahāvagga* ("Great Chapter")—rules for ordination, Observance Day, rainy-season retreat, clothing, food, medicine, and procedures of the Sangha.
      b. *Cullavagga* ("Lesser Chapter")—judicial procedures, miscellaneous rules, ordination and instruction of nuns, history of the First and Second Councils.
   3. *Parivāra* ("Appendix")—summaries and classifications of the rules. This is a late supplement.

II. *Sutta-piṭaka* ("Basket of Discourses")
   1. *Dīgha-nikāya* ("Collection of Long Discourses")—34 suttas.
   2. *Majjhima-nikāya* ("Collection of Medium Discourses")—152 suttas.
   3. *Saṃyutta-nikāya* ("Collection of Connected Discourses")—56 groups of suttas.

4. *Anguttara-nikāya* ("Collection of Item-More Discourses")—more than 2,300 suttas grouped by the number of factors in their topics.
5. *Khuddaka-nikāya* ("Collection of Little Texts")
   a. *Khuddaka-pāṭha* ("Little Readings")—a breviary.
   b. *Dhammapada* ("Verses on Dharma")—423 verses in 26 chapters.
   c. *Udāna* ("Utterances")—80 exalted pronouncements of the Buddha, with circumstantial tales.
   d. *Itivuttaka* ("Thus-saids")—112 short suttas.
   e. *Sutta-nipāta* ("Collection of Suttas")—short suttas, mostly in verse of high poetic quality.
   f. *Vimāna-vatthu* ("Tales of Heavenly Mansions")—gods tell the deeds that earned them celestial rebirths.
   g. *Peta-vatthu* ("Tales of Ghosts")—how various persons attained that unfortunate rebirth.
   h. *Thera-gāthā* ("Verses of the Elders")—stanzas attributed to 264 early monks.
   i. *Therī-gāthā* ("Verses of the Eldresses")—stanzas attributed to 73 early nuns.
   j. *Jātaka* ("Lives")—tales ostensibly reporting the former lives of Śākyamuni. The verses in each tale are supposed to have been uttered by the Buddha, and so are considered canonical; but the 547 tales themselves are extracanonical.
   k. *Niddesa* ("Exposition")—verbal notes to part of the *Sutta-nipāta*. The *Niddesa* is second or third century C.E.
   l. *Paṭisambhidā-magga* ("The Way of Discrimination")—scholastic treatment of doctrinal topics.
   m. *Apadāna* ("Stories")—lives and former lives of the saints.
   n. *Buddhavaṃsa* ("Lineage of the Buddhas")—lives of 24 previous Buddhas, of Śākyamuni, and of Maitreya, presented as being told by Śākyamuni.
   o. *Cariya-piṭaka* ("Basket of Conduct")—verse retellings of jātakas illustrating the Bodhisattva's practice of the perfections.

III. *Abhidhamma-piṭaka* ("Basket of Scholasticism")
1. *Dhamma-sangini* ("Enumeration of Dharmas")
2. *Vibhanga* ("Analysis")—more on sets of dharmas.
3. *Dhātu-kathā* ("Discussion of Elements")
4. *Puggala-paññatti* ("Designation of Persons")—classifies types of individuals according to their spiritual traits and stages.
5. *Kathā-vatthu* ("Subjects of Discussion")—arguments about theses in dispute among the Hīnayāna and early Mahāyāna schools.
6. *Yamaka* ("The Pairs")—arranged in pairs of questions; deals with distinctions among basic sets of categories.
7. *Paṭṭhāna* ("Conditional Relations")—24 kinds of causal relation and their almost infinite permutations.

B. The Chinese Canon: The *Ta-ts'ang-ching* ("Great Scripture-Store")

The first printed edition, produced in Szechuan in 972–983 C.E., consisted of 1,076 texts in 480 cases. The standard modern edition is the *Taishō Shinshū Daizōkyō* (*Ta-ts'ang-ching* newly edited in the Taishō reign-period). It was published in Tokyo, 1924–1929, and consists of 55 Western-style volumes containing 2,184 texts. A supplement consists of 45 volumes. The following analysis is of the Taishō edition.

I. *Āgama* Section, vol. 1–2, 151 texts. Contains the Long, Medium, Mixed (= Connected) and Item-more Āgamas (Nikāyas), plus some individual texts corresponding to parts of the Pali Khuddaka.
II. Story Section, vol. 3–4, 68 texts. *Jātakas,* lives of various Buddhas, fables, and parables.
III. *Prajñā-pāramitā* Section, vol. 5–8, 42 texts.
IV. *Saddharma-puṇḍarīka* Section, vol. 9, 16 texts. Three complete versions of the *Lotus Sūtra,* plus some doctrinally cognate Sūtras.
V. *Avataṃsaka* Section, vol. 9–10, 31 texts.
VI. *Ratnakūṭa* Section, vol. 11–12, 64 texts. A set of 49 Mahāyāna Sūtras, some in more than one translation.
VII. *Mahāparinirvāṇa* Section, vol. 12, 23 texts. The Mahāyāna account of Śākyamuni's last days and words.
VIII. Great Assembly Section, vol. 13, 28 texts. A collection beginning with the Great Assembly Sūtra, which is itself a suite of Mahāyāna Sūtras.
IX. Sūtra-collection Section, vol. 14–17, 423 texts. A miscellany of Sūtras, mostly Mahāyāna.
X. Tantra Section, vol. 18–21, 572 texts. Vajrayana Sutras, Tantras, ritual manuals, and spells.
XI. Vinaya Section, vol. 22–24, 86 texts. Vinayas of the Mahīśāsakas, Mahāsanghikas, Dharmaguptakas, Sarvāstivādins, and Mūla-sarvāstivādins. Also some texts on the Bodhisattva discipline.
XII. Commentaries on Sūtras, vol. 24–26, 31 texts on Āgamas and on Mahāyāna Sūtras, by Indian authors.
XIII. Abhidharma Section, vol. 26–29, 28 texts. Scholastic treatises of the Sarvāstivādins, Dharmaguptakas, and Sautrāntikas.
XIV. Mādhyamika Section, vol. 30, 15 texts.
XV. Yogācāra Section, vol. 30–31, 49 texts.
XVI. Collection of Treatises, vol. 32, 65 texts. Works on logic, anthologies from the Sūtras, and sundry treatises.
XVII. Commentaries on the Sūtras, vol. 33–39, by Chinese authors.
XVIII. Commentaries on the Vinaya, vol. 40, by Chinese authors.
XIX. Commentaries on the Śāstras, vol. 40–44, by Chinese authors.
XX. Chinese Sectarian Writings, vol. 44–48.
XXI. History and Biography, vol. 49–52, 95 texts.
XXII. Encyclopedias and Dictionaries, vol. 53–54, 16 texts.
XXIII. Non-Buddhist Doctrines, vol. 54, 8 texts. Sāṃkhya, Vaiśeṣika, Manichean, and Nestorian Christian writings.

XXIV. Catalogs, vol. 55, 40 texts. Successive catalogs of the Canon beginning with that of Seng-yu published in 515 C.E.

C. The Tibetan Canon

I. *Bka'-'gyur (Kanjur)* ("Translation of Buddha-word"). The number of volumes and order of sections differ slightly from edition to edition. The following is according to the Snar-thang (Narthang) version.
   1. *Vinaya,* 13 vols.
   2. *Prajñā-pāramitā,* 21 vols.
   3. *Avataṃsaka,* 6 vols.
   4. *Ratnakūṭa,* 6 vols. A set of 49 Mahāyāna Sūtras.
   5. *Sūtra,* 30 vols., 270 texts, three-quarters Mahāyāna Sūtras and one-quarter Hīnayāna ones.
   6. *Tantra,* 22 vols., over 300 texts.

II. *Bstan-'gyur (Tenjur)* ("Translation of Teachings"). In the Peking edition, this consists of 224 volumes and 3,626 texts, divided into:
   1. *Stotras* (hymns of praise), 1 vol., 64 texts.
   2. *Commentaries on mantras,* 86 vols., 3,055 texts.
   3. *Commentaries on Sūtras,* 137 vols., 567 texts.
      a. *Prajñā-pāramitā* commentaries, 16 vols.
      b. *Mādhyamika* treatises, 17 vols.
      c. *Yogācāra* treatises, 29 vols.
      d. *Abhidharma,* 8 vols.
      e. Miscellaneous, 4 vols.
      f. *Vinaya* Commentaries, 16 vols.
      g. Tales and dramas, 4 vols.
      h. Technical treatises: logic (21 vols.), grammar (1 vol.), lexicography and poetics (1 vol.), medicine (5 vols.), chemistry and sundry (1 vol.), supplement (old and recent translations, indices; 14 vols.).

Pronunciation Guide

As a pan-Asian religion, Buddhism has made use of the major languages of an entire continent. None of these languages is natively written in the Roman alphabet, but all can be transliterated into it. Each system of transliteration carries its own set of pronunciation difficulties. The following guidelines are intended simply to help the student overcome some of the more blatant hurdles to approximating correct pronunciation. They are not complete phonetic guidelines.

Sanskrit and Pali. A few basic rules for pronouncing words in these languages are as follows:

1. Marked vowels: A bar (called a macron) over a vowel makes it long, not so much in quality as in the length of time it is pronounced. Thus:

   ā as in "father"

   ī as in "machine"

   ū as in "rule"

2. Unmarked vowels:

   a as in "about"

   e as in "they"

   i as in "is"

o as in "go"

u as in "rhubarb"

3. Unmarked consonants are generally pronounced as they are in English, with a few exceptions:

c as in "ancient"

k unaspirated as in "skin"

kh aspirated as the *k* in "kin"

ñ as the *ny* in "canyon"

p unaspirated as in "spot"

ph as in "upholstery"

t unaspirated as in "stop"

th as in "Thomas"

4. Retroflex dots under letters—as in **ṭ, ḍ, ṇ**—mean that those letters should be pronounced with the tip of the tongue curled back up into the middle of the mouth, giving them a nasal quality. Exceptions to this rule:

ṣ is pronounced as the *sh* in "sheep"

ḷ as the *l* in "apple"

ṛ as the *ri* in "rig"

5. Other marked consonants:

ś as the *sh* in "sheep"

ṃ as a humming sound, pronounced in the nose and the back of the mouth, much like the *ng* in "sing"

Chinese. Aside from modern place names, such as Beijing, Chinese words in this book are transliterated using the Wade-Giles system, as this is the system found in most scholarly books on Chinese Buddhism. A few peculiarities of the system are as follows:

1. Initials:

ch unaspirated as the *c* in "ancient"

ch' as the *ch* in "chest"

hs as the *sh* in "shirt"

j as the *sur* in "leisure"

k unaspirated as in "skin"

k' aspirated as the *k* in "kin"

p unaspirated as in "spot"

p' aspirated as the *p* in "pot"

t unaspirated as in "stop"

t' aspirated as the *t* in "top"

ts/tz as the *ds* in "reads"

ts'/tz' as the *ts* in "its"

2. Vowels and finals:

a as in "father"

ai as the *i* in "high"

ao as the *ou* in "out"

ei as the *e* in "they"

en as the *un* in "unable"

eng as the *ung* in "rung"

i as in "sit"

ih as the *ur* in "church"

ou as the *o* in "go"

u as in "rhubarb"

ü as it is pronounced in German

ui as the entire word "way"

Japanese. The transliteration system used in this book is the Hepburn system, which has few peculiarities, but the following principles should be kept in mind:

1. Vowels are pronounced as in Italian. Thus **o, e, i, a** are sounded as in "do, re, mi, fa," although the **e** in "re" should be short and clipped. **U** is generally like the *u* in "rhubarb," although often, especially at the end of a word, it is barely pronounced at all. Vowels written with macrons—**ō, ū**—have the same quality as if they were written without macrons, but are sounded for a longer period of time. **Y** is pronounced as in "quickly," and not as in "why."
2. Consonants:

r as the unaspirated *tt* in the American pronunciation of "little"

g as in "go"

3. Double consonants—**nn, pp, kk**—should be pronounced distinctly as double, like the *nn* in "unnecessary."

Tibetan. Like English, Tibetan has a spelling system in which many of the consonants are silent. The Wylie transliteration reproduces all of the letters used to spell a word, but is absolutely useless as a guide to pronunciation. In this book, words and names are introduced in a phonetic rendering, followed by the Wylie transliteration in parentheses, after which the phonetic rendering is used alone. Vowels and consonants in the phonetic rendering are pronounced much as they are in English; vowels with an umlaut—**ü** and **ö**—are pronounced as they are in German.

Korean. Vowels and consonants in the standard Korean transcription system are pronounced much as they are in English, with the following peculiarities:

ae as the *e* in "they"

e as in "let"

ŏ as the *o* in "song"

ŭ as the *u* in "curl"

ŭi as the *i* in "machine"

ch' unaspirated as the *c* in "ancient"

ch as in "chop"

t' unaspirated as the *t* in "stop"

t as in "top"

Other languages. Words in Sinhalese, Khmer, Thai, Burmese, and Vietnamese are rendered in a phonetic form. Two general observations:

a as in "father"

th as in "Thomas"

Glossary

Learning about another vision of life, such as that of Buddhists, requires learning some of the language in which the vision is conceptualized. Often our English equivalents for specific terms carry connotations unwarranted for a different worldview. Thus, it is necessary to view the terms in their context in order to understand them properly. For this reason, the following glossary is an interlocking one. Many of the key terms are defined using terms defined elsewhere in the glossary. If not already known, these other terms—which are italicized—should be consulted as well. Numbers given in brackets indicate sections of the text that provide further background for the term in question.

Unless otherwise noted, all foreign-language terms are in Sanskrit. When the Pali form of the term is sufficiently different from the Sanskrit as to cause possible confusion, the Pali form follows in parentheses. A word immediately following in quotation marks is the literal English meaning of the term, but not necessarily a good translation equivalent. Generally, the first word or phrase that follows the literal equivalent is the translation equivalent chosen for this text.

Abhidhamma Piṭaka. Collection of seven scholastic works of the *Theravāda* school, one of the three traditional portions of the Pali Canon [3.1.3].

Abhidharma (Abhidhamma). "Higher dharma." Systematic analysis of the component factors of experience, based on teachings in the *Sūtras,* explaining physical and mental events without reference to an abiding self [3.2].

Ālaya-vijñāna. Store-consciousness. The Yogācārin teaching of a level of consciousness that contains the seeds of past karma together with pure seeds that will eventually lead to Awakening [4.3].

Anātman (Anattā). Not-self. A term applied to all phenomena with which one may develop a sense of self-identification. In the *Sūtra Piṭaka,* the anātman teaching is used as part of a strategy of diagnosis and therapy to undercut all craving and attachment for the *skandhas.* Beginning with the *Abhidharma* period, it came to take on the status of a metaphysical doctrine denying the existence of a self or soul underlying the phenomena of experience [2.3.1, 3.2].

Anitya (Anicca). Impermanent; inconstant. An attribute of all conditioned phenomena [2.3.1].

Arhant (Arahant). "One who is deserving [of reverence]; worthy"; perfected saint; a person who has attained *nirvāṇa,* destroyed the *āsravas,* achieved the goal of *bodhi,* and who is destined for no further rebirth. In the *Hīnayāna* schools, this term is applied both to the *Buddha* and to the highest level of his noble disciples (śrāvaka); in the *Mahāyāna* schools, it is applied only to the highest level of śrāvakas, who are viewed as seeking a "se̩lfish" *nirvāṇa* [2.2, 5.5.2].

Āsrava (Āsava). Binding influence; effluent; pollutant; fermentation, the ending of which is equivalent to attaining the goal of Buddhist practice. Listed either as three or four: sensuality, becoming, (speculative views), and ignorance [1.4].

Avidyā (Avijjā). Ignorance, particularly of the Four Noble Truths. This is the root cause of *duḥkha* and the first link in the causal chain of *pratītya-samutpāda* leading to recurrent rebirth in *saṃsāra;* its opposite is *bodhi* or *prajñā* [1.4.3].

Bardo (Tibetan). Intermediate state. There are four in all: the mental space between two events, the space between two thoughts, the space between sleeping and waking (the dream bardo), and the space after death (the death bardo). Each of these spaces can form the opening to altered states of consciousness [11.5].

Bhikṣu (Bhikkhu). Buddhist monk.

Bhikṣu Sangha. The Order of Buddhist monks.

Bhikṣuṇī (Bhikkhuṇī). Buddhist nun.

Bhikṣuṇī Sangha. The Order of Buddhist nuns.

Bodhi. Awakening. Comprehension of the nature of Conditioned reality and direct experience of the Unconditioned [1.4.3].

Bodhicitta. Thought or mind of (aspiration for) *bodhi.* In *Mahāyāna* practice, this is the mental attitude the candidate arouses when aspiring to the *bodhisattva* Path [5.1].

Bodhisattva. A being who is to become Awakened (achieve *bodhi),* especially as applied to Gautama, the future Buddha. More generally, in *Mahāyāna* the term applies to (1) those who have aroused *bodhicitta* and (2) those who have attained *bodhi* but who have taken a special vow to continue being reborn into *saṃsāra* rather than entering *nirvāṇa* so as to deliver others from their suffering by aiding in their attainment of Awakening [5.1].

Bon (Tibetan). A semi-indigenous religion of Tibet that combined elements of Buddhism from the First Propagation with native shamanic practices and beliefs [11.2.2].

Brahmā. A god; inhabitant of the heavens of form or formlessness. A state to be attained through the practice of *dhyāna* and the development of the four "Brahmā vihāras" (Sublime Attitudes): goodwill, compassion, appreciation, and equanimity [1.4.2].

Brahmin. Ritual priest of the old Aryan religious tradition. Continued into present times as the upper, sacerdotal caste of the Hindu social system. Related to Brahmanism [1.1].

Buddha. Awakened One. One of several titles from Indian religious tradition that

Gautama claimed as the result of his Awakening (see also *Tathāgata).* Later Buddhist tradition recognized three types of Buddhas: samyak-sambuddhas, rightly self-Awakened teaching Buddhas; pratyeka-buddhas, "private" Buddhas who gain Awakening without a teacher but are unable to formulate teachings to show the Path to others; and śrāvaka-buddhas, or arhants. According to *Hīnayāna* theory, there can be only one samyak-sambuddha at a time; Gautama is the fourth of our current era and will be followed by the final one of the era, Maitreya; also, there are no pratyeka-buddhas when the teachings of a samyak-sambuddha are still extant. According to *Mahāyāna* theory, there are innumerable world systems in the cosmos; although each may be home to only one Buddha at a time, they may all contain Buddhas simultaneously [2.1, 5.5].

Buddhology. (1) Theory of Buddhahood [1.3, 3.2.1, 4.3, 6.3.2–3.3, 8.5.2, 10.4]. (2) The academic study of Buddhism [12.2.1].

Caitya (Cetiya) (in Thai, chedi; in Burmese, zedi). A memorial shrine, especially to the *Buddha* or his disciples, containing relics, sacred objects, or sacred texts. Buddha-images are also classed as caityas [2.5, 3.4.5, 7.5.1].

Ch'an (Chinese). The first syllable of the Chinese word Ch'an-na, which transliterates the Sanskrit *dhyāna.* Originally, this referred simply to one of several vocations open to a monastic. During the T'ang dynasty, several Ch'an lineages developed. Those that survived into the Sung dynasty were regarded as "houses" of a more or less unified Ch'an school [8.5.5].

Ḍākinī. A powerful female deity, capable of flight, associated with Buddhist and non-Buddhist Tantric traditions and derived from earlier pre-Aryan Indian folklore [6.3.4].

Dependent co-arising. See *pratītya-samutpāda.*

Deva. A deity; inhabitant of the heavens of sensual pleasure [1.4.2].

Deva-yoga. The Tantric ritual whereby the initiate takes on the identity of a higher being—in Buddhist cases, a *bodhisattva* or a *Buddha*—thus assuming his/her powers and knowledge [6.1, 6.3.2, 11.5].

Dhāraṇī. "Holding"; a spell or incantation, often formed of syllables from passages or lists of Dharma-topics and said to "hold" the power of those topics. Used to fix the meditator's mind or to invoke a god or goddess (see *mantra)* or to generate beneficial *karma* or power [6.3.1].

Dharma (Dhamma). This word has many meanings in Buddhist texts, depending on context. Meanings occurring in this textbook are (1) Dharma, the teaching of the *Buddha;* the practice of those teachings; the attainment of *nirvāṇa* as a result of that practice [1.4.3]; moral law [3.3]; and (2) dharmas, the basic constituents of all phenomena, mental or physical, in the conditioned realm [3.2].

Dharma-kāya. "Dharma-body." In *Hīnayāna* schools, Dharma-kāya denotes the entirety of the Buddha's teachings; in *Mahāyāna* teachings, Dharma-kāya denotes the cosmic principle of *bodhi* embodied by the *Buddha* and the principle of Buddhahood innate in all beings [4.3].

Dhyāna (Jhāna). Meditative absorption; steady, mindful concentration in a single physical sensation or mental notion [1.3.5, 2.3.2]. Sometimes used to denote meditation in general, rather than specific states of absorption.

Duḥkha. "Dis-easeful"; usually translated as suffering, ill, or stressful. One of the common characteristics of all conditioned reality; all the suffering that beings experience in *saṃsāra* as a result of *avidyā, tṛṣṇā,* and attachment to the five *skandhas* [2.3.1].

Guru. Spiritual teacher; mentor.

Hīnayāna. The Small ("Inferior") Vehicle or Course. The *Mahāyāna* pejorative to denote all Buddhists who rejected the *Mahāyāna* texts and followed the teachings of the early schools of Buddhism that arose between the first and fourth centuries after the death of the *Buddha.* Hīnayānists numbered in the majority throughout the history of Indian Buddhism. Only one Hīnayāna sect, *Theravāda,* survives today, mainly in Sri Lanka and Southeast Asia [4.1].

Kami (Japanese). Spirit; charismatic force, object, or being [10.1].

Karma (Kamma). Intentional act, performed by body, speech, or mind, which—in line with the intention it embodies—will result in happiness or *duḥkha* in this or a future rebirth [1.4].

Kuan-yin (Chinese). The Chinese translation of Avalokiteśvara, the *bodhisattva* of compassion. During the Sung dynasty (960–1279), this *bodhisattva* changed from male to female but later became male again in Japan. Kuan-yin is petitioned for earthly favors such as money, good luck, and children.

Lama (Tibetan; in Sanskrit, *guru*). Spiritual teacher; mentor; master of Tantric ritual [11.5].

Mādhyamika. "Middle School," so called because it claimed to teach the doctrine of *śūnyatā* as a middle position between 'being' and 'non-being'; a *Mahāyāna* school based on the writings of Nāgārjuna [4.2].

Mahāyāna. The Great Vehicle or Course. The self-bestowed name of the teachings of the *bodhisattva* Path that began to appear between 100 B.C.E. and 100 C.E. [4.1].

Maṇḍala. Power circle; cosmoplan used in Tantric meditation and ritual [6.3.1].

Mantra. "Instrument"; short verse or collection of syllables used to evoke a deity, to gain protection against evil or adverse forces, or as a meditation object, especially in *Tantra* [6.3.1].

Māra. "Destroyer," "Tempter," the personification of evil or attachment to conditioned reality; the god of desire and death; defilement and the *skandhas* as personifications of obstacles to release from *saṃsāra.* In Buddhist iconography, Brahmā, Viṣṇu, Śiva, and Indra are occasionally depicted as four forms of Māra, indicating the Buddhist antipathy for the Hindu gods of worldly continuance.

Māyā. Illusion, trick. A term favored by *Mahāyāna* writers to describe the apparent "reality" of *saṃsāra,* which, because it lacks any substantial independent reality, is akin to a bubble or a mirage [4.2].

Mudrā. Sign, seal token; especially a position of the fingers and hands characterizing images of the *Buddha* or other Buddhist figures and practiced in Tantric ritual performance [5.3, 6.3.1].

Nembutsu (Japanese). Japanese translation of the Chinese *nien-fo* [10.5.2].

Neo-Confucianism (Chinese). A renewal and development of Confucianism in the Sung dynasty (960–1279), inspired partly in reaction to Buddhism but also incorporating many Buddhist ideas. This "new" Confucianism received definitive interpretation in the hands of Chu Hsi (1130–1200) and remained the official state orthodoxy until the ushering in of the Republic in 1912 [8.6].

Nien-fo (Chinese). "Reciting *Buddha's* name," "concentrating on the *Buddha*"; eventually the practice of reciting the name of the *Buddha* Amitābha as an expression of having received his saving grace [8.5.3].

Nikāya. (1) Grouping of *Sūtras* found in the *Sūtra Piṭaka,* also called Āgama, text, scripture [3.1.1]; (2) school of early Buddhism [3.2].

Nirmāṇa-kāya. The "apparition-body" of a *Buddha,* corresponding to his physical body and to the apparitions of him that may appear to human beings in visions or dreams [4.3].

Nirvāṇa (Nibbāna). "Unbinding, the extinguishing of a fire." Metaphorical name for the Buddhist goal, conveying connotations of stilling, cooling, limitless emancipation, and peace; release from the limitations of *saṃsāra* through the extinguishing of the "fires" of passion, aversion, and delusion, and through the ending of the *āsravas* [2.3.2].

Pāramitā. "Supremacy"; perfection, practice of a virtue to the point of supreme perfection, especially by a *bodhisattva* [5.1].

Parinirvāṇa (Parinibbāna). Total *nirvāṇa;* denotes (1) the attainment of release from *avidyā, tṛṣṇā,* and attachment to the five *skandhas;* and (2) the utter release from *saṃsāra* attained at the death of a *Buddha* or *arhant* [2.5].

Perfection of Wisdom. In this text, the translation equivalent for the Sanskrit term *prajñā-pāramitā.*

Phenomenology. Study of the phenomena of consciousness as they are directly experienced, without reference to the question of whether or not they correspond to anything outside of experience.

Poṣadha (Uposatha). Observance Day, determined by the phases of the moon. For the laity, these days are times to observe the Eight Precepts and listen to the *Dharma;* they occur on the days of the full, new, and half moons. For monastics, they are times to listen to the *Prātimokṣa,* occurring on the days of the full and new moons.

Prajñā (Paññā). Discernment; wisdom. (The first of these equivalents is closer to the original meaning, as the word is related to the Pali verb pajānāti, which means to discern. Thus this is the equivalent used in this textbook to translate *prajñā* in *Theravāda* and other *Hīnayāna* contexts. "Wisdom," however, has been the established usage in English-language discussions of *Mahāyāna* for so long that to change the usage would amount to an affectation.) Understanding of the true nature of reality, leading to release from bondage to *saṃsāra.* The final step in the stages of the practice, it depends on the previous ones while at the same time strengthening and perfecting them [2.3.1, 5.1].

Prajñā-pāramitā. The perfection of *prajñā.* The *Mahāyāna* designation of the supreme degree of *prajñā,* which views all *dharmas* as *śūnya,* devoid of *svabhāva;* also the designation of the earliest *Mahāyāna Sūtras* [4.1, 5.1].

Prātimokṣa (Pāṭimokkha). The code of monastic discipline [3.1.2, 3.4.1].

Pratītya-samutpāda (Paṭicca-samuppāda). Dependent co-arising; also translated in other works as dependent origination, conditioned genesis, and variations on these. The specific formula analyzing the preconditions (nidāna) in the causal loops connecting *avidyā* with the consequents of birth, aging, death, and the whole mass of samsaric *duḥkha* [1.4.3].

Private Buddha (Pratyeka-buddha). See *Buddha.*

Pudgala. "Person." A designation of relative status—neither ultimate nor conventional truth—to describe what gives cohesion to the personality, transmigrates, and attains *nirvāṇa.* A doctrine asserted by the Pudgalavādins (Personalists) [3.2.2].

Samādhi. Concentration; a mindful state characterized by singleness of object, calm, stability, and absence of distraction; right concentration is equivalent to the four states of *dhyāna* [2.3.2].

Saṃsāra. "The wandering-on"; the round of death and rebirth, into which beings driven by craving *(tṛṣṇā)* are repeatedly born; characterized as *anitya, duḥkha, anātman,* and *śūnya* [1.4.2, 4.2].

Saṃbhoga-kāya. The "recompense-body" or "enjoyment-body"; the glorified body that the Buddha attains as a reward for his *bodhisattva* practices; a transfigured form that the great *bodhisattvas* apprehend when they see him [4.3].

Sangha. "Assemblage, community." This word has two levels of meaning: (1) On the ideal (ārya) level, it denotes all of the *Buddha's* followers, lay or ordained, who have attained at least the level of *srotāpanna;* (2) on the conventional (samvṛti) level, it denotes the Orders of *Bhikṣus* and *Bhikṣuṇīs* [2.4].

Satori (Japanese). Awakening.

Shintō (Japanese). Native, pre-Buddhist beliefs in Japan, centered on the worship of *kami* [10.1].

Śīla. Morality, virtue; precepts of behavior conducive to the development of *samādhi* and *prajñā* [2.3.1, 3.4.4].

Skandha (Khandha). "Heap, mass, aggregate." A term to indicate that all factors with which one might identify one's "self" are in fact impermanent, causally produced aggregations. The five skandhas are (1) form (rūpa, the body or physical skandha); (2) feeling (vedanā); (3) perception, mental label (saṃjñā); (4) thought formations (saṃskāras, plural); and (5) sensory consciousness (vijñāna). These five skandhas constitute the phenomenal world and person; are the five bases for clinging to (taking sustenance from) conditioned existence, resulting in continued rebirth; and are characterized by *anitya, duḥkha,* and *anātman* [2.3.1].

Soteriology. The study or doctrine of salvation; studies of or theories about savior figures such as the *Mahāyāna bodhisattvas.*

Śramaṇa (Samaṇa). "Striver." A member of the renunciant sects of early India (after 800 B.C.E.) whose rule usually required abandoning social and ritual status and whose doctrines denied the validity of Vedic revelation in favor of truths discovered directly from nature through the use of reason or meditative experiences. The early Buddhist etymology for this word comes from "sama," which means "in tune," in the sense that the proper śramaṇa way of life was in tune with what was naturally right [1.2].

Srotāpanna (Sotapanna). Streamwinner, one who has entered the stream leading to *nirvāṇa,* will never relapse, and is destined to be reborn at most seven more times, never in any of the lower realms; the lowest of the four grades of Noble Disciples or saints, which are, in ascending order, (1) srotāpanna; (2) sakṛd-āgāmin (sakadāgāmin), once returner, one who will have to be reborn in the human world only once more to become an *arhant;* (3) anāgāmin, nonreturner, one who will never have to be reborn in this world but who will be spontaneously reborn in the highest *Brahmā* realms, to attain *nirvāṇa* there; and (4) *arhant,* one totally freed from the processes of renewed becoming and birth [2.3.2].

Sthavira (Thera). "Elder." See *Theravāda.*

Stūpa. Memorial shrine or reliquary, especially to the deceased *Buddha* [2.5, 3.4.5].

Sukhāvatī. "Happiness-having"; Pure Land or *Buddha*-realm of the *Buddha* Amitābha (Amita) [5.5.4].

Śūnya. "Empty, zero"; devoid of any substantial independent underlying reality (see *svabhāva).* This is the favorite *Mahāyāna* explication of the earlier *anātman* doctrine, extending it from the *Abhidharma* principle that the person, being composed of *dharmas,* is devoid of self, to the more radical principle that even *dharmas* are devoid of any own-nature [4.2].

Śūnyatā. "Emptiness."

Śūnyavāda. The *Mahāyāna* teaching that all *dharmas* are *śūnya.*

Śūnyavādin. Follower of *Śūnyavāda.*

Superknowledge (in Sanskrit, abhijñā). Knowledge attained through meditation. The six superknowledges are (1) psychic powers, (2) clairvoyance, (3) knowledge of others' minds, (4) memory of one's former lives, (5) clairaudience, and (6) ending of the *āsravas.* In Buddhism, only the last attainment is considered transcendent [1.3.5].

Sūtra (Sutta). A Buddhist text, especially a dialogue or discourse attributed to the *Buddha.*

Sūtra (Sutta) Piṭaka. The collection of discourses included in the early canons [3.1.1, 4.1].

Svabhāva. "Own-nature." In *Hīnayāna Abhidharma* theory, this is the defining characteristic that distinguishes one dharma-type from all others. *Mahāyāna* thinkers attacked this notion on the grounds that no phenomenon dependent on conditions could have an independent nature of its own [3.2, 4.2].

Tantra. Ritual manual, for which the school of Buddhist Tantra is named [6.3].

Tao (Chinese). The Way, the order of the universe, the way one ought to act to be in harmony with the cosmos. A native Chinese concept used to translate a number of Buddhist terms, including *bodhi, Dharma,* and mārga (Path) [8.3, 8.4.1].

Taoism (Chinese). A complex of several systems of practice all claiming as authoritative the early works attributed to Lao-tzu and Chuang-tzu, including philosophical Taoism, alchemical Taoism, and magical/popular Taoism, the latter two being very much interested in physical immortality.

Tārā. "Savioress." Female manifestation of the protective aspect of Buddhahood, especially popular in Tibet. Perhaps her name, taken to mean "star," relates her to the Babylonian Istar, "saving or lucky star" [5.4.4].

Tathāgata. "He who has come or gone thus [that is, on the Path of all the *Buddhas]"* or "He who has reached or become what is really so, the True." The term the *Buddha* used to speak of himself after Awakening.

Tathāgata-garbha. The "womb of Tathāgatahood"; the innate potential for

Buddhahood that, according to later *Mahāyāna* doctrine, is present in all beings [4.3].

Terma (Tibetan). Hidden treasure texts reputedly placed underground, underwater, in the sky, or in "mind" (conceived as the *Dharmakāya* of the *Yogācārins)* by spiritually advanced beings, and discovered by later generations [11.2.2].

Theravāda (Pali for Sthaviravāda). The Teaching of the Elders. An early Buddhist sect that became established in Sri Lanka at the Great Monastery of Anuradhapura about 240 B.C.E.; later to become the dominant form of Buddhism in Sri Lanka and Southeast Asia beginning with the eleventh century C.E. [7.3].

Theravādin. One who holds to the teachings of the Elders.

Tripiṭaka (Tipiṭaka). "Three Baskets"; early Buddhist canon, composed of collections of *Sūtras, Vinaya,* and *Abhidharma.* The Pali Canon is the only complete early canon still extant. In extended usage, this term also applies to later comprehensive collections of Buddhist texts, such as the Tibetan, Chinese, and Korean Tripiṭakas, even though these collections are not divided into three collections [3.1, 8.6, 9.4, 11.3.2].

Tṛṣṇā (Taṇhā). "Thirst," craving, the cause of *duḥkha.* Includes craving for sensuality, for becoming, and for no-becoming. Because tṛṣṇā is the cause for clinging to the round of *saṃsāra,* it must be abandoned to gain *nirvāṇa* [1.4.3, 2.3.1].

Tülku (Tibetan). The reincarnation of a spiritually advanced person, usually a *lama,* who on maturity resumes the office of his/her previous incarnation. In some cases, the tülku is regarded as the *nirmāṇakāya* of a *bodhisattva* [11.3.4].

Uji (Japanese). Clan; tribe [10.1].

Upaniṣad. Sanskrit speculative texts, the earliest of which were roughly contemporaneous with early Buddhism; later accepted into orthodox Brahmanism and Hinduism [1.2].

Vajra. Diamond; thunderbolt. A symbol of unfettered spiritual power used by the *Vajrayāna* to denote both the means of the practice, in which the vajra stands for firm compassion, and the goal, in which the Vajra Realm stands for the ground of all Buddhahood [6.3.2].

Vajrayāna. Adamantine (Diamond) Vehicle or Course. Path of *bodhisattva* practice, originally formulated in approximately the seventh century C.E., based primarily on Yoga and Unexcelled Yoga *Tantras,* claiming to be faster and more direct, if somewhat riskier, than older *Mahāyāna* practices [6.1, 6.3].

Vihāra. Monastic residence.

Vinaya. Monastic discipline.

Vinaya Piṭaka. Collection of texts containing rules for monastic discipline included in the early canons [3.1.2].

Vipaśyanā (Vipassanā). Insight. This term covers (1) particular forms of meditation that are said to provoke insight into the three characteristics of *anitya, duḥkha,* and *anātman,* and (2) the insight itself [2.3.1].

Wat (Thai). Temple-monastery complex [7.5.1].

Wings to Awakening (in Sanskrit, bodhipakṣya-dharma; in Pali, bodhipakkhiya-dhamma). Seven sets of *dharmas,* totaling 37 factors in all, which early canons say constitute the essential part of *Buddha's* teaching that would have to be practiced and maintained intact in order to keep his message alive: (1) the four foundations of mindfulness, (2) the four right exertions, (3) the four bases for attainment, (4) the five strengths, (5) the five faculties, (6) the seven factors of Awakening, and (7) the Noble Eightfold Path [2.3.1, 2.5].

Yogācāra. "Yoga practice." *Mahāyāna* school of meditative practice and the syncretic scholastic theories that developed around that practice [4.3].

Yogācārin. Follower of the *Yogācāra* school.

Yogin (feminine, yoginī). Practitioner of yoga and meditative self-discipline.

Zen (Japanese). Japanese pronunciation of the Chinese *Ch'an* [10.5.1, 10.7].

Select Bibliography

This selection is drawn primarily from the large body of academic literature on Buddhism, augmented with popular works where the academic literature has gaps. These works provide material that will supplement the discussion in this text, in some cases agreeing with the interpretations presented here, in some cases not. Citations are gathered under the chapters to which they are most relevant, preceded by a list applicable to the entire text.

Study aides for this book can be found on the World Wide Web at **http://www.wp.com/buddrel.** Also, three of the best sites on the Internet for materials on Buddhism are:

http://coombs.anu.edu.au/WWWVL-Buddhism.html

http://www.newciv.org/TigerTeam

http://world.std.com/˜metta/

GENERAL BOOKS ON BUDDHISM

Auboyer, Jeannine. *Buddha: A Pictorial History of His Life and Legacy*. New York: Crossroad, 1983.

Basham, A. L. *The Wonder That Was India*. New York: Macmillan, 1954.

Bechert, Heinz, and Richard Gombrich, eds. *The World of Buddhism: Monks and Nuns in Society and Culture*. London: Thames and Hudson, 1984.

Cabezon, Jose Ignacio, ed. *Buddhism, Sexuality, and Gender*. Albany: SUNY Press, 1992.

Conze, Edward. *Buddhist Scriptures: A Bibliography*. Edited and revised by Lewis Lancaster. New York: Garland, 1982.

———. *A Short History of Buddhism*. Oxford: Oneworld Publications, 1993.

Fu, Charles Wei-hsun, and Sandra A. Wawrytko, eds. *Buddhist Behavioral Codes and the Modern World: An International Symposium*. Westport, Conn.: Greenwood Press, 1994.

———, eds. *Buddhist Ethics and Modern Society: An International Symposium*. New York: Greenwood Press, 1991.

Harvey, Peter. *An Introduction to Buddhism: Teachings, History, and Practices*. Cambridge: Cambridge University Press, 1990.

Hirakawa, Akira. *A History of Indian Buddhism*. Honolulu: University of Hawaii Press, 1990.

Kitagawa, Joseph, and Mark Cummings, eds. *Buddhism and Asian History*. New York: Macmillan, 1989.

Kohn, Michael H., trans. *The Shambhala Dictionary of Buddhism and Zen*. Boston: Shambhala, 1991.

Liebert, Gosta. *Iconographic Dictionary of the Indian Religions*. Leiden, Netherlands: E. J. Brill, 1976.

Lopez, Donald S., Jr., ed. *Buddhism in Practice*. Princeton: Princeton University Press, 1995.

———, ed. *Buddhist Hermeneutics*. Honolulu: University of Hawaii Press, 1988.

Malalasekera, G. P., ed. *Encyclopedia of Buddhism*. Colombo, Sri Lanka: Government of Sri Lanka, 1961.

Pal, Pratapaditya. *Light of Asia: Buddha Sakyamuni in Asian Art*. Los Angeles: County Museum of Art, 1984.

Prebish, Charles S. *Historical Dictionary of Buddhism*. Metuchen, N.J.: Scarecrow Press, 1993.

———, ed. *Buddhism: A Modern Perspective*. University Park: Pennsylvania State University Press, 1978.

———, ed. *Buddhist Ethics: A Cross-Cultural Approach*. Dubuque, Iowa: Kendall/Hunt, 1992.

Queen, Christopher, and Sallie B. King. *Engaged Buddhism: Buddhist Liberation Movements in Asia*. Albany: SUNY Press, 1996.

Reynolds, Frank E. *Guide to the Buddhist Religion*. Boston: G. K. Hall, 1981.

Snellgrove, David L., ed. *The Image of the Buddha*. Tokyo: Kodansha International/UNESCO, 1978.

Strong, John. *The Experience of Buddhism: Sources and Interpretations*. Belmont, Calif.: Wadsworth, 1995.

Sutherland, Stewart, et al. *The World's Religions*. Boston: G. K. Hall, 1988.

Warder, A. K. *Indian Buddhism*. 2d ed. Delhi: Motilal Banarsidass, 1980.

Zwalf, W. *Buddhism: Art and Faith*. London: British Museum Publications, 1985.

CHAPTERS 1 AND 2: THE BUDDHA'S AWAKENING; THE BUDDHA AS TEACHER

Collins, Steven. *Selfless Persons: Imagery and Thought in Theravada Buddhism*. Cambridge: Cambridge University Press, 1982.

Cook, Elizabeth, ed. *Holy Places of the Buddha*. Berkeley: Dharma Publishing, 1994.

Cummings, Mary. *The Lives of the Buddha in the Art and Literature of Asia*. Ann Arbor: University of Michigan, 1982.

Gethin, R. M. L. *The Buddhist Path to Awakening: A Study of the Bodhi-Pakkhiya Dhamma*. Leiden, Netherlands: E. J. Brill, 1992.

Gunaratana, Henepola. *The Path of Serenity and Insight: An Explanation of the Buddhist Jhanas*. Delhi: Motilal Banarsidass, 1985.

Jayatilleke, K. N. *Early Buddhist Theory of Knowledge*. London: George Allen & Unwin, 1963.

Johnston, E. H., trans. *The Buddhacarita, or, Acts of the Buddha*. 3d ed. Delhi: Motilal Banarsidass, 1984.

Jones, John Garrett. *Tales and Teachings of the Buddha: The Jataka Stories in Relation to the Pali Canon*. London: George Allen & Unwin, 1979.

Kalupahana, David J. *Causality: The Central Philosophy of Buddhism*. Honolulu: University of Hawaii Press, 1975.

Karetsky, Patricia Eichenbaum. *The Life of the Buddha: Ancient Scriptural and Pictorial Traditions*. Lanham-Seabrook, Md.: University Press of America, 1992.

Katz, Nathan. *Buddhist Images of Human Perfection: The Arahant of the Sutta Pitaka Compared with the Bodhisattva and the Mahasiddha*. Delhi: Motilal Banarsidass, 1982.

Ñanamoli Bhikkhu. *The Life of the Buddha According to the Pali Canon*. Kandy, Sri Lanka: Buddhist Publication Society, 1978.

Thanissaro Bhikkhu. *The Mind Like Fire Unbound: An Image in the Early Buddhist Discourses*. Barre, Mass.: Dhamma Dana Publications, 1993.

———. *The Wings to Awakening: An Anthology from the Pali Canon*. Barre, Mass.: Dhamma Dana Publications, 1996.

CHAPTER 3: THE DEVELOPMENT OF EARLY INDIAN BUDDHISM

Barua, Dipak Kumar. *Viharas in Ancient India: A Survey of Buddhist Monasteries*. Calcutta: Indian Publications, 1969.

Chakravarti, Uma. *The Social Dimensions of Early Buddhism*. Delhi: Oxford University Press, 1987.

Dutt, Nalinaksha. *Buddhist Sects in India*. Delhi: Motilal Banarsidass, 1978.

Dutt, Sukumar. *Buddhist Monks and Monasteries of India: Their History and Their Contribution to Indian Culture*. London: George Allen & Unwin, 1962.

Hirakawa, Akira. *Monastic Discipline for the Buddhist Nuns: An English Translation of the Chinese Text of the Mahasamghika-Bhiksuni-Vinaya*. Patna, India: Kashi Prasad Jayaswal Research Institute, 1982.

Lamotte, Etienne. *History of Indian Buddhism: From the Origins to the Saka Era*. Louvain-La-Neuve: Institut Orientaliste, 1988.

Lancaster, Lewis. "Buddhist Literature: Its Canon, Scribes, and Editors." In *The Critical Study of Sacred Texts*. Edited by Wendy D. O'Flaherty. Berkeley: Berkeley Religious Studies Series, 1979, pp. 215–29.

Mitra, Debala. *Buddhist Monuments*. Calcutta: Sahitya Samsad, 1971.

Norman, K. R. *The Elders' Verses II: Therigatha*. London: Luzac and Company, 1971.

———. *Pali Literature, Including the Canonical Literature in Prakrit and Sanskrit of All Hinayana Schools of Buddhism*. Weisbaden, Germany: Otto Harrassowitz, 1983.

Nyanatiloka Mahathera. *A Guide through the Abhidhamma Pitaka*. Kandy, Sri Lanka: Buddhist Publication Society, 1971.

Olivelle, Patrick. *The Origin and Early Development of Buddhist Monachism*. Colombo, Sri Lanka: Gunasena, 1974.

Prebish, Charles S. *Buddhist Monastic Discipline: The Sanskrit Pratimoksa Sutras of the Mahasamghikas and Mulasarvastivadins*. University Park: Pennsylvania State University Press, 1975.

Ray, Reginald A. *Buddhist Saints in India: A Study in Buddhist Values and Orientations*. Oxford: Oxford University Press, 1994.

Seneviratna, Anuradha, ed. *King Asoka and Buddhism*. Kandy, Sri Lanka: Buddhist Publication Society, 1994.

Snodgrass, Adrian. *The Symbolism of the Stupa*. Ithaca: Cornell University Southeast Asian Studies Program, 1985.

Strong, John. *The Legend of King Asoka*. Princeton: Princeton University Press, 1983.

Thanissaro Bhikkhu. *The Buddhist Monastic Code: The Patimokkha Training Rules Translated and Explained*. Valley Center, Calif.: Metta Forest Monastery, 1994.

Tharpar, Romila. *Asoka and the Decline of the Mauryas*. Delhi: Oxford University Press, 1983.

Wijayaratna, Mohan. *Buddhist Monastic Life According to the Texts of the Theravada Tradition*. Translated by Claude Grangier and Steven Collins. Cambridge: Cambridge University Press, 1990.

Zysk, Kenneth G. *Asceticism and Healing in Ancient India: Medicine in the Buddhist Monastery*. New York: Oxford University Press, 1991.

CHAPTER 4: THE RISE AND DEVELOPMENT OF MAHĀYĀNA BUDDHISM

Anacker, Stefan. *Seven Works of Vasubandhu*. Delhi: Motilal Banarsidass, 1984.

Conze, Edward, trans. *The Large Sutra on Perfect Wisdom*. Berkeley: University of California Press, 1975.

Huntington, C. W., Jr. *The Emptiness of Emptiness: An Introduction to Early Indian Madhyamika*. Honolulu: University of Hawaii Press, 1989.

Kalupahana, David. *The Principles of Buddhist Psychology*. Albany: SUNY Press, 1987.

Khoroche, Peter, trans. *Once the Buddha Was a Monkey: Arya Sura's Jatakamala*. Chicago: University of Chicago Press, 1989.

Nagao, Gadjin. *Madhyamika and Yogacara. A Study of Mahayana Philosophies*. Albany: SUNY Press, 1991.

Napper, Elizabeth. *Dependent-Arising and Emptiness*. Boston: Wisdom Publications, 1989.

Robinson, Richard H. *Early Madhyamika in India and China*. Madison: University of Wisconsin Press, 1967.

Streng, Frederick. *Emptiness: A Study in Religious Meaning*. Nashville: Abingdon Press, 1967.

Sutton, Florin Giripescu. *Existence and Enlightenment in the Lankavatara Sutra: A Study in the Ontology and Epistemology of the Yogacara School of Mahayana Buddhism*. Albany: SUNY Press, 1991.

Warder, A. K. *Indian Kavya Literature*. Vol. 2, *The Origins and Formation of Classical Kavya*. 2d ed. Delhi: Motilal Banarsidass, 1990.

Williams, Paul. *Mahayana Buddhism: The Doctrinal Foundations*. London: Routledge & Kegan Paul, 1989.

Willis, Janice Dean. *On Knowing Reality: The Tattvartha Chapter of Asanga's Bodhisattvabhumi*. New York: Columbia University Press, 1982.

CHAPTER 5: SOTERIOLOGY AND PANTHEON OF THE MAHĀYĀNA

Bhattacharyya, Dipak Chandra. *Studies in Buddhist Iconography*. New Delhi: Manohar, 1978.

Birnbaum, Raoul. *The Healing Buddha*. Boston: Shambhala, 1989.

Paul, Diana. *Women in Buddhism: Images of the Feminine in the Mahayana Tradition*. Berkeley: University of California Press, 1985.

Sharma, R. C. *Buddhist Art: Mathura School*. New Delhi: Wiley Eastern Limited, 1995.

Sponberg, Alan, and Helen Hardacre, eds. *Maitreya: The Future Buddha*. Cambridge: Cambridge University Press, 1988.

Weiner, Sheila L. *Ajanta: Its Place in Buddhist Art*. Berkeley: University of California Press, 1977.

CHAPTER 6: VAJRAYĀNA AND LATER INDIAN BUDDHISM

Das Gupta, Shashibhusan. *Obscure Religious Cults*. Calcutta: Firma K. L. Mukhopadhyay, 1969.

Dowman, Keith. *Masters of Mahamudra: Songs and Histories of the Eighty-Four Buddhist Siddhas*. Albany: SUNY Press, 1985.

George, Christopher S. *The Candamaharosana Tantra*. New Haven, Conn.: American Oriental Society, 1974.

Lorenzen, David L. *The Kapalikas and Kalamukhas: Two Lost Saivite Sects*. Berkeley: University of California Press, 1972.

Shaw, Miranda. *Passionate Enlightenment: Women in Tantric Buddhism*. Princeton: Princeton University Press, 1994.

Snellgrove, D. L. *Indo-Tibetan Buddhism: Indian Buddhists and Their Tibetan Successors*. Vol. 1. Boston: Shambhala, 1987.

———. *The Hevajra Tantra*. Oxford: Oxford University Press, 1959.

CHAPTER 7: BUDDHISM IN SRI LANKA AND SOUTHEAST ASIA

Adikaram, E. W. *Early History of Buddhism in Ceylon*. Dehiwala, Sri Lanka: Buddhist Cultural Centre, 1994.

Aronson, Harvey B. *Love and Sympathy in Theravada Buddhism*. Delhi: Motilal Banarsidass, 1980.

Bartholomeusz, Tessa J. *Women under the Bo Tree: Buddhist Nuns in Sri Lanka*. Cambridge: Cambridge University Press, 1994.

Bond, George. *The Buddhist Revival in Sri Lanka*. Delhi: Motilal Banarsidass, 1992.

Bunnag, Jane. *Buddhist Monk, Buddhist Layman: A Study of Buddhist Monastic Organization in Central Thailand*. Cambridge: Cambridge University Press, 1973.

Carrithers, Michael. *The Forest Monks of Sri Lanka*. Delhi: Oxford University Press, 1983.

Gombrich, Richard F. *Buddhist Precept and Practice*. Delhi: Motilal Banarsidass, 1991.

———. *Theravada Buddhism: A Social History from Ancient Benares to Modern*

Colombo. London: Routledge & Kegan Paul, 1988.

Gombrich, Richard F., and Gananath Obeyesekere. *Buddhism Transformed: Religious Change in Sri Lanka*. Princeton: Princeton University Press, 1988.

Gomez, Luis O., and Hiram W. Woodward, eds. *Barabudur: History and Significance of a Buddhist Monument*. Berkeley: Berkeley Buddhist Studies Series, 1981.

Holt, John Clifford. *Buddha in the Crown: Avalokitesvara in the Buddhist Traditions of Sri Lanka*. New York: Oxford University Press, 1991.

Kornfield, Jack. *Living Dharma: Teachings of Twelve Buddhist Masters*. Boston: Shambhala, 1996.

Ñanamoli Thera, trans. *The Path of Purification* (Visuddhimagga). Kandy, Sri Lanka: Buddhist Publication Society, 1991.

Strachan, Paul. *Pagan: Art and Architecture of Old Burma*. Whiting Bay, Scotland: Kiscadale Publications, 1989.

Strong, John. *The Legend and Cult of Upagupta: Sanskrit Buddhism in North India and Southeast Asia*. Princeton: Princeton University Press, 1992.

Swearer, Donald K. *The Buddhist World of Southeast Asia*. Albany: SUNY Press, 1995.

Tambiah, Stanley. *Buddhism and Spirit Cults in Northeast Thailand*. Cambridge: Cambridge University Press, 1970.

Taylor, J. L. *Forest Monks and the Nation-state*. Singapore: Institute for Southeast Asian Studies, 1993.

CHAPTER 8: BUDDHISM IN CENTRAL ASIA AND CHINA

CENTRAL ASIA

Puri, B. N. *Buddhism in Central Asia*. Delhi: Motilal Banarsidass, 1987.

Snellgrove, David L. *Indo-Tibetan Buddhism: Indian Buddhists and Their Tibetan Successors*. Vol. 2. Boston: Shambhala, 1987.

Whitfield, Roderick, and Anne Farrer. *Caves of the Thousand Buddhas: Chinese Art from the Silk Route*. New York: George Braziller, 1990.

CHINA

Chappell, David W., ed. *T'ien-t'ai Buddhism*. Tokyo: Daiichi-Shobo, 1983.

Ch'en, Kenneth. *Buddhism in China: A Historical Survey*. Princeton: Princeton University Press, 1964.

———. *The Chinese Transformation of Buddhism*. Princeton: Princeton University Press, 1973.

Ching, Yu-ing. *Master of Love and Mercy: Cheng Yen*. Nevada City, Calif.: Blue Dolphin Publishing, 1995.

Cook, Francis H. *Hua-yen Buddhism: The Jewel Net of Indra*. University Park: Pennsylvania State University Press, 1977.

Ebrey, Patricia Buckley, and Peter Gregory, eds. *Religion and Society in T'ang and Sung China*. Honolulu: University of Hawaii Press, 1993.

Faure, Bernard. *The Rhetoric of Immediacy: A Cultural Critique of Chan/Zen Buddhism*. Princeton: Princeton University Press, 1991.

Gernet, Jacques. *Buddhism in Chinese Society: An Economic History (Fifth to Tenth Century)*. Translated by Franciscus Verellen. New York: Columbia University Press, 1995.

Gregory, Peter N., ed. *Sudden and Gradual: Approaches to Enlightenment in Chinese Thought*. Honolulu: University of Hawaii Press, 1987.

———, ed. *Traditions of Meditation in Chinese Buddhism*. Honolulu: University of Hawaii Press, 1986.

———. *Tsung-mi and the Sinification of Buddhism*. Princeton: Princeton University Press, 1991.

Lai, Whalen, and Lewis R. Lancaster, eds. *Early Ch'an in China and Tibet*. Berkeley: University of California Press, 1983.

McRae, John R. *The Northern School and the Formation of Early Ch'an Buddhism*. Honolulu: University of Hawaii Press, 1986.

Powell, William F. *The Record of Tung-shan*. Honolulu: University of Hawaii Press, 1986.

Robinson, Richard H. *Early Madhyamika in India and China*. Madison: University of Wisconsin Press, 1967.

Teiser, Stephen F. *The Ghost Festival in Medieval China*. Princeton: Princeton University Press, 1988.

Tsai, Kathryn Ann. *Lives of the Nuns: Biographies of Chinese Buddhist Nuns from the Fourth to Sixth Centuries*. Honolulu: University of Hawaii Press, 1994.

Weinstein, Stanley. *Buddhism under the T'ang*. Cambridge: Cambridge University Press, 1987.

Zürcher, Erik. *The Buddhist Conquest of China: The Spread and Adaptation of Buddhism in Early Medieval China*. Leiden, Netherlands: E. J. Brill, 1972.

CHAPTER 9: BUDDHISM IN KOREA AND VIETNAM

KOREA

Buswell, Robert E., Jr. *The Korean Approach to Zen: The Collected Works of Chinul*. Honolulu: University of Hawaii Press, 1983.

———. *The Zen Monastic Experience: Buddhist Practice in Contemporary Korea*. Princeton: Princeton University Press, 1992.

Cleary, J. C. *A Buddha from Korea: The Zen Teachings of T'aego*. Boston: Shambhala, 1988.

Lancaster, Lewis R., and C. S. Yu, eds. *Assimilation of Buddhism in Korea: Religious Maturity and Innovation in the Silla Dynasty*. Berkeley: Asian Humanities Press, 1991.

———, eds. *Introduction of Buddhism to Korea: New Cultural Patterns*. Berkeley: Asian Humanities Press, 1989.

Mu Soeng. *Thousand Peaks: Korean Zen—Traditions and Teachers*. Cumberland, R.I.: Primary Point Press, 1991.

Tae-heng Se Nim. *Teachings of the Heart: Zen Teachings of Korean Woman Zen Master Tae-Heng Se Nim*. Occidental, Calif.: Dai Shin Press, 1990.

VIETNAM

Chan Khong (Cao Ngoc Phuong). *Learning True Love: How I Learned and Practiced Social Change in Vietnam.* Berkeley: Parallax Press, 1993.

Nhat Hanh, Thich. *Vietnam: Lotus in a Sea of Fire.* New York: Hill and Wang, 1967.

Thien-An, Thich. *Buddhism and Zen in Vietnam in Relation to the Development of Buddhism in Asia.* Tokyo: Charles Tuttle, 1975.

Thien-Tam, Thich. *Buddhism of Wisdom and Faith: Pure Land Principles and Practice.* Sepulveda, Calif.: International Buddhist Monastic Institute, 1991.

CHAPTER 10: BUDDHISM IN JAPAN

Colcutt, Martin. *Five Mountains: The Rinzai Zen Monastic Institution in Medieval Japan.* Cambridge: Harvard University Press, 1981.

Dobbins, James C. *Jodo Shinshu: Shin Buddhism in Medieval Japan.* Bloomington: Indiana University Press, 1989.

Hakeda, Yoshito S. *Kukai: Major Works.* New York: Columbia University Press, 1972.

Hardacre, Helen. *Kurozumikyo and the New Religions of Japan.* Princeton: Princeton University Press, 1986.

Isshu, Miura, and Ruth Fuller Sasaki. *The Zen Koan: Its History and Use in Rinzai Zen.* New York: Harcourt, Brace & World, 1965.

Kasulis, T. P. *Zen Action, Zen Person.* Honolulu: The University of Hawaii Press, 1981.

Ketelaar, James Edward. *Of Heretics and Martyrs in Meiji Japan: Buddhism and Its Persecution.* Princeton: Princeton University Press, 1990.

Kitagawa, Joseph M. *Religion in Japanese History.* New York: Columbia University Press, 1966.

Kraft, Kenneth. *Eloquent Zen: Daito and Early Japanese Zen.* Honolulu: University of Hawaii Press, 1992.

———, ed. *Zen: Tradition and Transition.* New York: Grove Press, 1988.

LaFleur, William. *The Karma of Words: Buddhism and the Literary Arts in Medieval Japan.* Berkeley: University of California Press, 1983.

McMullin, Neil. *Buddhism and the State in Sixteenth Century Japan.* Princeton: Princeton University Press, 1988.

Sanford, James H. *Zen-man Ikkyu.* Chico, Calif.: Scholars Press, 1981.

Tanabe, George J., Jr. *Myoe the Dreamkeeper: Fantasy and Knowledge in Early Kamakura Buddhism.* Cambridge: Harvard University Press, 1992.

Yampolsky, Philip B. *The Zen Master Hakuin: Selected Writings.* New York: Columbia University Press, 1971.

CHAPTER 11: BUDDHISM IN THE TIBETAN CULTURAL AREA

Allione, Tsultrim. *Women of Wisdom.* London: Arkana, 1986.

Beyer, Stephan V. *The Cult of Tara.* Berkeley: University of California Press, 1973.

Cabezon, Jose Ignacio. *Buddhism and Language: A Study of Indo-Tibetan Scholasticism.* Albany: SUNY Press, 1994.

Cozart, Daniel. *Highest Yoga Tantra: An Introduction to the Esoteric Buddhism of Tibet.* Ithaca: Snow Lion Publications, 1986.

Dowman, Keith. *Sky Dancer: The Secret Life and Songs of the Lady Yeshe Tsogyel.* London: Routledge & Kegan Paul, 1984.

Havnevik, Hanna. *Tibetan Buddhist Nuns: History, Cultural Norms, and Social Reality.* Oslo: Norwegian University Press, 1989.

Hopkins, Jeffrey. *Meditation on Emptiness.* London: Wisdom Publications, 1983.

Karmay, Samten Gyaltsen. *The Great Perfection: A Philosophical and Meditative Teaching of Tibetan Buddhism.* Leiden, Netherlands: E. J. Brill, 1988.

Klein, Anne Carolyn. *Meeting the Great Bliss Queen: Buddhists, Feminists, and the Art of the Self.* Boston: Beacon Press, 1995.

Napper, Elizabeth. *Dependent-Arising and Emptiness.* Boston: Wisdom Publications, 1989.

Rhie, Marylin M., and Robert A. F. Thurman. *Wisdom and Compassion: The Sacred Art of Tibet.* New York: Harry H. Abrams, 1991.

Samuel, Geoffrey. *Civilized Shamans: Buddhism in Tibetan Societies.* Washington, D.C.: Smithsonian Institution Press, 1993.

Snellgrove, David L. *Four Lamas of Dolpo.* Cambridge: Harvard University Press, 1967.

———. *Indo-Tibetan Buddhism: Indian Buddhists and Their Tibetan Successors.* Vol. 2. Boston: Shambhala, 1987.

Taring, Rinchen Dolma. *Daughter of Tibet.* London: Wisdom Publications, 1986.

Willis, Janice D. *Feminine Ground: Essays on Women and Tibet.* Ithaca: Snow Lion Publications, 1989.

CHAPTER 12: BUDDHISM COMES WEST

Four periodicals dealing with Buddhism in the West may be of interest to students. They are *Shambhala Sun: Creating Enlightened Society; Tricycle: The Buddhist Review; Insight;* and *Inquiring Mind.*

Batchelor, Stephen. *The Awakening of the West: The Encounter of Buddhism and Western Culture.* Berkeley: Parallax Press, 1994.

Boucher, Sandy. *Turning the Wheel: American Women Creating the New Buddhism.* Boston: Beacon Press, 1993.

Butterfield, Stephen T. *The Double Mirror: A Skeptical Journey into Buddhist Tantra.* Berkeley: North Atlantic Books, 1994.

Fields, Rick. *How the Swans Came to the Lake: A Narrative History of Buddhism in America.* Boston: Shambhala, 1992.

Friedman, Lenore. *Meetings with Remarkable Women: Buddhist Teachers in America.* Boston: Shambhala, 1987.

Gross, Rita M. *Buddhism after Patriarchy: A Feminist History, Analysis, and Reconstruction of Buddhism.* Albany: SUNY Press, 1993.

Lang, David Marshall. *The Wisdom of Balahvar: A Christian Legend of the Buddha.* New York: Macmillan, 1957.

Lopez, Donald S., Jr., ed. *Curators of the Buddha: The Study of Buddhism under Colonialism.* Chicago: University of Chicago Press, 1995.

Numrich, Paul David. *Old Wisdom in the New World: Americanization in Two Immigrant Theravada Buddhist Temples.* Knoxville: University of Tennessee Press, 1996.

Prebish, Charles S. *American Buddhism.* Belmont, Calif.: Wadsworth, 1979.

Tsomo, Karma Lekshe. *Sakyadhita: Daughters of the Buddha.* Ithaca: Snow Lion Publications, 1988.

Tworkov, Helen. *Zen in America.* New York: Kodansha America, 1994.

Index

The names, subjects, and cross-cultural themes listed in this index have been chosen to supplement, with a minimum of duplication, the citations already given in the Table of Contents and Glossary.